Microsoft®

Windows® 98

Illustrated Introductory

Microsoft®

Windows® 98

Illustrated Introductory

Neil J. Salkind
Steven M. Johnson

COURSE
TECHNOLOGY

ONE MAIN STREET, CAMBRIDGE, MA 02142

an International Thomson Publishing company I(T)P®

Cambridge • Albany • Bonn • Boston • Cincinnati • London • Madrid • Melbourne • Mexico City
New York • Paris • San Francisco • Singapore • Tokyo • Toronto • Washington

Microsoft Windows 98—Illustrated Introductory

is published by Course Technology

Managing Editor:	Nicole Jones Pinard
Senior Product Manager:	Jeanne Herring
Production Editors:	Ellina Beletsky, Melissa Lima
Developmental Editors:	Mary Kemper, Jennifer Duffy
Composition House:	GEX, Inc.
QA Manuscript Reviewers:	Alex White
Text Designer:	Joseph Lee
Cover Designer:	Joseph Lee

© 1999 by Course Technology — I(T)P®

For more information contact:

Course Technology
One Main Street
Cambridge, MA 02142

ITP Europe
Berkshire House 168-173
High Holborn
London WCIV 7AA
England

Nelson ITP, Australia
102 Dodds Street
South Melbourne, 3205
Victoria, Australia

ITP Nelson Canada
1120 Birchmount Road
Scarborough, Ontario
Canada M1K 5G4

International Thomson Editores
Seneca, 53
Colonia Polanco
11560 Mexico D.F. Mexico

ITP GmbH
Königswinterer Strasse 418
53227 Bonn
Germany

ITP Asia
60 Albert Street, #15-01
Albert Complex
Singapore 189969

ITP Japan
Hirakawacho Kyowa Building, 3F
2-2-1 Hirakawacho
Chiyoda-ku, Tokyo 102
Japan

Trademarks

Disclaimer

ISBN 0-7600-6008-8

Printed in the United States of America

2 3 4 5 6 7 8 9 BM 03 02 01 00 99

Exciting New Illustrated Products

The Illustrated Projects™ Series: The Quick, Visual Way to Apply Computer Skills

Looking for an inexpensive, easy way to supplement almost any application text and give your students the practice and tools they'll need to compete in today's competitive marketplace? Each text includes more than 50 real-world, useful projects—like creating a resume and setting up a loan worksheet—that let students hone their computer skills. These two-color texts have the same great two-page layout as the Illustrated Series.

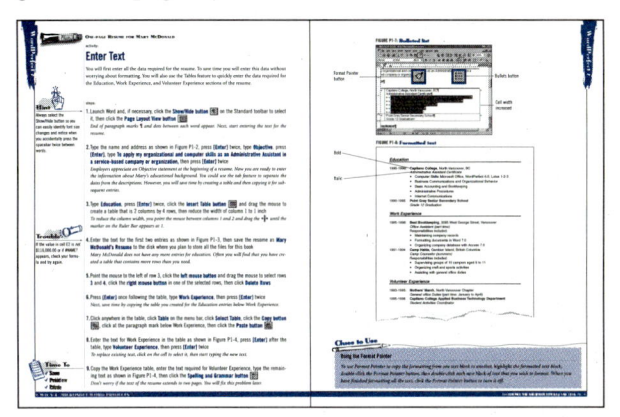

Illustrated Projects titles are available for the following:

- Microsoft Access
- Microsoft Excel
- Microsoft Office Professional
- Microsoft Publisher
- Microsoft Word
- Creating Web Sites
- World Wide Web
- Adobe PageMaker
- Corel WordPerfect

Illustrated Interactive™ Series: The Safe, Simulated Way to Learn Computer Skills

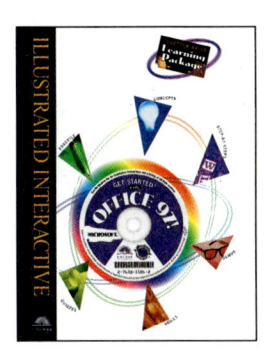

The Ilustrated Interactive Series uses multimedia technology to teach computer concepts and application skills. Students learn via a CD-ROM that simulates the actual software and provides a controlled learning environment in which every keystroke is monitored. Plus, all products in this series feature the same step-by-step instructions as the Illustrated Series. An accompanying workbook reinforces the skills that students learn on the CD.

Illustrated Interactive titles are available for the following applications:*

- Microsoft Office 97
- Microsoft Word 97
- Microsoft Excel 97
- Microsoft Access 97
- Microsoft PowerPoint 97
- Computer Concepts

Standalone & networked versions available. Runs on Windows 3.1, 95, and NT. CD-only version available for Computer Concepts and Office 97.

CourseKits™: Offering You the Freedom to Choose

Balance your course curriculum with Course Technology's mix-and-match approach to selecting texts. CourseKits provide you with the freedom to make choices from more than one series. When you choose any two or more Course Technology products for one course, we'll discount the price and package them together so your students pick up one convenient bundle at the bookstore.

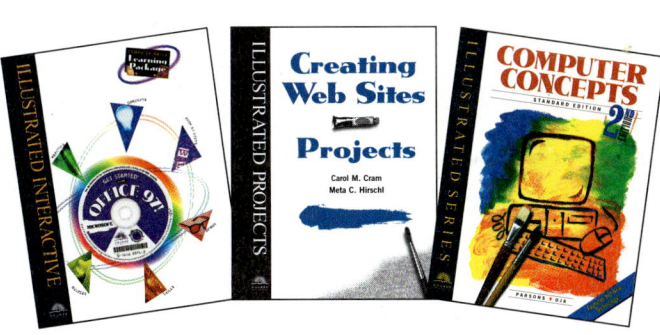

Contact your sales representative to find out more about these Illustrated products.

Preface

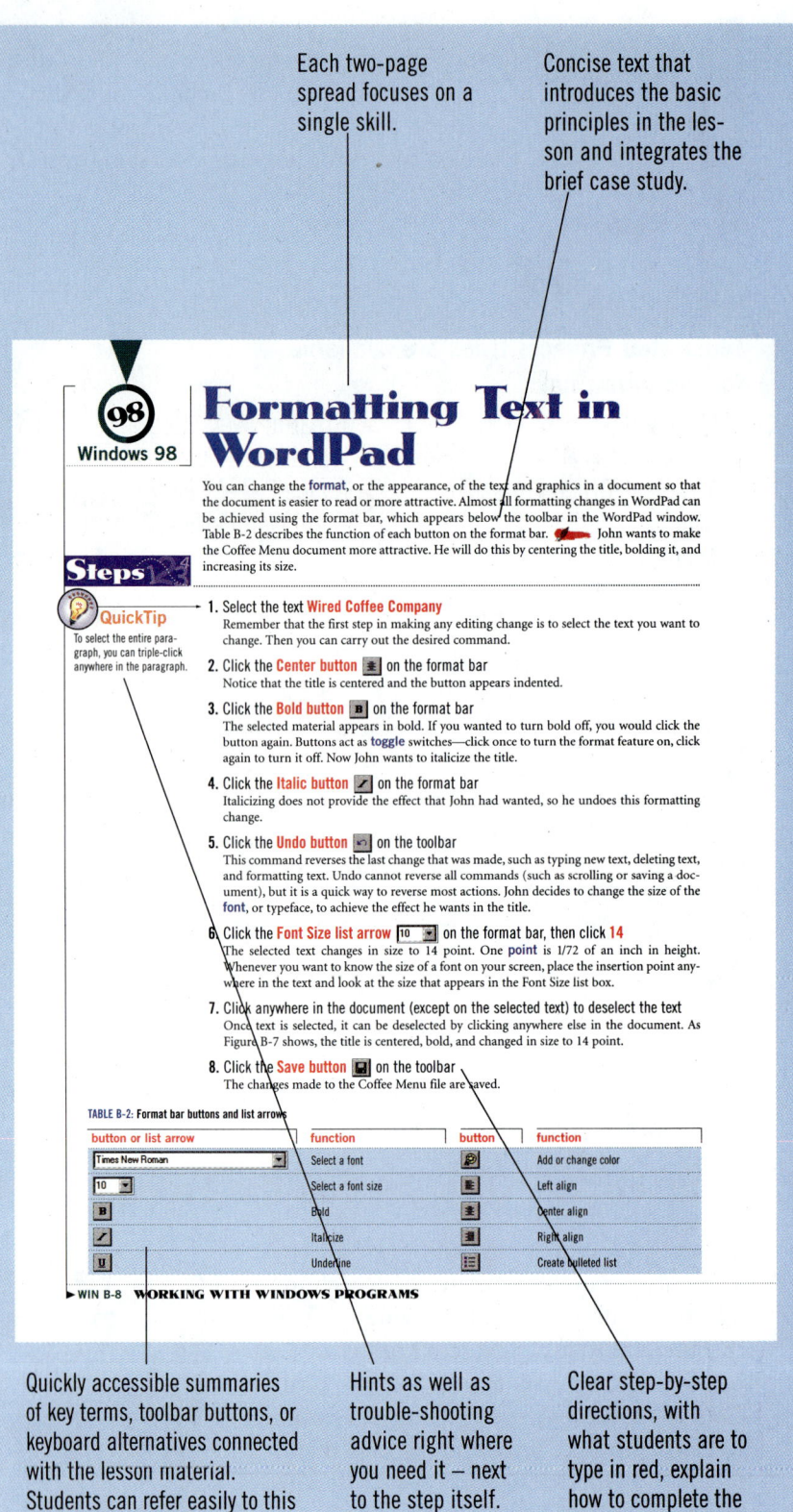

Welcome to *Microsoft Windows 98 – Illustrated*! This book in our highly visual design offers new users a hands-on introduction to Microsoft Windows 98 and also serves as an excellent reference for future use.

▶ Organization and Coverage

The Introductory book contains eight units that cover basic Microsoft Windows 98 skills. In these units students learn basic Windows skills along with how to work with programs and manage files using both My Computer and Windows Explorer. They also learn how to access the Internet and explore the World Wide Web using Internet Explorer, send and receive messages using Outlook Express, work with Windows 98 on a network, and much more!

▶ About this Approach

What makes the Illustrated approach so effective at teaching software skills? It's quite simple. Each skill is presented on two facing pages, with the step-by-step instructions on the left page, and large screen illustrations on the right. Students can focus on a single skill without having to turn the page. This unique design makes information extremely accessible and easy to absorb, and provides a great reference for students after the course is over. This hands-on approach also makes it ideal for both self-paced or instructor-led classes. The modular structure of the book also allows for great flexibility; you can cover the units in any order you choose.

Each lesson, or "information display," contains the following elements:

Each two-page spread focuses on a single skill.

Concise text that introduces the basic principles in the lesson and integrates the brief case study.

Formatting Text in WordPad

98 Windows 98

You can change the **format**, or the appearance, of the text and graphics in a document so that the document is easier to read or more attractive. Almost all formatting changes in WordPad can be achieved using the format bar, which appears below the toolbar in the WordPad window. Table B-2 describes the function of each button on the format bar. John wants to make the Coffee Menu document more attractive. He will do this by centering the title, bolding it, and increasing its size.

Steps

QuickTip
To select the entire paragraph, you can triple-click anywhere in the paragraph.

1. Select the text **Wired Coffee Company**
   Remember that the first step in making any editing change is to select the text you want to change. Then you can carry out the desired command.

2. Click the **Center button** on the format bar
   Notice that the title is centered and the button appears indented.

3. Click the **Bold button** on the format bar
   The selected material appears in bold. If you wanted to turn bold off, you would click the button again. Buttons act as **toggle** switches—click once to turn the format feature on, click again to turn it off. Now John wants to italicize the title.

4. Click the **Italic button** on the format bar
   Italicizing does not provide the effect that John had wanted, so he undoes this formatting change.

5. Click the **Undo button** on the toolbar
   This command reverses the last change that was made, such as typing new text, deleting text, and formatting text. Undo cannot reverse all commands (such as scrolling or saving a document), but it is a quick way to reverse most actions. John decides to change the size of the **font**, or typeface, to achieve the effect he wants in the title.

6. Click the **Font Size list arrow** on the format bar, then click **14**
   The selected text changes in size to 14 point. One **point** is 1/72 of an inch in height. Whenever you want to know the size of a font on your screen, place the insertion point anywhere in the text and look at the size that appears in the Font Size list box.

7. Click anywhere in the document (except on the selected text) to deselect the text
   Once text is selected, it can be deselected by clicking anywhere else in the document. As Figure B-7 shows, the title is centered, bold, and changed in size to 14 point.

8. Click the **Save button** on the toolbar
   The changes made to the Coffee Menu file are saved.

TABLE B-2: Format bar buttons and list arrows

button or list arrow	function	button	function
Times New Roman	Select a font		Add or change color
10	Select a font size		Left align
B	Bold		Center align
/	Italicize		Right align
U	Underline		Create bulleted list

► WIN B-8 **WORKING WITH WINDOWS PROGRAMS**

Quickly accessible summaries of key terms, toolbar buttons, or keyboard alternatives connected with the lesson material. Students can refer easily to this information when working on their own projects at a later time.

Hints as well as trouble-shooting advice right where you need it – next to the step itself.

Clear step-by-step directions, with what students are to type in red, explain how to complete the specific task.

Every lesson features large, full-color representations of what the screen should look like as students complete the numbered steps.

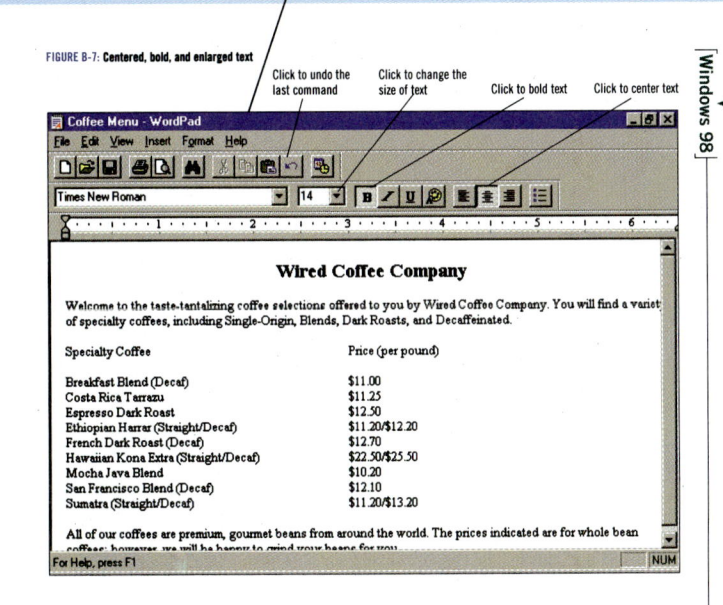

FIGURE B-7: Centered, bold, and enlarged text

Click to undo the last command
Click to change the size of text
Click to bold text
Click to center text

Windows 98

Coffee Menu - WordPad

File Edit View Insert Format Help

Times New Roman   14   B I U

· · · · · 1 · · · · · 2 · · · · · 3 · · · · · 4 · · · · · 5 · · · · · 6 · ·

Wired Coffee Company

Welcome to the taste-tantalizing coffee selections offered to you by Wired Coffee Company. You will find a variety of specialty coffees, including Single-Origin, Blends, Dark Roasts, and Decaffeinated.

Specialty Coffee   Price (per pound)

Breakfast Blend (Decaf) $11.00
Costa Rica Tarrazu $11.25
Espresso Dark Roast $12.50
Ethiopian Harrar (Straight/Decaf) $11.20/$12.20
French Dark Roast (Decaf) $12.70
Hawaiian Kona Extra (Straight/Decaf) $22.50/$25.50
Mocha Java Blend $10.20
San Francisco Blend (Decaf) $12.10
Sumatra (Straight/Decaf) $11.20/$13.20

All of our coffees are premium, gourmet beans from around the world. The prices indicated are for whole bean coffees; however, we will be happy to grind your beans for you.

For Help, press F1   NUM

CLUES TO USE

Formatting text as you type

As you've learned in the Steps, one way to format text is to select it, and then apply a change of format. Another way is to first select the formatting you want, and then enter text. This approach is helpful when you are starting a new document and are familiar with the effect that different formatting options create. For example, if you were creating a new list of items and knew that you wanted the title to be 24-point, underlined text, you would click the Underline button U on the format bar, and then select 24 from the Font Size list box. Anything that you type from that point will have those format characteristics. When you finish typing the title, you can change the font back to a smaller point size and click the Underline button to toggle the option off, then continue typing.

WORKING WITH WINDOWS PROGRAMS   WIN B-9

Clues to Use Boxes provide concise information that either expands on the major lesson skill or describes an independent task that in some way relates to the major lesson skill.

The page numbers are designed like a road map. WIN indicates that it's a Windows unit, B indicates Unit B, and 9 indicates the page within the unit. This map allows for the greatest flexibility in content — each unit stands completely on its own.

Other Features

The two-page lesson format featured in this book provides the new user with a powerful learning experience. Additionally, this book contains the following features:

▶ Real-World Case

The case study used throughout the textbook, a fictitious coffee company called Wired Coffee Company, is designed to be "real-world" in nature and introduces the kinds of activities that students will encounter when working with Microsoft Windows 98. With a real-world case, the process of solving problems will be more meaningful to students.

▶ End of Unit Material

Each unit concludes with a Concepts Review that tests students' understanding of what they learned in the unit. A Skills Review follows the Concepts Review and provides students with additional hands-on practice of the skills they learned in the unit. The Skills Review is followed by Independent Challenges, which pose case problems for students to solve. The Visual Workshop that follows the Independent Challenges helps students to develop critical thinking skills. Students are shown a completed screen or document and are asked to recreate it from scratch.

Instructor's Resource Kit

The Instructor's Resource Kit is Course Technology's way of putting the resources and information needed to teach and learn effectively into your hands. With an integrated array of teaching and learning tools that offer you and your students a broad range of technology-based instructional options, we believe this kit represents the highest quality and most cutting edge resources available to instructors today. Many of these resources are available at www.course.com. The resources available with this book are:

Course Test Manager Designed by Course Technology, this cutting-edge Windows-based testing software helps instructors design, administer, and print tests and pre-tests. A full-featured program, Course Test Manager also has an online testing component that allows students to take tests at the computer and have their exams automatically graded.

Instructor's Manual Quality assurance tested and includes:
- Solutions to all lessons and end-of-unit material
- Detailed lecture topics for each unit with teaching tips
- Information for each unit about the differences between Windows 95 and Windows 98
- Extra Independent Challenges
- Task References
- Transparency Masters

WWW.COURSE.COM We encourage students and instructors to visit our Web site at www.course.com to find articles about current teaching and software trends, featured texts, interviews with authors, demos of Course Technology's software, Frequently Asked Questions about our products, and much more. This site is also where you can gain access to the Faculty Online Companion for this text — see below for more information.

Course Faculty Online Companion Available at www.course.com, this World Wide Web site offers Course Technology customers a password-protected Faculty Lounge where you can find everything you need to prepare for class including the Instructor's Manual in an electronic Portable Document Format (PDF) file and Adobe Acrobat Reader software. Periodically updated items include any updates and revisions to the text and Instructor's Manual, links to other Web sites, and access to student files, x-tra files, and solution files. This site will continue to evolve throughout the semester. Contact your Customer Service Representative for the site address and password.

Student Files To use this book students must have the Student Files. See the inside front or inside back cover for more information on the Student Files. Adopters of this text are granted the right to post the Student Files on any stand-alone computer or network.

X-tra files Now it's even easier to teach the skills **you** want to teach! Every two-page spread requiring a student file now includes a student file **or** an X-tra file. A student file is a file you open at the beginning of the unit and use to work through all, or a group of the lessons in that unit. An X-tra file is a student file in the exact format needed to work through that one particular lesson. X-tra files are not available for lessons in which student files are not needed, or in which a student file is explicitly opened as part of the lesson steps.

The filename of each X-tra file is the page number for the lesson with an "X" in front of it. For instance, the X-tra file for the lesson on page WIN B-6 is **XWIN B-6**. As the name implies, these files are "extra" and you can choose whether or not to make them available to your students. The X-tra files for this book are provided separately from the Student Files in the Instructor's Resource Kit and on the Faculty Online Companion.

Brief Contents

Contents

 ▶ ⌈ **Windows 98** ⌉

Contents

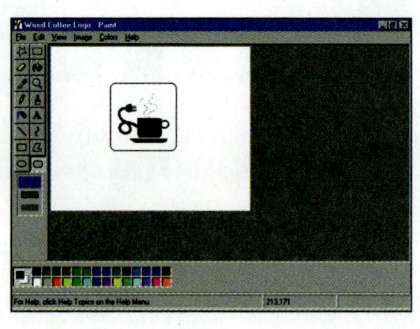

Managing Files Using My Computer   WIN C-1

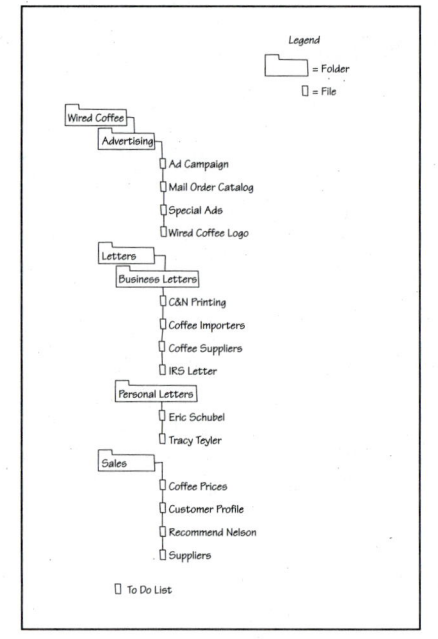

Managing Folders and Files Using Windows Explorer   WIN D-1

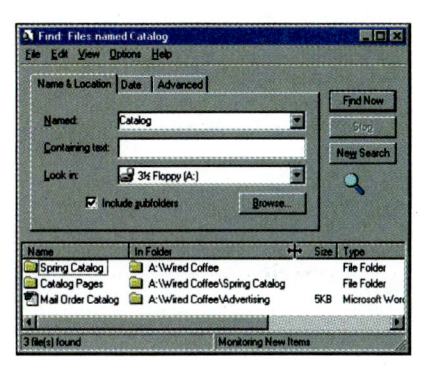

Contents

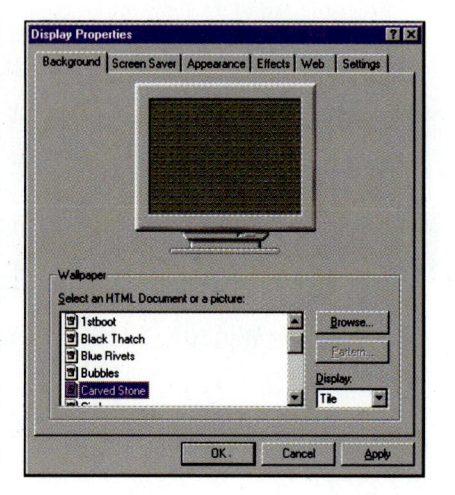

Exchanging Mail and News   WIN G-1

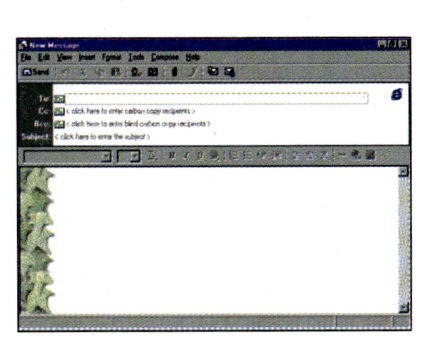

Contents

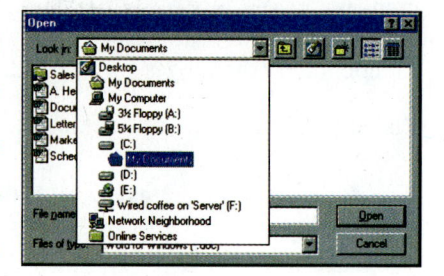

Getting
Started with Windows 98

- ► **Start Windows and view the Windows Active Desktop**
- ► **Use the mouse**
- ► **Get started with the Windows desktop**
- ► **Move and resize windows**
- ► **Use menus and toolbars**
- ► **Use scroll bars**
- ► **Use dialog boxes**
- ► **Use Windows Help**
- ► **Shut down Windows**

Microsoft Windows 98 is an **operating system**, a computer program that controls the basic operation of your computer and the programs you run on it. **Programs**, also known as **applications**, are task-oriented software you use to accomplish specific tasks, such as word processing, managing files on your computer, and performing calculations. When you work with Windows 98, you will notice many **icons**, small pictures on your screen intended to be meaningful symbols of the items they represent. You will also notice **windows** (thus the name of the operating system), rectangular frames on your screen that can contain several icons, the contents of a file, or other usable data. A **file** is an electronic collection of information, such as a resume or a database of addresses. This use of icons and windows is called a **graphical user interface** (**GUI**, pronounced "gooey"), meaning that you interact ("interface") with the computer through the use of graphics: icons and other meaningful words, symbols, and windows. ◄━━━ This unit introduces you to basic Windows skills.

Starting Windows and Viewing the Windows Active Desktop

When you first start Windows, you see the Windows Active Desktop. The **Active Desktop** is an on-screen version of a regular desk, containing all the information and tools you need to accomplish your tasks. From the desktop, you can access, store, share, and explore information in a seamless manner, whether it resides on your computer, a network, or the Internet. (The **Internet** is a worldwide collection of over 40 million computers linked together to share information.) The desktop is called "active" because (unlike other Windows desktops) it allows you to access the Internet and view Internet content directly from it. Figure A-1 shows what the desktop looks like when you start Windows 98 for the first time. The bar at the bottom of your screen is called the **taskbar**, which allows you to start programs and switch among currently running programs. (At the moment, none are running.) At the left end of the taskbar is the **Start button**, which you use to start programs, find and open files, access Windows Help, and so on. Next to the Start button on the taskbar is the **Quick Launch toolbar**, which contains buttons you use to quickly start Internet related programs and show the desktop. The bar on the right side of your screen is called the **Channel Bar**, which shows buttons you use to access the Internet and view channels (like those on television) that display Internet content. Use Table A-1 to identify the icons and other elements you see on your desktop. Windows 98 automatically starts when you turn on your computer. If Windows is not currently running, follow the steps below to start it now.

1. **Turn on your computer**
   Windows automatically starts, and the desktop appears, as shown in Figure A-1. If you are working on a network at school or at an office, you might see a network password dialog box. If so, continue to Step 2. If not, continue to the next lesson.

2. **Type your password in the Password box**
   When you enter a valid password, you are given privileges to use the network.

Trouble?

If you don't know your password, ask your instructor or technical support person for assistance.

3. **Click OK**
   Once the password is accepted, the Windows desktop appears on your screen, as shown in Figure A-1.

FIGURE A-1: Windows Active Desktop

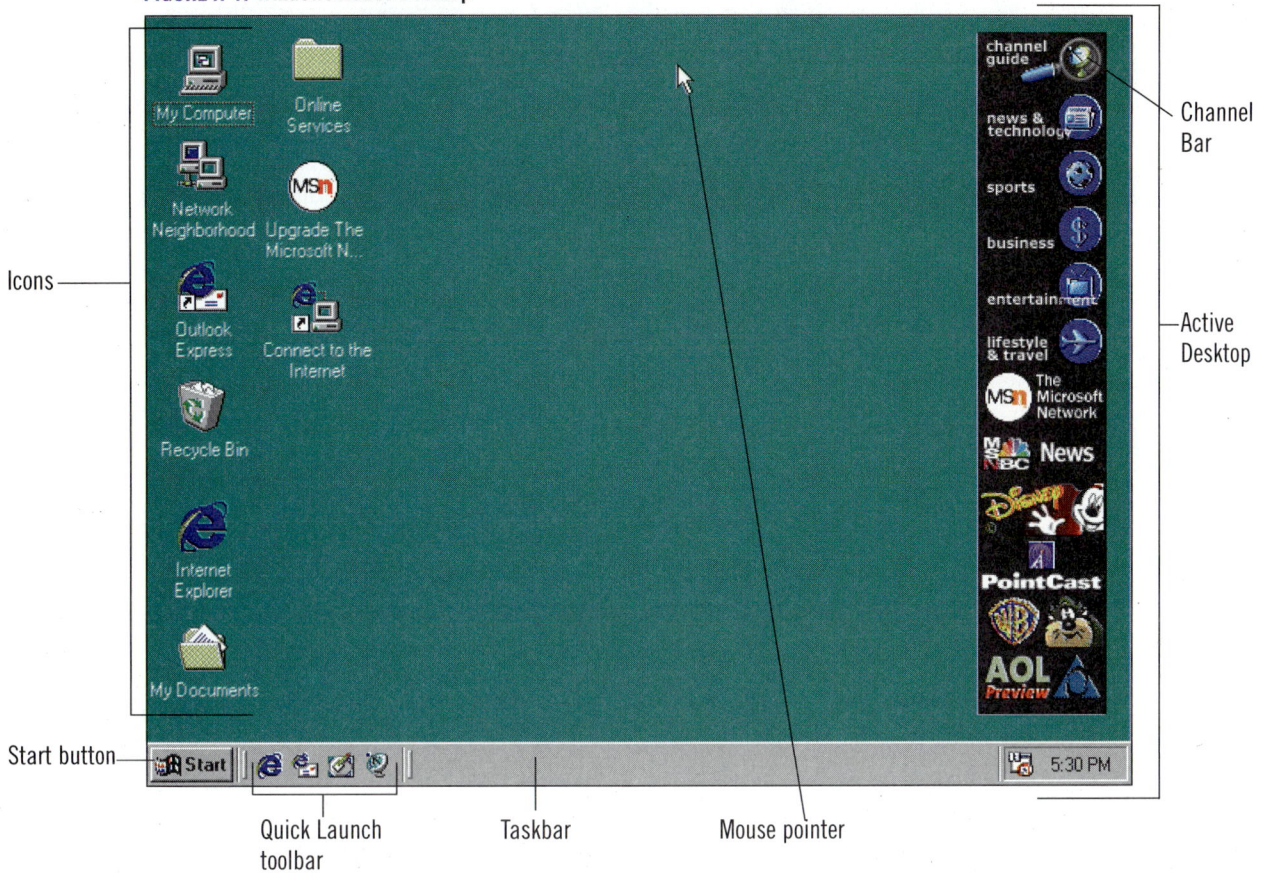

Icons —
Start button —
Quick Launch toolbar
Taskbar
Mouse pointer
Channel Bar
Active Desktop

TABLE A-1: Elements of the Windows Active Desktop

desktop element	allows you to
My Computer	Work with different disk drives and printers on your computer system
Network Neighborhood	Work with different disk drives and printers on a network
Outlook Express	Start Outlook Express, an electronic mail program
Connect to the Internet	Create a connection to the Internet using a phone or network
Recycle Bin	Delete and restore files
Internet Explorer	Start Internet Explorer, a program you use to access the Internet
My Documents folder	Store programs, documents, graphics, or other files
Online Services folder	Store programs to access online services such as CompuServe, America Online, and Prodigy
Upgrade The Microsoft Network	Start setup program for The Microsoft Network, an online service
Taskbar	Start programs and switch among open programs
Start button	Start programs, open documents, find a file, and more
Channel Bar	Start Internet Explorer and open channels
Quick Launch toolbar	Start Internet Explorer, start Outlook Express, show the desktop, and view channels

Windows 98

Use the Mouse

A **mouse** is a handheld input device you roll across a flat surface (such as a desk or a mousepad) to position the **mouse pointer**, the small symbol that indicates the pointer's relative position on the desktop. When you move the mouse, the mouse pointer on the screen moves in the same direction. The shape of the mouse pointer changes to indicate different activities. Table A-2 shows some common mouse pointer shapes. Once you move the mouse pointer to a desired position on the screen, you use the **mouse buttons**, shown in Figure A-2, to "tell" your computer what you want it to do. Table A-3 describes the basic mouse techniques you'll use frequently when working in Windows. ▬▬▬ Try using the mouse now to become familiar with these navigational skills.

1. Place your hand on the mouse, locate the mouse pointer ▧ on the desktop, then move the mouse back and forth across your desk
   As you move the mouse, the mouse pointer moves correspondingly.

2. Move the mouse to position the mouse pointer over the **My Computer icon** in the upper-left corner of the desktop
   Positioning the mouse pointer over an icon or over any specific item on the screen is called **pointing**.

3. Press and release the **left mouse button**
   The act of pressing a mouse button once and releasing it is called **clicking.** The icon is now highlighted, or shaded differently than the other icons on the desktop. The act of clicking an item, such as an icon, indicates that you have **selected** it to perform some future operation on it. To perform any type of operation on an icon (such as moving it), you must first select it. Now try a skill called **dragging**, which you use to move icons and other Windows elements.

4. Point to the **My Computer icon**, press and hold down the **left mouse button**, move the mouse down and to the right, then release the mouse button
   The icon moves with the mouse pointer. This is called dragging. Next you will use the mouse to display a shortcut menu.

5. Point to the **My Computer icon**, then press and release the **right mouse button**
   Clicking the right mouse button is known as **right-clicking**. Right-clicking an item on the desktop displays a **pop-up menu**, shown in Figure A-3. This menu displays the commands most commonly used for the item you have clicked; the available commands are not therefore the same for every item.

6. Click anywhere outside the menu to close the pop-up menu

7. Move the **My Computer icon** back to its original position in the upper-left corner of the desktop using the pointing and dragging skills you have just learned

8. Point to the **My Computer icon**, then click the **left mouse button** twice quickly
   The My Computer window opens, containing several icons. Clicking the mouse button twice is known as **double-clicking**, and it allows you to open a window, program, or file that an icon represents. Leave the desktop as it is, and move on to the next lesson.

QuickTip

This book assumes you are using Windows 98 default mouse settings.

QuickTip

When a step tells you to "click," it means, by default, to left-click. The direction will say "right-click" if you are to click with the right mouse button.

FIGURE A-2: The mouse

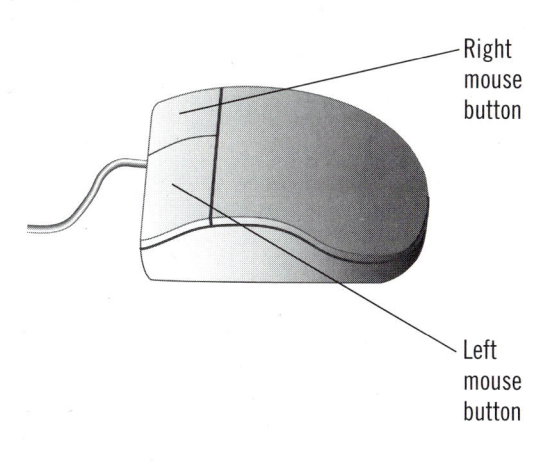

Right mouse button

Left mouse button

FIGURE A-3: Displaying a pop-up menu

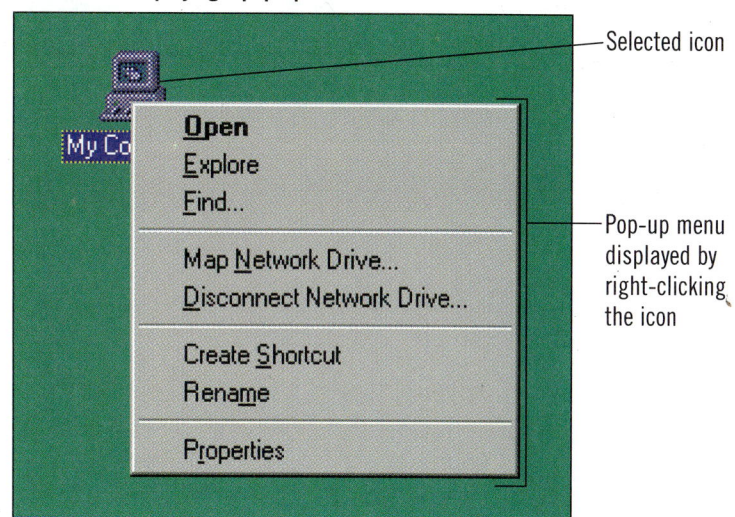

Selected icon

Pop-up menu displayed by right-clicking the icon

My Co...

Open
Explore
Find...
Map Network Drive...
Disconnect Network Drive...
Create Shortcut
Rename
Properties

TABLE A-2: Common mouse pointer shapes

shape	used to
▶	Select items, choose commands, start programs, and work in programs
I	Position mouse pointer for editing or inserting text; called the insertion point or cursor
▶⌛	Indicate Windows is busy processing a command
↔	Position mouse pointer on the border of a window for changing the size of a window
🖑	Position mouse pointer for selecting and opening Web-based content

TABLE A-3: Basic mouse techniques

task	what to do
Pointing	Move the mouse to position it over an item on the desktop
Clicking	Press and release the left mouse button
Double-clicking	Press and release the left mouse button twice quickly
Dragging	Point to an item, press and hold the left mouse button, move the mouse to a new location, then release the mouse button
Right-clicking	Point to an item, then press and release the right mouse button

CLUES TO USE

Using the mouse with the Internet

When you use the standard Windows operating system, you click an item to select it and double-click the item to open it. However, when you use the Internet, you point to an item to select it and single-click the item to open it. Because Windows 98 integrates use of the Internet with its other functions, it allows you to choose whether you want to extend the way you click on the Internet to the rest of your computer work. Therefore, Windows 98 gives you two choices for selecting and opening icons using the mouse buttons: single-click (known as the Internet or Web style) or double-click (known as the Classic style). To change from one style to the other, click the Start button on the taskbar, point to Settings, click Folder Options, then click the Web style, Classic style, or Custom option. Windows 98 is set by default to double-click using custom settings.

Windows 98

Getting Started with the Windows Desktop

The key to getting started with the Windows desktop is learning how to use the Start button on the taskbar. Clicking the Start button on the taskbar displays the **Start menu**, which is a list of commands that allows you to start a program, open a document, change a Windows setting, find a file, or display Help information. Table A-4 describes the available commands on this menu that are installed with Windows 98. As you become more familiar with Windows you might want to customize the Start menu to include additional items that you use most often and change Windows settings in the Control Panel to customize your Windows desktop. Begin by viewing the Start menu and opening the **Control Panel**, a window containing various programs that allow you to specify how your computer looks and performs.

1. **Click the Start button on the taskbar**

   The Start menu opens. You use the Settings command on the Start menu to change a Windows system setting.

2. **Point to Settings on the Start menu**

   An arrow next to a menu indicates a **cascading menu**, or a **submenu**—a list of commands for the menu item with the arrow next to it. Pointing at the arrow displays a submenu from which you can choose additional commands. The Settings submenu opens, shown in Figure A-4, listing commands to open the Control Panel and Printers; change settings for the taskbar, Start menu, folders, and icons; and customize the Windows desktop.

3. **Click Control Panel on the submenu**

   The Control Panel opens, shown in Figure A-5, containing icons for various programs that allow you to specify how your computer looks and performs. Leave the Control Panel open for now, and continue to the next lesson.

TABLE A-4: Start menu commands

command	description
Windows Update	Connects to a Microsoft Web site and updates your Windows 98 files as necessary
Programs	Opens programs included on the Start menu
Favorites	Connects to favorite Web sites, or opens folders or documents that you previously selected
Documents	Opens a list of documents most recently opened and saved
Settings	Allows user preferences for system settings, including Control Panel, printers, taskbar, Start menu, folders, icons, and Active Desktop
Find	Locates programs, files, folders, or computers on your computer network, or finds information or people on the Internet
Help	Displays Windows Help information by topic, alphabetical index, or search criteria
Run	Opens a program or file based on a location and filename that you type or select
Log Off	Allows you to log off the system and log on as a different user
Shut Down	Provides options to shut down the computer, restart the computer in Windows mode, or restart the computer in MS-DOS mode

FIGURE A-4: Cascading menu

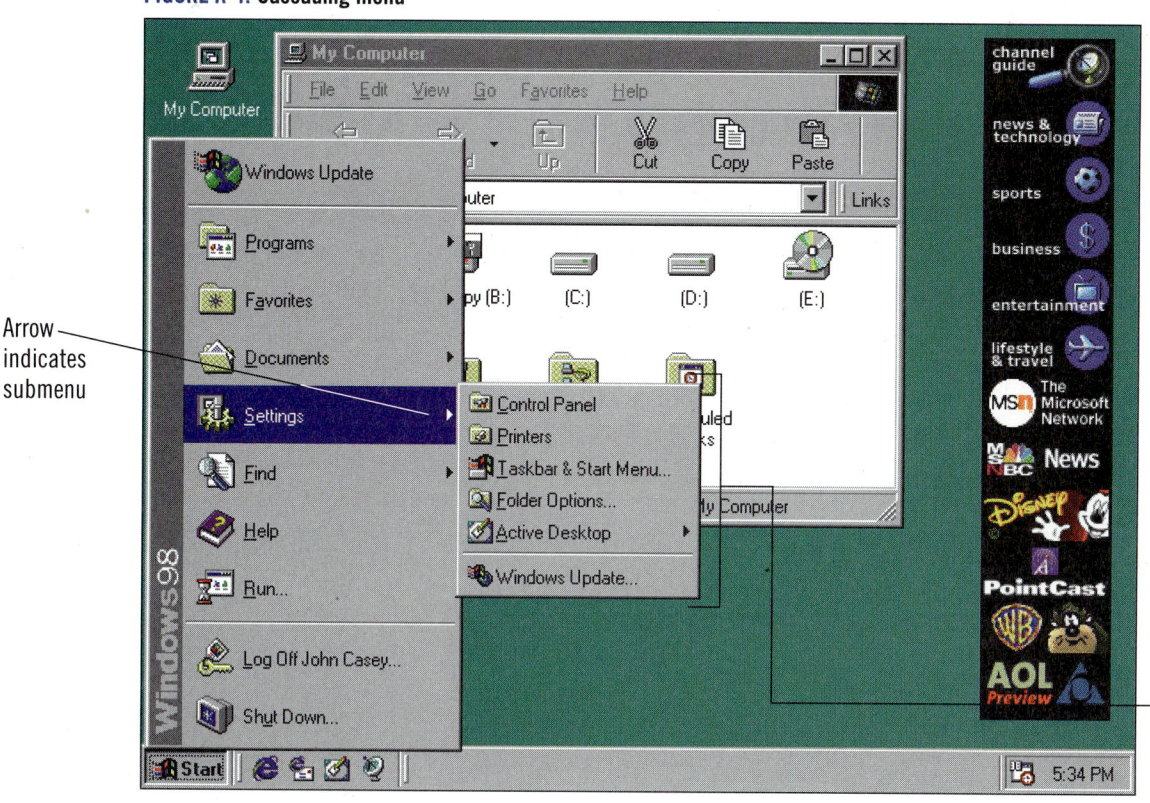

Arrow indicates submenu

Cascading menu, also called submenu

FIGURE A-5: Control Panel

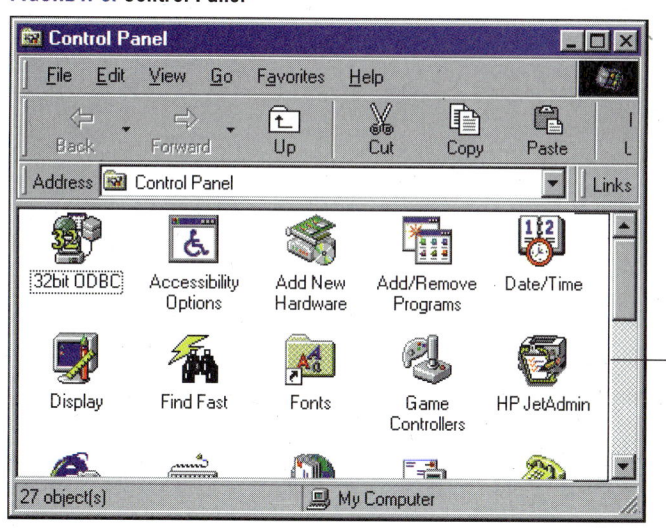

Icons for various programs to change Windows settings

Accessing the Internet from the Active Desktop

One of the important differences between Windows 98 and other versions of Windows is that Windows 98 allows you to access the Internet right from the desktop. This is possible because a program called Internet Explorer is integrated into the Windows 98 operating system. **Internet Explorer** is an example of a **browser**, a computer program designed to access the Internet. For example, commands on the Find submenu, On the Internet and People, and the Favorites command on the Start menu make it easy to find and access places on the Internet you visit frequently. For additional Internet access, you can use the Quick Launch toolbar on the taskbar to launch Internet-related programs, and the Channel Bar is available on the desktop to help you view channels. Windows 98 makes it easier than ever to access the Internet.

Windows 98

Moving and Resizing Windows

One of the powerful things about the Windows operating system is that you can open more than one window or program at once. This means, however, that the desktop can get cluttered with many open windows for the various windows and programs you are using. To organize your desktop, sometimes it is necessary to change the size of a window or move it to a different location. Each window, no matter what it contains, is surrounded by a standard border that you can drag to move the window or change its size. Each window also has three standard buttons in the upper-right corner that allow you to change the size of windows. Table A-5 shows the different mouse pointer shapes that appear when resizing windows. Try moving and resizing the Control Panel window now.

1. **Click anywhere in the My Computer window or click the My Computer button on the taskbar**
The My Computer window moves in front of the Control Panel window. The My Computer window is now **active**; this means that any actions you perform will take place in this window. At times, you might want to hide a window so that it isn't visible on the desktop but is still open.

2. **Click the Minimize button in the My Computer window**
The window no longer appears on the desktop, but you can still see a button named My Computer on the taskbar. When you **minimize** a window, you do not close it but merely reduce it to a button on the taskbar so that you can work more easily in other windows. The button on the taskbar reminds you that the program is still running.

3. **Point to the title bar on the Control Panel**
The **title bar** is the area along the top of the window that contains the name of the file and the program used to create it. When a window is active, the title bar color changes from gray to blue. You can move any window to a new location on the desktop by dragging the window's title bar.

4. **With the mouse pointer over any spot on the title bar, click and drag the window to center it on the desktop**
This action is similar to dragging an icon to a new location. The window is relocated.

5. **Click the Maximize button in the Control Panel**
When you **maximize** a window, it takes up the entire screen.

6. **Click the Restore button in the Control Panel**
The **Restore button** returns a window to its previous size, as shown in Figure A-6. The Restore button only appears when a window is maximized. Now try making the window smaller.

7. **Position the mouse pointer on the lower-right corner of the Control Panel window until the pointer changes to ⬉, as indicated in Figure A-6, then drag the corner up and to the left**
The window is now resized. In the next lesson you will work with the menus and toolbars in the Control Panel, so you can close My Computer now.

8. **Click the My Computer button on the taskbar**
The My Computer window is returned to the size it was before it was minimized and is now active. When you are finished using a window, you can close it with the Close button.

9. **Click the Close button, located in the upper-right corner of the My Computer window**
The My Computer window closes. You will learn more about My Computer in later lessons.

QuickTip

You can click the Show the Desktop button on the Quick Launch toolbar to minimize all open windows and programs in order to show the desktop.

QuickTip

You can resize windows by dragging any corner, not just the lower left. You can also drag any border to make the window taller, shorter, wider, or narrower.

FIGURE A-6: Restored Control Panel window

Title bar · Active window · Sizing buttons

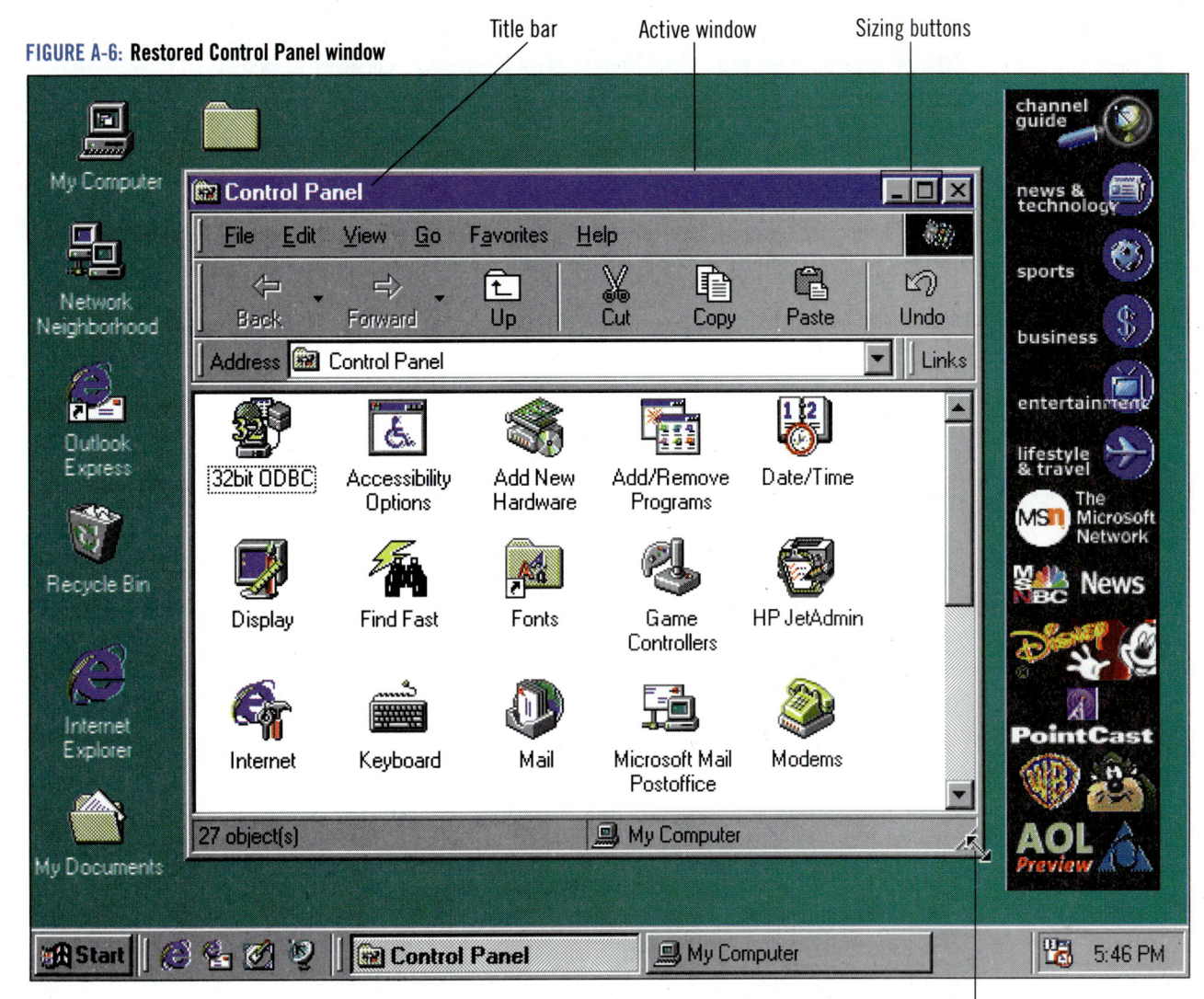

Drag here to size
both height and
width

TABLE A-5: Mouse pointer shapes that appear when resizing windows

mouse pointer shape	use to
↔	Drag the right or left edge of a window to change its width
↕	Drag the top or bottom edge of a window to change its height
⬉ or ⬈	Drag any corner of a window to change its size proportionally

CLUES TO USE

Moving and resizing the taskbar

In addition to windows, you can also resize and move other elements on the desktop, such as the taskbar, using the methods in this lesson. You can move the taskbar by dragging it to any edge (right, left, top, or bottom) of the desktop. You can also change the size of the taskbar by dragging its edge.

Using Menus and Toolbars

A **menu** is a list of commands that you use to accomplish certain tasks. You've already used the Start menu to open the Control Panel. A **command** is a directive that provides access to a program's feature. Each Windows program also has its own set of menus, which are located on the menu bar along the top of the program window. The **menu bar** organizes commands into groups of related operations. Each group is listed under the name of the menu, such as "File" or "Help." To access the commands in a menu, you click the name of the menu. See Table A-6 for examples of items on a typical menu. Some of the most frequently used commands on a menu can also be carried out by clicking a button on a toolbar. A **toolbar** contains buttons that are convenient shortcuts for menu commands. ➤ Use a menu and toolbar button to change how the Control Panel window's contents are displayed.

1. Click **View** on the menu bar
   The View menu appears, displaying the View commands, as shown in Figure A-7. When you click a menu name, a general description of the commands available on that menu appears in the status bar. On a menu, a **check mark** identifies a feature that is currently selected (that is, the feature is enabled or "on"). To disable ("turn off") the feature, you click the command again to remove the check mark. A **bullet mark** also indicates that an option is enabled. To disable a command with a bullet mark next to it, however, you must select another command (within the menu section) in its place. In the next step, you will select a command.

2. On the View menu, click **Small Icons**
   The icons are now smaller that they were before, taking up less room in the window. Since the Control Panel window has been resized, the toolbar buttons across the top do not fit in the window. To display all the buttons, you can maximize the Control Panel window or reduce the size of the toolbar buttons. To reduce the size of the toolbar buttons, you remove the text labels at the bottom of the buttons.

3. Click **View** on the menu bar, then point to **Toolbars**
   The Toolbars submenu appears, displaying check marks next to the toolbar commands. To remove the text labels on the toolbar buttons, you click Text Labels to turn the feature off.

4. Click **Text Labels**
   The Control Panel toolbar appears without text labels below the menu bar. This toolbar includes buttons for the commands that you use most frequently while you are in the Control Panel. When you position the mouse pointer over a button, the name of the button, known as a **ScreenTip**, appears. Use the ScreenTip feature to explore a button on the toolbar.

5. On the Control Panel toolbar, position the pointer over the **Views button** 📇 to display the ScreenTip
   Some toolbar buttons appear with an arrow, which indicates the button contains several choices. You click the button arrow to display the choices.

6. On the Control Panel toolbar, click the **Views button list arrow** 📇▾ as shown in Figure A-8, then click **Details**
   The Details view includes a description of each Control Panel program. In the next lesson you will use scroll bars in the Control Panel to view and read the description of each Control Panel program.

FIGURE A-7: View menu in the Control Panel

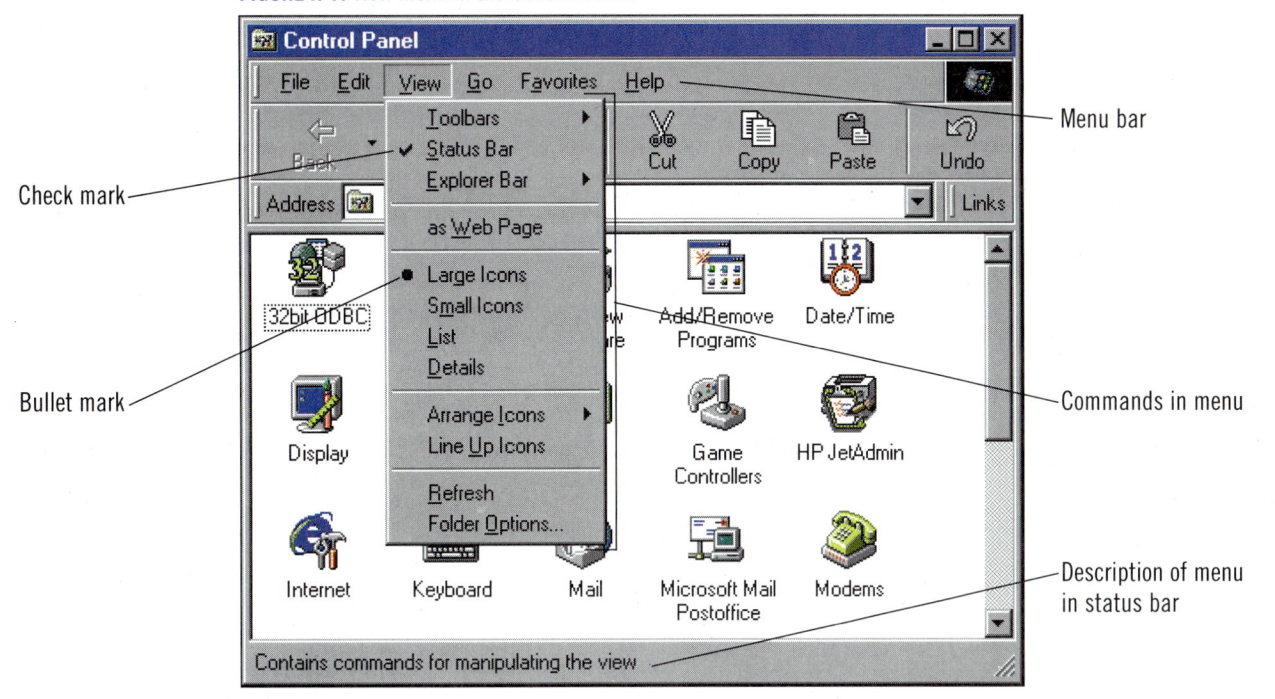

Menu bar

Check mark

Bullet mark

Commands in menu

Description of menu in status bar

FIGURE A-8: Control Panel toolbars

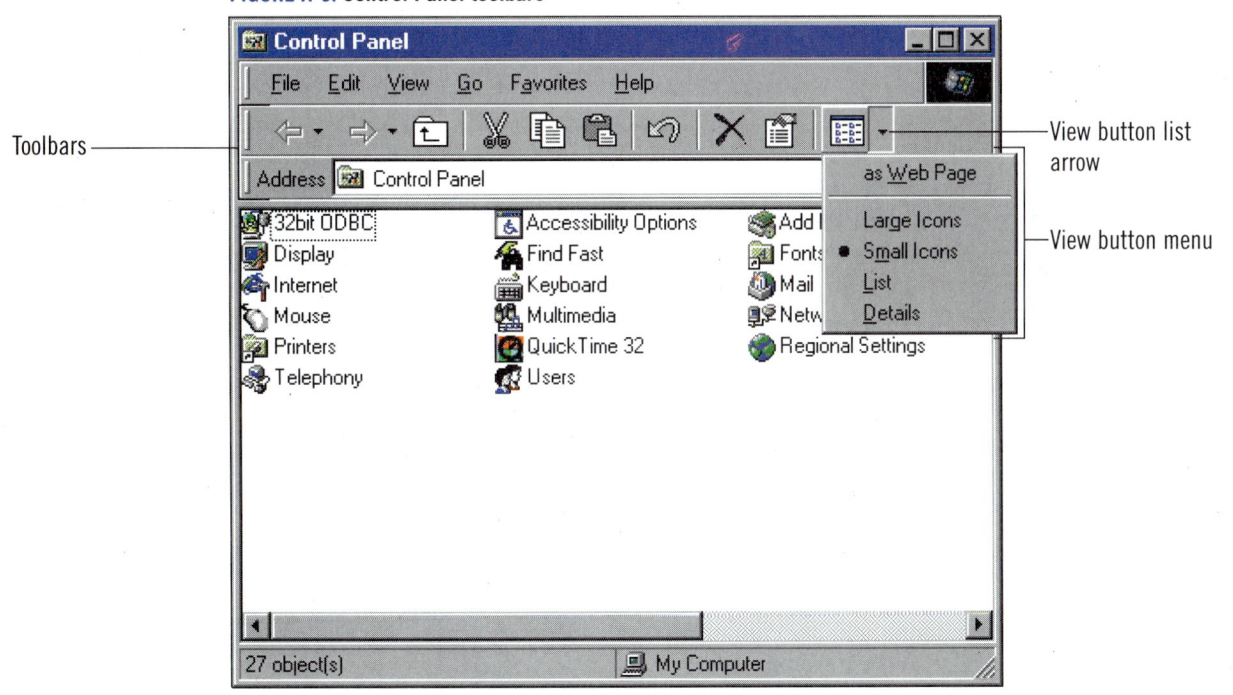

Toolbars

View button list arrow

View button menu

TABLE A-6: Typical items on a menu

item	description	example
Dimmed command	A menu command that is not currently available	Undo Ctrl+Z
Ellipsis	Indicates that a dialog box will open that allows you to select from several options	Save As...
Triangle	Indicates that a cascading menu will open containing an additional list of commands	Zoom ▶
Keyboard shortcut	An alternative to using the mouse for executing a command	Paste Ctrl+V
Underlined letter	Indicates the letter to press while holding down the [Alt] key for a keyboard shortcut	Print Preview

Using Scroll Bars

When you cannot see all of the items available in a window, scroll bars appear on the right and/or bottom edges of the window. **Scroll bars** allow you to display the additional contents of the window. See Figure A-9 for the components of the scroll bars. The vertical scroll bar moves your view up and down through a window; the horizontal scroll bar moves your view from left to right. There are several ways you can use the scroll bars. When you need to scroll only a short distance, you can use the scroll arrows. When you need to scroll more quickly, you can click in the scroll bar above or below the **scroll box**, which moves the view up or down one window's height (the line that was at the bottom of the screen is moved to the top, and vice versa). Dragging the scroll box moves you even more quickly to a new part of the window. See Table A-7 for a summary of the different ways to use scroll bars. You can use the scroll bars to view and read the description of each Control Panel program.

QuickTip

When scroll bars don't appear in a window, it means that all the information fits completely in the window.

1. In the Control Panel, click the **down scroll arrow** in the vertical scroll bar, as shown in Figure A-9
   Clicking this arrow moves the view down one line. Clicking the up arrow moves the view up one line at a time.

2. Click the **up scroll arrow** in the vertical scroll bar
   The view moves up one line.

3. Click anywhere in the area below the scroll box in the vertical scroll bar
   The contents in the window scroll down in a larger increment.

4. Click the area above the scroll box in the vertical scroll bar
   The contents in the window scroll back up. To move in even greater increments, you can drag the scroll box to a new position.

5. Drag the **scroll box** in the horizontal scroll bar to the middle of the bar
   The scroll box indicates your relative position within the window, in this case, the halfway point. After reading the Control Panel program descriptions, you restore the Control Panel to its original display.

6. On the Control Panel toolbar, click the **Views button list arrow** ⊞▾ , then click **Large Icons**

7. Click **View** on the menu bar, point to **Toolbars**, then click **Text Labels**
   In the next lesson you will open a Control Panel program to learn how to work with dialog boxes.

FIGURE A-9: Scroll bars in Control Panel

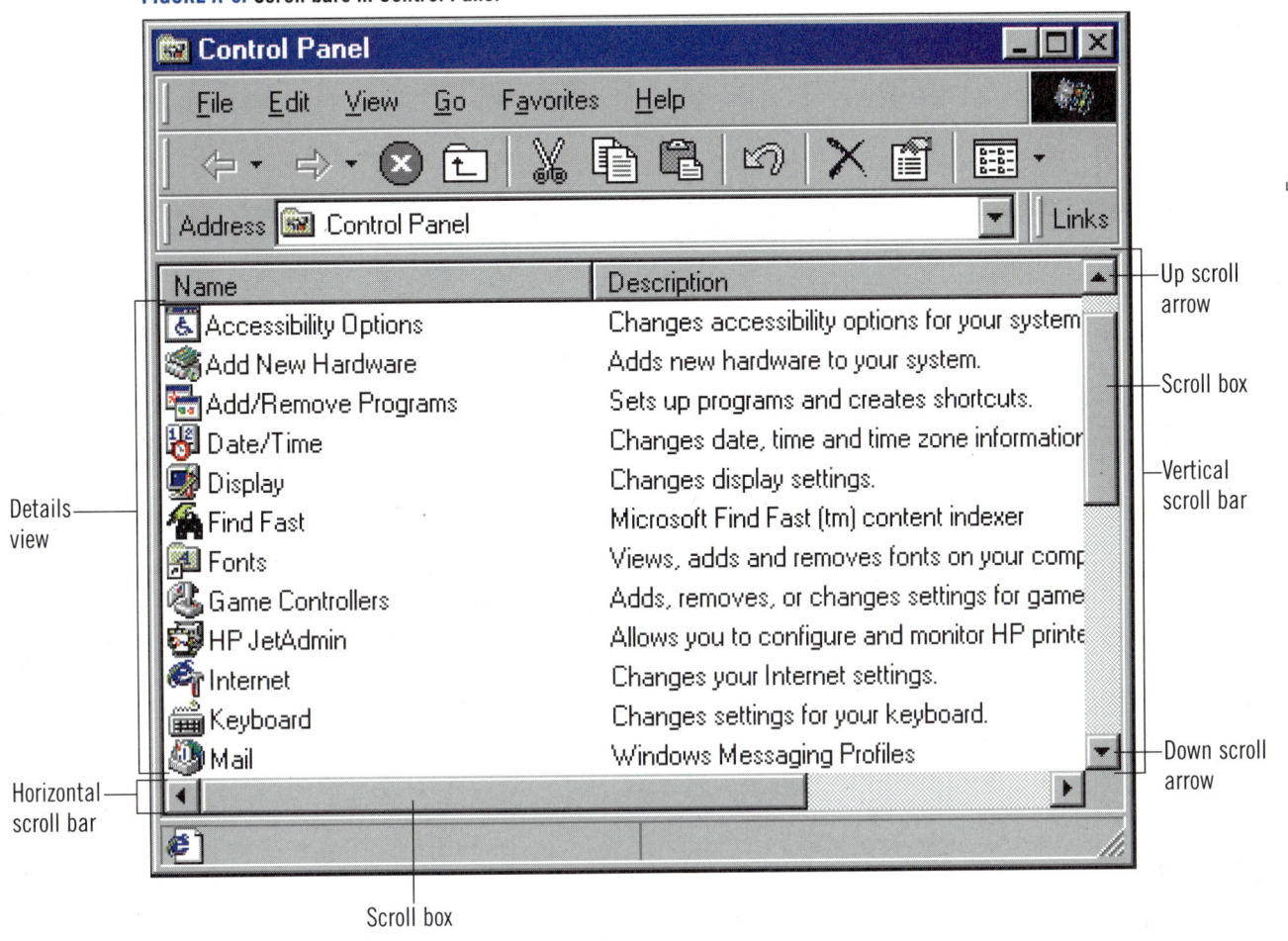

Details view

Horizontal scroll bar

Up scroll arrow

Scroll box

Vertical scroll bar

Down scroll arrow

Scroll box

TABLE A-7: Using scroll bars in a window

to	do this
Move down one line	Click the down arrow at the bottom of the vertical scroll bar
Move up one line	Click the up arrow at the top of the vertical scroll bar
Move down one window's height	Click in the area below the scroll box in the vertical scroll bar
Move up one window's height	Click in the area above the scroll box in the vertical scroll bar
Move up or down a greater distance in the window	Drag the scroll box in the vertical scroll bar
Move a short distance side to side in a window	Click the left or right arrows in the horizontal scroll bar
Move to the right one window's width	Click in the area to the right of the scroll box in the horizontal scroll bar
Move to the left one window's width	Click in the area to the left of the scroll box in the horizontal scroll bar
Move left or right a greater distance in the window	Drag the scroll box in the horizontal scroll bar

Using Dialog Boxes

A **dialog box** is a window that opens when you choose a command from a menu that is followed by an ellipsis (. . .). The ellipsis indicates that more information is required before the program can carry out the command you selected. Dialog boxes open in other situations as well, such as when you open a program in the Control Panel. In a dialog box, you specify the options you want using a variety of elements. See Figure A-10 and Table A-8 for some of the typical elements of a dialog box. ▰▰▰ Practice using a dialog box to control your mouse settings.

Steps

1. **In the Control Panel, double-click the Mouse icon** (you might need to scroll down the Control Panel window to find this icon)
   The Mouse Properties dialog box opens, shown in Figure A-11. The options in this dialog box allow you to control the way the mouse buttons are configured, select the types of pointers that are displayed, choose the speed of the mouse movement on the screen, and specify what type of mouse you are using. **Tabs** at the top of the dialog box separate these options into related categories.

2. **Click the Motion tab**
   This tab has two boxes. The first, labeled Pointer speed, has a slider for you to set how fast the mouse pointer moves on the screen in relation to how you move the mouse in your hand. The second, Pointer trail, has a check box you can select to make the mouse pointer easier to see, especially on certain types of computer screens, such as laptop computers. The slider lets you specify the degree to which the option is in effect—the length of the pointer trail. You will experiment with the pointer trail options.

3. **In the Pointer trail box, click the Show pointer trails check box to select it, then drag the slider below the check box all the way to the right**
   As you move the mouse, notice the long pointer trails.

4. **Click the other tabs in the Mouse Properties dialog box and examine the options that are available in each category**
   Now, you need to select a command button to carry out the options you've selected. The two most common command buttons are OK and Cancel. Clicking OK accepts your changes and closes the dialog box; clicking Cancel leaves the original settings intact and closes the dialog box. The third command button in this dialog box is Apply. Clicking the Apply button accepts the changes you've made and keeps the dialog box open so that you can select additional options. Because you might share this computer with others, it's important to return the dialog box options back to the original settings.

5. **Click Cancel to leave the original settings intact and close the dialog box**

6. **Click the Close button in the upper-right corner of the Control Panel**

FIGURE A-10: Dialog box elements

List box   List arrow

Check box

Option button

Spin box

Command button

Text box

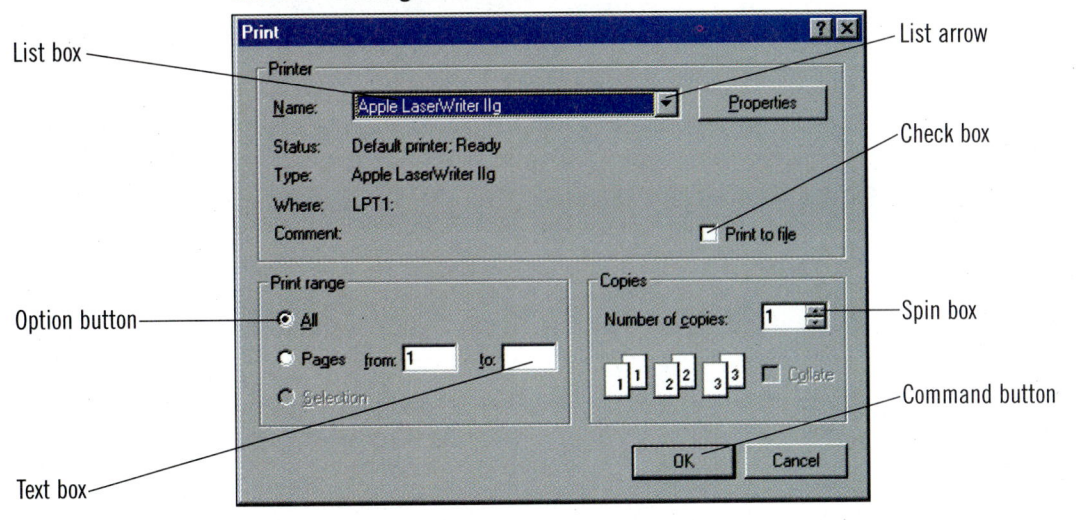

FIGURE A-11: Mouse Properties dialog box

Tabs

Button configuration section

Slider

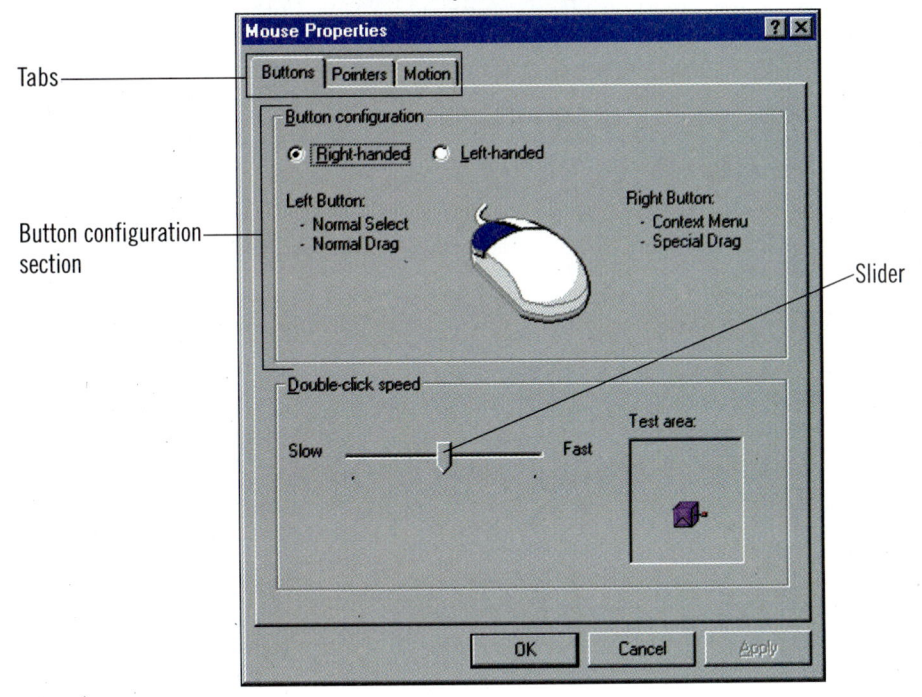

TABLE A-8: Typical items in a dialog box

item	description
Check box	A square box that turns an option on (when the box is checked) and off (when the box is blank)
Command button	A rectangular button with the name of the command on it; it carries out a command in a dialog box
List box	A box containing a list of items; to choose an item, click the list arrow, then click the desired item
Option button	A small circle that selects a single dialog box option; you cannot check more than one option button in a list
Spin box	A box with two arrows and a text box; allows you to scroll numerical increments or type a number
Slider	A shape that you drag to set the degree to which an option is in effect
Tab	A place to organize related options
Text box	A box in which you type text

Using Windows Help

When you have a question about how to do something in Windows 98, you can usually find the answer with a few clicks of your mouse. There are a variety of different ways to access **Windows Help**, which is like a book stored on your computer, complete with an index and a table of contents to make finding information easier. You can click Help on the Start menu to open the main Windows Help dialog box. To get help on a specific program, you can click Help on the program's menu bar. You can also access **context-sensitive help**, help specifically related to what you are doing, using a variety of methods such as pointing to or right-clicking an object. Use Help to find out about the Control Panel that comes with Windows.

1. Click the **Start button** on the taskbar, then click **Help**

   The main Help command is located on the Start menu. While there are other ways to get help, this is the easiest way to access the list of all Help topics that are available. The Windows Help dialog box opens, shown in Figure A-12, with the Contents tab in front. The Contents tab provides you with a list of Help categories. Each book icon has several "chapters" (subcategories) that you can see by clicking the book icon or the name of the Help category next to the book.

2. Click the **Contents tab** (if necessary), point to the **Exploring Your Computer** category, then click to display the subcategories underneath

   When you point to a Help category, the mouse changes to the hand pointer and the Help category text is selected. The text changes to gray and is underlined. This is similar to the way selecting on the Internet works. You continue to click subcategories to find the Help topic you want.

QuickTip

You can hide the left pane of the Help window to make reading the information easier. Click the Hide button on the Help toolbar to hide the left pane; click the Show button to redisplay it.

3. Click the **The Windows Desktop** subcategory, then click the **Getting Started with Windows Desktop Update** topic

   The Help topic appears in the right pane, as shown in A-13. **Panes** divide a window into two or more sections. Read the help information on the Windows desktop. You can move back and forth between Help topics you have already visited by clicking the Back button and the Forward button on the Help toolbar.

4. Click the **Index tab**

   The Index tab provides you with an alphabetical list of all the Help topics that are available, much like an index at the end of a book. You can find out about any Windows feature by either entering the topic in the text box, or by scrolling down to the topic for which you want help, selecting a topic, and then clicking Display.

5. Click the **Search tab**

   The Search tab helps you locate the topic you need using keywords. You can find a topic by entering a keyword in the text box, clicking List Topics, selecting a topic, and then clicking Display. If you cannot find the information you need, you can look on the Internet, where Microsoft has updated information on Windows 98.

QuickTip

To print all or part of the Windows Help information, click the Options button on the Help toolbar, then click Print.

6. Click the **Web Help button** on the Help toolbar

   Windows Update Web site information appears in the right pane. You can access the Windows Update Web site by clicking the "Support Online" underlined text. When you click the underlined text, you connect to the Windows Update Web site. The Web site provides links to Internet resources, including Online Help, Troubleshooting Wizards, the Microsoft Knowledge Base, the Microsoft Technical Support for Windows Home Page, and the Windows Update Manager. Once you've read the information, you can close the window.

7. Click the **Close button** in the Windows Help window

   The Help window closes.

FIGURE A-12: Windows Help dialog box

Help tabs

Help toolbar

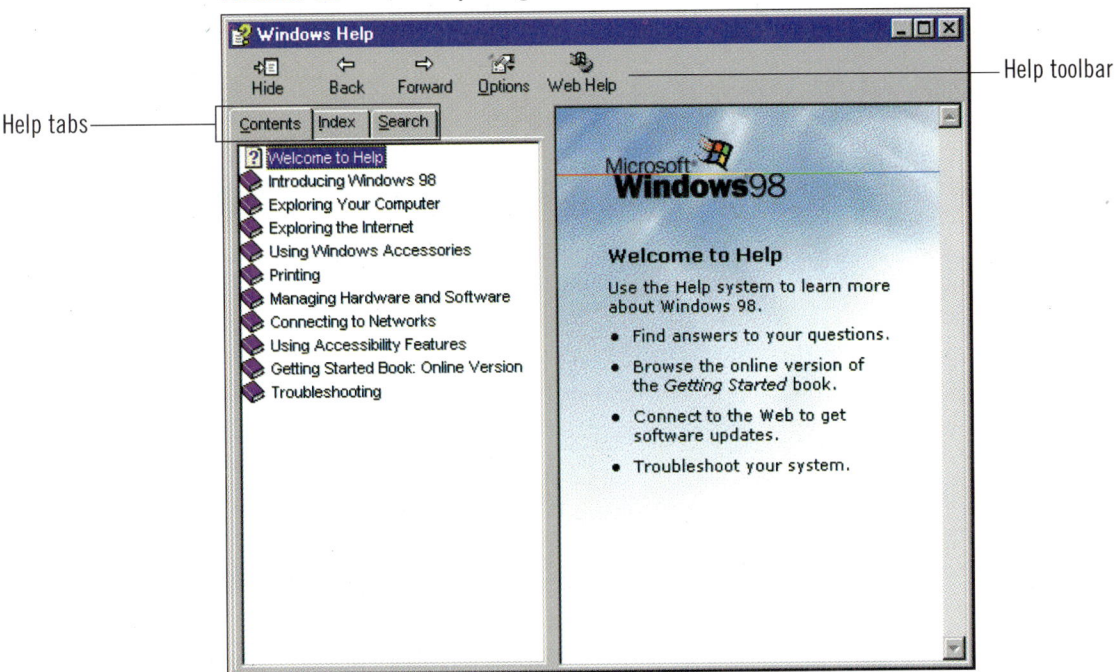

FIGURE A-13: Specific help on a particular topic

Help topic

Hand pointer

Left pane displays
Help categories

Right pane displays
help on the topic
you select

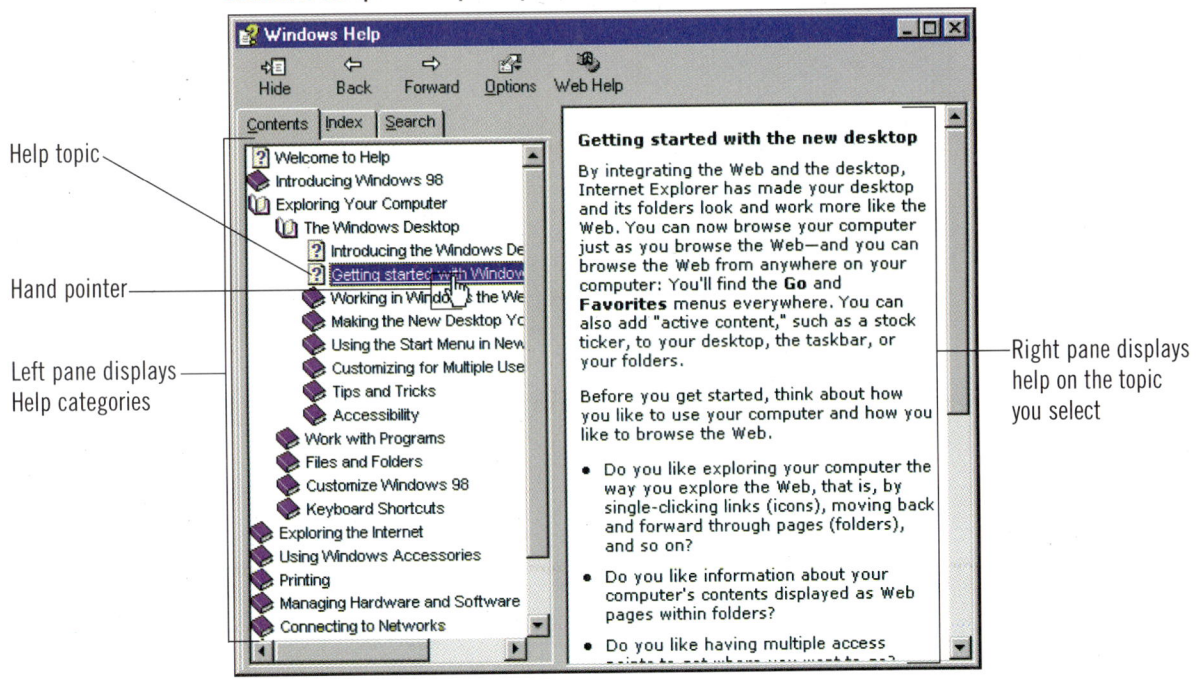

Context-sensitive help

To receive help in a dialog box, click the Help button [?] in the upper-right corner of the dialog box; the mouse pointer changes to ▷?. Click on the item in the dialog box for which you need additional information. A pop-up window opens, providing a brief explanation of the selected feature. You can also click the right-mouse button on an item in a dialog box, then click the What's This? Button to display the explanation. In addition, when you click the right mouse button in a Help topic window, you can choose commands to annotate, copy, and print the contents of the topic. Help windows always appear on top of the currently active window, so you can see Help topics while you work.

Windows 98

Shutting Down Windows

When you are finished working at your computer, you need to make sure to **shut down**, or exit, the machine properly. This involves several steps: saving and closing all open files, closing all open windows, exiting all running programs, shutting down Windows itself, and, finally, turning off the computer. If you turn off the computer while Windows or other programs are running, you could lose important data. Once all files, windows and programs are closed, you choose the Shut Down command from the Start menu. The Shut Down Windows dialog box, shown in Figure A-14, opens with three options. See Table A-9 for a description of each option. ✏️ Close all your open files, windows, and programs, and then exit Windows.

1. If you have any open windows or programs, click the **Close button** ☒ in the upper-right corner of the window
   Complete the remaining steps to shut down Windows and your computer only if you have been told to do so by your instructor.

2. Click the **Start button** on the taskbar, then click **Shut Down**
   The Shut Down Windows dialog box opens as shown in Figure A-14. In this dialog box, you have the option to shut down the computer, restart the computer in Windows mode, or restart the computer in MS-DOS mode. You choose the Shut Down option.

3. Click the **Shut Down option button**, if it isn't already selected

4. If you are working in a lab, click **Cancel** to return to the Windows desktop; if you are working on your own machine or if your instructor told you to shut down Windows, click **OK** to exit Windows

5. When you see the message "It's now safe to turn off your computer," turn off your computer and monitor

Logging off Windows

For a quick change between users of the same computer, you can choose the Log Off command on the Start menu. This command identifies the name of the user who is currently logged on. When you choose this command, Windows 98 shuts down and automatically restarts to the Enter Network Password dialog box. When the new user enters a user name and password, Windows will provide access to network capabilities.

FIGURE A-14: Shut Down Windows dialog box

Click to shut down Windows

Click to restart computer in Windows mode

Click to restart computer in MS-DOS mode

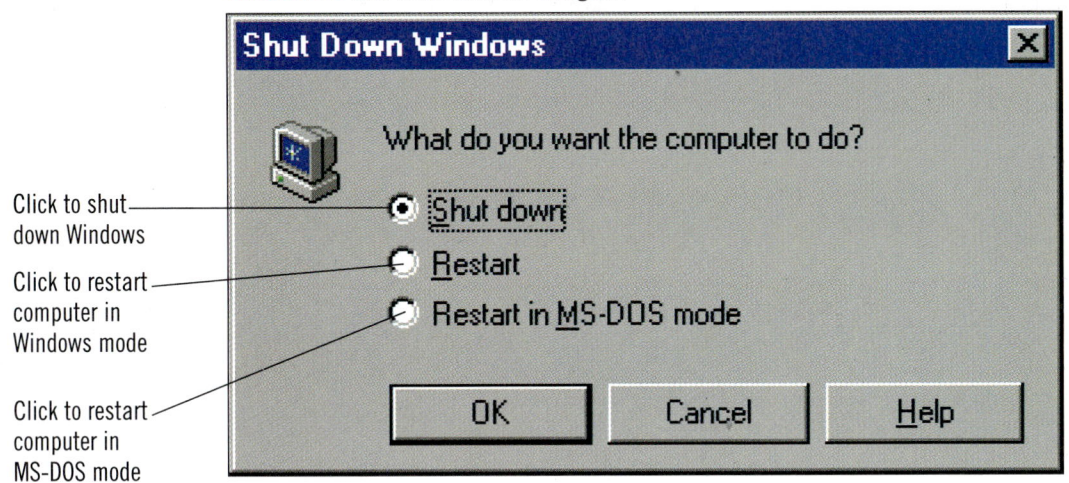

TABLE A-9: Shut down options

shut down option	function	when to use it
Shut down	Prepares the computer to be turned off	When you are finished working with Windows and you want to shut off your computer
Restart	Restarts the computer and reloads Windows	When you want to restart the computer and begin working with Windows again; (your programs might have frozen or stopped working)
Restart in MS-DOS mode	Starts the computer in the MS-DOS mode	When you want to run programs under MS-DOS or use DOS commands to work with files

Practice

▶ Concepts Review

Label each of the elements of the screen shown in Figure A-15.

FIGURE A-15

Match each of the terms with the statement that describes its function.

6. Allows for minimizing, maximizing, and restoring windows
7. The item you first click to start a program
8. Used to point at screen elements and make selections
9. Where the name of the program and file appear
10. Where deleted files are placed
11. Displays the Start button and buttons for currently open programs and windows

a. Recycle Bin
b. Sizing buttons
c. Start button
d. Taskbar
e. Title bar
f. Mouse

Select the best answer from the following list of choices.

12. The term for moving an item to a new location on the desktop is
    a. Pointing.
    b. Clicking.
    c. Dragging.
    d. Restoring.

13. The Maximize button is used to
   a. Return a window to its original size.
   b. Expand a window to fill the entire screen.
   c. Scroll slowly through a window.
   d. Reduce a window to a button on the taskbar.

14. The Minimize button is used to
   a. Return a window to its original size.
   b. Expand a window to fill the entire screen.
   c. Scroll slowly through a window.
   d. Reduce a window to a button on the taskbar.

15. The Menu bar provides access to a program's functions through
   a. Toolbar buttons.
   b. Scroll buttons.
   c. Commands.
   d. Dialog box elements.

16. To move the contents of the window up one screen,
   a. Click the up scroll arrow.
   b. Click the down scroll arrow.
   c. Click in the scroll bar above the scroll box.
   d. Click in the scroll bar below the scroll box.

17. An ellipses after a menu command indicates
   a. The menu command is not currently available.
   b. A dialog box will open.
   c. Another menu will display.
   d. A keyboard shortcut to that command.

18. Which is not a method for getting Help?
   a. Click the Start button on the taskbar, then click Help
   b. Click the question mark button in a dialog box
   c. Click Help on a program's menu bar
   d. Right-click in a dialog box, then use the Help pointer to point to what you need help with

► Skills Review

1. **Identify Windows items on the screen.**
   a. Identify and write down as many items on the desktop as you can, without referring to the lesson.
   b. Compare your results with Figure A-1.

2. **Practice using the mouse.**
   a. Move the mouse on your desk and watch how the mouse pointer moves across the screen.
   b. Point at the My Computer icon on the desktop.
   c. Click the My Computer icon once. Notice that the icon's title is highlighted.
   d. Press and hold down the mouse button, then drag the My Computer icon to the opposite side of the desktop. Release the mouse button when you are finished.
   e. Drag the My Computer icon back to the original location.
   f. Practice clicking and dragging other icons on the desktop.
   g. Double-click the My Computer icon.

3. **Get started with Windows.**
   a. Click the Start menu.
   b. Point to Settings.
   c. Click Control Panel.

4. **Move and resize windows.**
   a. Click the My Computer window.
   b. Click the Minimize button.
   c. Point to the title bar on the Control Panel window, then drag the window to the center of the desktop.
   d. Click the Maximize button.
   e. Click the Restore button.
   f. Position the mouse pointer on any corner of the Control Panel window, and drag to make the window smaller.
   g. Click the My Computer button on the taskbar.
   h. Click the Close button on the My Computer window.

5. **Practice working with menus and toolbars.**
   a. Click View on the menu bar, point to Toolbars, then click Text Labels.
   b. Click View on the menu bar, then click List.
   c. Click the Views button arrow on the toolbar, then click Details.

6. **Practice using scroll bars.**
   a. Click below the vertical scroll box.
   b. Click the vertical up scroll arrow.
   c. Drag the horizontal scroll box to the middle of the scroll bar.
   d. Click the View button arrow on the toolbar, then click Large Icons.
   e. Click View on the menu bar, point to Toolbars, then click Text Labels.

7. Practice using dialog boxes.

   a. Double-click the Display icon.

   b. Click the Appearance tab.

   c. Click the Scheme list arrow, then select a color scheme.

   d. Click Apply (but don't click OK yet).

   e. Click the Scheme list arrow, then click Windows Standard to return the color scheme back to the way it was.

   f. Click OK, then close the Control Panel.

8. Use Windows Help.

   a. Click the Start button, then click Help.

   b. Click the Index tab.

   c. Type "dialog boxes."

   d. Click Display.

   e. Select "To get help in a dialog box", then click Display again to see the topic.

   f. Read the Help topic in the right pane.

   g. Click the Close button.

9. Exit Windows.

   a. Click the Start button, then click Shut Down.

   b. Click the Restart option button.

   c. Click OK if you are not working in a lab or if your lab manager approves of shutting down the computer. Otherwise, click Cancel.

▶ Independent Challenges

1. Windows 98 provides extensive online help. At anytime, you can select Help from the Start menu and get the assistance you need. Use the Help options to learn about the topics listed below.

   To complete this independent challenge:

1. Locate help on My Computer.
2. Locate help on adjusting the double-click speed of the mouse.
3. Locate help on changing the color of the desktop.
4. Locate help on changing the appearance of scroll bars.
5. Locate help on exiting programs.
6. If you have a printer connected to your computer, print one or more of the Help topics.
7. Close the Windows Help window.

2. You can customize many Windows features to suit your needs and preferences. One way you do this is to change the appearance of the taskbar on the desktop.

To complete this independent challenge:

1. Position the mouse pointer over the top border of the taskbar. When the pointer changes shape, drag upwards to increase the size of the taskbar.
2. Position the mouse pointer over a blank area of the taskbar, and then drag to the top of the screen to move the taskbar.
3. Click the Start button, point to Settings, and click Taskbar & Start menu. On the Taskbar Options tab, click the Show Clock check box to deselect the option, and then observe the effect on the taskbar.
4. Print the Screen (Press the Print Screen key to make a copy of the screen, open Paint, click Edit on the menu bar, click Paste to paste the screen into Paint, then click Yes to paste the large image, if necessary. Click File on the menu bar, click Print, then click OK.)
5. Restore the taskbar to its original setting, size, and location on the screen.

3. You have accepted a new job in New York City. After moving into your new home and unpacking your stuff, you decide to set up your computer. Once you set up and turn on the computer, you decide to change the date and time settings to reflect New York.

To complete this independent challenge:

1. Open the Control Panel window.
2. Double-click the Date/Time icon.
3. Click the Time Zone tab.
4. Select Eastern Time (US & Canada) from the list.
5. Click the Date & Time tab.
6. Change the month and year to September 1999, then click Apply.
7. Print the screen. (See Independent Challenge 1, Step 4 for screen printing instructions)
8. Return the date and time zone back to their original settings.
9. Click OK.
10. Close the Control Panel window.

4. You are a student in a Windows 98 course. After learning basic Windows 98 Active Desktop skills, you want to learn how to customize the desktop. Use the online version of the Getting Started Book in Windows Help to find information on customizing your desktop and then print the related Help topics.

To complete this independent challenge:

1. Open the Windows Help window.
2. Display Getting Started Book: Online Version.
3. Display Microsoft Windows 98 Getting Started.
4. Open Getting Started.
5. Display Customizing Your Desktop.
6. Display Choosing a Desktop Style.
7. Print the Overview.
8. Close the Windows Help window.

Working
with Windows Programs

Objectives

- ▶ Start a program
- ▶ Open and save a WordPad document
- ▶ Edit text in WordPad
- ▶ Format text in WordPad
- ▶ Use Paint
- ▶ Copy data between programs
- ▶ Print a document
- ▶ Play a video clip
- ▶ Play a sound

Now that you know how to work with common Windows graphical elements, you're ready to work with programs. Windows comes with several **Accessories**: built-in programs that, while not as feature-rich as many programs sold separately, are extremely useful for completing basic tasks. In this unit, you will work with some of these accessories. John Casey, the owner of Wired Coffee Company, will use several Accessories to prepare a coffee menu.

Windows 98

Starting a Program

A Windows program is software designed to run on computers using the Windows operating system. To start a program in Windows 98, you click the Start button, point to Programs to open the Programs submenu, point to a submenu (if necessary), and then click the program you want to start. In this lesson, you'll start a Windows Accessory called WordPad, a word processing program that comes with Windows. Throughout the rest of this unit, you'll work with WordPad and other Windows Accessories to learn essential Windows skills.

Steps

1. **Click the Start button on the taskbar**
   The Start menu opens.

2. **Point to Programs on the Start menu**
   The Programs submenu opens, listing the programs and submenus for programs installed on your computer. WordPad is in the submenu called Accessories.

3. **Point to Accessories on the Programs submenu**
   The Accessories submenu opens, as shown in Figure B-1. Locate WordPad on this submenu.

4. **Click WordPad on the Accessories submenu**
   Your mouse pointer will change momentarily to an hourglass, indicating that you are to wait while Windows starts the WordPad program. The WordPad window then appears on your desktop, as shown in Figure B-2. The WordPad window includes two toolbars, called the toolbar and format bar, as well as a ruler, a work area, and a status bar. A blinking cursor, known as the **insertion point**, appears in the work area of the WordPad window, indicating where new text will appear. The WordPad program button appears in the taskbar, indicating that the WordPad program is now running.

5. **Click the Maximize button in the WordPad window**
   WordPad expands to fill the screen. In the next lesson you will open and save a document in WordPad.

FIGURE B-1: Starting WordPad using the Start menu

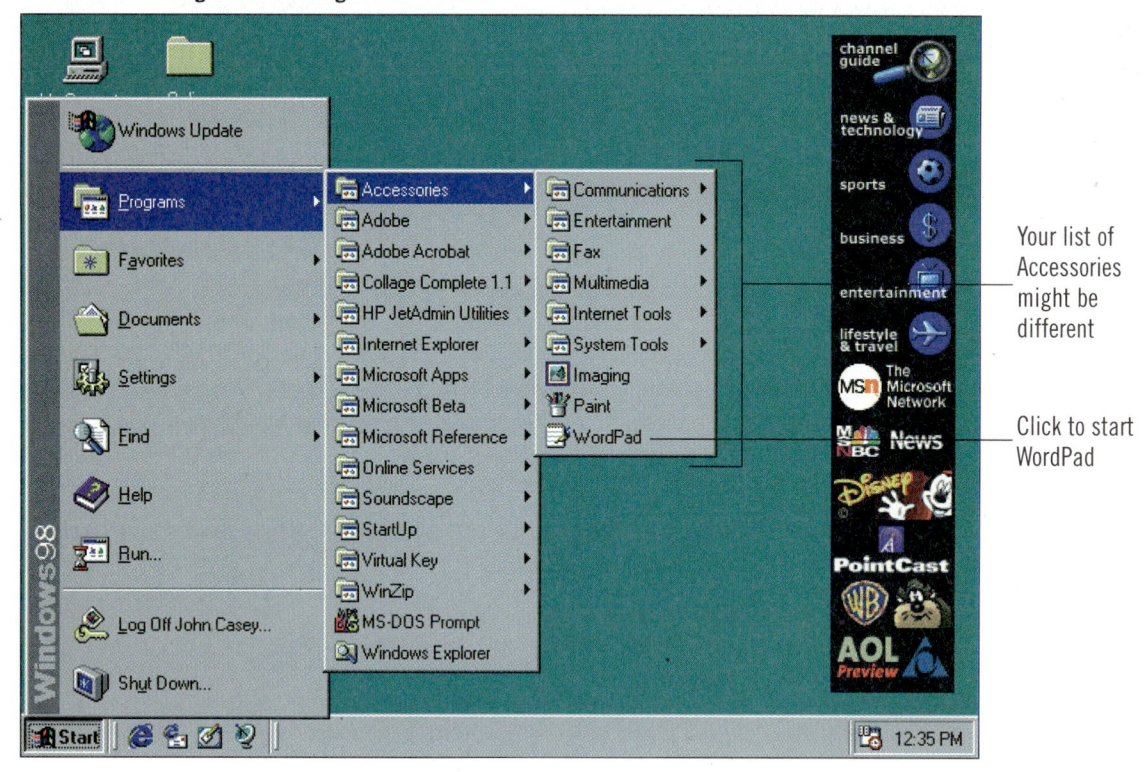

Your list of
Accessories
might be
different

Click to start
WordPad

FIGURE B-2: Windows desktop with the WordPad window open

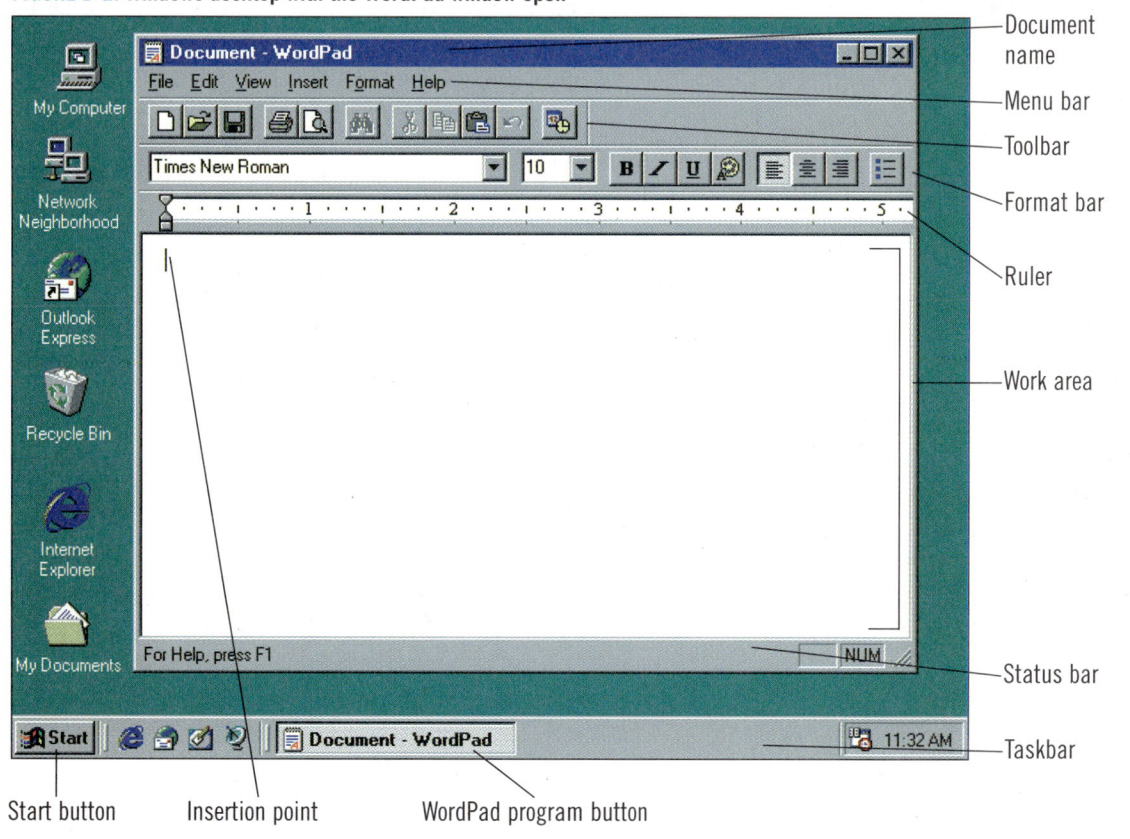

Document
name

Menu bar

Toolbar

Format bar

Ruler

Work area

Status bar

Taskbar

Start button   Insertion point   WordPad program button

Opening and Saving a WordPad Document

A **document** is the result of your work using a word processing program. You can use WordPad to create documents such as letters, memos, and resumes. When you start WordPad, a blank document appears in the work area of the WordPad window, known as the **document window**. You can enter new information to create a new document and save the result as a file, or you can open an existing file and save the document with any changes you made. In this unit you will open a document that John created. To prevent any accidental changes to the original file, you will save it with a new name. This makes a copy of the document so you can make changes to the new document and leave the file John created unaltered. This way you can repeat a lesson. ✒ John wants to open an existing WordPad document (a coffee menu), make some changes, and then save the results.

1. **Insert your Student Disk into the appropriate drive, then click the Open button**  **on the WordPad toolbar**
   The Open dialog box opens, as shown in Figure B-3. In this dialog box, you locate and choose the file you wish to open. The file John created is stored on your Student Disk.

2. **Click the Look in list arrow, then click the drive that contains your Student Disk**
   A list of the files and folders stored on the Student Disk appears in the file list.

3. **In the file list, click Win B-1, then click Open**
   The file named Win B-1 opens. This is a menu for the coffee company. Save this file under a new name so you don't make any changes to the original file. You will use a more descriptive name for the file so you can identify its contents more easily.

4. **Click File on the menu bar, then click Save As**
   The Save As dialog box opens, as shown in Figure B-4. The Save As command allows you to save an existing document under a new name. Now specify a new name.

5. **If Win B-1 is not already selected, click in the File name text box, then select the entire filename by dragging the mouse pointer over it**
   In WordPad, as in most other Windows programs, you must select text before you can modify it. When you **select** text, the selection appears **highlighted** (white text on a black background) to indicate that it has been selected. Any action you now take will be performed on the selected text.

6. **Type Coffee Menu to replace the selected text**
   As soon as you start typing, the selected text is replaced by the text you are typing. John decides to store the Coffee Menu document on the Student Disk.

7. **Click Save**
   Once you click Save, the file is saved under the new name, Coffee Menu, which you should now see in the title bar of the WordPad window. The original file, called Win B-1, is automatically closed.

QuickTip

When an existing document is open, you can click the New button □ on the toolbar to create a blank new document. The original existing document is automatically closed.

FIGURE B-3: Open dialog box

List of files and folders stored in the drive or folder selected in the Look in list box; your list might be different

Type filename here

Select type of file here

Click to specify the location of file to be opened

Click to open selected file

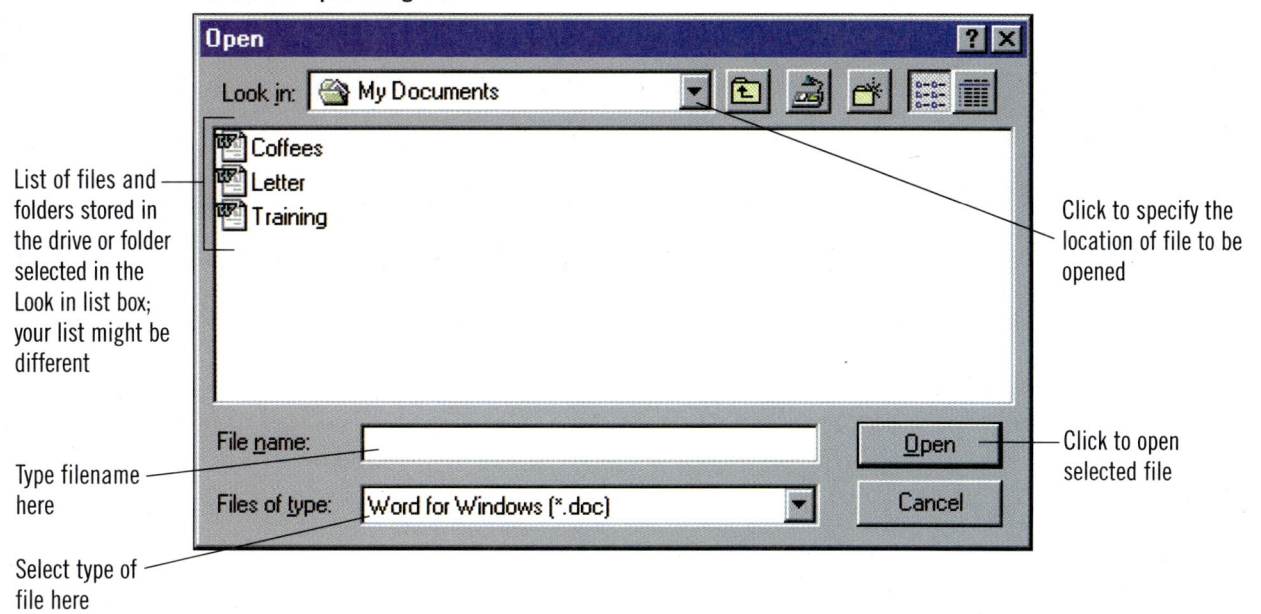

FIGURE B-4: Save As dialog box

Type new filename here

Click to save file

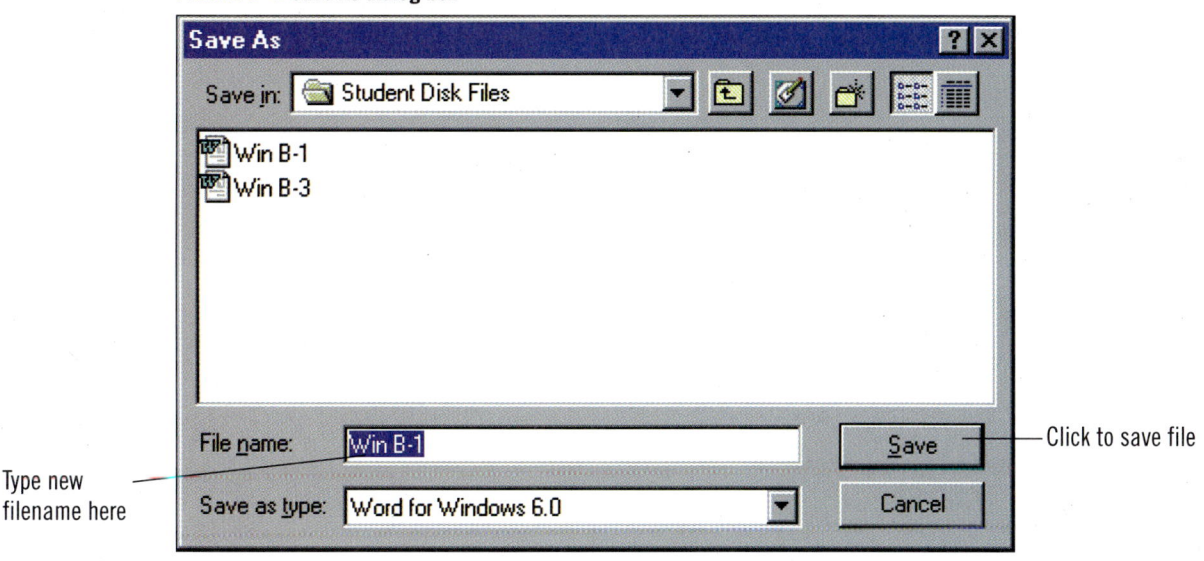

About saving files

Until you save them, the documents you create are stored in the computer's random access memory (RAM). **RAM** is a temporary storage space that is erased when the computer is turned off. To store a document permanently, you must save it as a file. A file is a collection of information that has a unique name, distinguishing it from other files. You can save files to a floppy disk that you insert into the disk drive of your computer (usually drive A: or B:) or a **hard disk**, which is built into the computer (usually drive C:). This book assumes that you will save all of your files to your Student Disk, which your instructor has provided to you. Windows 98 lets you save files using names that have up to 255 characters, including spaces.

Editing Text in WordPad

One of the major advantages of using a word processing program is that you can **edit**, or change, the contents of a document without having to retype it. You can also move whole sections of a document from one place to another using the Cut and Paste commands. John wants to add a greeting and change the price for a pound of coffee in the Coffee Menu document. He also wants to change the order of the menu items so that the coffees are listed in alphabetical order.

1. **Press ↓ three times, or click Ι in the fourth line**
   Figure B-5 shows the insertion point in the location where you want to insert new text. Repositioning the insertion point in a document (called **navigating**) is an important skill to learn. In addition to the arrow keys, WordPad offers another set of keys and key combinations, as shown in Table B-1, that enable you to navigate a document quickly.

Trouble?

If you make a mistake while typing, press [Backspace] (which deletes the character to the left of the insertion point) until you have deleted your mistake, then retype the text.

2. **Type Welcome to the taste-tantalizing coffee selections offered to you by Wired Coffee Company. You will find a variety of specialty coffees, including Single-Origin, Blends, Dark Roasts, and Decaffeinated., then press [Enter]**
   WordPad automatically puts the text that won't fit on one line onto the next line, using a feature called **wordwrap**. Now John wants to change the price of the Breakfast Blend coffee from $11.90 to $11.00.

3. **In the price of the Breakfast Blend coffee, click to the right of the last digit, 0**
   This number needs to be changed from "11.90" to "11.00."

4. **Press [Backspace] twice, then type 00**
   Now John wants to rearrange the list so that the coffees are listed in alphabetical order. The fourth coffee in the list (Espresso Dark Roast) needs to be moved so it comes before the third (Ethiopian Harrar). To do this, John first has to select the name of the fourth coffee; only then he can move the text up the list. You can select text three different ways. You can drag the mouse to highlight the text you want to select. If you need to select just a word, you can double-click it. If you need to select a line or paragraph, you can position the pointer to the left of the first character in the line or paragraph, and then click once to select a line or twice to select an entire paragraph.

5. **Position the pointer to the left of the first character in the line "Espresso Dark Roast"**
   The pointer changes from Ι to ↰ .

QuickTip

To select the entire paragraph, you can triple-click anywhere in the paragraph.

6. **Click once**
   The entire line is selected. Now John can move the line.

7. **Click the Cut button on the toolbar**
   When selected text is **cut** from a document, Windows removes it from the document and places it on the **Clipboard**, a temporary storage place where it remains available to be pasted somewhere else. When text is **copied**, a copy of it is placed in the Clipboard to be pasted in another location, but the text also remains in its original place in the document.

8. **Press ↑ once to move up one line in the list**
   This is where John wants to paste the line he cut.

9. **Click the Paste button on the toolbar, then click the Save button on the toolbar**
   Figure B-6 shows the information pasted into the list with all the coffees in alphabetical order. The changes you made to the file are saved.

FIGURE B-5: Positioning the insertion point

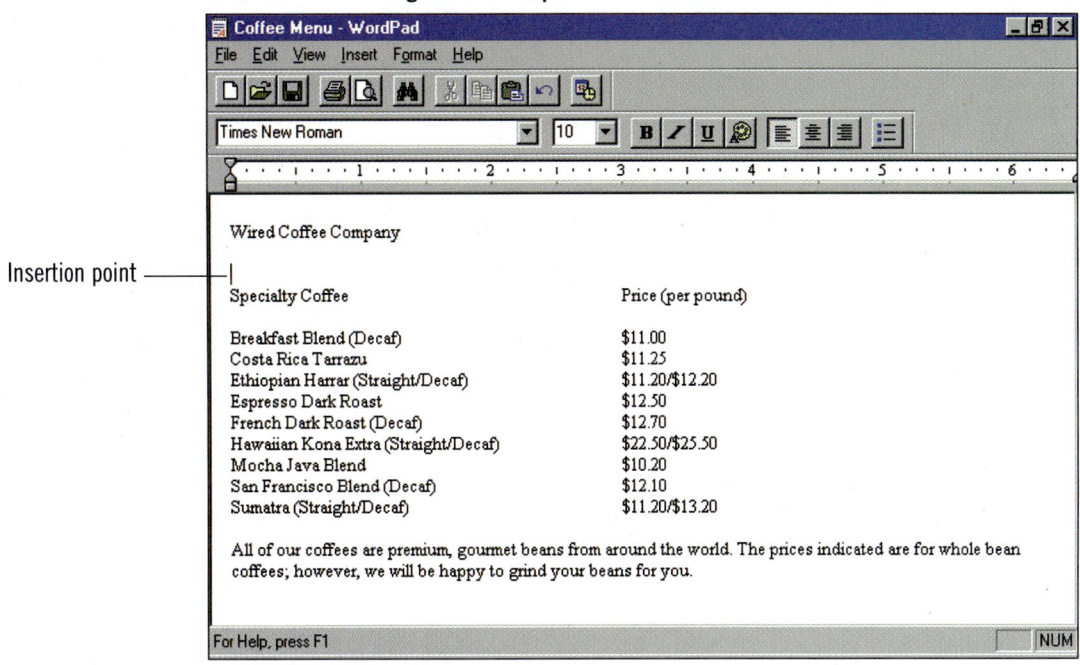

Insertion point

FIGURE B-6: Editing a WordPad file by cutting and pasting

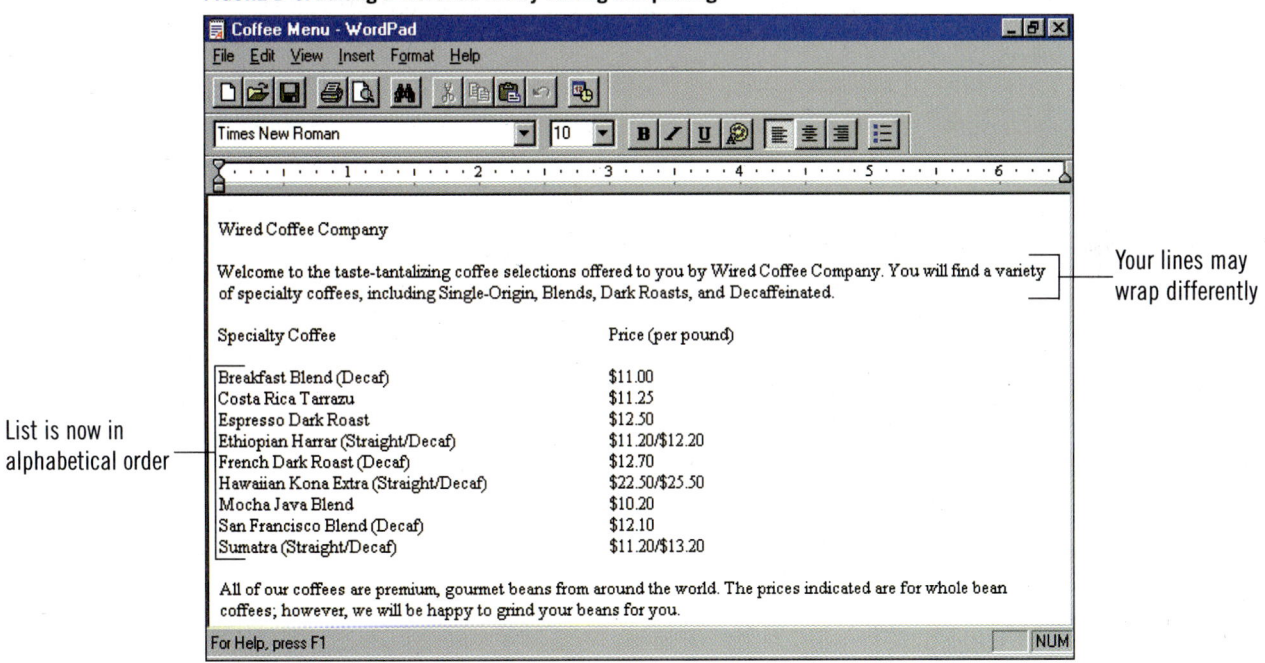

Your lines may wrap differently

List is now in alphabetical order

TABLE B-1: Keys to use to move around a WordPad document

key(s)	navigation	key(s)	navigation
↑	Move up one line	[PdDn]	Move to the next page
↓	Move down one line	[Ctrl][End]	Move to the end of the document
←	Move left one character	[Ctrl][Home]	Move to the beginning of the document
→	Move right one character	[Ctrl][→]	Move to the beginning of the next word to the right
[PgUp]	Move to the previous page	[Ctrl][←]	Move to the beginning of the previous word to the left

Windows 98

Formatting Text in WordPad

You can change the **format**, or the appearance, of the text and graphics in a document so that the document is easier to read or more attractive. Almost all formatting changes in WordPad can be achieved using the format bar, which appears below the toolbar in the WordPad window. Table B-2 describes the function of each button on the format bar. John wants to make the Coffee Menu document more attractive. He will do this by centering the title, bolding it, and increasing its size.

1. **Select the text Wired Coffee Company**
   Remember that the first step in making any editing change is to select the text you want to change. Then you can carry out the desired command.

2. **Click the Center button** ≡ **on the format bar**
   Notice that the title is centered and the button appears indented.

3. **Click the Bold button** B **on the format bar**
   The selected material appears in bold. If you wanted to turn bold off, you would click the button again. Buttons act as **toggle** switches—click once to turn the format feature on, click again to turn it off. Now John wants to italicize the title.

4. **Click the Italic button** / **on the format bar**
   Italicizing does not provide the effect that John had wanted, so he undoes this formatting change.

5. **Click the Undo button** ↶ **on the toolbar**
   This command reverses the last change that was made, such as typing new text, deleting text, and formatting text. Undo cannot reverse all commands (such as scrolling or saving a document), but it is a quick way to reverse most actions. John decides to change the size of the **font**, or typeface, to achieve the effect he wants in the title.

6. **Click the Font Size list arrow** [10 ▼] **on the format bar, then click 14**
   The selected text changes in size to 14 point. One **point** is 1/72 of an inch in height. Whenever you want to know the size of a font on your screen, place the insertion point anywhere in the text and look at the size that appears in the Font Size list box.

7. **Click anywhere in the document (except on the selected text) to deselect the text**
   Once text is selected, it can be deselected by clicking anywhere else in the document. As Figure B-7 shows, the title is centered, bold, and changed in size to 14 point.

8. **Click the Save button** 🖫 **on the toolbar**
   The changes made to the Coffee Menu file are saved.

TABLE B-2: Format bar buttons and list arrows

button or list arrow	function	button	function
Times New Roman ▼	Select a font	🎨	Add or change color
10 ▼	Select a font size	≡	Left align
B	Bold	≡	Center align
/	Italicize	≡	Right align
U	Underline	☰	Create bulleted list

FIGURE B-7: Centered, bold, and enlarged text

Click to undo the last command

Click to change the size of text

Click to bold text

Click to center text

Coffee Menu - WordPad

File   Edit   View   Insert   Format   Help

Times New Roman   14   **B** *I* U   ≡ ≡ ≡   ≣

Wired Coffee Company

Welcome to the taste-tantalizing coffee selections offered to you by Wired Coffee Company. You will find a variety of specialty coffees, including Single-Origin, Blends, Dark Roasts, and Decaffeinated.

Specialty Coffee	Price (per pound)
Breakfast Blend (Decaf)	$11.00
Costa Rica Tarrazu	$11.25
Espresso Dark Roast	$12.50
Ethiopian Harrar (Straight/Decaf)	$11.20/$12.20
French Dark Roast (Decaf)	$12.70
Hawaiian Kona Extra (Straight/Decaf)	$22.50/$25.50
Mocha Java Blend	$10.20
San Francisco Blend (Decaf)	$12.10
Sumatra (Straight/Decaf)	$11.20/$13.20

All of our coffees are premium, gourmet beans from around the world. The prices indicated are for whole bean coffees; however, we will be happy to grind your beans for you.

For Help, press F1   NUM

CLUES TO USE

Formatting text as you type

As you've learned in the Steps, one way to format text is to select it, and then apply a change of format. Another way is to first select the formatting you want, and then enter text. This approach is helpful when you are starting a new document and are familiar with the effect that different formatting options create. For example, if you were creating a new list of items and knew that you wanted the title to be 24-point, underlined text, you would click the Underline button U on the format bar, and then select 24 from the Font Size list box. Anything that you type from that point will have those format characteristics. When you finish typing the title, you can change the font back to a smaller point size and click the Underline button to toggle the option off, then continue typing.

Using Paint

You use each Windows Accessory to perform a certain task. When it comes to creating and working with images, the Windows Accessory Paint is a useful tool. You can draw images and manipulate them with commands such as rotate, stretch, and invert colors. You can open more than one Accessory at a time, so while WordPad is still running, you can open Paint and work on drawings and images. This is called **multitasking**. John already created a logo for his coffee company. Now he wants to review the logo and revise it as necessary before using it on his promotional materials.

1. Click the **Start button** on the taskbar, point to **Programs**, point to **Accessories**, click **Paint**, then click the **Maximize button** in the Paint window
   The Paint window opens and is maximized in front of the WordPad window. You can find buttons for frequently used commands in the Paint Toolbox, located along the left edge of the window. Table B-3 describes these tools. Now you open the file with John's logo in it.

2. Click **File** on the menu bar, click **Open**, click the **Look in list arrow**, then click the drive that contains your Student Disk
   A list of the files stored on the Student Disk appears.

3. In the file list, click **Win B-2**, then click **Open**
   The file named Win B-2 opens, shown in Figure B-8. If you cannot see the logo on your screen, use the scroll buttons to adjust your view. John decides the logo could use some final modifications. Before he makes any changes, he wants to save this file (using a more meaningful name) so the original file won't be affected.

4. Click **File** on the menu bar, click **Save As**, then save the file as **Wired Coffee Logo** on your Student Disk
   John wants to add a rounded border around the logo. First he selects the proper tool from the Toolbox, and then he can "draw" the border.

5. Click the **Rounded Rectangle tool** in the Toolbox, then move the pointer into the Paint work area
   When you move the mouse pointer into the work area, it changes to ✛, indicating that the Rounded Rectangle tool is active.

6. Beginning above and to the left of the logo, drag ✛ so that a rounded rectangle surrounds the image, then release the mouse button when the pointer is below and to the right of the image, as shown in Figure B-9
   John likes this new look. The logo is complete but needs to be saved.

7. Click **File** on the menu bar, then click **Save**
   Now John can use the logo in his other documents.

FIGURE B-8: Company logo in Paint

Paint Toolbox

Click to select
the Rounded
Rectangle tool

Work area

Logo

Paint Fill bar

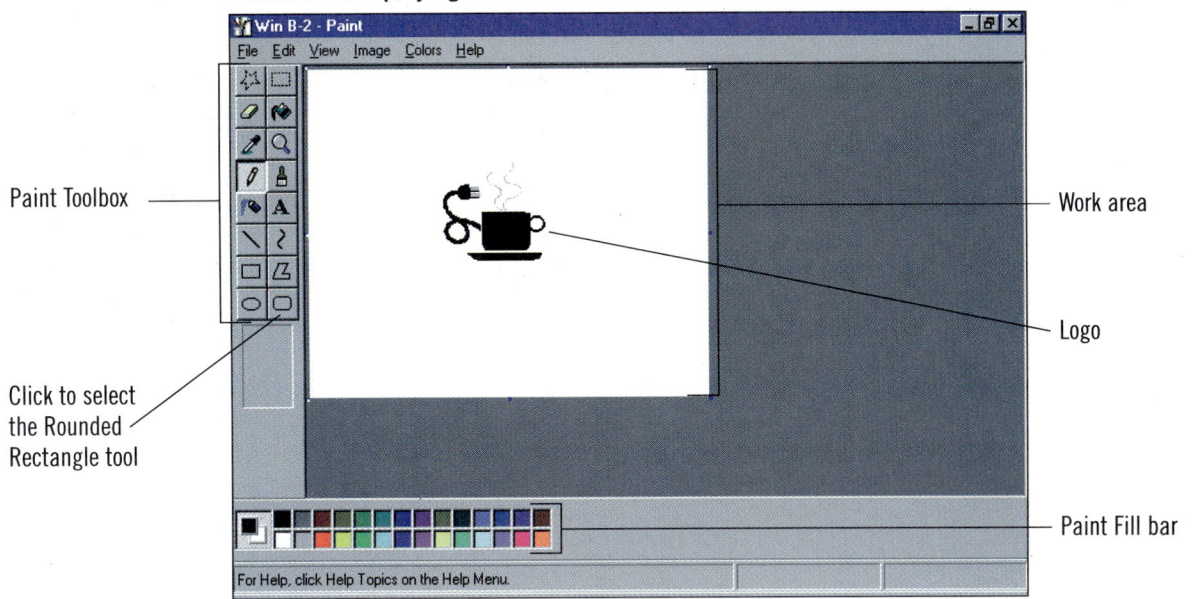

FIGURE B-9: Company logo with rounded rectangle

Start rectangle here

End rectangle here

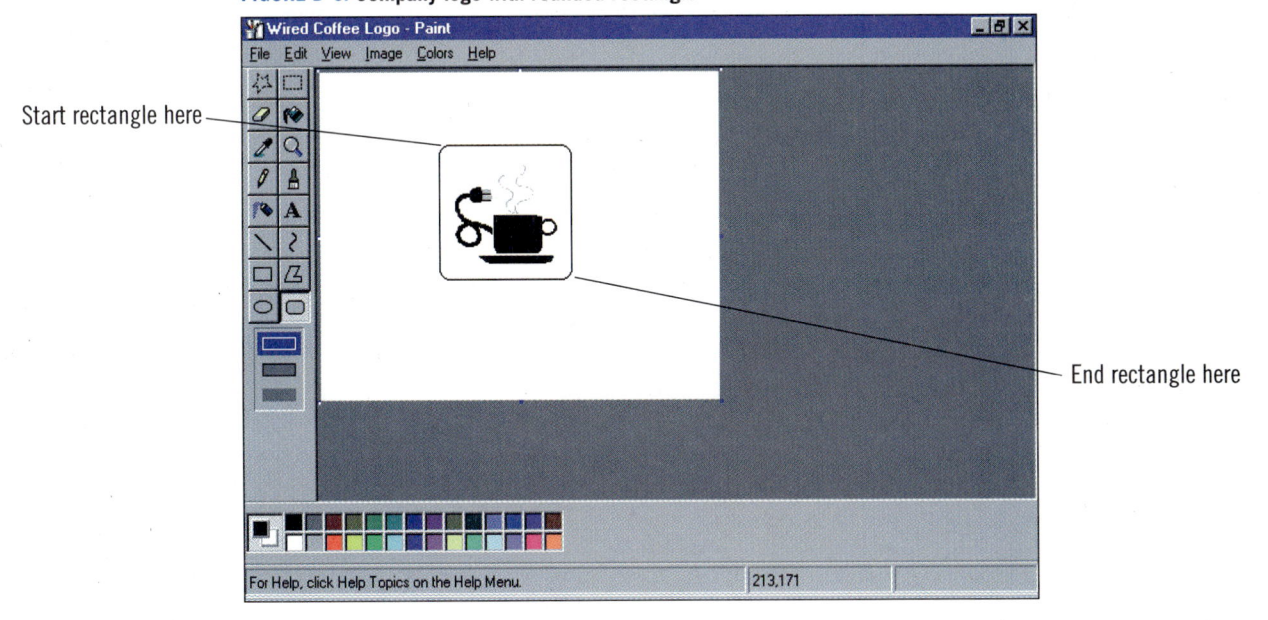

TABLE B-3: Tools in the Paint Toolbox

tool	description	tool	description
	Selects a shape that is not regular		Creates dispersed lines and patterns
	Selects a shape that is regular	A	Enters text in drawings
	Erases part of a drawing		Draws a straight line
	Fills a shape with a color or texture		Draws a free form line
	Picks up a color from the picture for drawing		Draws a regular shape
	Magnifies part of an image		Draws an irregular shape
	Draws freehand		Draws an oval or circle
	Designates the size and shape brush to draw with		Draws a rectangle or square with rounded corners

Copying Data Between Programs

One of the most useful features that Windows offers is the ability to use data created in one document in another document, even if the two documents were created in different Windows programs. To work with more than one program or document at a time, you simply need to open them on your desktop. Any window that is open on the desktop is represented by a **program button** on the taskbar. When you want to switch from one open window to another, click the correct program button on the taskbar. Just as you worked with the Cut and Paste commands to rearrange the coffee list, you can use the same commands to move and copy data between two different documents. Table B-4 reviews the Cut, Copy and Paste commands and their associated keyboard shortcuts. John wants to add the company logo, which he created with Paint, to the Coffee Menu document, which he created with WordPad. He'll first go back to WordPad, which is still running. Then he'll copy and paste the Paint logo into the WordPad document.

Steps

Trouble?

If your windows don't appear tiled, click the program button on the taskbar for each program (Paint and WordPad) to ensure that both windows are maximized, then repeat Step 1.

QuickTip

When windows are tiled, you can drag a selected item from one program window to another to copy the item between programs.

1. Make sure both WordPad and Paint are open, place the mouse pointer on an empty area of the taskbar, **right-click**, then click **Tile Windows Vertically** on the shortcut menu
   The windows (Paint and WordPad) are arranged next to one another vertically, as shown in Figure B-10, so that John can maneuver quickly between them while working.

2. Click the **Paint program button** on the taskbar, or click anywhere in the Paint window
   The Paint program becomes the **active program** (the title bar changes from gray to blue). To copy the logo, John selects it first. To select an image, you need to choose the Select tool from the Toolbox and drag the mouse pointer over the image.

3. Click the **Select tool** ⬚ in the Toolbox, then drag a rectangle around the coffee logo to select it

4. Click **Edit** on the Paint menu bar, then click **Copy**
   The logo is copied to the Clipboard, but the original remains in your Wired Coffee Logo file.

5. Click the first line of the WordPad document
   The WordPad program becomes active, and the insertion point is placed on the WordPad page, where John wants the logo to appear. If you cannot see enough of the page, use the scroll buttons to adjust your view.

6. Click the **Paste button** 📋 on the WordPad toolbar
   The logo is pasted into the document, as shown in Figure B-11. Now John wants to center the logo on the page to match the title.

7. Click the **Maximize button** in the WordPad window, click the **Center button** ≣ on the format bar, then click below the logo to deselect it
   The logo is centered in the document. Now save the WordPad file for future use.

8. Click the **Save button** 💾 on the toolbar
   The document is complete and ready for John to print.

9. Click the **Paint program button** on the taskbar, then click the **Close button** in the Paint window

FIGURE B-10: Tiled windows

Click to activate the Paint program

Right-click to open pop-up menu and tile windows vertically

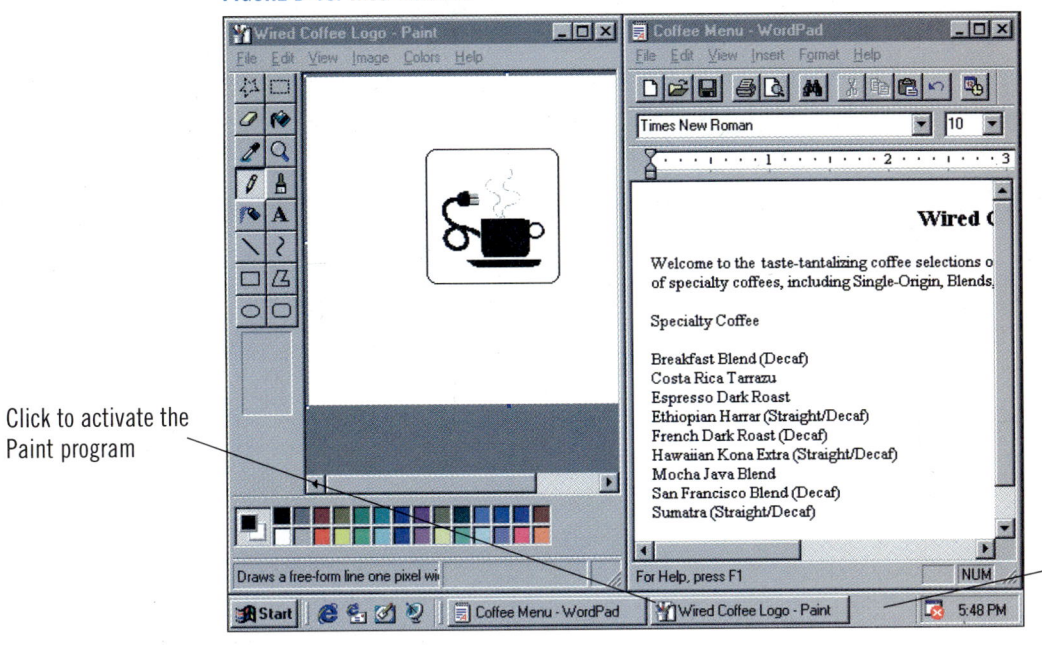

FIGURE B-11: Copying a logo between programs

Copy selected logo from Paint file

Paste logo in WordPad document

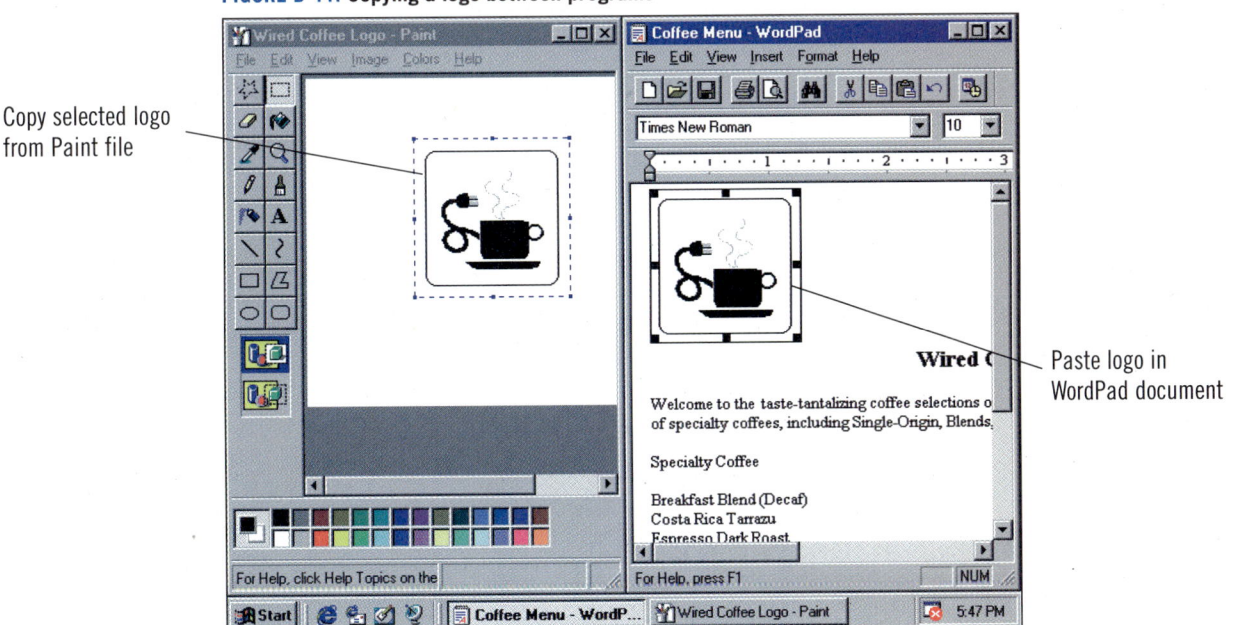

TABLE B-4: Overview of cutting, copying, and pasting

function	toolbar button	keyboard shortcut	drag-and-drop method *(for use within a file or between files if the windows are tiled)*
Cut: Removes selected information from a file and places it on the Clipboard	✂	[Ctrl][X]	Press and hold [Shift] as you drag selected text and it will be moved
Copy: Places a copy of selected information on the Clipboard, leaving the file intact	📋	[Ctrl][C]	Press and hold [Ctrl] as you drag selected text and it will be copied
Paste: Inserts whatever is currently on the Clipboard into another location (within the same file or in a different file)	📋	[Ctrl][V]	Release the left mouse button

Printing a Document

Printing a document creates a **printout** or **hard copy**, a document on paper that you can share with others or review as a work in progress. Most Windows programs have a print option that you access through the Print dialog box and a Print button on the toolbar. Although your printing options vary from program to program, the process works similarly in all of them. It is a good idea to use the **Print Preview** feature to look at the layout and formatting of a document before you print it. You might catch a mistake, find that the document fits on more pages than you wanted, or notice formatting that you want to do differently. Making changes before you print saves paper. John decides to preview the coffee menu before printing the document. Satisfied with the result, John prints the Coffee Menu document.

Steps

1. In the WordPad window, click the **Print Preview button** on the toolbar
A reduced but proportionate image of the page appears in the Preview window, shown in Figure B-12.

2. Click **Zoom In** in Print Preview
The preview image of the page appears larger, easier to see. John notices extra space around the dotted rectangle, the area determined by the **margin** setting. You can change the margin setting to decrease or increase the area outside the dotted rectangle with the Page Setup command. Before you can make the change, you need to close Print Preview.

3. Click **Close** in Print Preview
The Preview window closes and you return to the Coffee Menu document.

4. Click **File** on the menu bar, then click **Page Setup**
The Page Setup dialog box opens. Table B-5 describes the Page Setup dialog box options. You can change other printing options here, such as paper size, page orientation, and printer source.

5. Select the number in the Top text box, then type **1.25**, select the number in the Bottom text box, type **1.25**, then click **OK**
You should verify that you like the new margins before printing.

6. Click
The menu is displayed with smaller margins. John likes this better, so he prints the document.

7. Click **Print** in Print Preview
The Print dialog box opens, as shown in Figure B-13, showing various options available for printing. Check to make sure you are printing to the correct printer. If you need to change printers, click the Name list arrow, and then select a printer. When you are done, accept all of the settings.

QuickTip

To quickly print a document, click the Print button on the toolbar.

8. Click **OK**
The WordPad document prints. To **close**, or quit, a program and any of its currently open files, you select the Exit command from the File menu. You can also click the Close button in the upper right corner of the program window.

9. Click the **Close button** in the WordPad window
If you have made any changes to the open file without saving them, you will be prompted to save your changes before the program quits.

FIGURE B-12: Coffee Menu in Print Preview

Click to print document

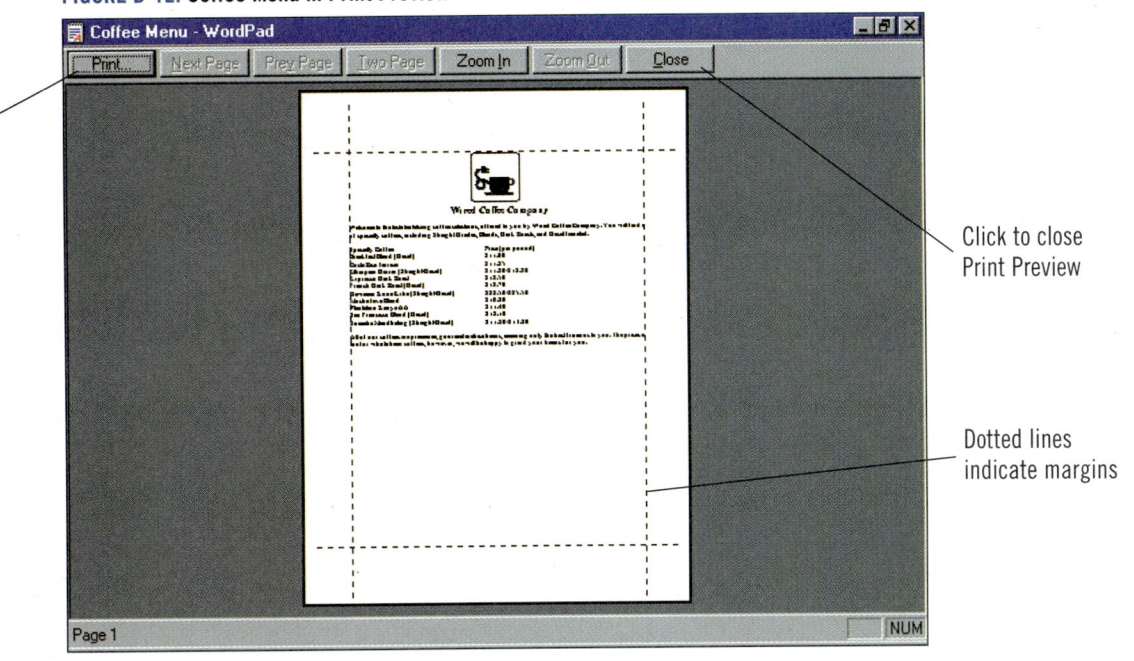

Click to close Print Preview

Dotted lines indicate margins

FIGURE B-13: Print dialog box

Printer information

In a multipage document, set which pages to print here

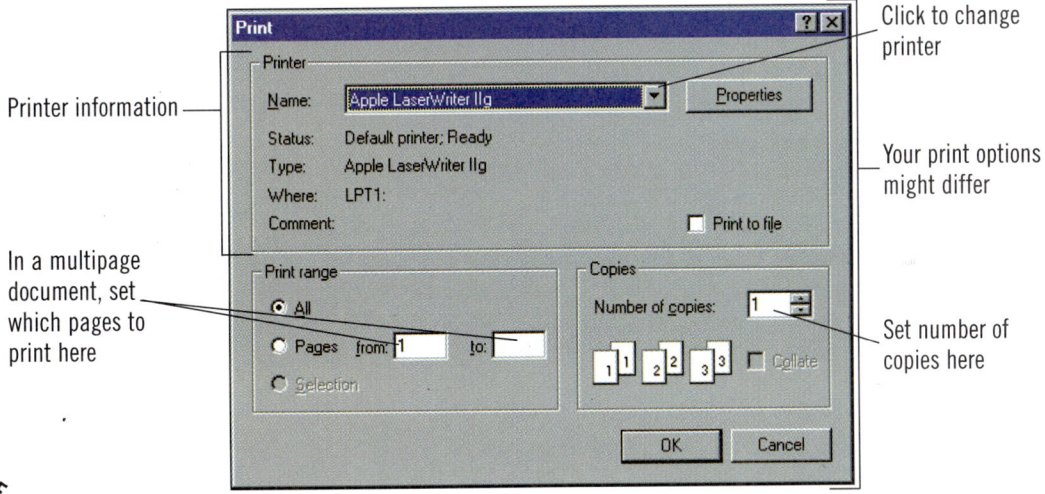

Click to change printer

Your print options might differ

Set number of copies here

Printer properties

You can select Properties from the Print dialog box and adjust several facets of the printing operation. For example, to control the intensity with which graphics images are printed, you would click the Graphics tab, then adjust the Intensity slider. You can also adjust fonts, paper sizes and other printing dimensions in the Properties dialog box.

TABLE B-5: Page Setup dialog box options

page setup option	function
Size	Defines the size of the paper on which you want to print
Source	Defines the location of the paper, such as a paper tray or an envelope feeder
Orientation	Allows you to select between Portrait (the page being taller than it is wide) and Landscape (the page being wider than it is tall)
Margins	Allows you to define top, bottom, left, and right page margins

Windows 98

Playing a Video Clip

Windows 98 comes with two built-in Accessories, ActiveMovie Control and Media Player, that you can use to play video and sound files. **ActiveMovie Control** is a new media application for Windows that delivers high-quality continuous video playback. You can use it to play movies, sounds, and other multimedia files from your computer, a local network, or the Internet. The **Media Player** gives you extended capabilities over the ActiveMovie Control. With the Media Player, you can play the same ActiveMovie videos and sounds, but you can also modify the media and control the settings for multimedia hardware devices. John experiments using the Media Player to play a sample video.

Steps 1 2 3 4

1. **Click the Start button on the taskbar, point to Programs, point to Accessories, point to Entertainment, then click Media Player**
   Media Player opens. You can open a specific type of video or sound file by choosing a command type on the Device menu or a general type by choosing the Open command on the File menu. John decides to open a video with the ActiveMovie type.

2. **Click Device on the menu bar, then click ActiveMovie, as shown in Figure B-14**
   The Open dialog box opens. John wants to play a video located on your Student Disk.

3. **Click the Look in list arrow, then click the drive that contains your Student Disk**
   A list of the files and folders stored on the Student Disk appears in the file list.

4. **In the file list, click Coffee Cup, then click Open**
   An hourglass appears, indicating that Media Player is opening the video file. The video opens in a separate window below the Media Player window. Table B-6 describes the function of each button on the Media Player toolbar.

5. **In the Media Player window, click the Play button ▶ on the toolbar**
   The video plays in the separate window. A slider in the Media Player window indicates the progress of the video, as shown in Figure B-15. You can drag the slider backward or forward to play different parts of the video. When the video is finished, close the video window.

6. **Click File on the menu bar, then click Close**
   The video window is closed, but the Media Player window remains open. John will use the Media Player to play a sound in the next lesson.

TABLE B-6: Buttons on the Media Player toolbar

button	description
▶ or ❙❙	Play or pause a video or sound
■	Stop a video or sound
▲	Eject a CD-ROM
◀◀❙	Move to the previous selection mark
◀◀	Rewind the video or sound
▶▶	Forward the video or sound
❙▶▶	Move to next selection mark
⊥	Start the selection of a video or sound you want to copy
⊤	End the selection of a video or sound you want to copy

FIGURE B-14: Media Player window with the Device menu

Click to open an
ActiveMovie file

FIGURE B-15: Media Player window and video window

Slider indicating
current play time

Toolbar

Click to play video

Length of video
in seconds

Playing a Sound

Besides playing videos, you can also play sounds using the Media Player or the ActiveMovie Control. In order to listen to sounds, your computer must have a sound card and self-powered speakers. Media Player and ActiveMovie Control can play a variety of sounds. To play a sound, you click the Play button. If you want to pause while playing the sound, you click the Pause button. If you want to change the starting position of the sound, you drag the slider. John enjoyed playing a video, so he decided to play a sound.

Trouble?

If Sound doesn't appear on the Device menu, Media Player doesn't detect a sound card on your computer. See your instructor or technical support person.

1. Make sure Media Player is open, click **Device** on the menu bar, then click **Sound**
The Open dialog box opens. John decides to play a sound located on your Student Disk.

2. Click the **Look in list arrow**, then click the drive that contains your Student Disk
A list of the files and folders stored on the Student Disk appears in the file list.

3. In the file list, click **Better Coffee**, then click **Open**
The time scale appears below the slider in the Media Player window.

4. In the Media Player window, click the **Play button** ▶ on the toolbar
The sound plays. See Figure B-16. The slider in the Media Player window moves indicating the current play time of the sound. John decides to pause the sound, change the starting position of the sound, and then resume playing.

5. Before the sound finishes, click the **Pause button** ▐▐ on the toolbar
You can drag the slider backward or forward to play different parts of the sound. John drags the slider backward to restart the sound.

6. Drag the **slider** back to the beginning, then click the **Play button** ▶ to restart the sound
When you are finished playing the sound, close the Media Player.

7. Click the **Close button** in the Media Player window

FIGURE B-16: Media Player window playing a sound

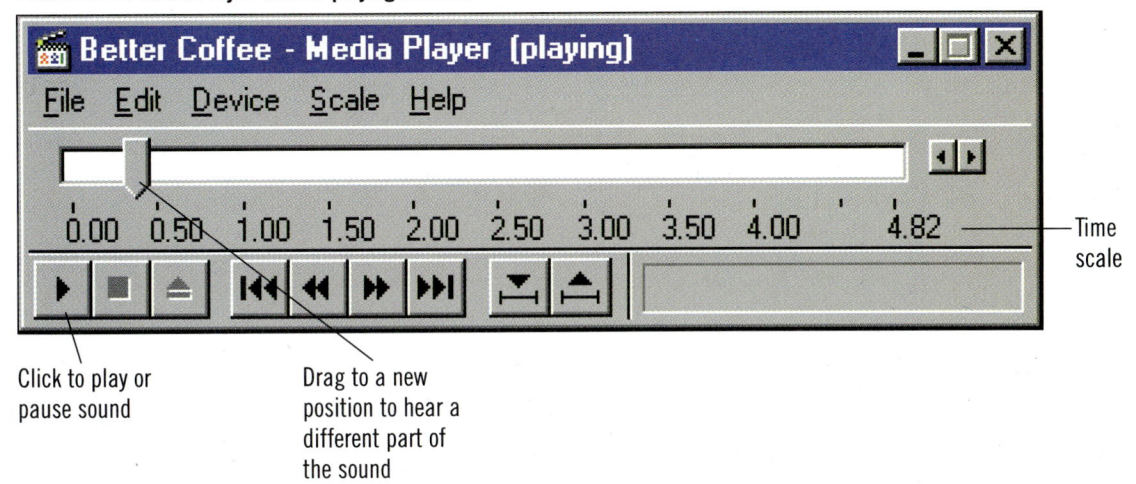

Time scale

Click to play or pause sound

Drag to a new position to hear a different part of the sound

Playing a music CD

To accommodate the many people who like to play audio CDs in their CD-ROM drives while working, Windows 98 includes the CD Player program in its accessories. The controls on the player, shown in Figure B-17, look just like those on a regular CD player. The Windows 98 CD Player supports many of the same features found in CD players, such as random play, programmable playback order, and the ability to save programs so that users don't have to recreate their playlists each time they play a CD. To play an audio CD, insert the CD in your CD-ROM drive; the CD Player will automatically start playing the audio CD. You can click the CD Player button on the taskbar to display the CD Player window.

FIGURE B-17: CD Player window

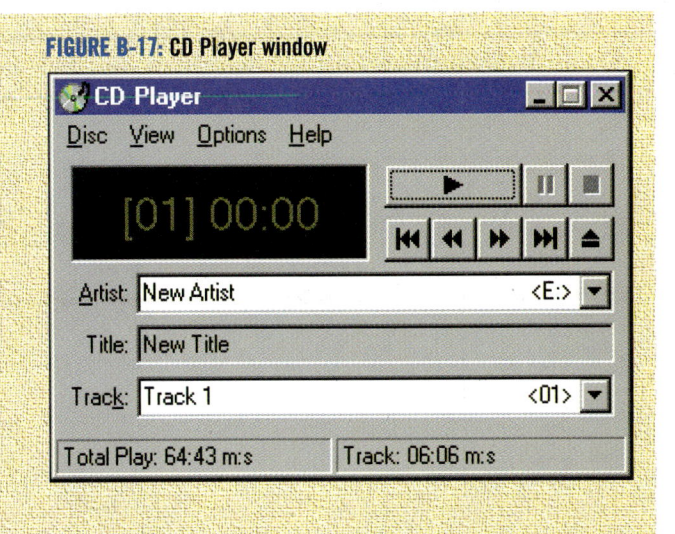

Practice

► Concepts Review

Label each of the elements of the screen shown in Figure B-18.

FIGURE B-18

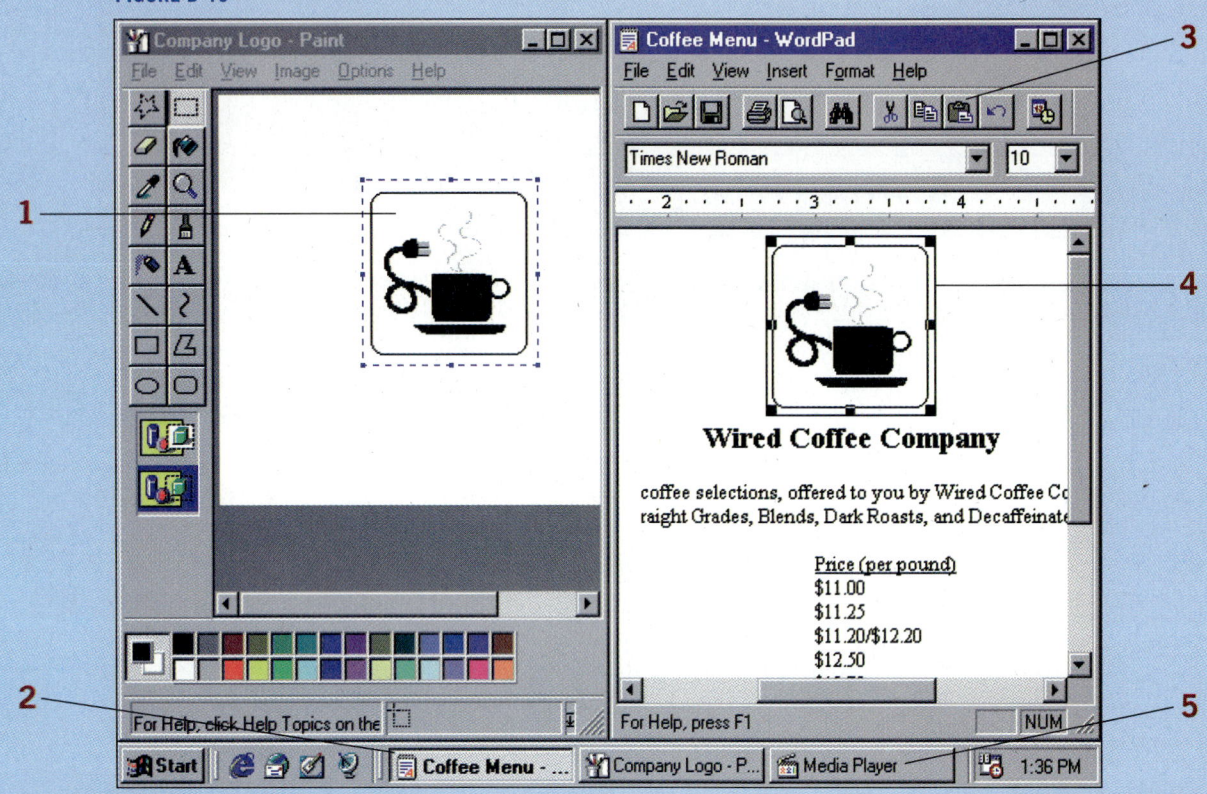

Match each of the terms with the statement that describes its function.

6. Removes selected text or an image from its current location   **a.** Copy
7. Copies selected text or an image from its current location   **b.** Accessories
8. A set of characters you assign to a collection of information   **c.** Cut
9. A collection of Windows programs that enable you to perform certain tasks   **d.** Select
10. What you must first do to existing text before you can format it   **e.** Filename

Select the best answer from the following list of choices.

11. The first step in starting any Windows Accessory is to click
    a. The Start button.   **b.** The taskbar.   **c.** The Open icon.   **d.** Anywhere on the desktop.

12. What program command makes a copy of a file?
    a. Save   **b.** Save As   **c.** Copy   **d.** Duplicate

13. When WordPad automatically moves words to the next line, it is called
    a. Wordwrap.   **b.** Format insert.   **c.** Margin.   **d.** Tab.

14. Which of the following is not a way to select text?
- **a.** Double-click a word.
- **b.** Drag over the text.
- **c.** Click File on the menu bar, then click Select.
- **d.** Click to the left of the first character in a line of text.

15. What is the name of the Windows location where information is placed after it is cut or copied?
- **a.** Clipboard
- **b.** Paint
- **c.** Start Up menu
- **d.** Hard drive

16. Which of the following is an option to change the size of the empty border around a document?
- **a.** Paper Size
- **b.** Paper Source
- **c.** Orientation
- **d.** Margins

▶ Skills Review

1. Create, edit, and save a WordPad document.
- **a.** Start WordPad.
- **b.** Open the WordPad file named Win B-3 on your Student Disk.
- **c.** Save the file as "Choose Coffee" on your Student Disk.

2. Edit a WordPad document.
- **a.** Change the spelling of the word "neuances" to "nuances" in the first paragraph.
- **b.** Insert a space between the characters *r* and *a* in the word, "ora" in the second paragraph.
- **c.** Delete the word "heavy" in the last line of text and replace it with "medium".

3. Format WordPad text.
- **a.** Select all the text in the file named Choose Coffee.
- **b.** Change it from the present font to Garamond, and change the size to 12 point.
- **c.** Center the title ("Wired Coffee") and change it to bold, 16 point.
- **d.** Underline each title ("How to Choose a Coffee" and "How to Taste the Difference") and change them to 14 point.
- **e.** Click anywhere in the WordPad window outside of the selected text.
- **f.** Save the document.

4. Modify a Paint image.
- **a.** Start Paint.
- **b.** Open the Paint file named Win B-2 on your Student Disk (this is the same file you used in the lessons).
- **c.** Save this file as "Wired Coffee Logo 2" on your Student Disk.
- **d.** Draw a circle around the logo.
- **e.** Use the Undo command or Eraser tool as necessary if the circle doesn't fit around the logo.
- **f.** Save the file.

5. Copy data between two documents.
- **a.** Tile the WordPad and Paint windows vertically. (*Hint:* Maximize both windows first.)
- **b.** Select the logo in the Paint window.
- **c.** Copy it to the Clipboard.
- **d.** In WordPad, insert the cursor at the beginning of the document.
- **e.** Maximize WordPad.
- **f.** Paste the logo in the newly inserted blank line.
- **g.** Center the logo.
- **h.** Save the Choose Coffee file.
- **i.** Close the Wired Coffee Logo 2 file and Paint.

6. **Print and close a document.**
   a. Print two copies of the file named Choose Coffee.
   b. Close all open documents.
   c. Close WordPad.

7. **Play a video.**
   a. Start Media Player.
   b. Open the Coffee Cup video on your Student Disk.
   c. Play the video.
   d. Close the video window.

8. **Play a sound.**
   a. Open the AM Coffee sound on your Student Disk.
   b. Play the video.
   c. Pause the sound.
   d. Drag the slider to the beginning of the sound.
   e. Replay the sound.
   f. Close the Media Player window.

▶ Independent Challenges

1. You just opened a small, independent bookstore and are working on your inventory. You need to create a list of books that can be consulted when customers come in and want to know what kind of books you carry. Start WordPad and create a new document that lists the first 10 books in your stock, including the name of your bookstore and its street address, city, zip code, and phone number, and for each book, the author's name (last name first), the title, and the date of publication.

To complete this independent challenge:

1. Start WordPad.
2. Enter the heading (the name of the bookstore, address, city, state, zip code, and phone number).
3. Center the heading information.
4. Enter the information for at least ten books, using the Tab key to create columns for the author's name, the title, and the date of publication. Be sure that the columns line up with one another.
5. Proofread your list and correct any errors you may have made.
6. Italicize the last and first names of each author.
7. Bold the title of each book.
8. Save the list as Book Inventory on your Student Disk.
9. Print two copies of the list.
10. Close WordPad.

2. Your parents are celebrating their twenty-fifth wedding anniversary. You want to create an invitation to a party for them. Using WordPad, create an invitation, including the invitation title, your parents' names, date and time of the party, location of the party (use "35 Crow Canyon Road" for the address), written directions to the party, your name, the date to respond by, and phone number to reach you. Using Paint, you will then paste a map of the party location into the invitation. Remember that you can open more than one program at a time and you can easily switch between programs using the taskbar.

To complete this independent challenge:

1. Start WordPad and type the information needed for the invitation.
2. Select the title text and click the Center button on the toolbar.

3. Change the title text to 18 point, bold.

4. Change the rest of the text to 14-point Arial.

5. Save the WordPad document as "Invitation" on your Student Disk.

6. Start Paint, then open the "Invitation Map" file from your Student Disk.

7. Copy the map to the Clipboard.

8. Place the insertion point above the written instructions in the Invitation document.

9. Click the Paste button on the toolbar.

10. Save the document, preview the document, make any necessary changes, then print the document.

11. Close WordPad and Paint.

3. As the vice president of Things-That-Fly, a kite and juggling store, you need to design a new type of logo, consisting of three simple circles, each colored differently. This logo will be used both in the new stationery and in all advertising for the store. You'll use Paint to design the logo, and then you will paste the logo into a WordPad document and name the document Stationery.

To complete this independent challenge:

1. Start Paint and create a small circle using the [Shift] key and the Ellipse tool.

2. Use the Select tool to surround the circle (thereby selecting it), and then select Copy from the Edit menu. Now you can paste the circle so you don't have to try to redraw the exact same shape.

3. Select Paste from the Edit menu, and use the mouse to drag the second circle below the first and a bit to the right of the first.

4. Select Paste from the Edit menu again, and use the mouse to drag the third circle below the first and a bit to the left of the first.

5. For each circle, click the Fill tool in the Toolbox, click the color you want the circle to be, then click inside the circle you want filled with that color.

6. Using the Select tool, select the completed logo, click Edit on the menu bar, then click Copy.

7. Open WordPad and click the Center button on the toolbar.

8. Click the Paste button on the toolbar, click to the right of the logo to deselect it, press [Enter] twice, then type "Things-That-Fly."

9. Using the format bar, change the text to 18 point, bold.

10. Save the document as "Stationery" on your Student Disk.

11. Preview the document, make any necessary changes, then print the document.

12. Close Wordpad and Paint.

4. As the creative director at Digital Arts, a computer music company, you need to find sample sounds to include on a demo CD. You'll use Media Player to open sound files located on your computer and play each one. You'll also use WordPad to keep track of the sounds you listened to and which ones you liked the best.

To complete this independent challenge:

1. Open Media Player.

2. Open all the sound files in the Media folder (in the Windows folder) on your computer.

3. Play each sound file.

4. In WordPad, create a list of the sound files that you played and indicate the sounds you liked the best.

5. Save the list as "Sound List" on your Student Disk.

6. Print the list.

7. Close Media Player.

► Visual Workshop

Re-create the screen shown in Figure B-19, which displays the Windows desktop with more than one program window open. You can use the file Win B-2 for the coffee cup logo (save it as "A Cup of Coffee" on your Student Disk). Create a new WordPad document, save it as "Good Time Coffee Club" on your Student Disk, and enter the text shown in the figure. Print the screen. (Press the Print Screen key to make a copy of the screen, open Paint, click Edit on the menu bar, click Paste to paste the screen into Paint, then click Yes to paste the large image, if necessary. Click File on the menu bar, click Print, then click OK.)

FIGURE B-19

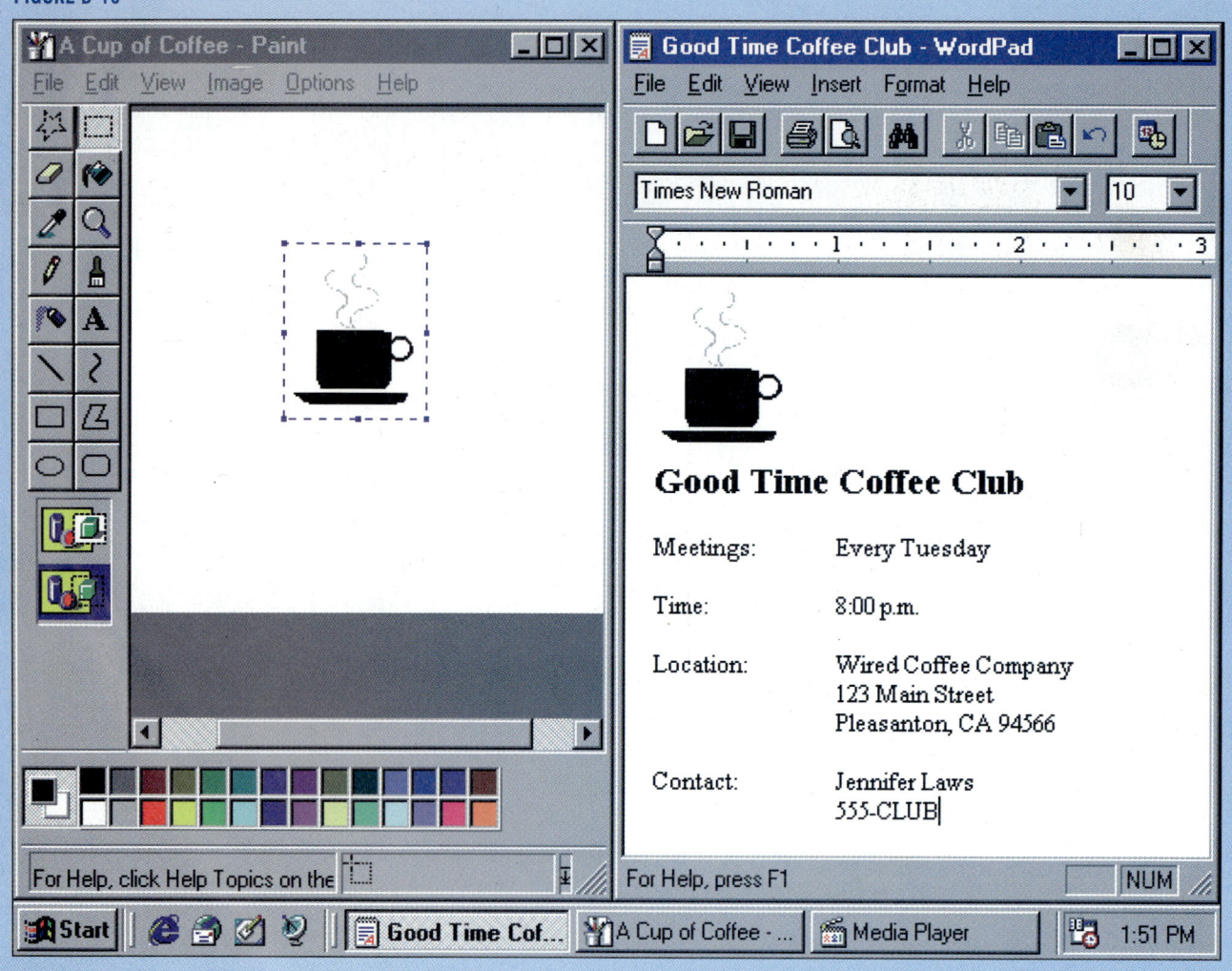

Managing
Files Using My Computer

Objectives

- ► **Understand file management**
- ► **Open and view My Computer**
- ► **View folders and files**
- ► **Create a folder**
- ► **Move files and folders**
- ► **Delete and restore files and folders**
- ► **Create a shortcut to a file**
- ► **Display drive information**

An important Windows 98 skill for you to learn is **file management**, which is being able to organize and keep track of files and folders. Windows 98 provides you with two file management programs: My Computer and Windows Explorer. You use both of these tools to view the files that are on your computer and how they are arranged. You can also use them to rearrange the files to fit the way that you work by creating new folders and by renaming and deleting files and folders. A **folder** is an electronic collection of files and other folders. This unit concentrates on My Computer while the next unit will focus on Windows Explorer. In this unit John Casey will learn about the files on his computer and how to keep them organized using My Computer.

Understanding File Management

Managing folders and files enables you to quickly locate any file that you have already created and need to use again. Not being able to manage files is like looking for a needle in a haystack—it is frustrating and time-consuming. The way your files are organized on disk is called a **file hierarchy**. Figure C-1 shows the files and folders that John uses in the course of running his business.

As you examine the figure, note that file management can help you do the following:

Organize folders and files in a file hierarchy, or a logical order, so that information is easy to locate and use

John stores all of his correspondence files in a folder called Letters. Within that folder are two more folders. One is named Business Letters and holds all business correspondence. The other is named Personal Letters and holds all of John's personal correspondence.

Save files to the folder in which you want to store them for future use

John has a folder named Sales in which he stores all information about sales for the current year. He also places files related to accounting information in this folder.

Create a new folder so you can reorganize information

Now that John is doing more advertising for Wired Coffee Company, he wants to create a new folder to store files related to these marketing efforts.

Delete files and folders that you no longer need

John deletes files once he is sure he will no longer use them again to free up disk space and keep his disk organized.

Create shortcuts

If a file or folder you use often is located several levels down in a file hierarchy (for example, if it is in a file within a folder within a folder), it might take you several steps to access it. To save you time in accessing the files and programs you use most frequently, you can create shortcuts to them. A **shortcut** is a link that you can place in any location that gives you instant access to a particular file, folder, or program on your hard disk or on a network. John creates a shortcut on the desktop to the Wired Coffee folder. To view or access the contents of his folder, all he will have to do is double-click the shortcut icon on the desktop.

Find a file when you cannot remember where it is stored

John knows he created a letter to a supplier earlier this week, but now that he is ready to revise the letter, he cannot find it. Using the Find command on the Start menu, he can quickly find that letter and revise it in no time.

Use Quick View to see the contents of a file without having to open it

John can view a WordPad file, Paint file, or almost any Windows file from My Computer using the Quick View feature, without having to first start each program and then open the file.

FIGURE C-1: How John uses Windows to organize his files

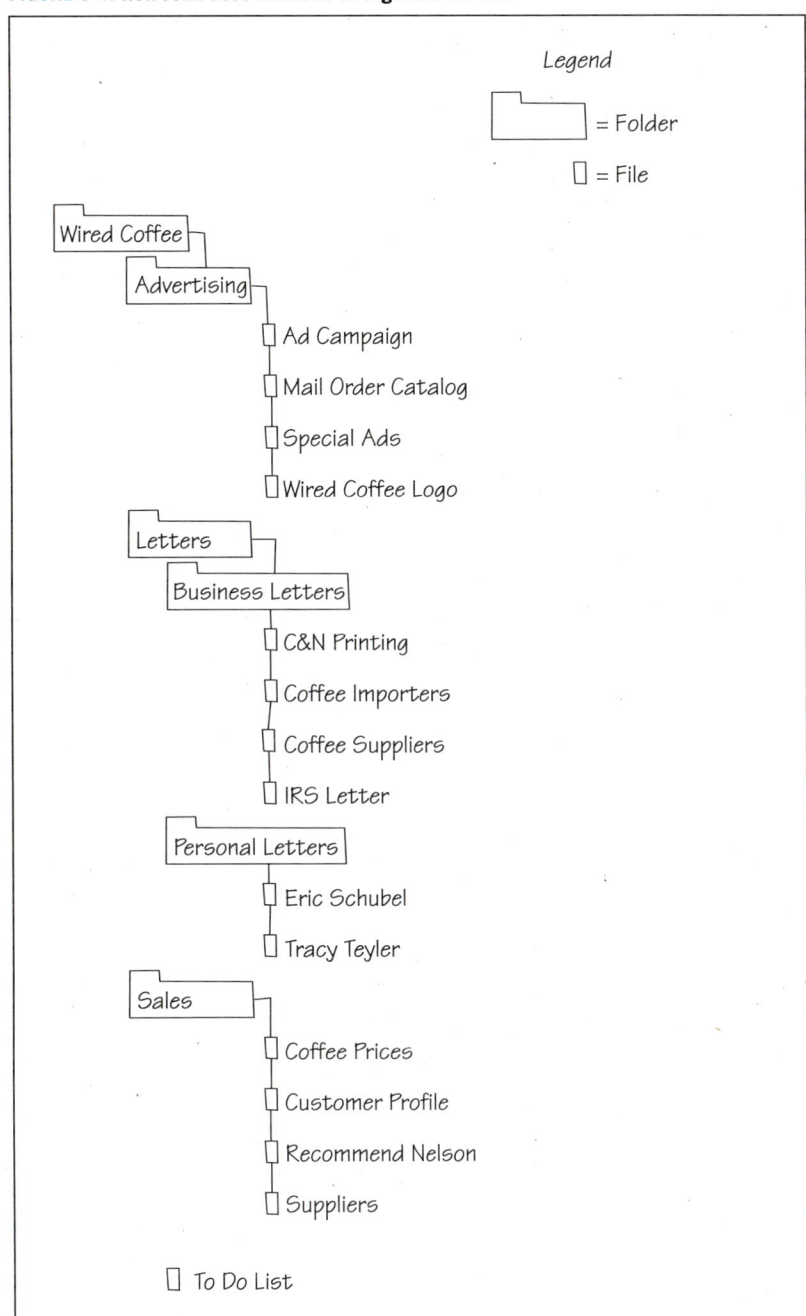

Legend

⬜ = Folder

▯ = File

Wired Coffee
- Advertising
  - Ad Campaign
  - Mail Order Catalog
  - Special Ads
  - Wired Coffee Logo
- Letters
  - Business Letters
    - C&N Printing
    - Coffee Importers
    - Coffee Suppliers
    - IRS Letter
  - Personal Letters
    - Eric Schubel
    - Tracy Teyler
- Sales
  - Coffee Prices
  - Customer Profile
  - Recommend Nelson
  - Suppliers
- To Do List

CLUES TO USE

What is a file hierarchy?

Windows 98 allows you to organize folders and files into a file hierarchy, imitating the way you would actually store paper documents in real folders. Just as a filing cabinet contains several folders each containing a set of related documents, and several dividers grouping related folders together, a file hierarchy allows you to place files into folders, then folders into other folders, so that your files are neat and organized. For example, Figure C-1 shows the file hierarchy of the Wired Coffee folder on your Student Disk. At the topmost level of the hierarchy is the name of the folder, Wired Coffee. This folder contains several files and folders. The folders are named Advertising, Letters, Business Letters, Personal Letters, and Sales, each containing files and folders related to each of these topics.

Opening and Viewing My Computer

The key to organizing folders and files effectively within a hierarchy is storing related things together and naming folders informatively. That way, you can get a good idea of what's on your system just by looking at the higher levels of your file hierarchy, and not having to examine every individual file or memorize a coding system. As the previous lesson showed, the file hierarchy on John's disk contains several folders and files organized by topic. Now he will use My Computer to review this organization and see if it needs to be changed.

QuickTip

Make a copy of your Student Disk before you use it. For assistance, see your instructor or technical support person.

Trouble?

If the toolbar is not visible, click View on the menu bar, point to Toolbars, then click Standard Buttons.

QuickTip

To go from My Computer to Windows Explorer, another file management tool that comes with Windows 98, right-click any disk or folder icon, then click Explore.

1. **Make sure your Student Disk is in the appropriate drive, then double-click the My Computer icon**
   This icon is usually located in the upper-left corner of the desktop. My Computer opens, displaying the contents of your computer, including all the disk drives and printers, as shown in Figure C-2. Since computers differ, your My Computer window will probably look different. There are icons that represent drives and icons that represent folders. As with most other windows, there is a toolbar, a status bar providing information about the contents of the window, a menu bar, and a list of contents in the My Computer window.

2. **If necessary, click the Maximize button in the My Computer window**
   This enables you to see the entire toolbar as you work. The toolbar contains a set of buttons that make using My Computer easier. Table C-1 lists what each of these buttons does and how they are used.

3. **Double-click the drive that contains your Student Disk**
   You can see the folders that are contained on the disk drive. When you open a disk drive or folder, the Address bar changes to indicate the new location. The Address bar changed from My Computer to disk drive A (A:\) and the title bar for the My Computer window changed to 3½ Floppy (A:). To see what's contained in the folders stored on the disk drive, you need to open them. John wants to see what files are contained in the Wired Coffee folder.

4. **Double-click the Wired Coffee folder**
   You can see the files and folders that are contained in the Wired Coffee folder. Files that are created using different applications are represented by a different type of icon. John wants to see what files are contained in the Sales folder.

5. **Double-click the Sales folder**
   You can now see the files contained in the Sales folder. These are files that John created using WordPad and saved in the Sales folder.

FIGURE C-2: My Computer window

Toolbar

Floppy disk
drives

Click to go to
a different
folder

CD-ROM drive

Your list of
folders might
be different

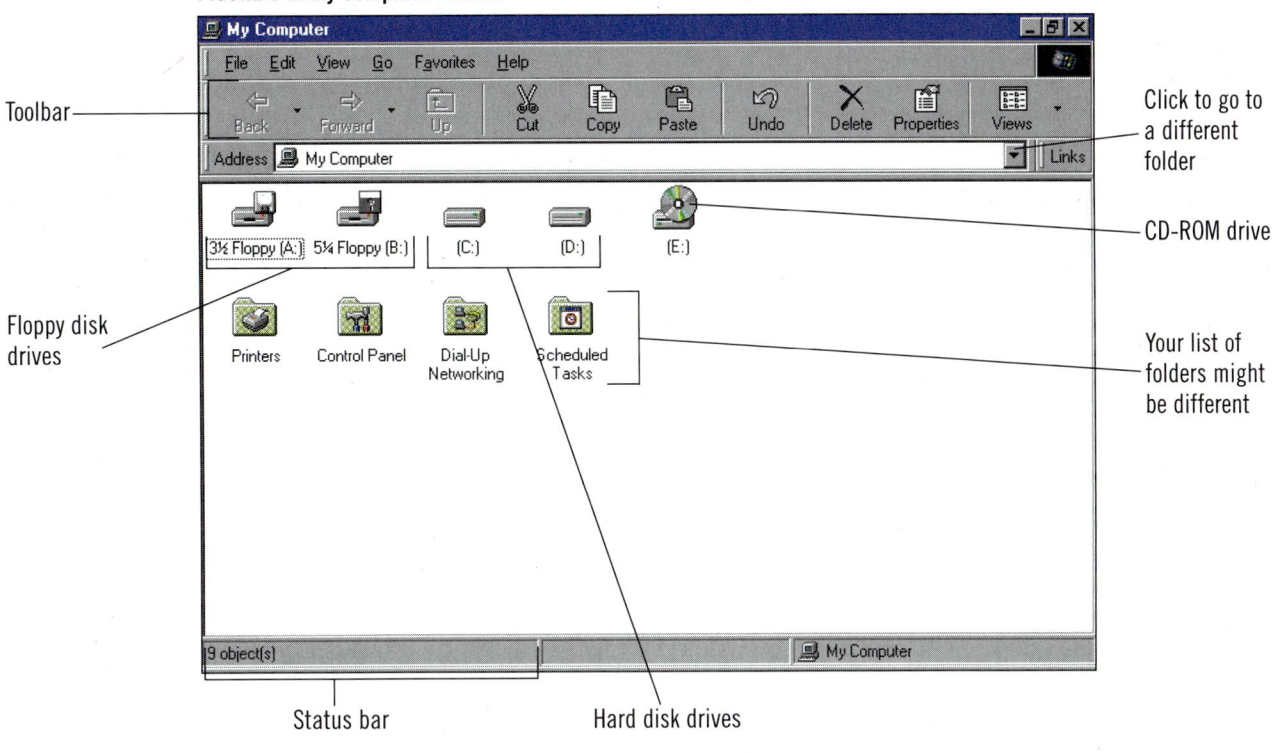

Status bar

Hard disk drives

TABLE C-1: My Computer toolbar buttons

button	function	button	function
⇐	Moves back to the previous location you have already visited	▨	Pastes a folder or file
⇒	Moves forward to the previous location you have already visited	↶	Undoes the most recent My Computer operation
▣	Moves up one level in the file hierarchy	✕	Deletes a folder or file
✂	Cuts a folder or file	▤	Shows the properties of a folder or file
▣	Copies a folder or file	▦	Lists the contents of My Computer using different views

CLUES TO USE

Formatting a disk

New floppy disks have to be formatted before they can be used. Sometimes the disk is preformatted, but if it is not, you can easily perform this function yourself. To format a floppy disk, select the disk drive in My Computer that contains the disk, click File on the menu bar, then click Format, or right-click the disk drive, then click Format. Specify the size of the disk and format type, then click Start. If you are format-ting a disk that has never been formatted, select the Full format type. If the disk has already been format-ted once and you simply want to clear its contents, select the Quick format type to reduce the time it takes. Be absolutely certain you want to format a disk before doing so, because formatting removes all the data from a disk.

Viewing Folders and Files

Once you have opened one or more folders, you can use buttons on the toolbar to help you move quickly between them in My Computer. If you want to move up one step in the hierarchy, you can click the Up One Level button. Each time you open a folder, Windows 98 keeps track of where you have been. If you want to go back or forward to a folder you have already visited, you can click the Back or Forward button. If you want to go to a folder you visited two or more locations ago, you can click the list arrow next to the Back or Forward button to display a menu of places you have been, and then select the place you want to go. When you view a folder in the My Computer window, you can use the View button on the toolbar to change the way folder and file icons are viewed. John moves between folders and changes the way he views folders and files depending upon the type of information that he needs.

QuickTip

You can also click the Address bar list arrow to move to another location up or down the file hierarchy.

1. Click the **Up One Level button** 📁 on the toolbar

The Wired Coffee folder and its contents appear in the Wired Coffee window. Each time you click on the Up One Level button, you move up one step in the hierarchy to the folder that contains the folders and files you currently see on the screen.

2. Click the 📁 again

You should now be at the topmost level of your disk drive file hierarchy showing several folders. See Figure C-3. Instead of double-clicking the Wired Coffee folder icon again to reopen the folder, you can click the Back button on the toolbar to go back to the previous folder (Wired Coffee) you visited.

3. Click the **Back button** ⬅ on the toolbar

The Wired Coffee folder and its contents appear in the My Computer window. At this point, you can open other folders. John opens the Advertising folder to see what's inside.

Trouble?

If Microsoft Word is installed on your computer, the Word icon will appear for the files, as shown in Figure C-4. If not, the WordPad icon will appear.

4. Double-click the **Advertising folder**

The Advertising folder and its contents appear in the My Computer window. John wants to go back to the Sales folder. Instead of using the Up One Level button to go back to the Wired Coffee folder and then clicking the Sales folder, you can click the list arrow next to the Back button to display a menu of places you have been, and then select the Sales folder.

5. Click the **Back button list arrow** ⬅▾ on the toolbar, then click **Sales**

The Back button list arrow, as shown in Figure C-4, displays the folders you have recently visited. You can click the Forward button on the toolbar to quickly return to the folder that you recently visited. In this case, you can return to the Wired Coffee folder.

QuickTip

You can click File on the menu bar, then click a folder or drive to open a location you have recently visited.

6. Click the **Forward button** ➡ on the toolbar

The Wired Coffee folder and its contents appear in the My Computer window. John wants to change the way the icons in the Wired Coffee folder are displayed.

7. Click the **Views button list arrow** ▦▾ on the toolbar, then click **Details**

In the Details view, the name, size of the object, type of file, and date on which each folder or file was last modified appear, as shown in Figure C-5. This might be the most useful view because it includes a great deal of information about the folder or file, in addition to the icon of the application that was used to create the file.

8. Click the **Views button** ▦ on the toolbar

The Large Icons view is displayed. Each time you click the Views button, the view changes, appearing in the following order: Large Icons, Small Icons, List, Details.

FIGURE C-3: Viewing folders and files in Large Icons view

Click to view
the next level
up in the folder
hierarchy

Click to go
back to the
previous folder

Address bar
changes to
reflect new
location

Large icons

Folders

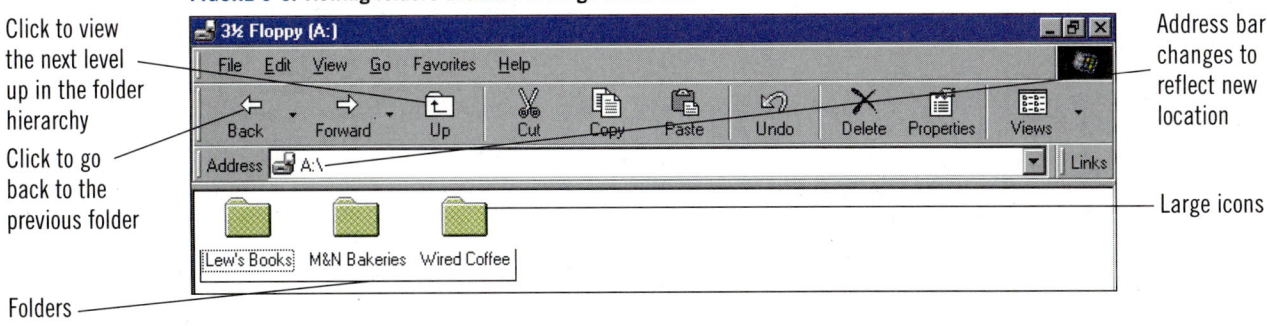

FIGURE C-4: Moving between folders

Back button
list arrow

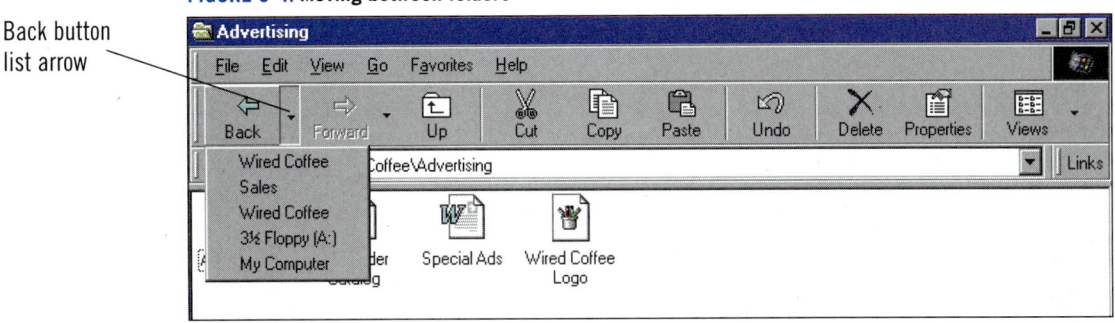

FIGURE C-5: Viewing folders and files in Details view

Click to
change views

Size of file

Type of file
or folder

Date file in folder
was last modified

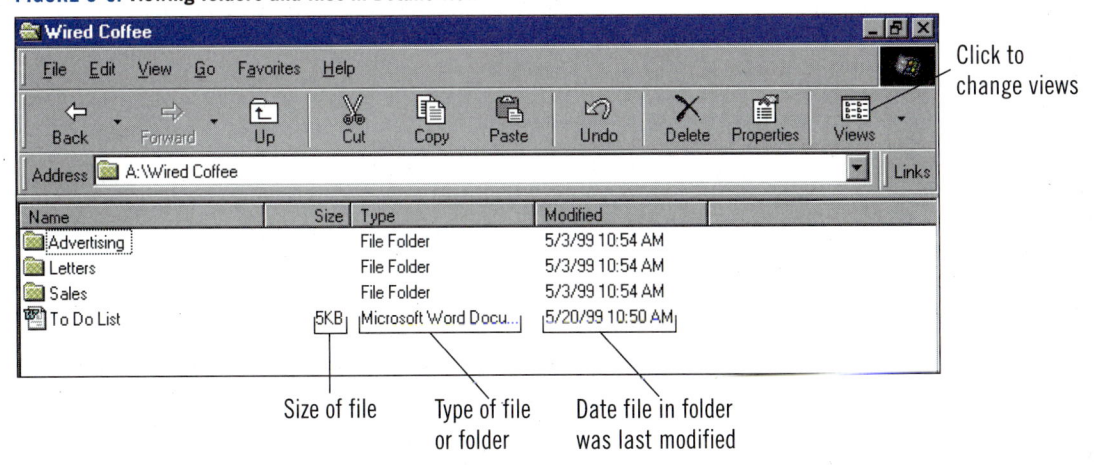

CLUES TO USE

Viewing files with Quick View

Quick View allows you to view the contents of a file without having to open that file. Although you cannot edit the contents of a file in Quick View, you can open the file for editing 🗐, increase the font size for easier reading A, decrease the font size A, or dis-

play new files in the Quick View window 🖻. To open a file with Quick View, right-click the file you want to open, then click Quick View on the pop-up menu. If you do not see a Quick View option on your pop-up menu, then you probably do not have this feature installed.

Creating a Folder

Creating a new folder is a necessary skill for successful file management. Creating a new folder can help you organize and keep track of files and other folders. There are two ways to create a folder in Windows 98. You can select the New command on the File menu, or you can right-click anywhere in any My Computer window and then select the New command. John needs to create two new folders. One will contain his To Do List, and the other will contain information about his employees.

Steps

1. **Click File on the menu bar, point to New, then click Folder**

   A new folder appears in the Wired Coffee window, shown in Figure C-6. All new folders are initially named New Folder. A border appears around the newly created folder, meaning that it is selected and ready to be renamed. Since this folder will hold important files relating to John's work week, he decides to call the folder "Important."

2. **Type Important and press [Enter]**

   The folder is now named "Important."

3. **Place the mouse pointer anywhere in the Wired Coffee window (except on a file or folder), right-click, then point to New**

   The pop-up menu opens, as shown in Figure C-7.

4. **Click Folder**

   A new folder appears, named New Folder, where you right-clicked the mouse in the My Computer window.

5. **Type Personnel and press [Enter]**

   The My Computer window now has two new folders, shown in Figure C-8. Once you create new folders, you can quickly rearrange them into orderly rows and columns.

6. **Click the View on the menu bar, point to Arrange Icons, then click By Name**

   The folder and file icons in the Wired Coffee folder are sorted by name in alphabetical order and automatically moved in line with the other icons. You can change the way individual files and folders are sorted by using other Arrange Icons options on the View menu. Table C-2 describes these options. John is ready to move files.

QuickTip

To rename a folder, right-click the folder you want to rename, click Rename, then type a new name.

TABLE C-2: Options on the View menu for arranging files and folders

option	arranges files and folders
By Name	Alphabetically
By Type	By type, such as all documents created using the WordPad program
By Size	By size, with the largest folder or file listed first
By Date	Chronologically by the date they were last modified, with the latest modification date listed last
Auto Arrange	Automatically in orderly rows and columns

FIGURE C-6: Creating a new folder

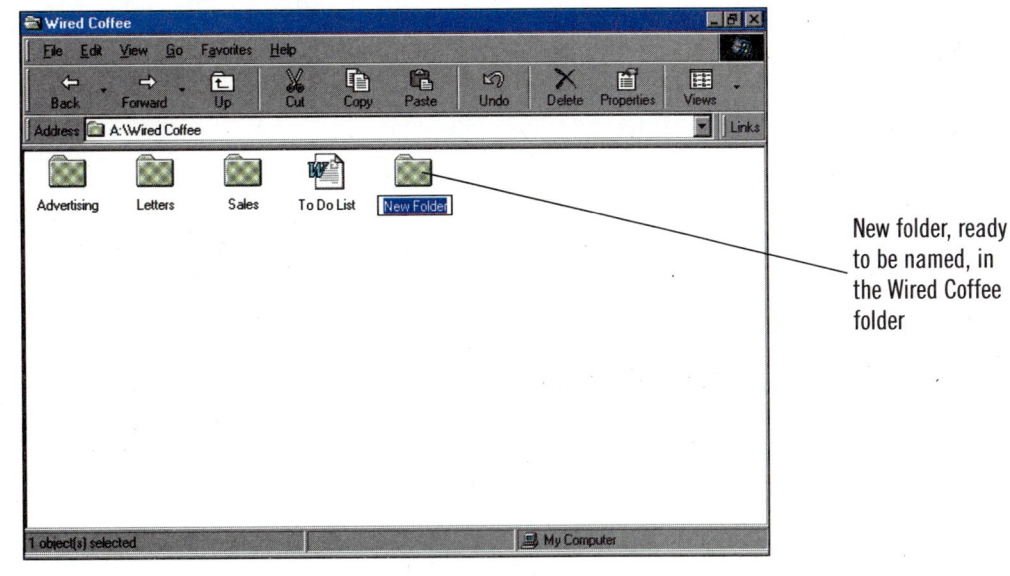

New folder, ready to be named, in the Wired Coffee folder

FIGURE C-7: Right-clicking to display a shortcut menu

Right-click in the blank part of the window to open the pop-up menu

Point to see the New options

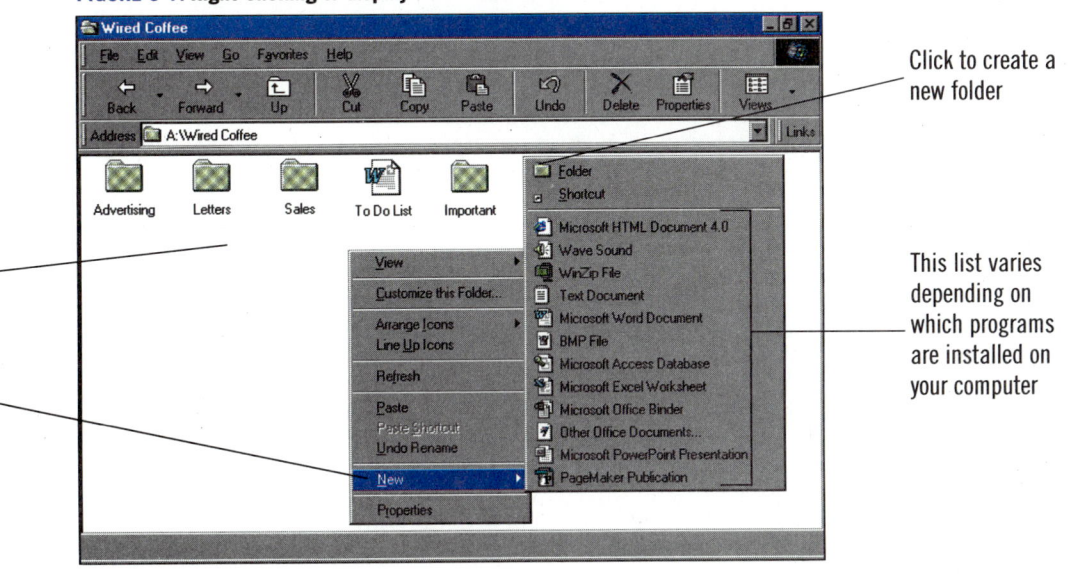

Click to create a new folder

This list varies depending on which programs are installed on your computer

FIGURE C-8: Two new folders

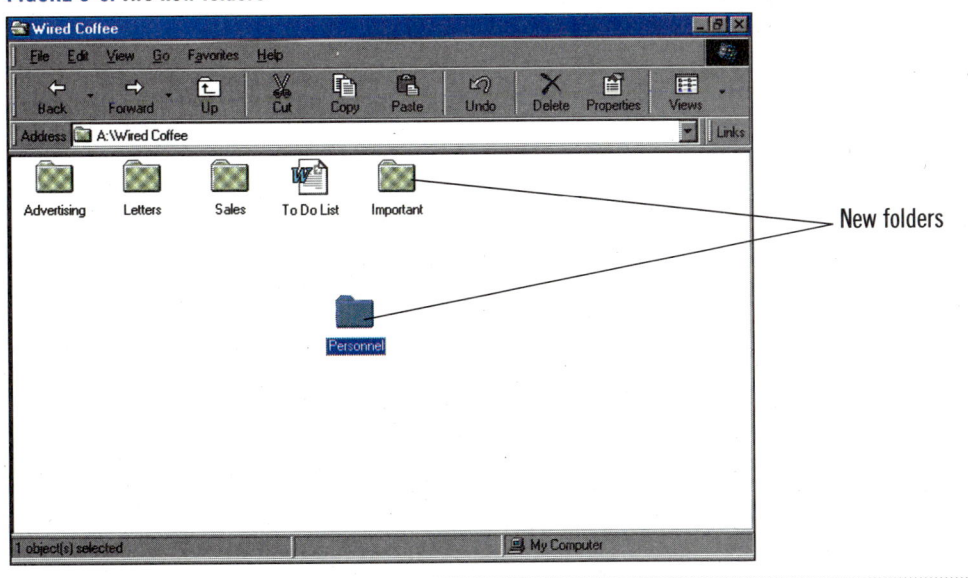

New folders

Moving Files and Folders

You can move a file or folder from one location to another using a variety of methods in My Computer (or Windows Explorer). If the file or folder and the location to which you want to move it are visible in a window or on the desktop, you can simply drag the item from one location to the other. When the location is not visible, you can use the Cut, Copy and Paste commands on the Edit menu or the buttons on the toolbar. Now that John has created a folder (which he named Important) for his weekly tasks, he is ready to move the To Do List file into it. He also needs to move a letter (a recommendation for a new marketing person) currently contained in the Sales folder to the new Personnel folder.

Steps

QuickTip

Dragging a file or folder from one place to another on the same disk will move it; whereas dragging it from one disk to another will copy it. If you want to copy the item on the same disk by dragging, simply press and hold [Ctrl] while you drag the mouse.

QuickTip

If you want to perform a file management operation such as moving or copying more than one file or folder at a time, first select all the files or folders by pressing and holding [Ctrl] and clicking each one you want to select. Then perform the operation.

1. Drag the **To Do List file** from the Wired Coffee window to the Important folder
   The icon representing the To Do List file is removed from the Wired Coffee folder and is placed in the folder named Important. Folders are moved in the same manner.

2. Double-click the **Important folder** and confirm that the file has been moved
   The folder named Important now contains John's To Do List. John now needs to move the file named Recommend Nelson, a personnel recommendation for one of his employees, from the Sales folder to the Personnel folder.

3. Click the **Back button list arrow** [←▾] on the toolbar, click **Sales**, then click the **Recommend Nelson file** to select it
   Since the Personnel folder is not visible, John uses the Cut and Paste commands to move a file from one folder to another.

4. Click the **Cut button** [✂] on the toolbar
   The file is removed from its original location and stored on the Windows Clipboard. When you cut or copy a file, the file icon turns gray, as shown in Figure C-9. John moves back to the Wired Coffee folder and then opens the Personnel folder to complete the file move.

5. Click the **Back button** [←] on the toolbar, then double-click the **Personnel folder**
   John is ready to use the paste command to move the file.

6. Click the **Paste button** [📋] on the toolbar
   The file is now pasted into the Personnel folder, shown in Figure C-10. After completing the move, John returns to the Wired Coffee folder.

7. Click [←] to return to the Wired Coffee folder

FIGURE C-9: Preparing to move a file

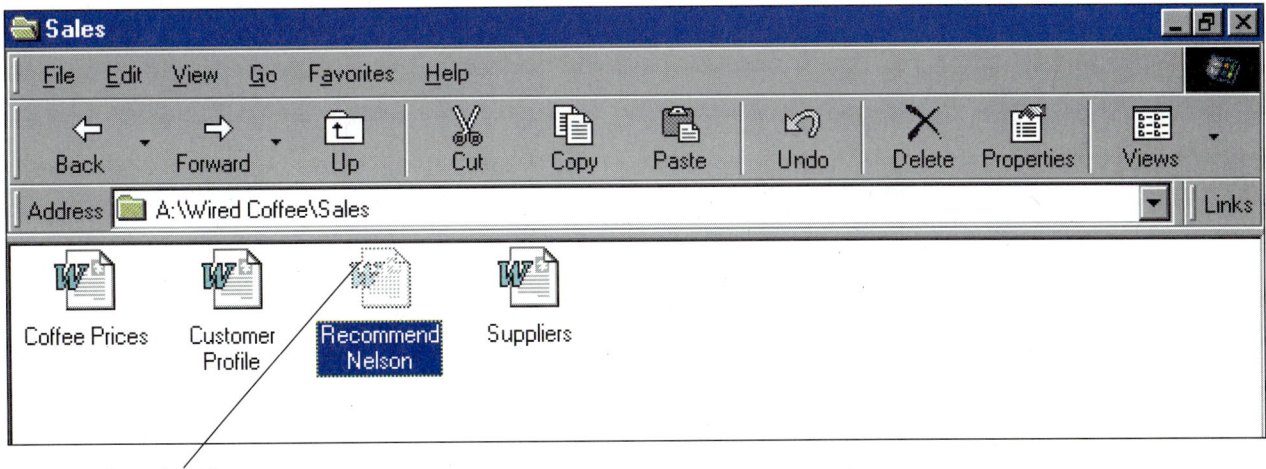

Grayed-out icon
indicates file has
been cut

FIGURE C-10: The relocated file

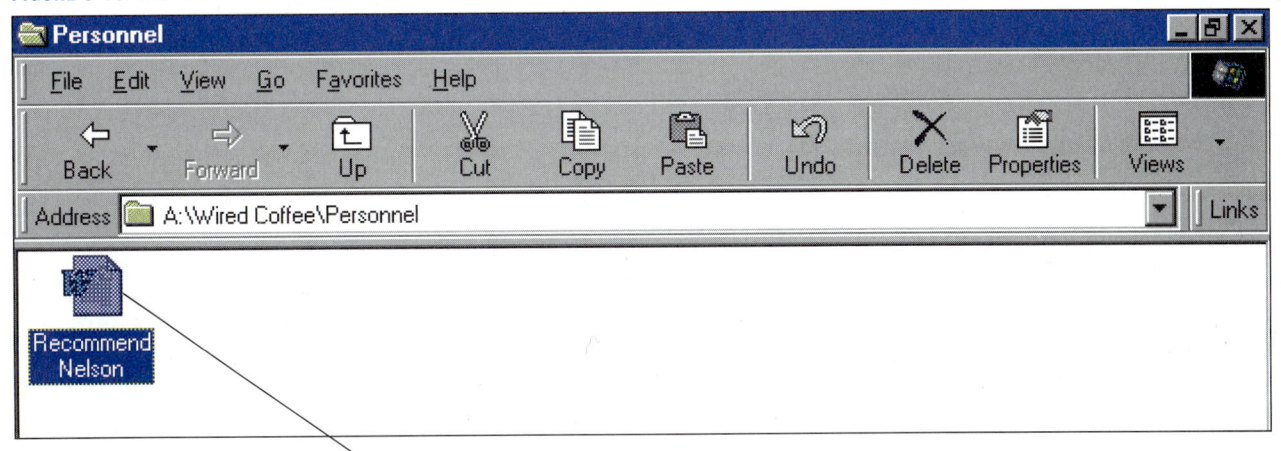

The file in its
new location

Sending files and folders

The Send To command, located on the pop-up menu of any desktop object, lets you "send" (or move) a file or folder to a new location on your computer. For example, you can send a file or folder to a floppy disk for making a quick backup copy of the file or folder, a mail recipient for receiving electronic messages, or the desktop for creating a shortcut. You can also use the Send To command to move a file or folder from one folder to another. To send a file or folder, right-click the file or folder you want to send, point to Send To on the pop-up menu, and then click the destination you want. You can determine the options that appear in the Send To command by creating a shortcut to the program or folder you want included and moving it to the SendTo folder, located within the Windows folder.

Deleting and Restoring Files and Folders

When you organize the contents of a folder, disk, or the desktop, you might find files and folders that you no longer need. You can **delete** these items, or remove them from the disk. If you delete a file or folder from the desktop or from the hard disk, it goes into the Recycle Bin. The **Recycle Bin**, located on your desktop, is a temporary storage area for deleted files. If you delete a file that you still need, you can restore it by moving it from the Recycle Bin to another location. Be aware that if you delete a file from your floppy disk it will not be stored in the Recycle Bin—it will be permanently deleted. See Table C-3 for a summary of the deleting and restoring options. To demonstrate how the Recycle Bin works, John first moves a file to the desktop, deletes that file, and then restores it.

Steps

Trouble?

Click the title bar in the My Computer window, then drag the window to the right to see the Recycle Bin.

1. **Double-click the Advertising folder, then click the Restore button in the Advertising window**
   The Advertising folder and its contents appear in the Advertising window. Before you can delete a file from a floppy disk to the Recycle Bin, you need to move it to the desktop or hard drive. If you want to delete a file directly from a floppy disk without the possibility of restoring it, you can drag the file directly to the Recycle Bin or press [Delete].

QuickTip

To quickly move files or folders from one disk to another, select the files or folder, press and hold [Shift], then drag the selected items to the new location.

2. **Right-click and hold the Ad Campaign file, drag it to the desktop from the Advertising folder on your Student Disk, then click Move Here**
   The file now appears on the desktop and can be moved to the Recycle Bin, as shown in Figure C-11.

3. **Drag the Ad Campaign file from the desktop to the Recycle Bin (you might have to move the Advertising window), then click Yes**
   The Recycle Bin icon should now look like it contains paper.

4. **Double-click the Recycle Bin icon**
   The Recycle Bin window opens. It contains the file that was deleted. The Recycle Bin window is like most other windows in that it contains a menu bar, a toolbar, and a status bar. Because John still needs this file he decides to restore it. The contents of the folders overlap, making it difficult for John to see both windows. He will first have to rearrange the desktop.

5. **Right-click an empty area of the taskbar, then click Tile Windows Vertically**
   This option allows you to see all open windows on the desktop at one time. The Recycle Bin window and the My Computer window appear side-by-side, as shown in Figure C-12.

QuickTip

Your deleted files remain in the Recycle Bin until you empty it. To empty the Recycle Bin, right-click the Recycle Bin icon, then click Empty Recycle Bin. This permanently removes the contents of the Recycle Bin from your hard disk.

6. **Select the Ad Campaign file in the Recycle Bin window, then drag it back to the Advertising window**
   The file is restored—it is intact and identical to the form it was in before you deleted it.

7. **Click the Close button in the Recycle Bin window**

FIGURE C-11: Selecting a file to drag to the Recycle Bin

Drag the selected icon here to delete the file

The selected file moved from the Advertising folder to the desktop

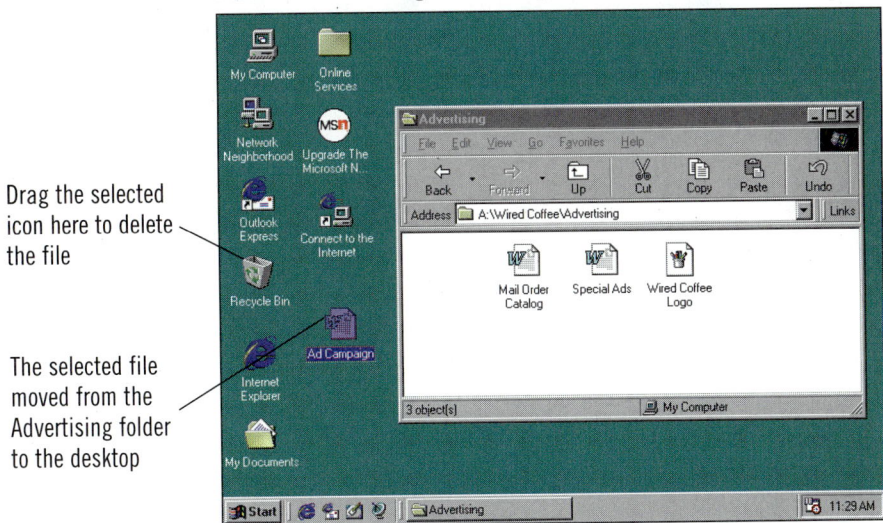

FIGURE C-12: The deleted file from the Advertising folder in the Recycle Bin

The contents of your Recycle Bin might be different

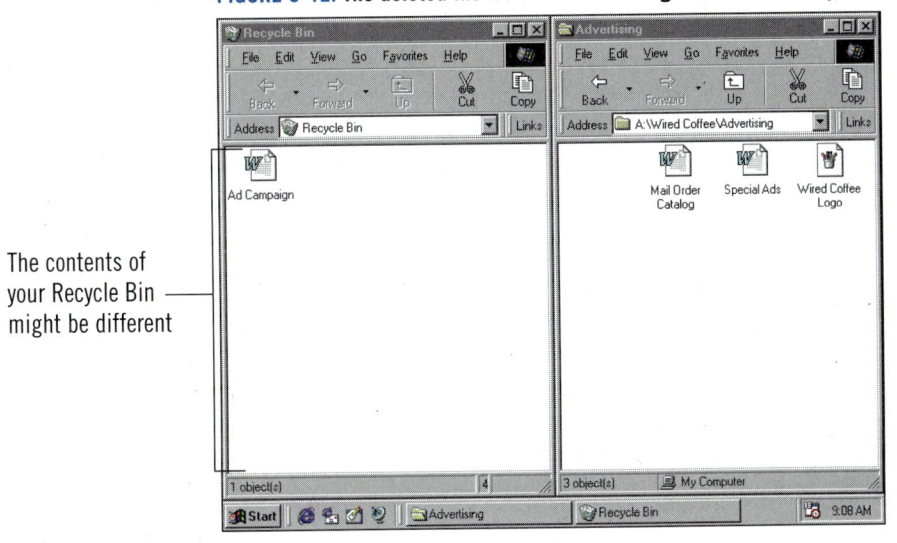

TABLE C-3: Deleting and restoring files

ways to delete a file	ways to restore a file from the recycle bin
Select the file, then click the Delete button on the toolbar	Click the Undo button on the Recycle Bin toolbar
Select the file, then press [Delete]	Select the file, click File, then click Restore
Right-click the file, then click Delete	Right-click the file, then click Restore
Drag the file to the Recycle Bin	Drag the file from the Recycle Bin to any location

CLUES TO USE

Recycle Bin properties

You can adjust several Recycle Bin settings by using the Properties option on the Recycle Bin shortcut menu. For example, if you do not want files to go to the Recycle Bin when you delete them, but, rather, want them to be immediately deleted, right-click the Recycle Bin, click Properties, then click the Do Not Move Files to the Recycle Bin check box to select the option. Also, if you find that the Recycle Bin is full and cannot accept any more files, you can increase the amount of disk space devoted to the Recycle Bin by moving the Maximum Size of Recycle Bin slider to the right. The percentage shown is of the drive on which the Recycle Bin is located.

Creating a Shortcut to a File

If a file or folder is buried several levels down in a file hierarchy, it could take you a while to access it. To save you time in getting to the items you use frequently, you can create shortcuts. A **shortcut** is a link between two points: a "home" folder where a file, folder, or program is actually stored and any other location where you want to access that file or program. The actual file, folder, or program remains stored in its original location, while you place the icon representing the shortcut in a convenient location, whether that is a folder or the desktop. John always uses his Wired Coffee logo in stationery, flyers, and general advertising materials. Rather than having to go through the steps to start Paint and then open the file, he'll simply place a shortcut for this Paint file on the desktop.

Steps

1. **In the Advertising folder, right-click Wired Coffee Logo, then click Create Shortcut**
   An icon for a shortcut to the Wired Coffee Logo now appears in the Advertising window. Compare your screen with Figure C-13. All shortcuts are named the same as the file on which they are based, but with the words "Shortcut to" in front of the original name. John wants the shortcut on his desktop for easy access to the file.

Trouble?

If you can't see an empty area of your desktop, your My Computer window is maximized. Click the Restore button to resize it.

2. **Right-click and hold the Shortcut to Wired Coffee Logo file, drag it from the Advertising folder to an empty area of the desktop, then click Move Here**
   The shortcut appears on the desktop, as shown in Figure C-14. A shortcut can be placed anywhere on the desktop. You should test the shortcut.

3. **Double-click the Shortcut to Wired Coffee Logo icon**
   The Paint program opens with the file named Wired Coffee Logo.

4. **Click the Close button in the Paint window**
   The logo file and the Paint program close. The shortcut to Wired Coffee Logo remains on the desktop until you delete it, so you can use it again and again. If you are working in a lab environment you should delete this shortcut.

5. **Right-click the Shortcut to Wired Coffee Logo icon**
   When you right-click folders and files (as opposed to the blank area in a window), a pop-up menu opens that offers several file management commands, as described in Table C-4. The commands on your pop-up menu might be different depending on the Windows 98 features installed on your computer.

6. **Click Delete on the pop-up menu, then click Yes in the Confirm File Delete dialog box**
   The shortcut is deleted from the desktop and placed in the Recycle Bin, where it will remain until John empties the Recycle Bin or restores the shortcut. When you delete a shortcut, only the shortcut is removed. The original file remains intact in its original location.

7. **Click the Maximize button in the Advertising window**

Placing shortcuts on the Start menu

You can place shortcuts to your favorite files and programs on the Start menu. To do this, simply drag the folder, file, or program to the Start button, and the item will appear on the first level of the Start menu.

FIGURE C-13: Creating a shortcut

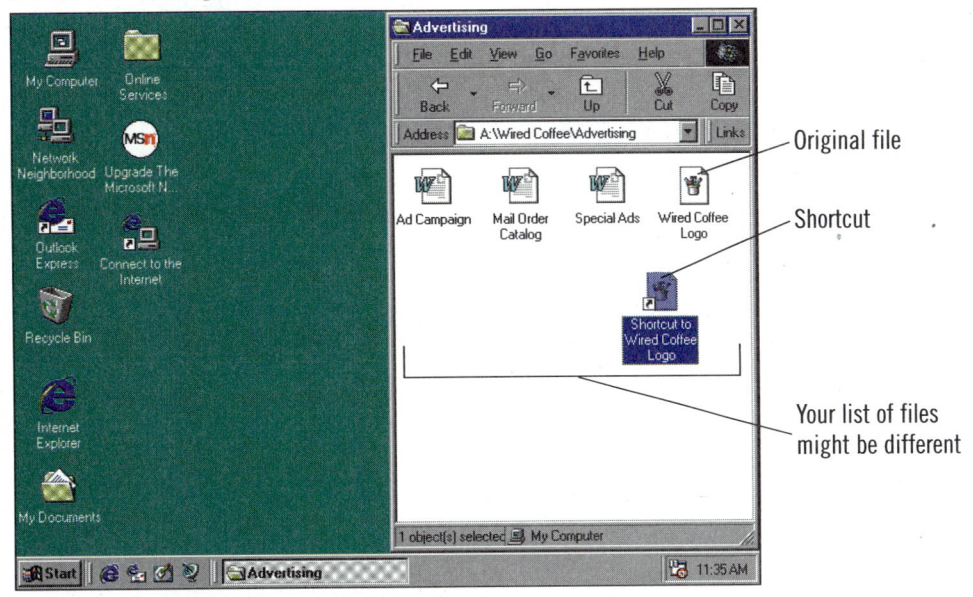

Original file

Shortcut

Your list of files might be different

FIGURE C-14: Dragging a shortcut to a new location

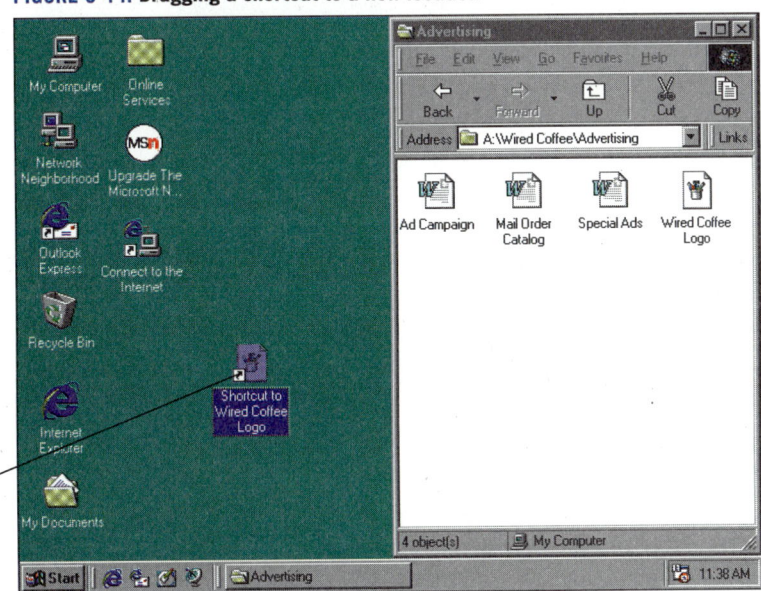

The relocated shortcut on the desktop

TABLE C-4: Shortcut menu options for files and folders

shortcut menu options	description	shortcut menu options	description
Open	Opens the file or folder	Create Shortcut	Creates a shortcut for the file or folder
Explore	Opens a folder or drive in Windows Explorer	Delete	Deletes the file or folder
Find	Finds files in a folder or drive	Print	Prints the file
Send To	Sends the file or folder to new location	Quick View	If installed, displays the contents of the file
Cut	Cuts the file or folder from its original location to the Clipboard	Rename	Renames the file or folder
Copy	Copies the file or folder to the Clipboard	Properties	Displays the properties of the file or folder
Paste	Pastes the file or folder from the Clipboard to a new location		

Displaying Drive Information

You should know as much about your system as possible. You might have to tell your instructor or technical support person certain information if you encounter a problem with your computer, or you might want to know how much space is left on a disk or want to change a **disk label** (a name you can assign to a hard or floppy disk). When you label a hard disk, the label will appear in the My Computer and Windows Explorer windows. Besides checking hard drive or floppy disk information, you can also use Windows 98 tools to check your disks for damage, optimize your disk for better performance, make copies of your disks for safe keeping, and share your disk contents with others. You can perform these activities by using the Properties command. John wants to find out how much free space is available on his floppy disk.

1. Click the **Back button list arrow** on the toolbar, then click **My Computer**
   John needs to display the 3½ Floppy disk icon in the My Computer window to examine property information.

2. Right-click the icon in the My Computer window for the drive which contains your Student Disk
   The icon representing the 3½ disk drive is highlighted, and the pop-up menu opens.

3. Click **Properties** on the pop-up menu
   The 3½ Floppy (A:) Properties dialog box opens with the General tab in front, as shown in Figure C-15. Click the General tab if it is not the frontmost tab. You can see a graphical representation of the amount of space being used relative to the amount available in the pie chart for the floppy disk. John reviews the chart and determines that the floppy disk contains plenty of free space. John wants to label this disk.

4. Click the **Label text box** if necessary, then type **StudentDisk**
   A disk label can contain up to 11 characters but no spaces.

5. Click the **Tools tab**
   The Tools tab becomes the frontmost tab, as shown in Figure C-16, showing you three utilities that can make Windows work more efficiently: error-checking, backup, and defragmentation. You can use the Defragmentation feature to speed up the performance of a disk. **Defragmenting** means that files will be rewritten to the disk in contiguous blocks rather than in random blocks. When you click any one of these options, Windows will update you as to when it was last used on the currently selected disk. Although these tools are mostly used for keeping a hard disk healthy, they can be used on a floppy disk as well. Table C-5 describes what each tool does.

6. Click **OK**
   The Properties dialog box closes.

7. Click the **Close button** in the My Computer window

Backing up files

The more you work with a computer, the more files you'll create. To protect yourself from losing critical information, it's important to **back up** (make copies on a separate disk) your files frequently. The Backup option in the disk drive Properties dialog box walks you through a series of dialog boxes to help you back up the files on your hard disk to a floppy or tape drive. You can back up the contents of an entire disk or only certain files.

FIGURE C-15: General tab options in the 3½ Floppy (A:) Properties window

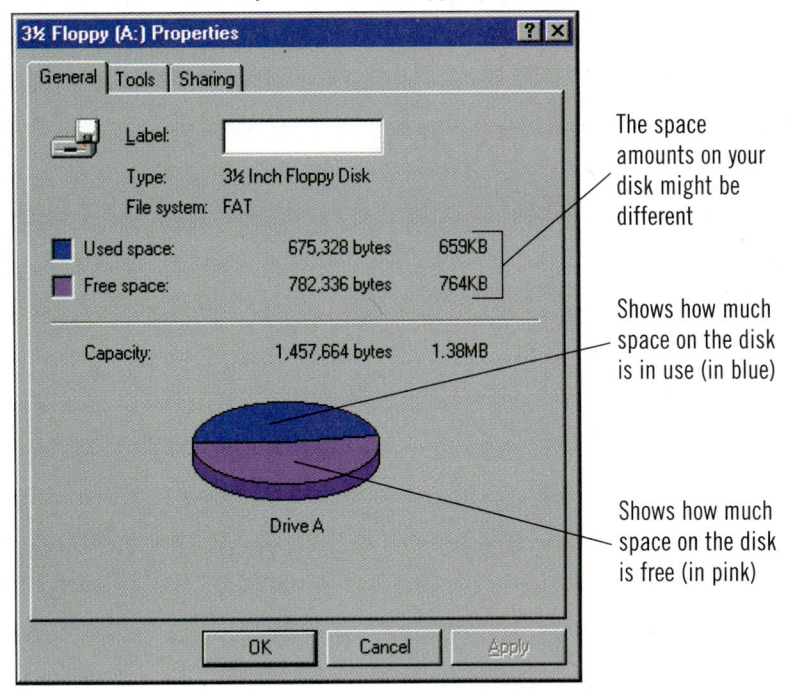

The space amounts on your disk might be different

Shows how much space on the disk is in use (in blue)

Shows how much space on the disk is free (in pink)

FIGURE C-16: Tools tab options in the 3½ Floppy (A:) Properties window

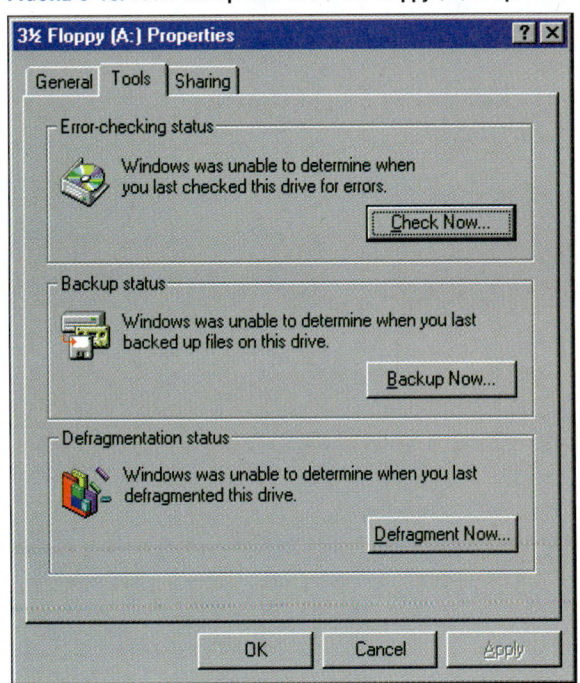

TABLE C-5: Tools in the Properties dialog box

tool	description
Error-checking status	Checks for the last time you checked the disk for damage and, if you want, attempts to correct files that are damaged
Backup status	Displays the last time you backed up the contents of the disk, and if you want, starts the Windows 98 backup program
Defragmentation status	Checks for the last time you optimized the disk, and if you want, starts the Windows 98 Defragmentation procedure

Practice

► Concepts Review

Label each of the elements of the screen shown in Figure C-17.

FIGURE C-17

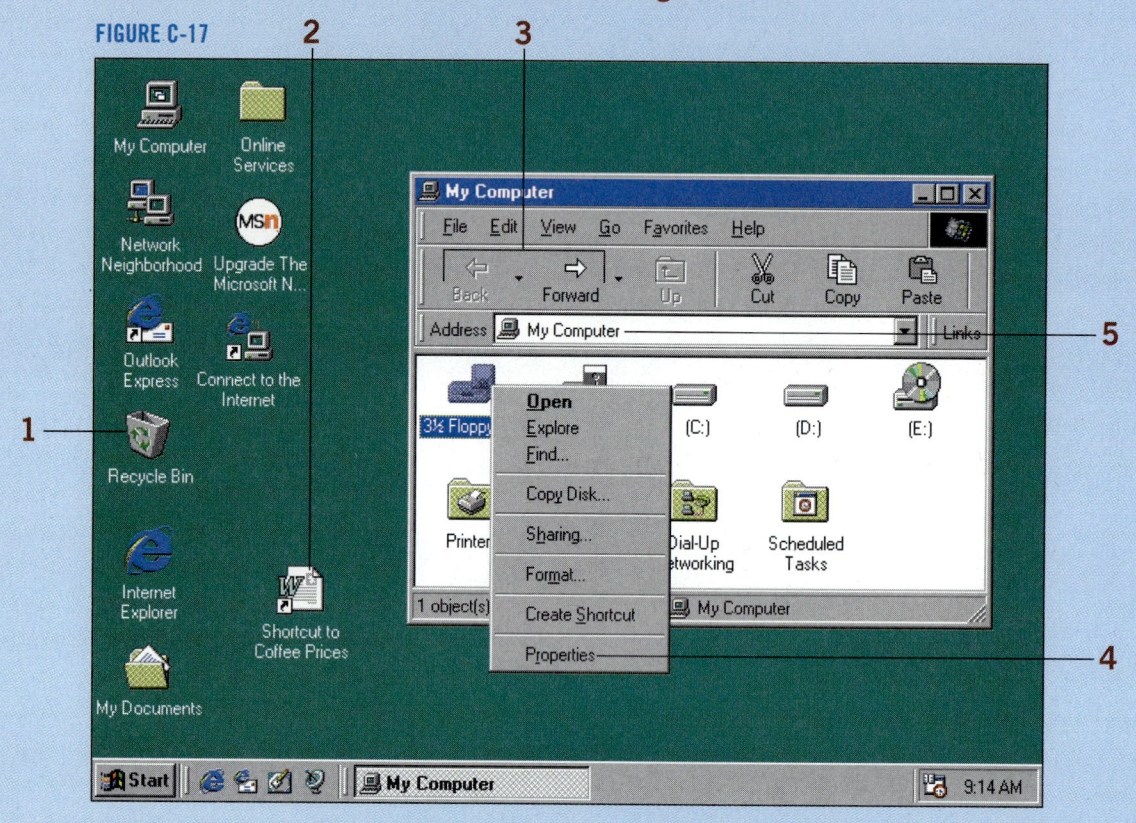

Match each of the terms with the statement that describes its function.

6. My Computer
7. Shortcut
8. File
9. Recycle Bin
10. Folder

a. A collection of files and folders
b. Location of deleted files
c. A file and folder management tool
d. A collection of information
e. A link to a file or folder

Select the best answer from the following list of choices.

11. When a file is deleted, it is placed in
    a. My Computer.
    b. Accessories.
    c. the Recycle Bin.
    d. the Desktop Container.

12. My Computer is used to
   a. manage files and folders.
   b. delete files.
   c. add folders.
   d. all of the above.

13. Which of the following is not an option for viewing files and folders?
   a. Large icons
   b. Small icons
   c. File names
   d. Details

14. When files and folders are arranged by date, they are arranged by
   a. the current date.
   b. the date they were last modified.
   c. the date they were created.
   d. the date they were last opened.

15. When right-clicking on a folder, which of the following cannot be done?
   a. Explore the folder
   b. Find a file
   c. Print the contents of the folder
   d. Create a shortcut

▶ Skills Review

1. Open and view My Computer.
   a. Insert your Student Disk in the appropriate disk drive.
   b. Double-click My Computer.
   c. Click the Maximize button in the My Computer window.
   d. Double-click the 3½ Floppy drive (A: or B:).
   e. Double-click the Wired Coffee folder.
   f. Double-click the Sales folder.

2. View files and folders.
   a. Click the Views button list arrow, then click List.
   b. Click the Up One Level button on the toolbar twice.
   c. Click the Back button on the toolbar.
   d. Open the Personnel folder.
   e. Click the Back button list arrow on the toolbar, then click Sales.
   f. Click the Forward button on the toolbar.
   g. Click View on the menu bar, then click Details.
   h. Click View on the menu bar, then click Large Icons.

3. Create folders.

a. Right-click a blank area of the window, point to New, then click Folder.

b. Type "Marketing" and press [Enter].

c. Click View on the menu bar, point to Arrange Icons, then click By Name.

4. Move files.

a. Double-click the Advertising folder.

b. Click the Mail Order Catalog file.

c. Click the Copy button on the toolbar.

d. Click the Back button on the toolbar.

e. Double-click the Marketing folder.

f. Click the Paste button on the toolbar.

g. Click the Back button on the toolbar.

5. Delete and restore files.

a. Click the Marketing folder.

b. Click the Restore button on the toolbar.

c. Right-click the Marketing folder, drag it to the desktop, then click Move Here.

d. Drag the Marketing folder from the desktop to the Recycle Bin, then click Yes.

e. Double-click the Recycle Bin.

f. Right-click an empty area of the taskbar, then click Title Windows Vertically.

g. Click File on the Recycle Bin menu bar, click Empty Recycle Bin, then click Yes. (To restore the Marketing folder, you would drag it back to the Wired Coffee folder).

h. Click the Close button in the Recycle Bin window.

6. Create shortcuts.

a. Double-click the Advertising folder.

b. Right-click the Special Ads file, then click Create Shortcut.

c. Right-click and drag the Shortcut to Special Ads file to the desktop, then click Move Here.

d. Right-click the Shortcut to Special Ads file, then click Delete.

e. Click Yes.

f. Right-click the Recycle Bin icon, then click Empty Recycle Bin.

g. Click Yes.

7. Examine disk capacity.

a. Click the Back button list arrow on the toolbar, then click My Computer.

b. Right-click the icon representing your Student Disk in the My Computer window, then click Properties.

c. Write down the capacity of the disk, how much capacity is being used, and how much is available for further use.

d. Click OK.

e. Click the Close button in the My Computer window.

▶ Independent Challenges

1. As a manager at Lew's Books and Cappuccino bookstore, you need to organize the folders and files currently on the store's computer. These are located on your Student Disk in the folder named Lew's Books.

To complete this independent challenge:

1. Open My Computer, and open and view the contents of the folder called Lew's Books on your Student Disk.
2. Create a new folder called Lew's Books & Cappuccino.
3. Using paper and pencil, draw out the organization for all folders and files in Lew's Books & Cappuccino.
4. In the Lew's Books folder, create four new folders named Q1, Q2, Q3, and Q4.
5. Take the quarterly folders in the 1999 and 2000 folders and place them in the respective Q1, Q2, Q3, and Q4 folders.
6. Create a shortcut for the Collectors' Newsletter file (located in the Letters folder) and place it in the Lew's Books folder.
7. In the folder named Store Locations, create a new folder and name it New Stores.
8. Move the New Store Locations file in the Letters folder to the New Stores folder.
9. Using paper and pencil, draw out the new organization of all the folders and files in the Lew's Books folder.
10. Close My Computer.

2. You are the vice president of a small carton manufacturing company, Apex Cartons, and you need to organize your Windows 98 folders and files. As with any typical business, you have folders for correspondence (business and personal), contracts, inventory, personnel documents, and payroll information. You may have other folders as well. Your job is to organize these separate folders.

To complete this independent challenge:

1. Open My Computer and create a new folder named Apex Cartons on your Student Disk, within which the rest of the organization of files and folders for this independent challenge will appear.
2. Create a folder named Manufacturing.
3. Create a folder named Material Suppliers.
4. Create two folders; one named East Coast and one named West Coast.
5. Move (not copy) the East Coast and West Coast folders into the folder named Material Suppliers.
6. Create a file using WordPad (it doesn't have to have any text in it) and save it as "Suppliers Bid" to the Manufacturing folder on your Student Disk.
7. Move the Suppliers Bid file into the Materials Suppliers folder.
8. Using paper and pencil, draw out the new organization of all the folders and files in your Apex Cartons folder.
9. Close My Computer.

3. You and your college roommate have decided to start a mail order PC business called MO PC, and you decide to use Windows 98 to organize the files for the business. Your job is to organize the following folders and files, as well as to create shortcuts.

To complete this independent challenge:

1. Open My Computer and create a new folder named MO PC on your Student Disk, within which the rest of the organization of files and folders for this independent challenge will appear.
2. Create a new folder named Advertising.
3. Create a new folder named Customers.
4. Use WordPad to create a form letter welcoming new customers (one paragraph long), save it as "Customer Letter" and place it in the Customers folder.
5. Use WordPad to create a list of tasks that need to get done before the business opens (at least five items), save it as "Business Plan," and place it in the MO PC folder.
6. Use Paint to create a simple logo, and place it in the Advertising folder.
7. Create a shortcut for the logo.
8. Delete the Business Plan file and then restore it.
9. Using paper and pencil, draw out the new organization of all the folders and files in your MO PC folder.
10. Close My Computer.

4. M & N Bakeries just opened. You have been hired to help the owners organize their recipes into different categories and work on the design of their company logo.

For this independent challenge, use the files Icing 1, Icing 2, Brownies, Passover/Easter Torte, located in the M&N Bakeries folder on your Student Disk.

To complete this independent challenge:

1. Open My Computer and open the folder called M&N Bakeries on your Student Disk, within which the rest of the organization of files and folders for this Independent Challenge will appear.
2. Create a folder named Cakes.
3. Create a folder named Flourless Cakes, and move it into the Cakes folder.
4. Create a folder named Flour Cakes, and move it into the Cakes folder.
5. In the M&N Bakeries folder, create a folder named Cookies & Bars.
6. Place the file named Brownies in the Cookies & Bars folder.
7. Place the file named Passover & Easter Torte into the Flourless Cakes folder.
8. Move the Icing 1 recipe file to your desktop, then drag the file to the Recycle Bin.
9. Double-click to open the Recycle Bin and restore the Icing 1 recipe file to the M&N Bakeries folder on your Student Disk.
10. Using paper and pencil, draw out the new organization of all the folders and files in your M&N Bakeries folder.
11. Close My Computer.

▶ Visual Workshop

Re-create the screen shown in Figure C-18, which displays the My Computer window for the floppy disk drive with the Student Disk. Use Figure C-1 to help you locate the Coffee Price file on your Student Disk. Print the screen. (Press the Print Screen key to make a copy of the screen, open Paint, click Edit on the menu bar, click Paste to paste the screen into Paint, then click Yes to paste the large image, if necessary. Click File on the menu bar, click Print, then click OK.)

FIGURE C-18

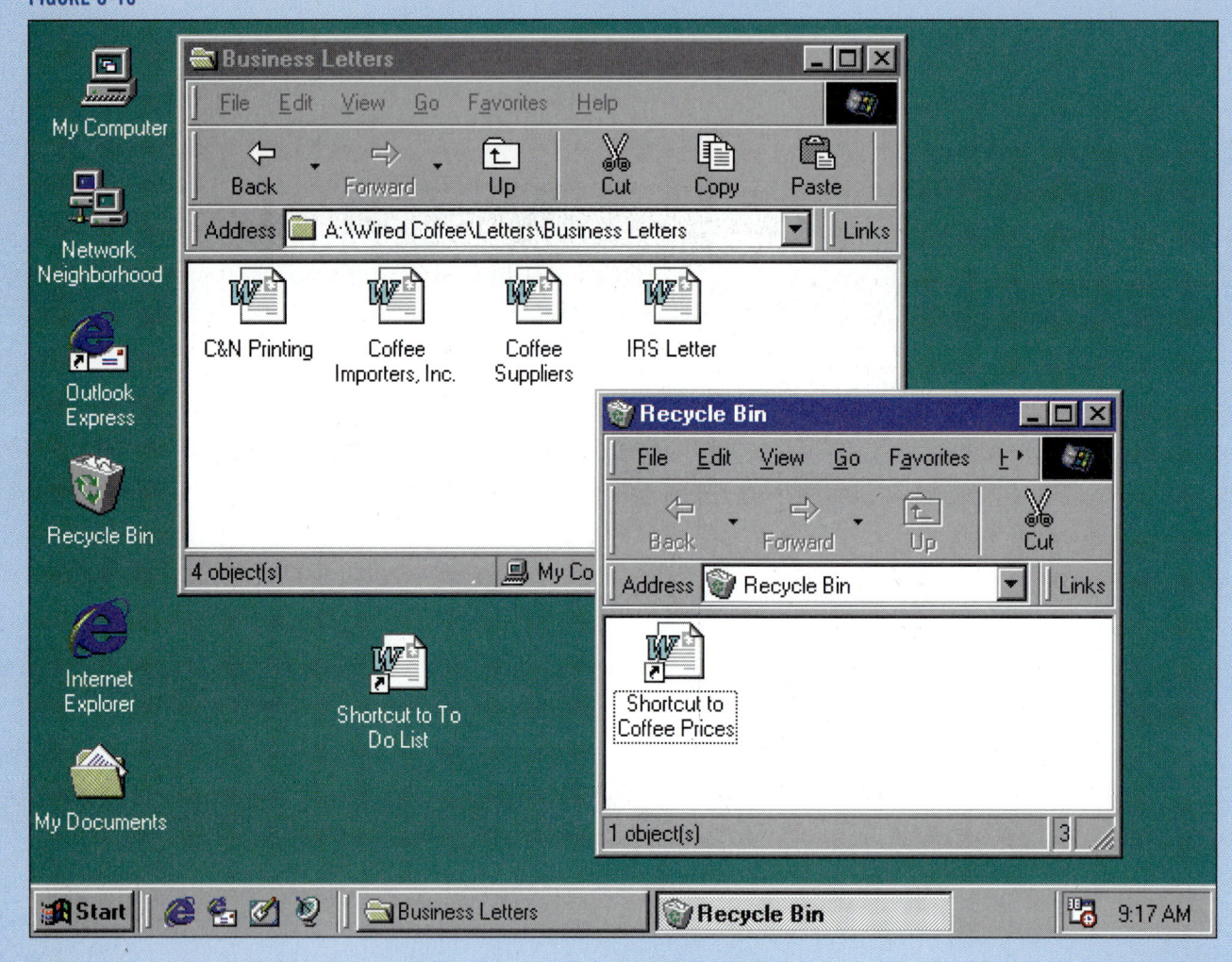

Managing

Folders and Files Using Windows Explorer

- ► View the Windows Explorer window
- ► Open and view folders in Windows Explorer
- ► Change the Windows Explorer window
- ► Create and rename folders in Windows Explorer
- ► Find a file
- ► Move and copy a file to a folder
- ► Restore a deleted file using Undo
- ► Customize a folder

Windows 98 offers another useful feature for managing files and folders, named Windows Explorer. Windows Explorer is more powerful than My Computer, offers more features, and most importantly, allows you to work with more than one computer, folder, or file at once. This is possible because the Windows Explorer window is split into two **panes**, or frames, to accommodate a comparison of information from two different locations. You can also use Windows Explorer to copy, move, delete, and rename files and folders, as you can with My Computer. In this unit John Casey will use Windows Explorer to perform some general file management tasks and also to prepare for the upcoming Wired Coffee Spring Catalog.

Viewing the Windows Explorer window

The most important aspect of the Windows Explorer window is the two panes shown in Figure D-1. The pane on the left side of the screen, known as the **Explorer Bar** (or simply "the left pane"), displays all drives and folders on the computer, and the right pane displays the contents of whatever drive or folder is selected in the Explorer Bar. This arrangement enables you to simultaneously view the overall structure of the contents of your computer (the "file hierarchy") and the contents of specific folders within that structure. 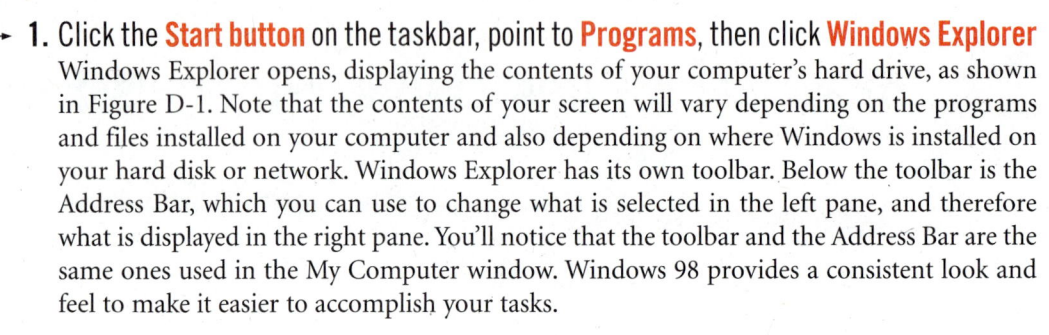 John wants to gain more experience working in Windows Explorer, so he starts the program and then views the contents of his computer.

Steps

Trouble?

If you do not see the toolbar, click View on the menu bar, point to Toolbars, then click Standard Buttons to place a check mark next to it and to display the toolbar. Follow the same procedure (clicking Address Bar instead of Standard Buttons) if you don't see the Address Bar.

QuickTip

You can change the size of the left and right panes. Place the mouse pointer on the vertical bar that separates the two panes of the Explorer window. When the mouse changes to ↔, you can drag the line to change the size of each pane.

1. **Click the Start button on the taskbar, point to Programs, then click Windows Explorer**
   Windows Explorer opens, displaying the contents of your computer's hard drive, as shown in Figure D-1. Note that the contents of your screen will vary depending on the programs and files installed on your computer and also depending on where Windows is installed on your hard disk or network. Windows Explorer has its own toolbar. Below the toolbar is the Address Bar, which you can use to change what is selected in the left pane, and therefore what is displayed in the right pane. You'll notice that the toolbar and the Address Bar are the same ones used in the My Computer window. Windows 98 provides a consistent look and feel to make it easier to accomplish your tasks.

2. **Click the Address list arrow on the Address Bar, then click Desktop**
   The icons on the desktop are listed in the right pane. The Address Bar makes it easy to open items on the desktop and the drives, and in the folders and system folders on your computer. As an alternative to using the Address Bar, you can change what is displayed in the right pane by clicking the drive or folder in the Explorer Bar, which is the left pane. In the same way you can view the contents of your computer using the My Computer window on your desktop, you can also view the contents of your computer using Windows Explorer.

3. **In the Explorer Bar, click the My Computer icon**
   The drives and system folders on your computer are listed in the right pane.

4. **Make sure your Student Disk is inserted in the appropriate disk drive, then in the right pane of Windows Explorer, double-click 3½ Floppy (A:) or (B:)**
   The 3½ floppy disk drive opens, as shown in Figure D-2. The contents of the drive are shown in the right pane of Windows Explorer. You can open a folder or open a document in the right pane of Windows Explorer. When you double-click a drive or folder in the right pane, the contents of that item are shown in the right pane of the Windows Explorer. When you double-click a document, the program associated with the program starts and opens the document. You can move back and forth to the last drive or folder you displayed by using the Back and Forward buttons on the toolbar in the Explorer window just as you did in the My Computer window.

5. **Click the Back button ⇦ on the toolbar**
   The contents of My Computer (the last location you displayed in Step 3) are listed in the right pane of Windows Explorer.

6. **Click the Forward button ⇨ on the toolbar**
   The contents of the 3½ floppy disk drive reappear in the right pane of Windows Explorer. Leave Windows Explorer open and move on to the next lesson.

FIGURE D-1: Displaying the contents of your computer's hard drive

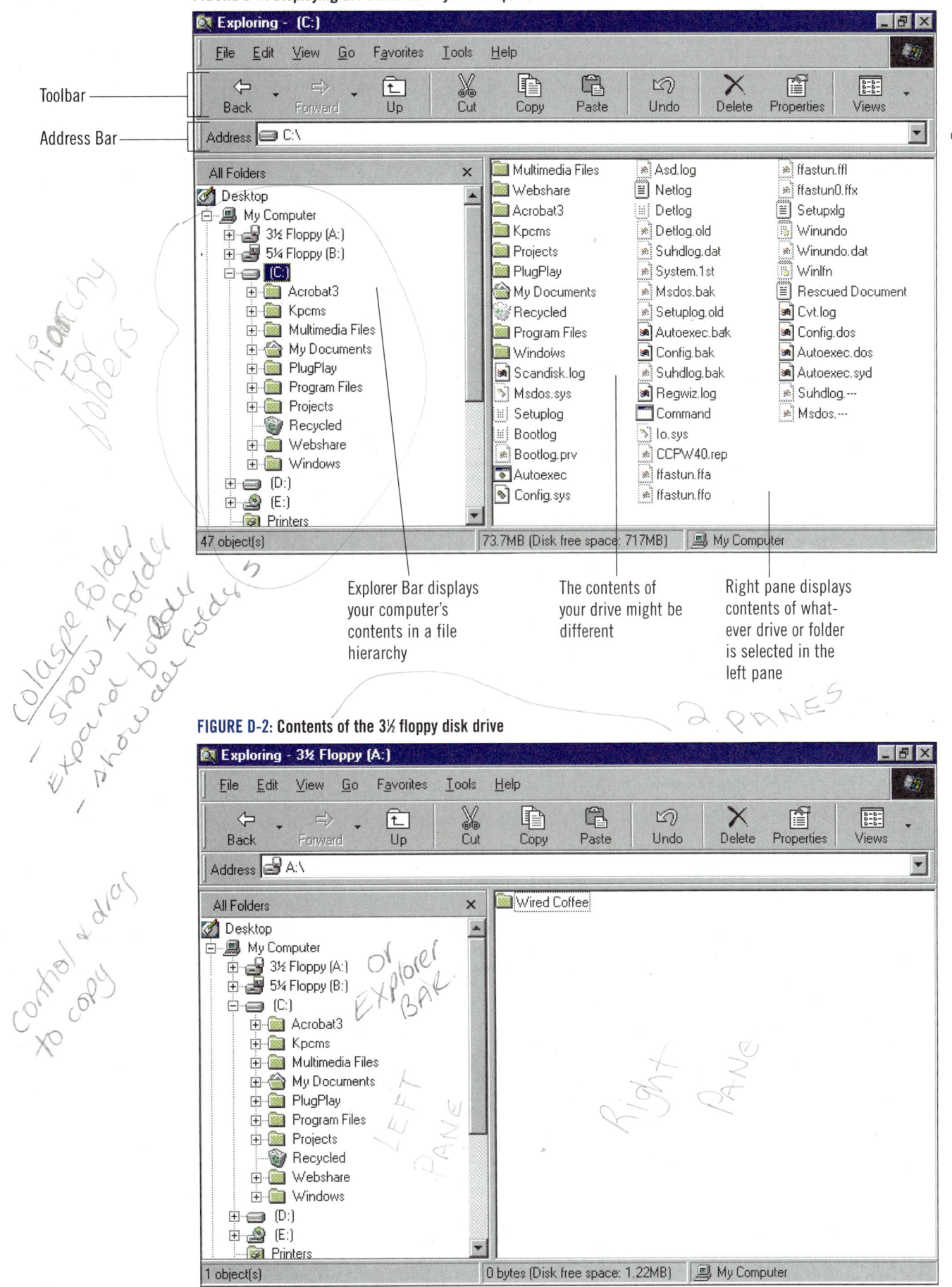

Toolbar

Address Bar

Explorer Bar displays your computer's contents in a file hierarchy

The contents of your drive might be different

Right pane displays contents of whatever drive or folder is selected in the left pane

FIGURE D-2: Contents of the 3½ floppy disk drive

Opening and Viewing Folders in Windows Explorer

The Explorer Bar (the left pane of Windows Explorer) displays your computer's contents in file hierarchy. The top of the file hierarchy is the desktop, followed by the drives, and then the folders. The dotted gray lines indicate the different levels. You can display or hide the different levels by clicking the plus sign (+) or the minus sign (–) to the left of an icon in the Explorer Bar so that you don't always have to look at the complicated structure of your entire computer or network. Clicking the + to the left of an icon displays (or expands the drive or folder) under the icon the contents of the drive or folder, and clicking the – hides them (or "collapses" the drive or folder). Clicking the icon itself displays the contents of the item in the right pane. When neither a + nor a – appears next to an icon, it means that the item does not have any folders in it (although it might have files, which you could display in the right pane by clicking the icon). Using the + and – in the Explorer Bar allows you to quickly display the file hierarchy of the drives and folders on your computer without having to open and display the contents of each folder. ◢ John wants to open the Personnel and Letters folders without having to open and display the contents of each folder in the file hierarchy.

Steps 1234

1. **Click the – (minus sign) next to the hard drive (C:) icon in the Explorer Bar**
   The folders on the hard drive collapse to display only the hard drive icon. The – changes to a + indicating the hard drive contains folders. Because you did not click the hard drive icon, the right pane still displays the contents of drive A as it did before. John decides to display the folders on the floppy disk drive.

QuickTip

Make a copy of your Student Disk before you use it. For assistance, see your instructor or technical support person.

2. **Click the + (plus sign) next to the 3½ Floppy drive icon in the Explorer Bar**
   The folder on the floppy disk drive, which is where your Student Disk is located, expands and appears in the Explorer Bar.

3. **Click the + next to the Wired Coffee folder in the Explorer Bar**
   The folders in the Wired Coffee folder expand and appear in the Explorer Bar, as shown in Figure D-3.

4. **Click the Personnel folder in the Explorer Bar**
   The contents of Personnel folder appear in the right pane, as shown in Figure D-4. When you click a folder in the Explorer Bar, the contents of that folder are displayed in the right pane of Windows Explorer.

5. **Click the Letters folder in the Explorer Bar, then double-click the Business Letters folder in the right pane of Windows Explorer**
   The Business Letters folder opens, as shown in Figure D-5. The contents of the Business Letters folder are shown in the right pane of Windows Explorer, and the folders in the Letters folder are expanded in the Explorer Bar.

FIGURE D-3: Folders on the 3½ floppy disk drive

Folders in the Wired Coffee folder expanded in the Explorer Bar

Contents of the 3½ floppy disk drive

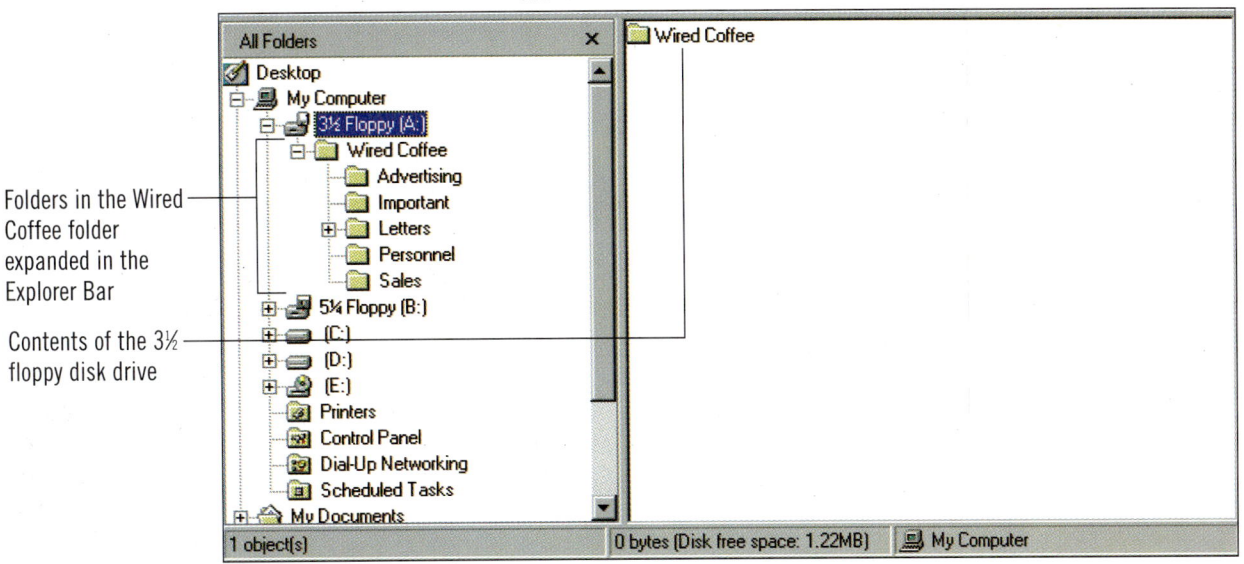

FIGURE D-4: Personnel folder

Contents of Personnel folder

Icon indicates the folder is open and its contents are displayed in the right pane

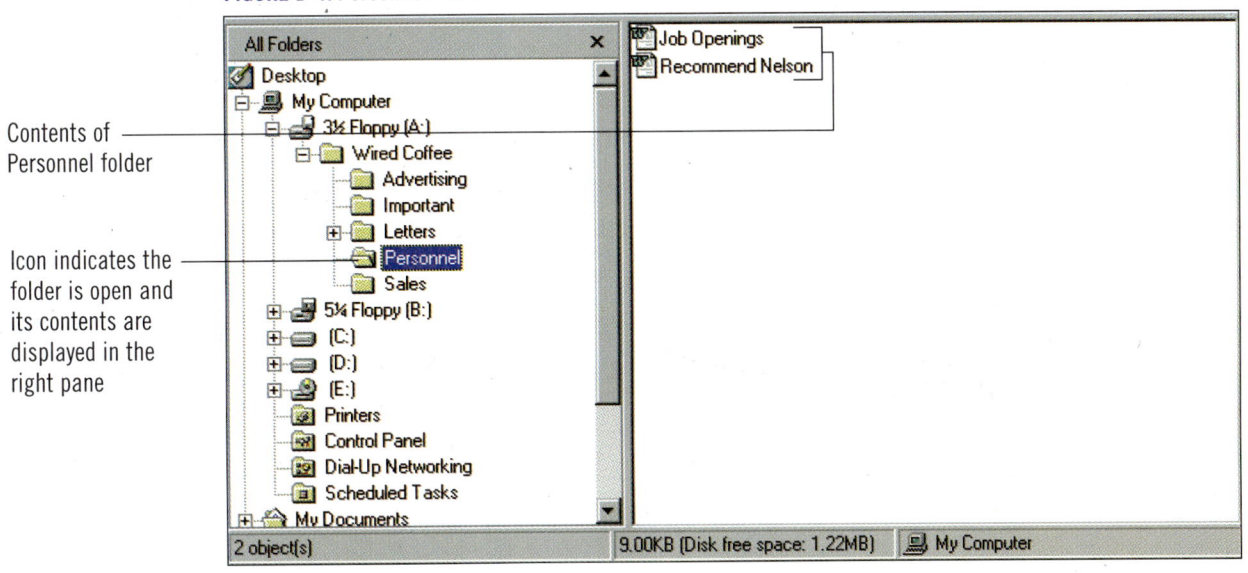

FIGURE D-5: Business Letters folder

Open folder

Contents of Business Letters folder

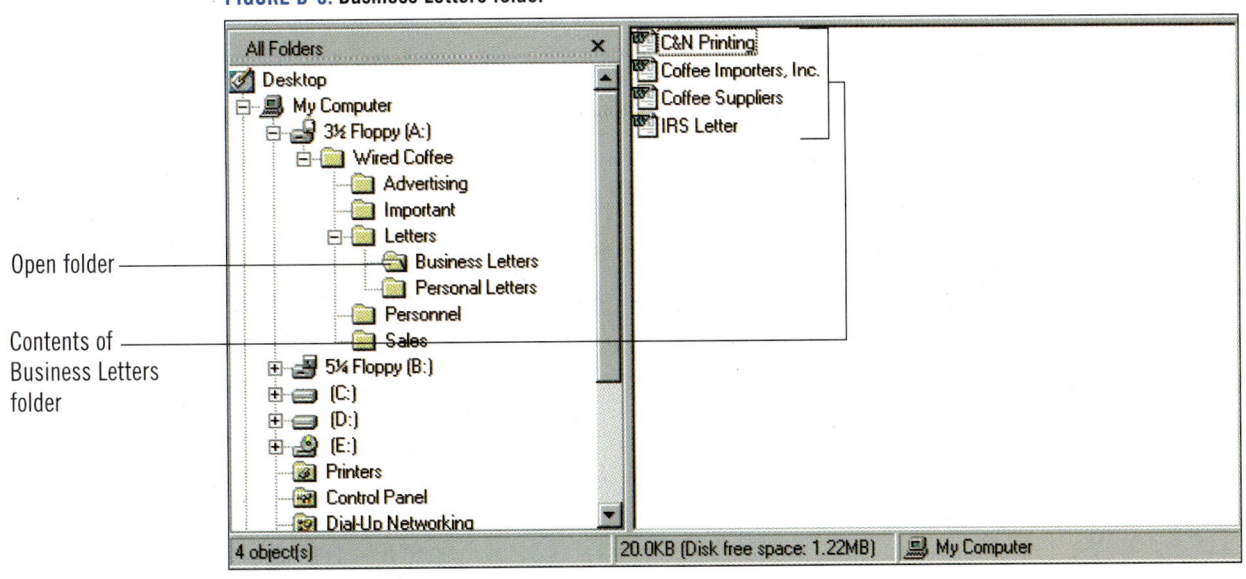

Changing the Windows Explorer Window

You can display Windows Explorer and your file hierarchy in a variety of different ways depending on what you want to see and do. For example, if you have a lot of files and folders to display, you can hide the Explorer Bar or the status bar to give you more room. If you need to change the way Windows Explorer sorts your files and folders, you can use the column indicator buttons in the right pane in Details view. When you click one of the column indicator buttons, such as Name, Size, Time, or Modified (date) in Details view, the folders and files are sorted by the type of information listed in the column. ◄━━━ John wants to find out the date he wrote a letter to the coffee suppliers so he decides to sort the files in the Business Letters folder by date.

1. Click the **Views button list arrow** 🔲▾ on the toolbar, then click **Details**

   The files and folders on your Student Disk (in the 3½ floppy disk drive) are displayed in Details view, shown in Figure D-6. John wants to sort his files and folders. First, to see the file and folder information better, he closes the Explorer Bar.

2. Click the **Close button** on the Explorer Bar

   The Explorer Bar closes. You can sort by any category listed by clicking the column indicator button located at the top of the folders and files list in the right pane. The files in the Business folder are currently sorted in alphabetical order. John decides to sort the files by date.

3. Click the **Modified column indicator button**

   The files and folders are sorted by the date they were last modified, from latest to earliest, as shown in Figure D-7. You can click the Modified column indicator again to sort the list by modification date from earliest to latest.

4. Click the **Modified column indicator button** again

   The files and folders are sorted by date from earliest to latest. When you click the Name column indicator button, the list is sorted in alphabetical order from A to Z, with folders appearing before files.

5. Click the **Name column indicator button**

   The files and folders are sorted by name in alphabetical order. John finds the Coffee Suppliers file and sees the date he last modified the file. After finding the information he needs, John decides to restore the Explorer Bar.

6. Click the **View** on the menu bar, point to **Explorer Bar**, then click **All Folders**

   In the Explorer Bar, you can also display Internet-related features to search for information, list favorite Web pages, list Web pages you've visited in the past, and list channels. You'll learn more about these Internet-related features in a later lesson.

FIGURE D-6: Windows Explorer in Details view

Click to select a different view

Column indicator buttons

Click to close the Explorer Bar

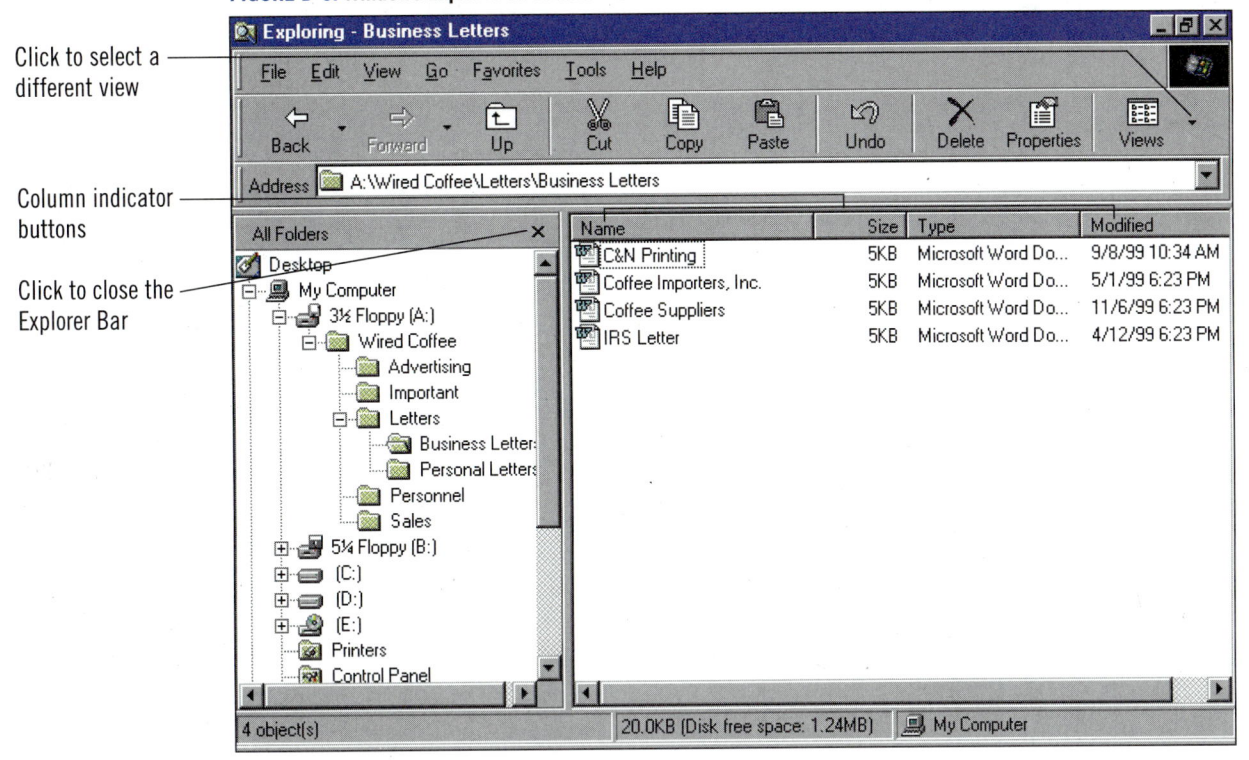

FIGURE D-7: Sorting files and folders by date

Click to sort alphabetically by name

Click to sort by date

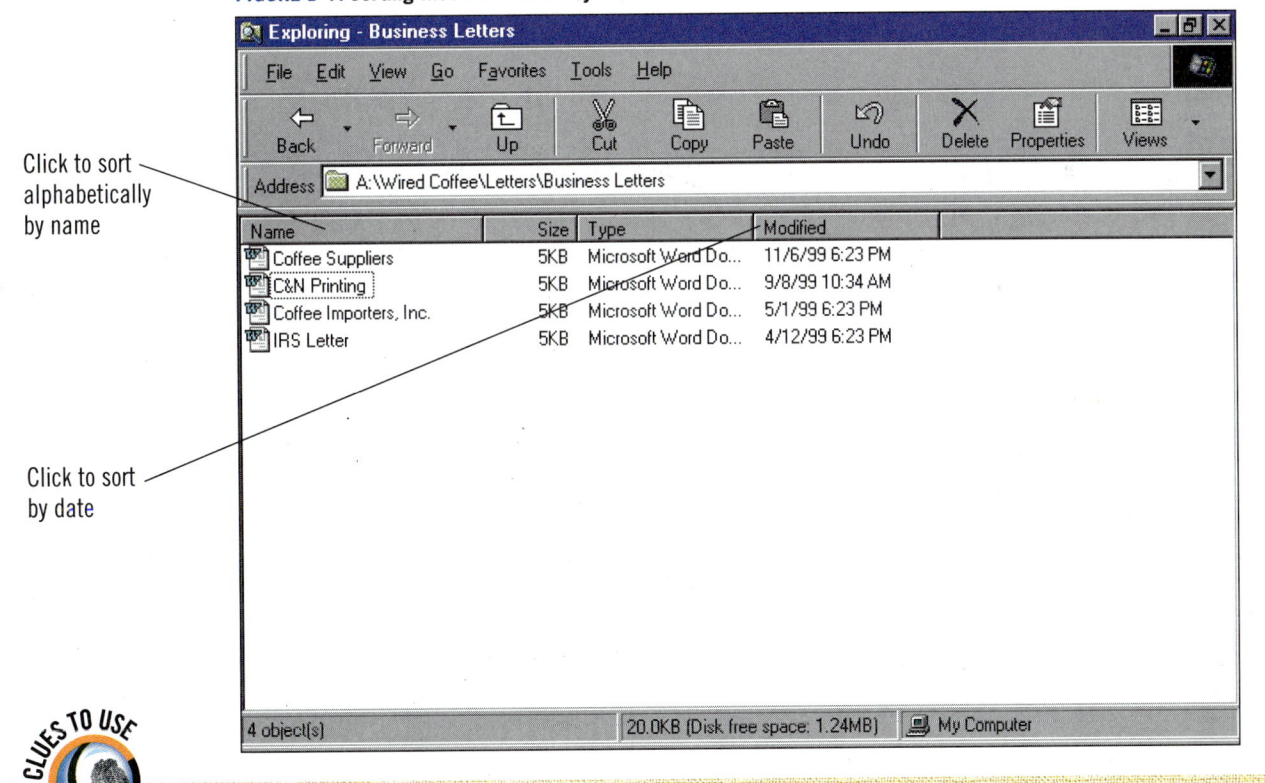

CLUES TO USE

Using the status bar

The status bar at the bottom of the Windows Explorer window gives you information about drives, folders, and files on your computer. You can quickly find out how many items a drive or folder contains, the total size of its contents, where it is located on your computer and (for drives) the amount of free disk space. If you don't want to use the status bar, you can turn the status bar off by clicking View on the menu bar, then click Status Bar to remove the check mark.

Windows 98

Creating and Renaming Folders in Windows Explorer

To effectively manage all the files on your computer, you need folders in convenient locations to store related files. You should give each folder a meaningful name so that merely glancing at the folder reminds you what is stored there. Creating a new folder in Windows Explorer is much like doing so from My Computer. First, select the location where you want the new folder, then create the folder, and finally, name the folder. You can create a folder in Windows Explorer by using the New command on the File menu, or by right-clicking in the right pane, clicking New, then clicking folder. You can rename a folder or file in Windows Explorer using the Rename command. To do this, right-click the file or folder you want to rename, click Rename on the pop-up menu, type the new name, and then press [Enter]. John wants to create a set of new folders that will hold the files related to the creation of the Wired Coffee Spring Catalog. He then renames one of the folders.

Steps 1 2 3 4

1. **Click the Wired Coffee folder in the Explorer Bar**
   To create a new folder, you must first select the drive or folder where you want the folder, which in this case is the Wired Coffee folder.

2. **Click File on the menu bar, point to New, then click Folder**
   A new folder, temporarily named New Folder, appears highlighted with a rectangle around the title in the right pane of Windows Explorer, as shown in Figure D-8. To enter a new folder name, you simply type the new name. John names it "Spring Catalog".

Trouble?

If nothing happens when you type the name, you pressed [Enter] or clicked outside the new folder. Select the folder, click the name "New Folder" so a rectangle surrounds it (with the insertion point inside), then repeat Step 3.

3. **Type Spring Catalog, then press [Enter] or click an empty area in the right pane**
   The Spring Catalog folder appears in both panes, as shown in Figure D-8. John wants to create folders within the Spring Catalog folder.

4. **In the right pane, double-click the Spring Catalog folder**
   Nothing appears in the right pane because the folder is empty; there have been no new files or folders created or moved here. Because Spring Catalog is the currently selected folder, the folders that John creates will be located here.

5. **Right-click anywhere in the right pane, point to New on the pop-up menu, then click Folder**
   A new folder, named New Folder, appears in the right pane of Windows Explorer.

6. **Type Catalog Text, then press [Enter]**
   The folder is now named Catalog Text, as shown in Figure D-9. Notice also that there is a + (or a – if the folder is expanded) next to the Spring Catalog folder in the left pane, indicating that this folder contains other folders or files. John decides to change the name of the new folder to Catalog Pages.

QuickTip

To rename a file, you can also select the item, click the name so a rectangle surrounds it, type the new name, then press [Enter].

7. **Right-click the Catalog Text folder in the right pane, then click Rename on the pop-up menu, as shown in Figure D-10**
   The folder appears highlighted with a rectangle around the title in the right pane of Windows Explorer.

8. **Type Catalog Pages, then press [Enter]**
   The folder is renamed from Catalog Text to Catalog Pages.

FIGURE D-8: Newly created folder

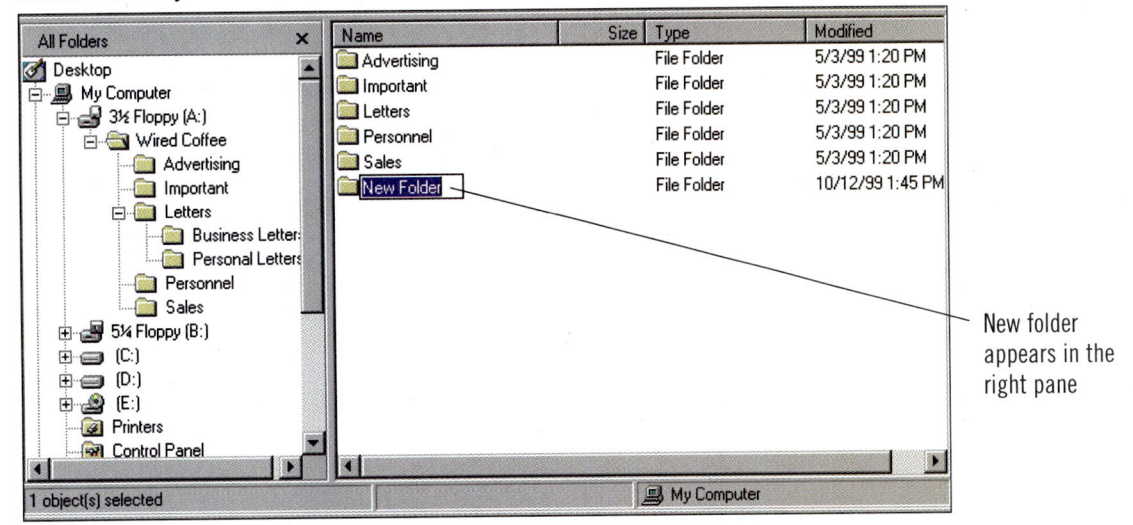

New folder
appears in the
right pane

FIGURE D-9: Creating a new folder using right-click method

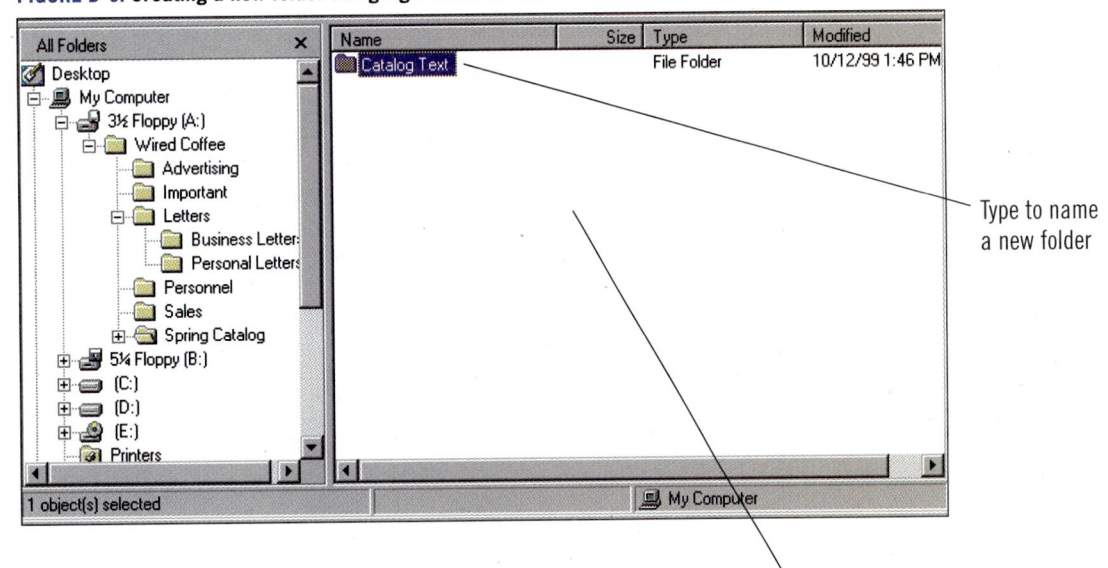

Type to name
a new folder

Click an empty area to complete the folder name

FIGURE D-10: Renaming a folder using right-click method

Right click
to display a
pop-up menu

+ (or −)
indicates that
this folder
contains other
folders

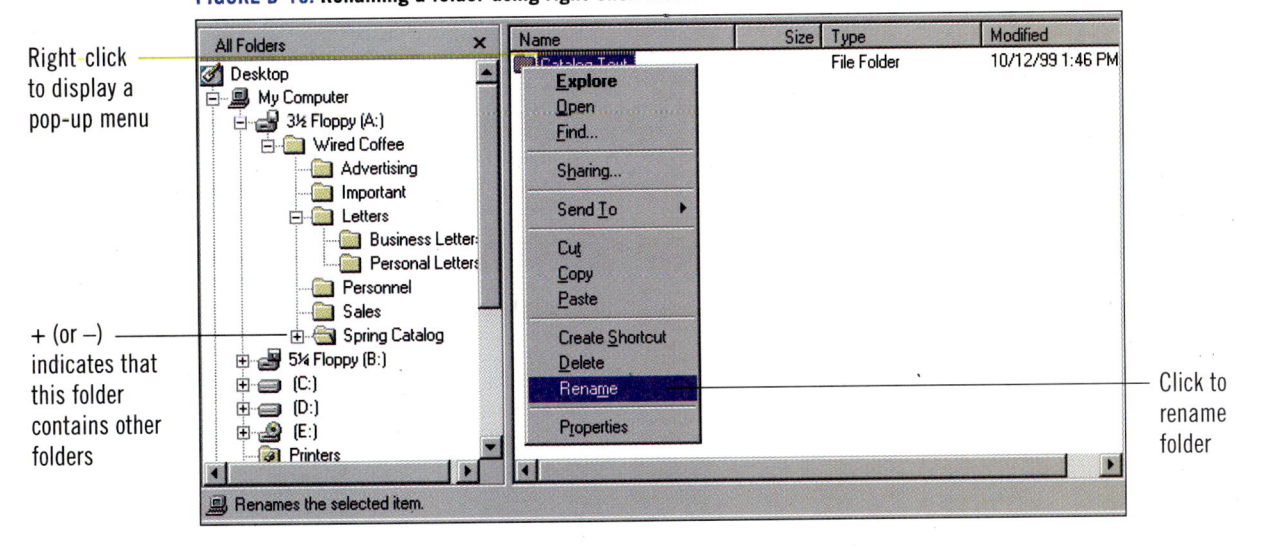

Click to
rename
folder

Finding a File

Sometimes it is difficult to remember precisely where you stored a file. Windows Explorer provides a Find program located on the Tools menu to help you find the files or folders you are looking for. The Find program gives you the option to find files or folders by name, location, size, type, and the date on which it was created or last modified. The Find program is also available on the Start menu to help you locate files and folders when you are not using Windows Explorer. To access the Find program on the Start menu, click the Start button on the taskbar, point to Find, and then click Files or Folders.  John wants to find a file he created several months ago with a preliminary outline for the Spring Catalog. He cannot remember the exact title of the file or where he stored it, so he needs to do a quick search.

Steps

1. **Click Tools on the menu bar, point to Find, then click Files or Folders**
   The Find: All Files window opens, shown in Figure D-11. Table D-1 lists the tabs in The Find: All Files window and describes the search options each offers. Since John remembers part of the name (but not the location) of the file he needs, he can use the Name & Location tab.

2. **Type Catalog in the Named text box**
   You can supply the full name of the folder or file you want to find, or only the part you're sure of. If, for example, John were unsure as to whether or not he had saved the file as Spring Catalog or Catalog Outline, he could type Catalog, since he's sure of that much of the name. If John didn't know the name of the file, but did know some text contained in the file, he could enter the text in the Containing text text box. Before you can start the search, you need to indicate where you want the Find program to search. The Find program initially begins searching in the open folder in Windows Explorer, but you can choose the location you want.

3. **Click the Look in list arrow, then click the drive that contains your Student Disk**

4. **Click Find Now**
   The Find program searches all the folders and files on your Student Disk and lists those folders and files whose names contain the word "Catalog" in the box at the bottom of the Find: All Files window. The full names, locations, sizes, types, and the dates on which the folders or files were created or last modified are listed.

5. **Position the pointer between the In Folder column indicator button and the Size column indicator button; when the pointer changes to ↔ drag to the right to display the location of the file, as shown in Figure D-12**
   At this point, John can either double-click the file to start the associated program and open the file, or he can note the file's location and close the Find: Files named Catalog window. He decides to note the file's location and close the window.

6. **Click the Close button in the Find: Files named Catalog window**

QuickTip

Insert the * (asterisk) wildcard symbol in a filename when you're unsure of the entire name. For example, type S*rs to find not only the file named Suppliers, but also all other files beginning with S and ending with rs (such as Stars and Sportscars).

CLUES TO USE

Performing an Advanced Search

You can also complete an advanced search that uses criteria, or information, beyond just the name or partial name of the file. If you have no idea what the name or content of the file is, but can recall the type of file (such as a WordPad document), then use the Advanced tab in the Find: All Files window, and select a file type using the Of type list arrow, shown in Figure D-13. When you click Find Now, Windows will search for and display all the files for the type you specified. This can take a long time, although probably less time than it would take to re-create the missing file.

FIGURE D-11: Find: All Files window

Enter name or partial name of the file you are looking for here

Enter text contained in the file here

Click to include all subfolders (folders within folders)

Options for searching using criteria

After specifying what to search for, click to begin search

Specify where you think the file is here

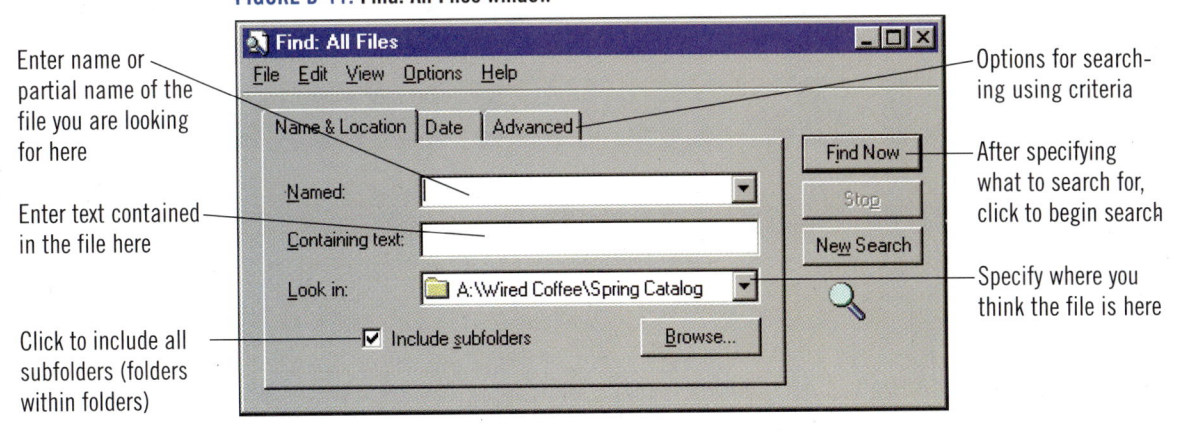

FIGURE D-12: Results of search for Catalog file

Click to start a new search

Drag to resize column size

Files that match your search

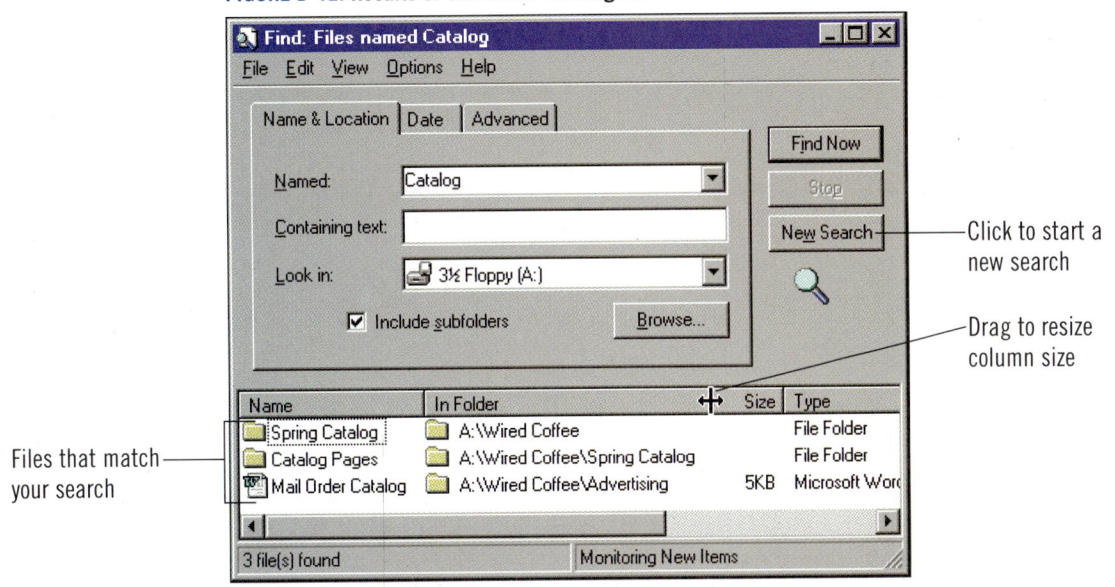

FIGURE D-13: Using advanced search features

Type of file

Size of file

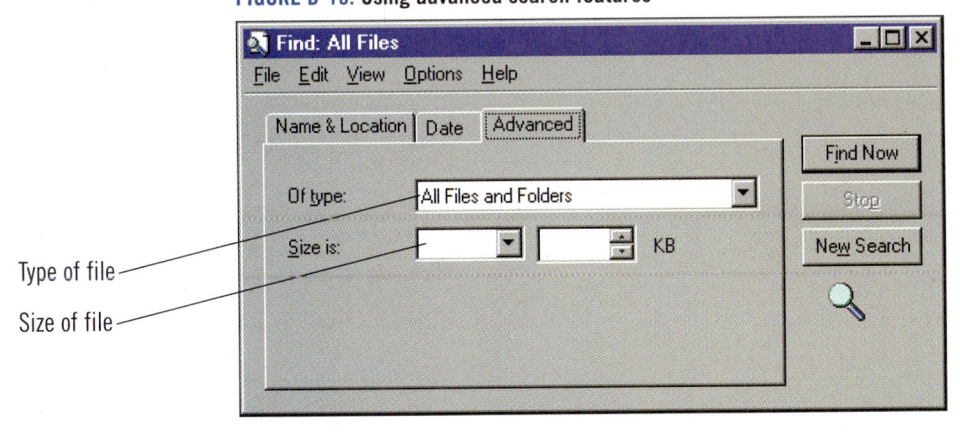

Table D-1: Tabs in the Find: All Files window

tab	use to
Name & Location	Find the file by name, location, and text the file contains; browse through directories for the file
Date	Search for files created during the previous number of days or months, or between a certain period of time that you specify
Advanced	Search for files by type (such as a WordPad file) or a file's size

Copying and Moving a File to a Folder

You should always store your files in the appropriate folders. Sometimes this means moving a file from one folder to another (removing it from the first and placing it in the second) and sometimes this means copying a file from one folder to another (leaving it in the first but placing a copy of it in the second). You can move and copy files and folders in several different ways in Windows Explorer. You can use the Cut, Copy, and Paste buttons on the Windows Explorer toolbar. Or you can "drag and drop" the file or folder while holding down a mouse button. A third way is to right-click the file or folder and choose the appropriate command from the pop-up menu. ▶ John plans to use text from the Mail Order Catalog file (currently located in the Advertising folder) in the Spring Catalog, so he wants to move the Mail Order Catalog file from the Advertising folder to the Catalog Pages folder. He also wants to make a copy of the Wired Coffee Logo file and place it in the Spring Catalog folder.

1. **Click the + next to the Spring Catalog folder in the Explorer Bar**
   The Spring Catalog folder expands displaying the folder it contains.

2. **Click the Advertising folder in the Explorer Bar**
   The contents of the folder are shown in the right pane of Windows Explorer. When moving or copying files or folders in Windows Explorer, make sure the files or folders you want to move or copy are displayed in the right pane. To move the Mail Order Catalog file, John will drag it from the right pane to the Catalog Pages folder in the Explorer Bar.

3. **Drag the Mail Order Catalog file across the vertical line separating the two panes to the Catalog Pages folder as shown in Figure D-14, then release the mouse button**
   Once you release the mouse button, the Mail Order Catalog file is relocated into the Catalog Pages folder. If you decide that you didn't want the file moved, you can move it back easily using the Undo button on the toolbar. Now John copies the Wired Coffee Logo file in the Advertising folder to the Spring Catalog folder.

4. **Point to the Wired Coffee Logo file, press and hold the right mouse button, drag the file across the vertical line separating the two panes to the Spring Catalog folder, then release the mouse button**
   As Figure D-15 shows, the pop-up menu offers a choice of options. The Copy Here option is listed second. You can also right-click a file in the right pane to open a pop-up menu—another way to copy or move the file to a new location.

5. **Click Copy Here**
   The original file named Wired Coffee Logo remains in the Advertising folder and a copy of the file has been placed in the Spring Catalog folder.

6. **Click the Spring Catalog folder in the Explorer Bar**
   The Wired Coffee Logo file was copied from the Advertising folder (where the original is still located) to the Spring Catalog folder (where the copy is located).

QuickTip

To quickly copy a file from one folder to another on the same disk, select the file, press and hold [Ctrl], then drag the file to the folder. You can also copy a file from a hard disk to a floppy disk by right-clicking the file, pointing to Send To, then clicking the appropriate disk drive icon.

FIGURE D-14: Moving a file from one folder to another

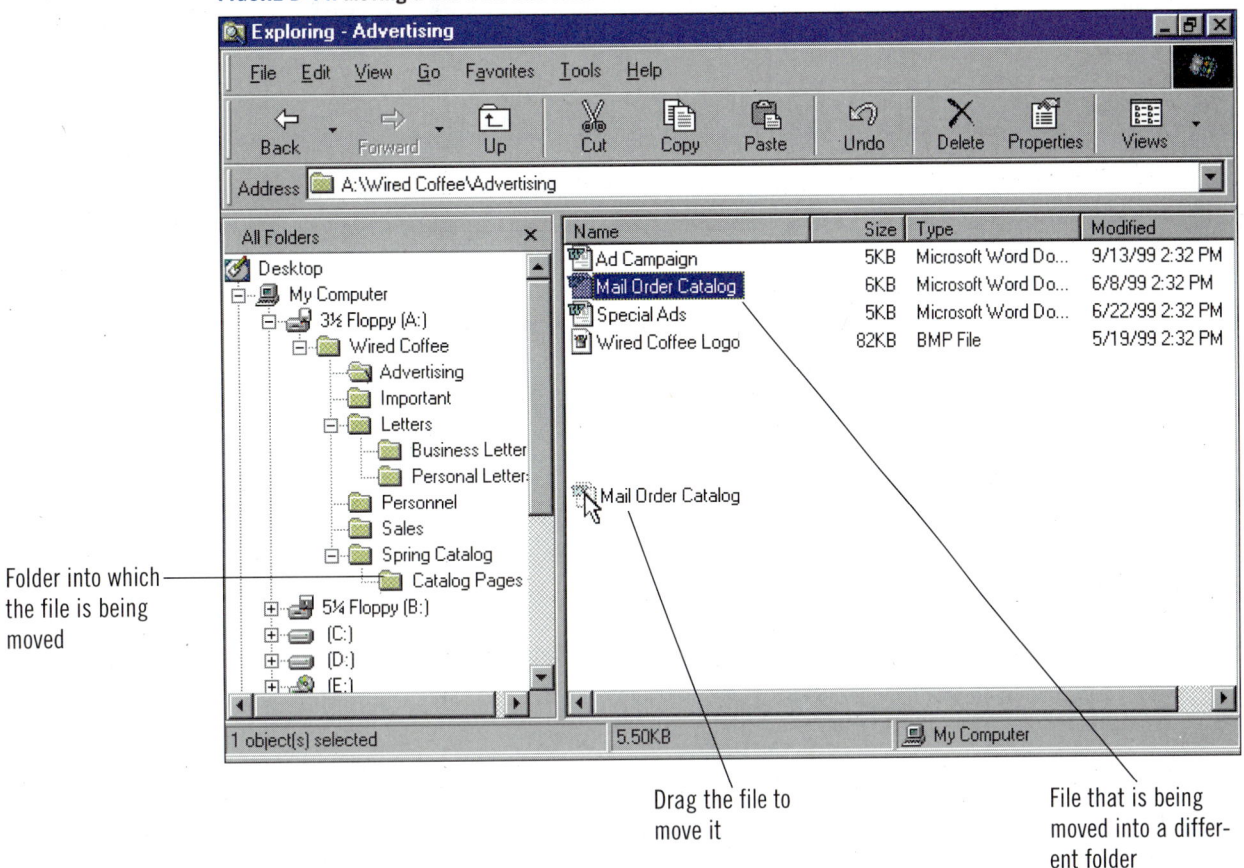

Folder into which the file is being moved

Drag the file to move it

File that is being moved into a different folder

FIGURE D-15: Copying a file from one location to another

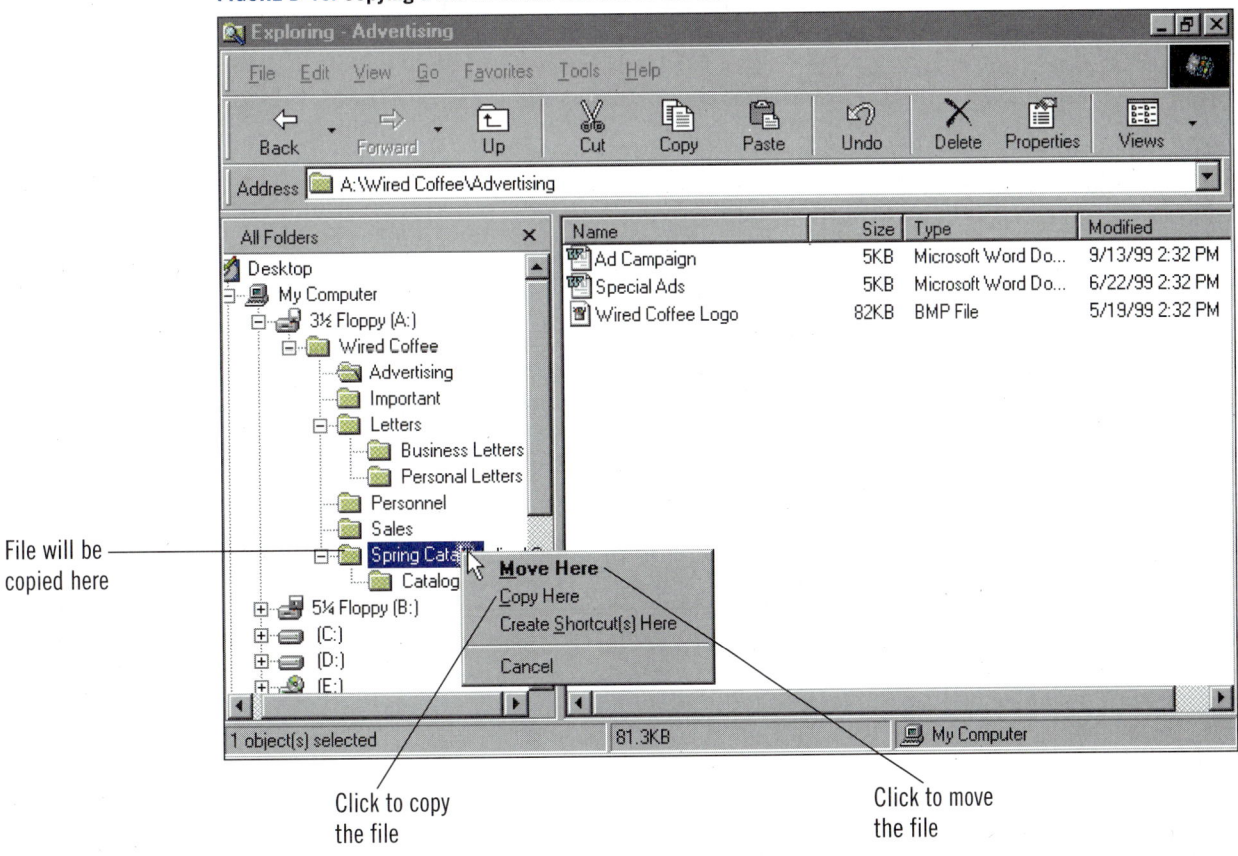

File will be copied here

Click to copy the file

Click to move the file

MANAGING FOLDERS AND FILES USING WINDOWS EXPLORER WIN D-13

Restoring a Deleted File Using Undo

To keep your files and folders manageable, you should delete files and folders you no longer need. All the items you delete from your hard disk are stored in the Recycle Bin, so that if you accidentally delete an item, you can move it out of the Recycle Bin to restore it, or you can use the Undo command. You cannot restore files and folders that you delete from a floppy disk or that you drag from a floppy disk to the Recycle Bin. Windows does not store items deleted from a floppy disk in the Recycle Bin, rather they are deleted (after a confirmation). See Table D-2 for the various methods of deleting and restoring items. ✒ In this lesson, you'll delete a file and then restore it using the Undo command. Because you cannot restore files deleted from a floppy disk, you will start by moving a file from your Student Disk to the desktop.

1. **Click the + next to the hard drive (C:) icon in the Explorer Bar**
   The hard drive is expanded in the left pane and the contents of the Spring Catalog folder appear in the right pane.

2. **Right-click the Wired Coffee Logo file in the right pane, drag it to the My Documents folder in the Explorer Bar, then click Move Here**
   The Wired Coffee file is now moved to the My Documents folder.

3. **Click the My Documents folder in the Explorer Bar**
   The My Documents folder is a general folder in which you can store files and folders. When you delete the Wired Coffee Logo file, it will be stored in the Recycle Bin, and you'll be able to restore it using the Undo command.

4. **Scroll to the bottom of the Explorer Bar, then drag the Wired Coffee Logo file in the right pane to the Recycle Bin in the Explorer Bar**
   You can also right-click the file and then click Delete, or select the file and then press [Delete]. A confirmation dialog box appears, as shown in Figure D-16.

5. **Click Yes**
   The Wired Coffee Logo file is now removed from the My Documents folder and is stored in the Recycle Bin.

6. **Click the Undo button [🔄] on the toolbar**
   The Wired Coffee Logo file is now restored to the My Documents folder. The Undo command also lets you reverse multiple actions, so you can use the Undo command again to move the Wired Coffee Logo file back into the Spring Catalog folder on your Student Disk.

7. **Click [🔄] again**
   The Wired Coffee Logo file is now moved back to the Spring Catalog folder.

8. **Scroll to the top of the Explorer Bar, then click the Spring Catalog folder in the Explorer Bar**
   The contents of the Spring Catalog folder, including the Wired Coffee Logo file, appear in the right pane, as shown in Figure D-17.

QuickTip

Some computers are set up so that the Recycle Bin isn't used—deleted files are removed from the hard drive immediately. To check whether your Recycle Bin is being used, right-click the Recycle Bin on the desktop, then click Properties. If the Do not move files to the Recycle Bin check box has a check in it, click the check box to turn this option off.

QuickTip

Files and folders that you delete from your hard drive remain in the Recycle Bin until you either restore them or empty the Recycle Bin. To empty the Recycle Bin, right-click it (on the desktop or in Windows Explorer), then click Empty Recycle Bin.

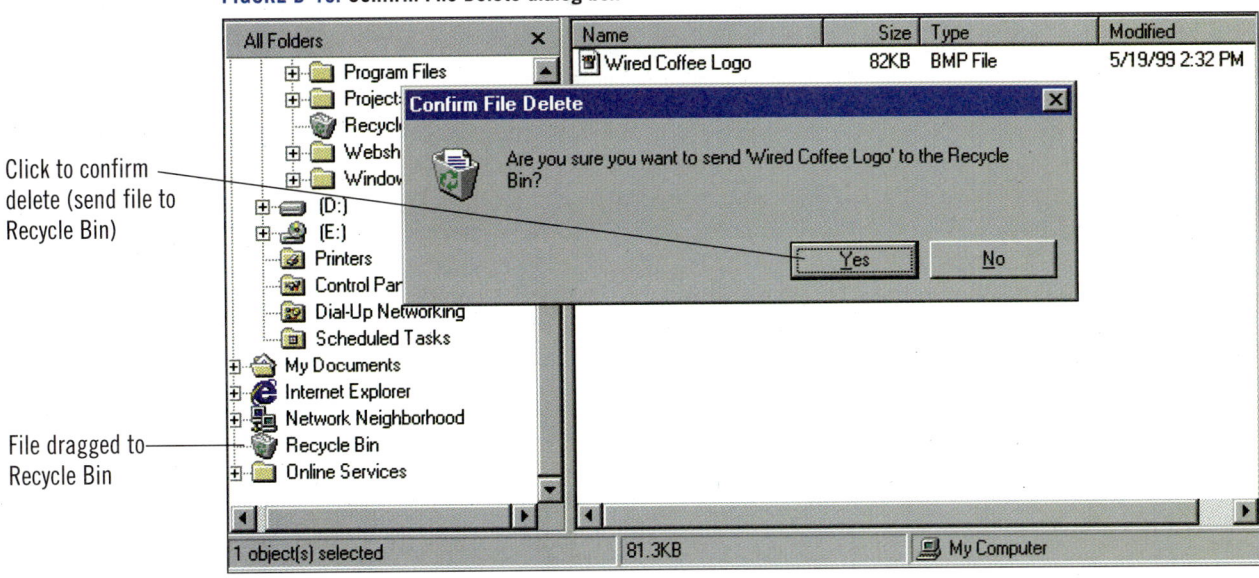

FIGURE D-16: Confirm File Delete dialog box

Click to confirm delete (send file to Recycle Bin)

File dragged to Recycle Bin

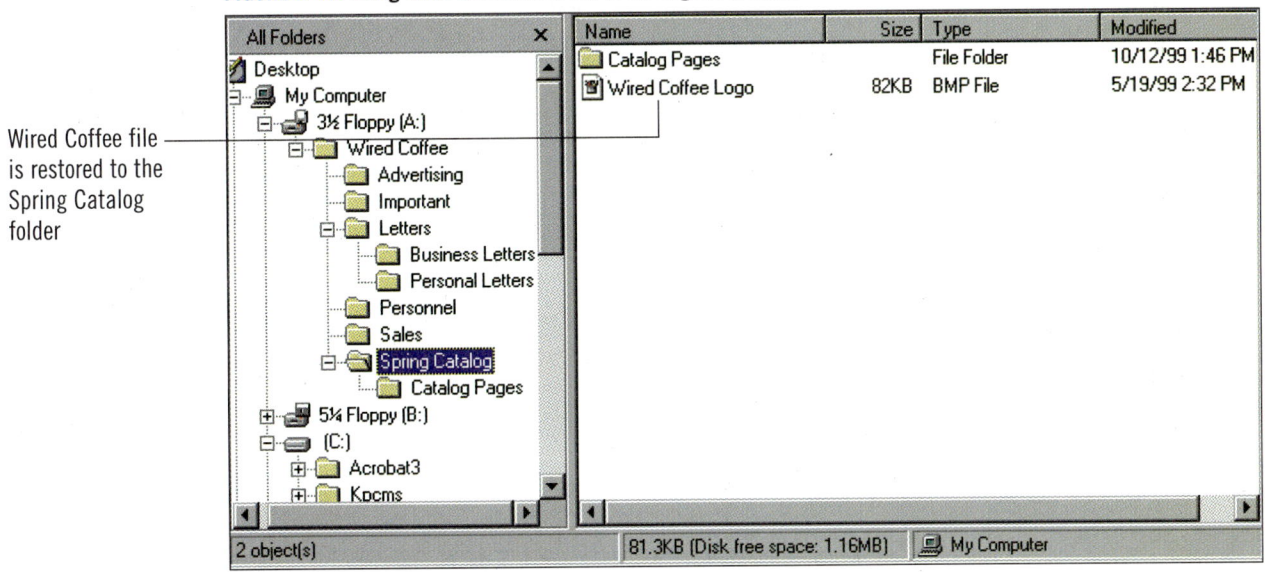

FIGURE D-17: Using Undo to restore a file to its original location

Wired Coffee file is restored to the Spring Catalog folder

TABLE D-2: Methods for deleting and restoring files in Windows Explorer

action	methods
Delete	• Right-click the file or folder you want to delete, then click Delete
	• Drag the file or folder to the Recycle Bin
	• Select the file or folder, click File on the menu bar, then click Delete
	• Select the file or folder you want to delete, then press [Del]
	• Select the file or folder you want to delete, then click the Delete button on the toolbar
Restore	Open the Recycle Bin, then
	• Select the file or folder you want to restore, click File on the menu bar, then click Restore
	• Right-click the file or folder you want to restore, then click Restore
	• Drag the file or folder to a new location on the desktop

Customizing a Folder

To make working in Windows Explorer more interesting and appealing, you can customize the way a folder looks when it is open (when its contents are displayed in the right pane). As you have seen, by default folders appear against a white background. You can change the background color, select a picture to use as a background, or even create your own Web page view of the folder. Windows Explorer comes with a **wizard** (a series of dialog boxes) that walks you through the steps of customizing a folder. John wants to customize the background of the Wired Coffee folder to display the Wired Coffee logo.

1. **Click the Wired Coffee folder in the Explorer Bar**
   The contents of Wired Coffee folder are listed in the right pane of Windows Explorer.

2. **Click View on the menu bar, then click Customize this Folder**
   The Customize this Folder Wizard opens, as shown in Figure D-18. This wizard helps you change the background appearance of the currently displayed folder. See Table D-3 for a description of the wizard options.

3. **Click the Choose a background picture option button, then click Next**
   Now you need to select a background picture for the Wired Coffee folder. You can select a picture from the list provided, or you can click the Browse button to select a picture stored elsewhere on your computer. John wants to select the Wired Coffee Logo file, which is stored on the Student Disk, so he clicks the Browse button.

4. **Click Browse**
   The Open dialog box opens, displaying the My Documents folder. John selects the Wired Coffee Logo file on the Student Disk.

5. **Click the Look in list arrow, click the drive that contains your Student Disk, double-click the Wired Coffee folder, double-click the Advertising folder, then double-click Wired Coffee Logo**
   The Wired Coffee Logo file is displayed in the left pane of the Customize this Folder dialog box and selected in the list of available background pictures.

6. **Click Next**
   The wizard displays the filename and location of the background picture you have selected. You can click the Back button to change the picture you have selected or click the Finish button to complete the wizard with the selected picture.

7. **Click Finish**
   The right pane of Windows Explorer displays the Wired Coffee logo in the background, as shown in Figure D-19. John is finished working with Windows Explorer, so he closes the program.

8. **Click the Close button in Windows Explorer**
   Windows Explorer closes.

FIGURE D-18: Customize this Folder Wizard

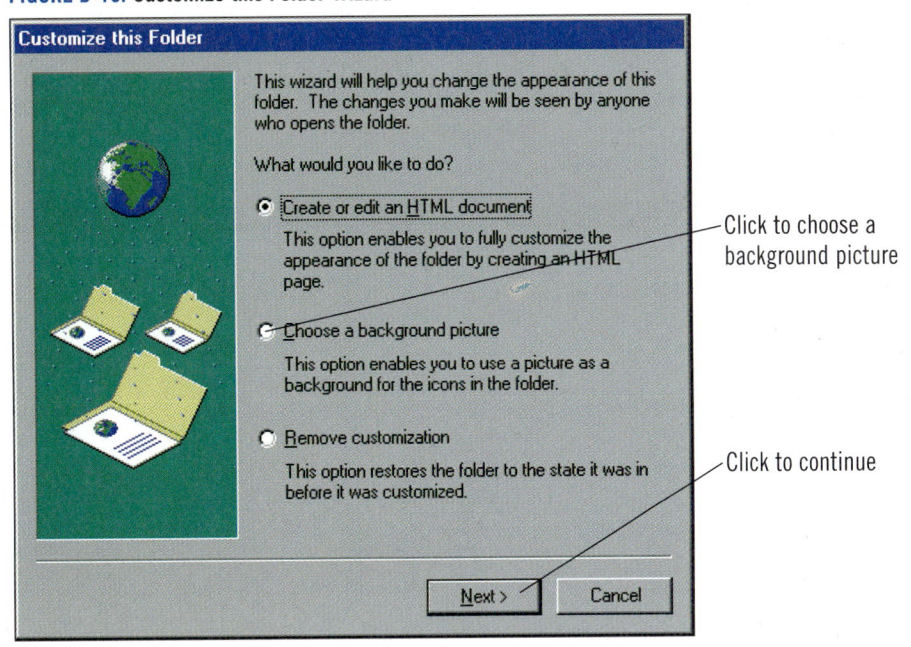

Click to choose a background picture

Click to continue

FIGURE D-19: Customized Wired Coffee folder

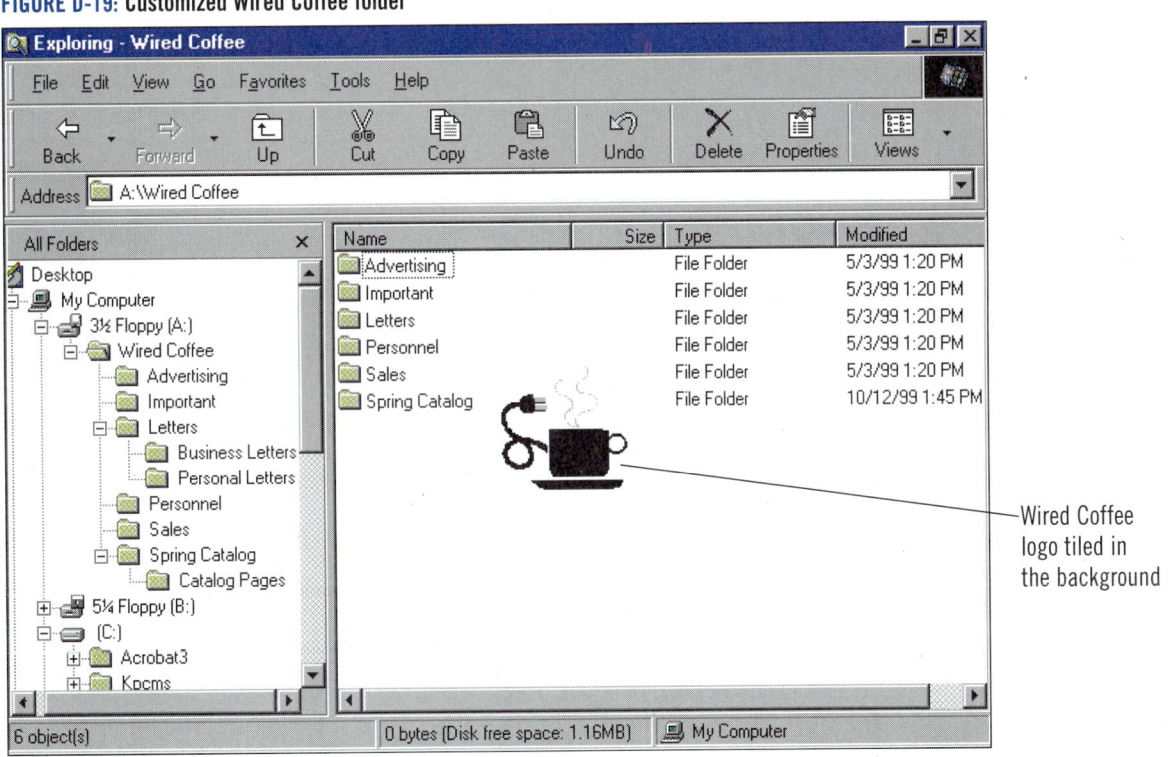

Wired Coffee logo tiled in the background

TABLE D-3: Customize this Folder Wizard options

option	allows you to...
Create or edit an HTML document	Create or edit an Internet document to view the folder as a Web page (you must know how to use HTML, a computer programming language, to use this option)
Choose a background picture	Change the background color or select a picture as a background for the folder
Remove customization	Remove the previous customization of the folder

Practice

▶ Concepts Review

Label each of the elements of the screen shown in Figure D-20.

FIGURE D-20

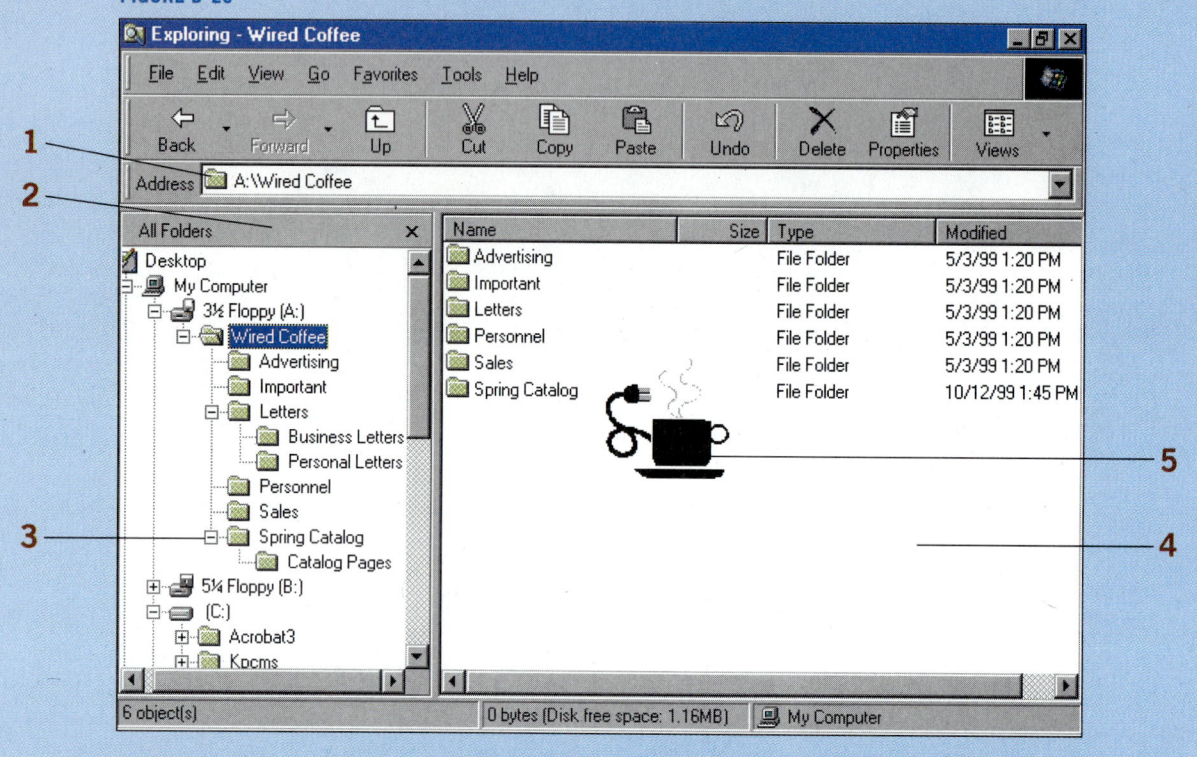

Match each of the terms with the statement that describes its function.

6. Move a file or folder to the Recycle Bin
7. Column indicator
8. Panes
9. + icon
10. Right-click an icon

a. Icon that is clicked to expand folder contents
b. Frames that display information from two different locations
c. Delete selected file or folder from a hard drive
d. Opens pop-up menu
e. Sorts files and folders

Select the best answer from the following list of choices.

11. Windows Explorer is different from My Computer in that it allows you to
    a. View the overall structure of your computer's contents.
    b. View the contents of a folder or drive.
    c. Change the view.
    d. Move between folders.

12. **Where is the Explorer Bar located in Windows Explorer?**
    a. Right pane
    b. Left pane
    c. Folder
    d. Hard drive

13. **In Windows Explorer, which of the following do you click to display the contents of a folder or drive in the Explorer Bar?**
    a. +
    b. −
    c. 🖿
    d. ⇦

14. **To sort files and folders in Windows Explorer, click**
    a. View on the menu bar, then click Sort.
    b. A column indicator button.
    c. The Views button list arrow on the toolbar, then click List.
    d. View on the menu bar, then click Arrange.

15. **Which of the following is NOT a valid search criterion for a file using the Find program?**
    a. Name
    b. Location
    c. Date modified
    d. Date opened

16. **To copy a folder or file in Windows Explorer**
    a. Double-click the folder or file.
    b. Left-click the folder or file, then click Copy.
    c. Press [Ctrl] and drag the folder or file.
    d. Drag the folder or file.

17. **When a folder or file is moved**
    a. The original is moved.
    b. A copy of the original is created.
    c. A copy of the original is created and moved.
    d. A shortcut is created and moved.

18. **Which of the following locations is NOT a valid place from which to delete a file to the Recycle Bin?**
    a. Hard drive
    b. My Computer
    c. Floppy disk
    d. My Documents folder

19. **Which of the following is NOT a Customize this Folder Wizard option?**
    a. Choose a background picture
    b. Create and edit an HTML document
    c. Remove customization
    d. Choose a color scheme

Skills Review

1. **View the Windows Explorer window and identify the items in it.**
   a. Insert your Student Disk in the appropriate disk drive.
   b. Click the Start button on the taskbar, point to Programs, then click Windows Explorer.
   c. Click the Address list arrow, then click My Computer.
   d. Double-click 3½ Floppy drive (A:) or (B:) to explore the contents of the floppy.
   e. Click the Back button on the toolbar.
   f. Click the Forward button on the toolbar.

2. **Open and view folders in Windows Explorer.**
   a. Click the − next to the hard drive (C:) icon in the Explorer Bar.
   b. Click the + next to the 3½ floppy drive icon in the Explorer Bar.
   c. Click the + next to the Wired Coffee folder in the Explorer Bar.
   d. Click the Personnel folder in the Explorer Bar.
   e. Click the Letters folder in the Explorer Bar.
   f. Double-click the Business Letters folder in the right pane.

3. **Change the Windows Explorer window and sort files and folders date and names.**
   a. Click the Views button list arrow on the toolbar, then click Details.
   b. Click the Close button in the Explorer Bar.
   c. Click the Modified column indicator button.
   d. Click the Name column indicator button.
   e. Click View on the menu bar, point to Explorer Bar, then click All Folders.

4. **Create and name new folders.**
   a. Click the Wired Coffee folder in the Explorer Bar.
   b. Right-click a blank area of the right pane of Windows Explorer.
   c. Point to New on the pop-up menu, then click Folder.
   d. Name the folder Money, then press [Enter].
   e. Click File on the menu bar, point to New, then click Folder.
   f. Name this folder Legal, then press [Enter].
   g. Right-click the Money folder, then click Rename.
   h. Rename this folder Financial, then press [Enter].

5. **Find a file.**
   a. Click Tools on the menu bar, point to Find, then click Files or Folders.
   b. Type "IRS" in the Named text box.
   c. Click the Look in list arrow, then click 3½ Floppy (A:) or (B:).
   d. Click Find Now.
   e. Write down the location of the IRS Letter file.
   f. Click the Close button in the Find: All Files window.

6. **Copy a file from one location to another.**
   a. Locate the IRS Letter file on your Student Disk.
   b. Drag the IRS Letter file in the right pane to the Financial folder in the Explorer Bar.
   c. Right-click and then drag the Coffee Importers, Inc. file from the Business folder in the right pane to the Legal folder in the Explorer Bar.
   d. Click Copy Here on the pop-up menu.
   e. Click the Legal folder in the Explorer Bar.

7. Restore deleted files using Undo.

   a. Click the + next to the hard drive (C:) icon in the Explorer Bar.

   b. Right-drag the Coffee Importers, Inc. file from the Legal folder in the right pane to the My Documents folder in the Explorer Bar, then click Move Here.

   c. Click the My Documents folder in the Explorer Bar.

   d. Scroll to the bottom of the Explorer Bar.

   e. Drag the Coffee Importers, Inc. file from the My Documents folder in the right pane to the Recycle Bin in the Explorer Bar.

   f. Click Yes.

   g. Click the Undo button on the toolbar.

   h. Click the Undo button on the toolbar again.

   i. Scroll to the top of the Explorer Bar.

8. Customize a folder.

   a. Click the Business Letters folder in the Explorer Bar.

   b. Click View on the menu bar, then click Customize this Folder.

   c. Click the Choose a background picture option button.

   d. Click Next, then click Browse.

   e. Select the Wired Coffee Logo file in the Advertising folder on your Student Disk.

   f. Click Open.

   g. Click Next.

   h. Click Finish.

   i. Click the Close button in Windows Explorer.

▶ Independent Challenges

1. You have just started Sewing Works, a sewing machine repair business, and want to use Windows 98 to organize your documents. For this challenge, you will create on your Student Disk a set of files that are relevant to the business and organize them in a set of folders that will make it easy for you to locate what you need when you need it.

   To complete this independent challenge:

1. Create a WordPad file named Wilson Letter thanking Mr. Wilson for his business. Save this file and the other files you create on your Student Disk.

2. Create another WordPad file named Suppliers. List the following suppliers in the file:
   Apex Sewing Machine Parts
   PO Box 3645
   Tempe, AZ 12345

   Jones Sewing Repair
   18th and 3rd Avenues
   Brooklyn, NY 09091

3. Create a third WordPad file and name it Bills. List the following information in the file:
Apex	16453	$34.56
Jones	47354	$88.45
Ott	44412	$98.56

4. On your Student Disk, create a folder named Sewing Works.

5. In the Sewing Works folder, create three new folders: Letters, Contacts, and Accounts.

6. Expand the Sewing Works folder in the Explorer Bar.

7. Move the file named Wilson Letter into the Letters folder, the file named Suppliers into the Contacts folder, and the file named Bills into the Accounts folder.

8. Open the Letters folder.

9. Print the screen. (Press the Print Screen key to make a copy of the screen, open Paint, click Edit on the menu bar, click Paste to paste the screen into Paint, then click Yes to paste the large image, if necessary. Click File on the menu bar, click Print, then click OK.)

10. Close Windows Explorer.

2. As manager of the summer program at a day camp, you need to keep your folders and files organized so information can be easily and quickly found. Your files fall into two main categories: children and activities. You need to create a folder for each category and place them in a separate folder named Camp 1999, to distinguish your work this year from other years you've managed the camp.

To complete this independent challenge:

1. On your Student Disk, create three folders: Camp 1999, Campers, and Activities.

2. Create a WordPad file named Camper Data. Save the file on your Student Disk. In this file, create information on five campers, including their name, age, bunk, and favorite sports. Here's a sample of two:

Name	Age	Bunk #	Sports
Bill Moore	11	3	Swimming, Horseshoes
Michael Morley	12	4	Basketball

3. Move the file named Camper Data into the folder named Campers.

4. Create a WordPad file named Activities Overview. Save the file on your Student Disk. In this folder, create information on five camp activities, including the name, equipment or supplies the children need to supply, number of children, and name of the activity leader. Here's a sample of two:

Activity	Children provide	Number allowed	Leader
Swimming	Swimsuit, water wings if needed	18	John Lee
Soccer	Shoes, shin guards	24	Madeline Harman

5. Move the file named Activities Overview into the folder named Activities.

6. Move the Activities folder and the Campers folder into the Camp 1999 folder.

7. Expand the Camp 1999 folder in the Explorer Bar.

8. Open the Campers folder.

9. Copy the Camper Data file to the Activities folder.

10. Open the Activities folder.

11. Print the screen. (See Independent Challenge 1, Step 9 for screen printing instructions.)

12. Close Windows Explorer.

3. The summer fine arts program that you manage has different categories of participation for young adults, including two-week and four-week programs. In order for you to keep track of who is participating in each program, you have to organize the following list into folders. For this challenge, you'll have to create new folders, create a list of participants, and then move the document lists into folders.

To complete this independent challenge:

1. On your Student Disk, create a folder named Summer Program 1999.

2. Within the Summer Program 1999 folder, create a folder named Arts.

3. Within the Arts folder, create two other folders named 2 Weeks and 4 Weeks.

4. Create a WordPad file named 2 Weeks Art on your Student Disk with the following information:
   Leni Welitoff   2 weeks   painting
   Tom Stacey   2 weeks   ceramics and jewelry
5. Create a WordPad file named 4 Weeks Art on your Student Disk with the following information:
   Kim Dayton   4 weeks   painting and landscape design
   Sara Jackson   4 weeks   set construction
6. Move the files you created into their respective folders named 2 Weeks and 4 Weeks.
7. Rename the folder Arts to Fine Arts.
8. Collapse and expand the Summer Program 1999 folder.
9. Expand Fine Arts folders.
10. Open the 4 Weeks folder located in the Fine Arts folder.
11. Use the Print Screen key to make a copy of the screen, then print it from the Paint program (see your instructor for details).
12. Find the files on your Student Disk that contain "painting" in the text (not the title).
13. Print the screen. (See Independent Challenge 1, Step 9 for screen printing instructions.)
14. Close Windows Explorer.

4. As the head of the graphics department in a small design firm, one of your jobs is to organize the clip art images used by the company. The two categories in which you want to place an image are Lines and Shapes. You can place clip art images in more than one category as well. For this challenge, you'll have to create several folders and Paint images, then move and copy them to different folders.
   To complete this independent challenge:

1. On your Student Disk, create four different Paint images and save them using the following names: Ellipses, Lines, and Curves.
2. On your Student Disk, create two folders named Lines and Shapes.
3. Move the Curves and Lines files to the Lines folder.
4. Move the Ellipses file to the Shapes folder.
5. Copy the Curves file into the Shapes folder.
6. Rename the Ellipses file to Ovals.
7. Customize the Lines folder with the Curves file.
8. Open the Lines folder.
9. Print the screen. (See Independent Challenge 1, Step 9 for screen printing instructions.)
10. Close Windows Explorer.

▶ **Visual Workshop**

Re-create the screen shown in Figure D-21, which displays the Windows Explorer. Print the screen. (See Independent Challenge 1, Step 9 for screen printing instructions.)

FIGURE D-21

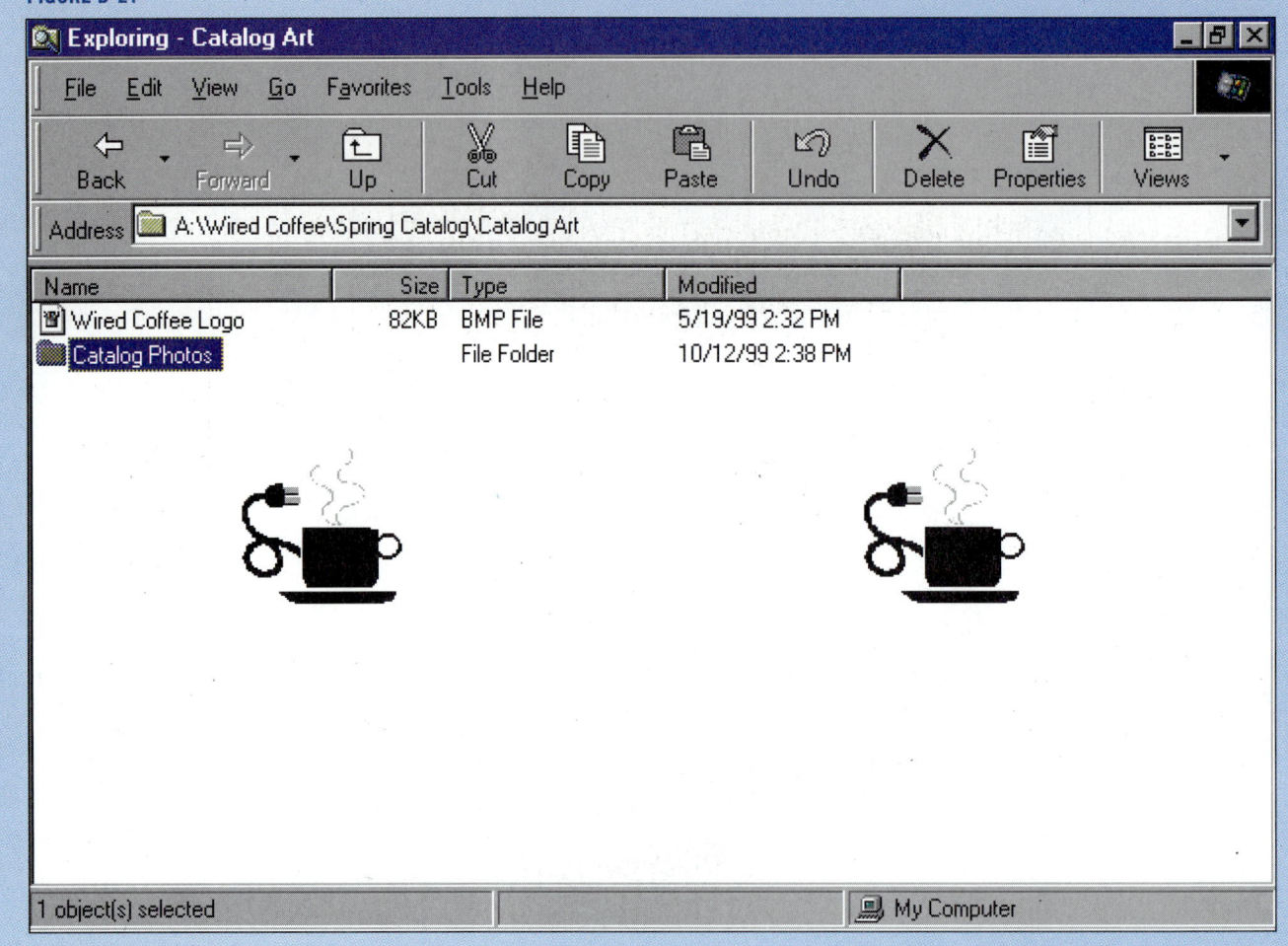

Customizing

Windows 98 Using the Control Panel

Objectives

- ▶ Customize the Active Desktop
- ▶ Change the Desktop Background and Screen
- ▶ Saver Setting
- ▶ Change the Desktop Color Scheme
- ▶ Set the Date and Time
- ▶ Work with Fonts
- ▶ Customize Mouse Operations
- ▶ Examine System Properties
- ▶ Customize the Taskbar
- ▶ Add an Item to the Start Menu

In this unit you'll learn how to customize Windows 98 to suit your personal needs and preferences. Most Windows features can be adjusted through the **Control Panel**, a central location where you can change Windows settings. The Control Panel contains several icons, each of which opens a dialog box for changing the **properties**, or characteristics, of a specific element of your computer, such as the mouse, the keyboard, or the desktop. John Casey needs to change some of the settings on his computer to make his computing environment more attractive and efficient. *If you are concerned about changing the aspects of Windows 98 at your location and do not wish to customize, simply read through this unit without completing the steps, or click the Cancel button in any dialog box where a change could be made.*

Customizing the Active Desktop

Because more and more people are using the Internet, Windows 98 includes the **Active Desktop**, a feature that allows you to view your desktop as you would documents on the Internet, and the Active Desktop items, such as the Channel Bar. **Active Desktop items** are elements you can place on the desktop to access or display information from the Internet. For example, you can add an Active Desktop item to continuously display stock prices or weather information. Using the Control Panel Display Properties dialog box, you can customize the desktop to display the Active Desktop items you want to use. In addition, you can also change the way you click on desktop icons. For example, you can change double-clicking to open an item to single-clicking. When you use this setting, your desktop looks and acts like a document on the Internet, known as a **Web page**. John wants to learn how to customize the Active Desktop.

QuickTip

To open the Display Properties dialog box from the Control Panel, double-click the Display icon.

QuickTip

You can quickly disable all Active Desktop items from the desktop by right-clicking the desktop, pointing to Active Desktop, then clicking View as Web Page to remove the check mark.

QuickTip

You can open the Folder Options dialog box directly by clicking the Start button, pointing to Settings, and then clicking Folders Options.

1. **Right-click in an empty area on the desktop, point to Active Desktop, then click Customize my Desktop**
   The Display Properties dialog box opens, displaying the Web tab, as shown in Figure E-1. The Web tab provides a list of Active Desktop items and a preview of those items. To enable or disable (turn on or off) items on the Active Desktop, you select or deselect the Active Desktop item check boxes. John decides to disable the Internet Explorer Channel Bar on the Active Desktop.

2. **Click the Internet Explorer Channel Bar check box to deselect it**
   The Internet Explorer Channel Bar is removed from the preview display. You can disable all Active Desktop items by clicking the View my Active Desktop as a Web page check box to deselect the option. John changes his mind and enables the Active Desktop item.

3. **Click the Internet Explorer Channel Bar check box to select it**
   The Internet Explorer Channel Bar is displayed in the preview display. Besides enabling and disabling Active Desktop items, you can also change the way you select and open folders and icons on the desktop and in My Computer and Windows Explorer.

4. **Click Folder Options, then click Yes to save and close the Display Properties dialog box**
   The Folder Options dialog box opens, displaying the General tab. The option buttons at the bottom of the dialog box determine how you click on desktop icons. Your desktop can have a classic look like it did in Windows 95, or it can have a Web page, or Internet, style look.

5. **Click the Web style option button**
   Notice the Preview box changes to show the Web style desktop view, as shown in Figure E-2. If you prefer a combination of the Web style and Classic style, you can select the Custom option. John decides to use the current custom settings.

6. **Click the Custom, based on settings you choose option button, then click Settings**
   The Custom Settings dialog box opens in which you can change the way you click items, open folders, and use the Active Desktop.

7. **Click OK, then click Close**
   The Custom Settings dialog box and the Folder Options dialog box close.

FIGURE E-1: Display Properties dialog box

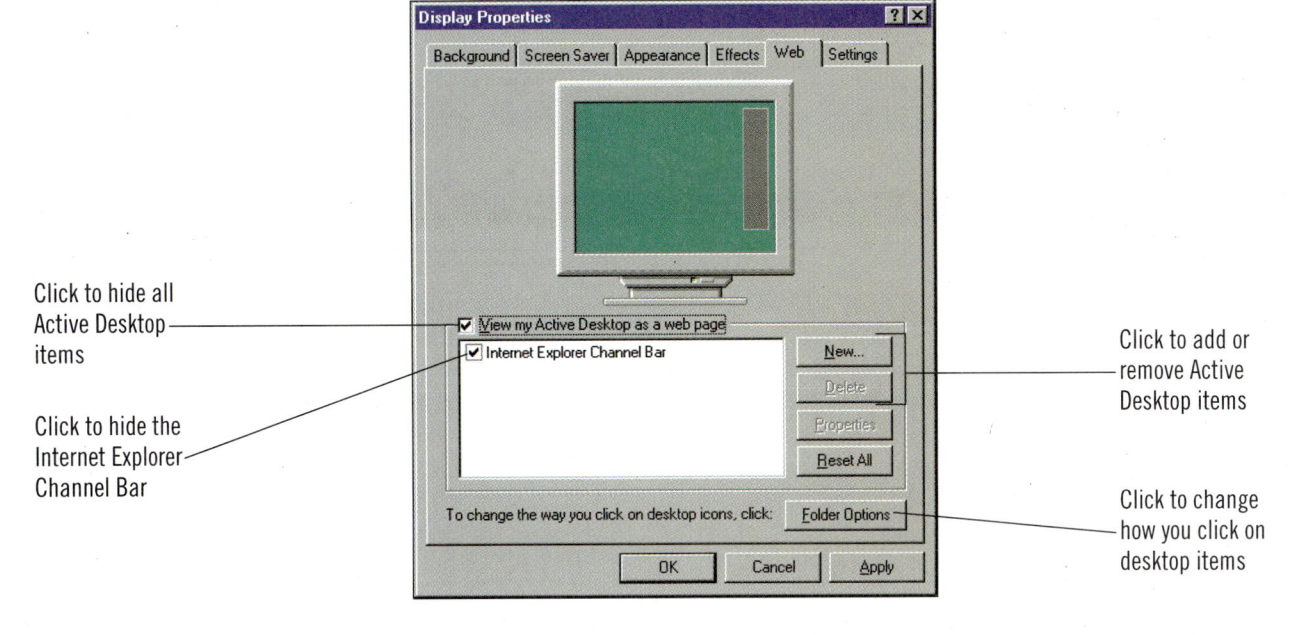

Click to hide all Active Desktop items

Click to hide the Internet Explorer Channel Bar

Click to add or remove Active Desktop items

Click to change how you click on desktop items

FIGURE E-2: Folder Options dialog box

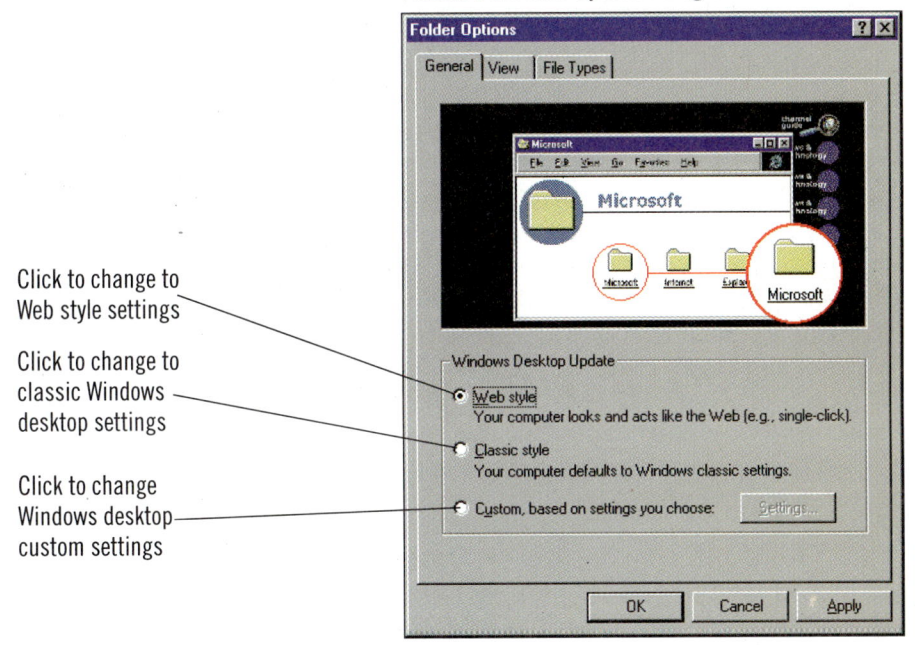

Click to change to Web style settings

Click to change to classic Windows desktop settings

Click to change Windows desktop custom settings

CLUES TO USE

Viewing a window as a Web page

If you prefer the look and feel of the Internet, you can view icons in a window as a Web page. When you view a window as a Web page, the panel along the left side of the window provides helpful information. When you select an icon, the panel displays a description or the properties of the item, as shown in the Control Panel window in Figure E-3. To view a window as a Web page, click the Views button list arrow ▦▾ on the toolbar, then click as Web Page. To return to the previous window view, click as Web Page again.

FIGURE E-3: Viewing the Control Panel as a Web page

Changing the Desktop Background and Screen Saver Settings

You can also change how your Windows desktop looks using the Display Properties dialog box. You can adjust the desktop's **background**, the basic surface on which icons and windows appear. You can use a **screen saver**, a moving display that protects your monitor from burn-in, which can occur when there is no movement on your screen for a long time. John chooses a background that he likes and makes sure that the screen saver is working. He'll select a new background and set one of the standard screen savers to start when his screen is idle for more than five minutes.

> **QuickTip**
>
> You can also open the Display Properties dialog box by right-clicking in an empty area of the desktop, then clicking Properties.

1. **Click the Start button on the taskbar, point to Settings, then click Control Panel**
   The Control Panel opens. Each icon represents an aspect of Windows that can be adjusted to fit your own working habits and personal needs.

2. **Double-click the Display icon in the Control Panel**
   The Display Properties dialog box opens with the Background tab active. Table E-1 describes the various tabs and what they do. John wants to experiment with wallpaper options.

3. **In the Wallpaper section, click the up or down scroll arrow, click Carved Stone (or a wallpaper of your choosing if this one is not available on your system)**
   You can preview the wallpaper you chose in the small monitor graphic, as shown in Figure E-4. **Wallpaper** is a picture that becomes your desktop's background. It is in the same format as a Paint file or an Internet document. You can use Paint to create new wallpaper designs or change existing ones. Besides the wallpaper, you can also choose a desktop **pattern**, a design that can be modified by clicking the None Wallpaper icon and then clicking the Pattern button. You can also determine how a wallpaper or pattern is displayed on the screen. Using the Display list arrow, you can select Tile, Center, or Stretch. **Tile** displays the wallpaper picture or pattern consecutively across the screen; **Center** displays the picture or pattern in the center of the screen; and **Stretch** displays the picture or pattern enlarged in the center of the screen. In addition to changing the background, John decides to change the screen saver settings.

4. **Click the Screen Saver tab**
   The default setting is for no screen saver, meaning that your screen will not be replaced by a constantly changing image no matter how long your computer remains idle. If someone else used this machine before you, a screen saver might already be set.

5. **Click the Screen Saver list arrow, then click 3D Flying Objects**
   The 3D Flying Objects screen saver appears in the small monitor graphic, as shown in Figure E-5.

6. **In the Wait box, click the up arrow (or down arrow) until it reads 5 minutes**
   This is the amount of time between when your computer detects no mouse or keyboard activity and when the screen saver begins to display.

7. **Click Preview**
   The entire desktop previews the screen saver pattern. To make it stop, move the mouse or press any key on the keyboard.

8. **Click Apply**
   The new wallpaper appears on the desktop, and the screen saver is in effect.

FIGURE E-4: Display Properties dialog box with Background tab

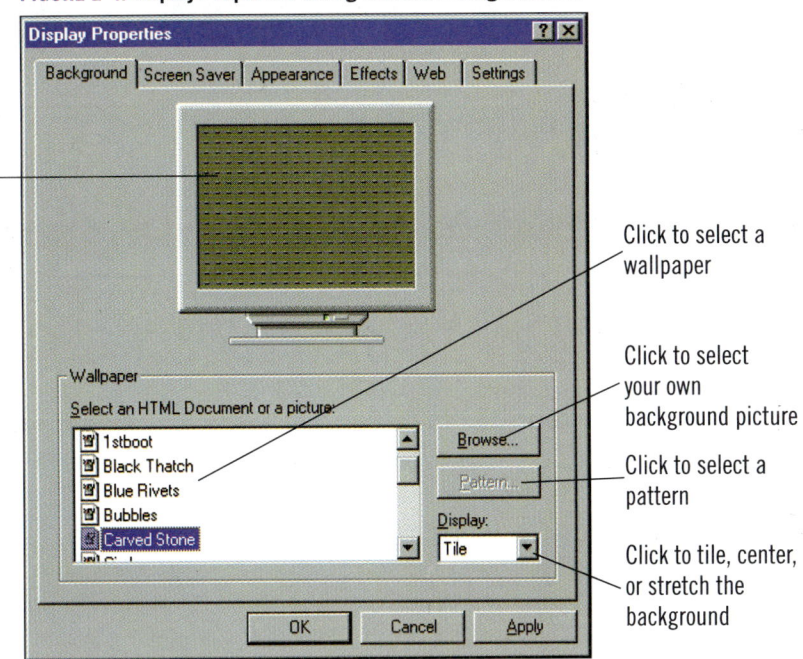

Preview selected wallpaper or pattern here

Click to select a wallpaper

Click to select your own background picture

Click to select a pattern

Click to tile, center, or stretch the background

FIGURE E-5: Display Properties dialog box with Screen Saver tab

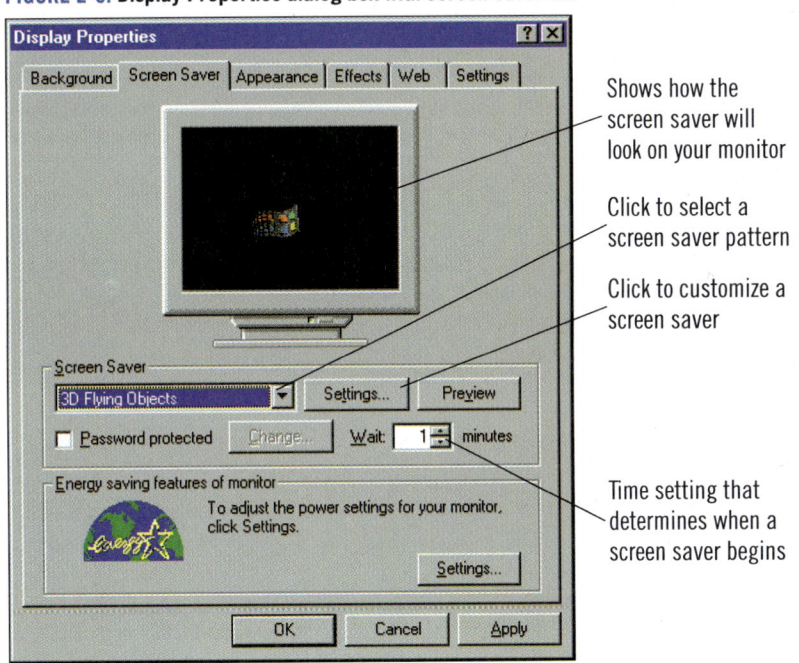

Shows how the screen saver will look on your monitor

Click to select a screen saver pattern

Click to customize a screen saver

Time setting that determines when a screen saver begins

TABLE E-1: Description of Display tab features

display tab	description
Background	Choose a picture or pattern to display on the desktop
Screen Saver	Choose and preview a screen saver pattern, and set pattern characteristics
Appearance	Choose colors, sizes, and font for Windows items
Effects	Change the appearance of desktop icons and visual settings
Web	Choose to view the desktop as a Web page, and add or delete Active Desktop items
Settings	Set the maximum number of colors viewable at one time, and change the screen resolution

Changing the Desktop Color Scheme

In addition to the background and screen saver, you can change the appearance of the color and fonts, or character designs, used for various window elements such as the title bar, icons, menus, border, and the desktop. There are thousands of custom combinations you can create in Windows. Each combination is called a **scheme**. You can select a predefined scheme or create one of your own. When you create a custom scheme, you can save the changes you make with a unique name. Other users of your computer can do the same, so each user can quickly customize the computer. ✎ Ray Adams, an employee of Wired Coffee, is visually impaired and needs a display configuration where the window elements are larger than the standard size. John can create a scheme for Ray so that Ray can switch to the scheme whenever he uses the computer.

Steps 1234

1. Click the **Appearance tab** in the Display Properties dialog box
   The Appearance tab, as shown in Figure E-6, allows you to change the color of various desktop elements, such as the menu bar, message box, and selected text. Rather than customizing each item individually, you can select one of several predefined schemes that Windows provides and modify it as necessary.

2. Click the **Scheme list arrow**, then click **Windows Standard (extra large)**
   In Figure E-7, you can see that the size of everything in the Preview box is increased from standard size to extra large. Now Ray can work more comfortably. However, he would prefer a light gray desktop to the teal one that comes with this preset scheme. John wants to change the desktop color; first he needs to select the desktop.

3. Click the **Item list arrow**, then click **Desktop**
   The desktop color can now be changed. Notice that the Item Size option and Font option are grayed out, indicating that these options do not apply to the desktop.

4. Click the **Color list arrow**, then click **light gray color box** in the top row
   You can select from a matrix of different colors. Before John saves the scheme, he wants to apply the scheme to the desktop to see how it looks.

5. Click **Apply**
   The desktop changes, but the dialog box remains open. Use the Apply button when you want to test your changes and the OK button when you want to keep your changes and close the dialog box. John saves the changes he made so Ray can use the scheme.

6. Click **Save As**, type **Ray**, then click **OK**
   The scheme is saved with the name Ray. Now, anytime Ray wants to use the computer, he can easily select this scheme.

7. Click **Delete** to remove the selected scheme
   The scheme is deleted. John has some work to do on the computer, so he wants to return to the Windows Standard scheme, which is the one he prefers.

8. Click the **Scheme list arrow**, click **Windows Standard**, then click **Apply**

9. Click the **Screen Saver tab**, click the **Screen Saver list arrow**, then click **(None)**

10. Click the **Background tab**, click **(None)** in the Wallpaper section, then click **OK**

FIGURE E-6: Display Properties dialog box with Appearance tab

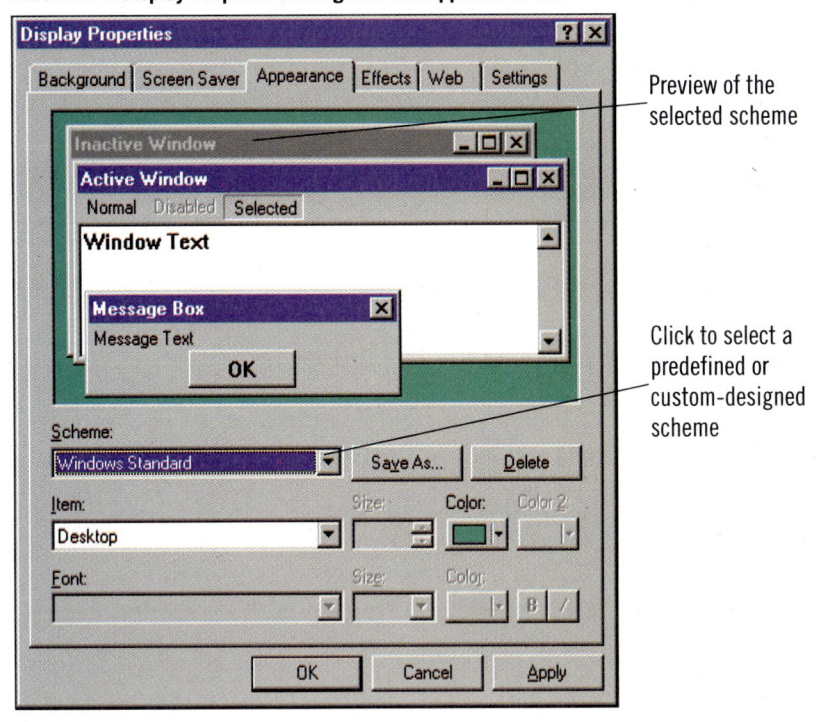

Preview of the selected scheme

Click to select a predefined or custom-designed scheme

FIGURE E-7: Changing the desktop color scheme

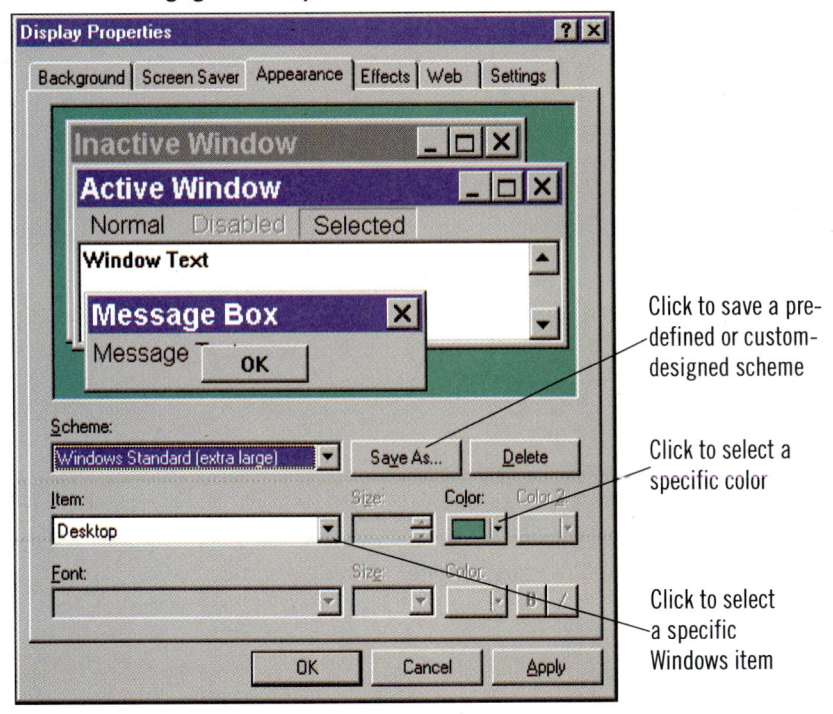

Click to save a pre-defined or custom-designed scheme

Click to select a specific color

Click to select a specific Windows item

Changing the size of the desktop

You can change the size of the desktop that appears on your monitor. In the Display Properties dialog box, click the Settings tab, then drag the Screen Area slider to the right. The settings available depend upon the hardware that Windows detects when it is installed. In some cases, you might even have higher settings than 640 × 480 or 800 × 600 (such as 1024 × 768) available. Note that a higher setting means higher resolution, and more information can fit on the screen.

Setting the Date and Time

Every so often, you need to change the date and time on your computer. The date and time you set in the Control Panel appears in the lower-right corner of the taskbar and is used by programs to establish the date and time that files and folders are created and modified. To change the date and time, you modify the date and time settings in the Date/Time Properties dialog box. In addition to changing the date and time, you can also change how the date and time is displayed. This can be handy if you are working on documents from a different country or region of the world. To change the date and time display, you modify the date or time settings on the Date/Time tab in the Regional Settings Properties dialog box. John is working on an international document and wants to change his date and time settings.

1. **Double-click the Date/Time icon in the Control Panel**
   The Date/Time Properties dialog box opens with the Date & Time tab displayed, as shown in Figure E-8. To change the time, you select the hours, minutes, or seconds you want to change in the text box in the Time section, and then type the new number or click the up or down arrows to select the new time. To change the date, you select the new month and year you want in the Date section, and then click the new date you want in the calendar. John wants to set his machine three hours ahead.

2. **Double-click the current hour in the text box in the Time section, then click the up arrow three times**
   The new time appears in the running clock. Now John wants to make the change.

3. **Click Apply**
   The new time appears in the right corner of the taskbar. You can also change your computer's time zone. To change the time zone setting, click the Time Zone tab, click the list arrow, and then select the time zone you want. After making the time change, John decides to restore his computer's time setting.

4. **Double-click the current hour, click the down arrow three times, then click OK**
   You can also change how the date and time is displayed. John reviews the regional setting to make sure the date and time are set correctly.

5. **Double-click the Regional Settings icon in the Control Panel**
   The Regional Settings dialog box opens, displaying tabs for Regional Settings, Number, Currency, Time, and Date. Using these tabs, you change the format and symbols used for numbers, currency, time, and date used in your files and programs. John wants to determine the date and time settings for his computer.

6. **Click the Date tab**
   You can click the short date or long date list arrows to change the two date formats, as shown in Figure E-9. John opens the Time tab to find out what time formats are being used.

7. **Click the Time tab**
   After reviewing the date and time display formats, John decides to keep the current settings.

8. **Click OK**

FIGURE E-8: Date/Time Properties dialog box

Click to change the time zone

Click to change the month

Click to change the date

Click to change year

Change time here

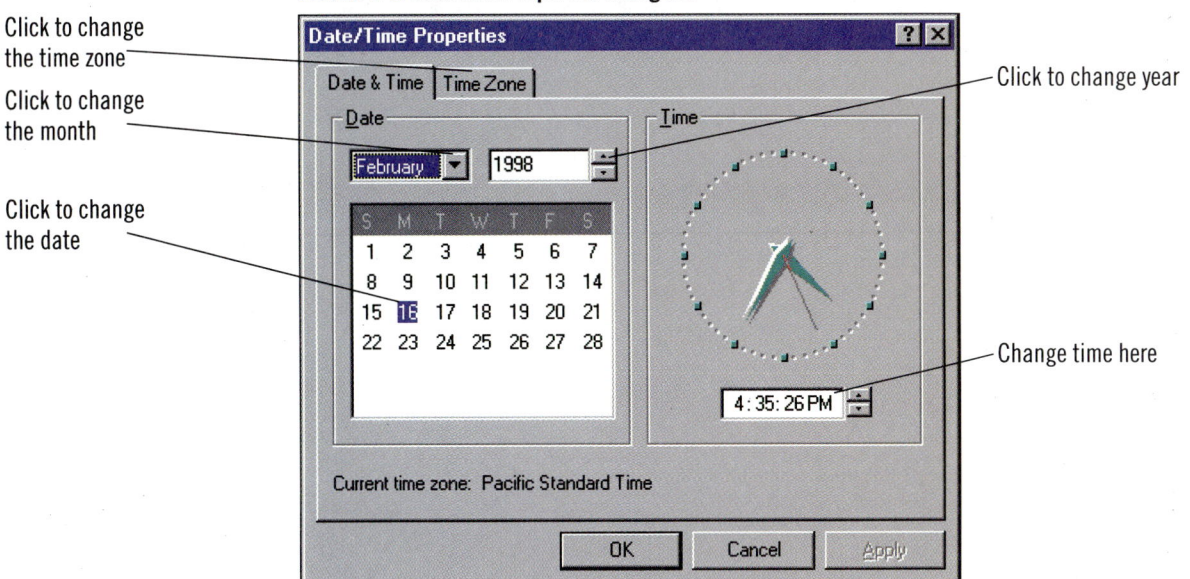

FIGURE E-9: Regional Settings Properties dialog box

Click to change short date display

Click to change long date display

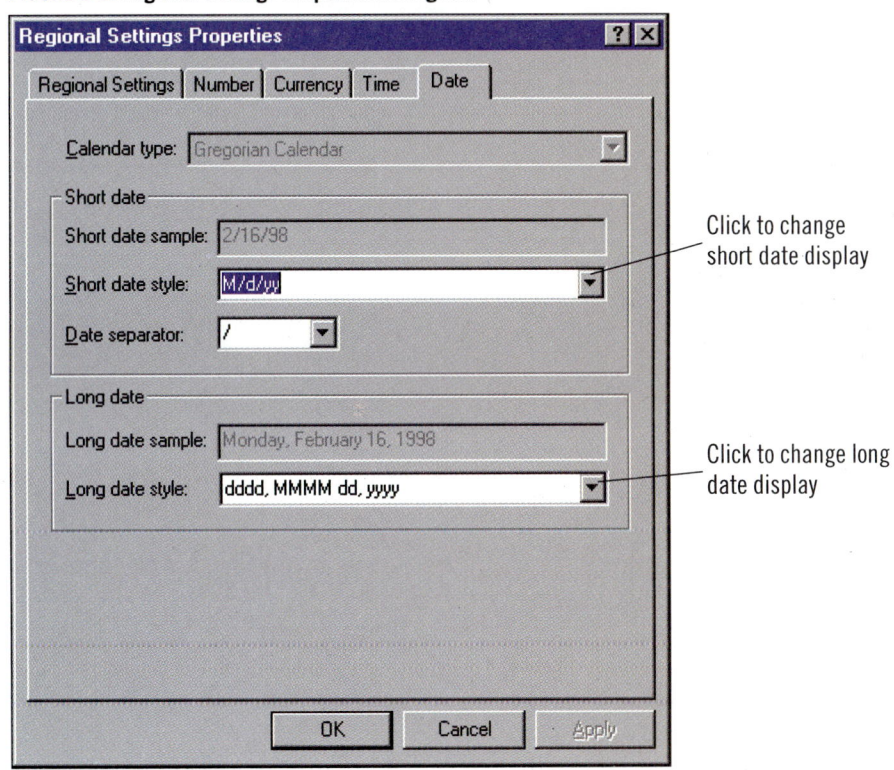

Adding a scheduled task

Task Scheduler is a tool that enables you to schedule tasks (such as Windows Tune-Up, a wizard to make your programs run faster) to run regularly, when it's most convenient for you. Task Scheduler starts each time you start Windows. When Task Scheduler is running on your computer, its icon appears next to the clock on the taskbar. You can double-click the Task Scheduler icon 🔳 on the taskbar to open Task Scheduler. With the Task Scheduler, you can schedule a task to run daily, weekly, monthly, or at certain times (such as when the computer starts or is idle), change the schedule for or turn off an existing task, or customize how a task will run at its scheduled time. To add a scheduled task, double-click the Add Scheduled Task icon and follow the step-by-step instructions.

Windows 98

Working with Fonts

Everything you type appears in a **font**, a particular design of letters. You might have heard of common font names such as Times New Roman, Arial, Courier, or Symbol. Windows comes with a variety of fonts that display and print in programs that are part of Windows, such as WordPad and Paint. Using the Fonts window, you can view these fonts, compare them to each other, see a sample of how a font would appear if printed, and even install new fonts. John wants to examine different fonts in preparation for an upcoming flyer he wants to create.

1. Double-click the **Fonts icon** in the Control Panel
   The Fonts window opens, as shown in Figure E-10. The window lists the fonts available on your system and indicates whether each is a TrueType or a screen font. A **TrueType font** is based on a mathematical equation so the curves of the letters are smooth and the corners are sharp. A **screen font** consists of **bitmapped characters**, small dots organized to form a letter. Table E-2 lists the various options on the Fonts toolbar and describes what they do.

2. If the Fonts window is not maximized, click the **Maximize button** in the Fonts window

3. Double-click the **Arial font**
   As shown in Figure E-11, the window displays information about this font and shows a sample of the font in different sizes. You can print a copy of this font information to use for further reference.

4. Click **Print** in the Arial (TrueType) window, then click **OK**
   A copy of the font information prints.

5. Click **Done**
   The Arial (TrueType) window closes. You can also use the tools in the Fonts window to find fonts that are similar to the selected font.

6. Click the **Similarity button** 🔲 on the Fonts toolbar
   All the fonts are listed by how similar they are to Arial, the font listed in the List fonts by similarity to box. You can choose a different font to check which ones are similar to it by clicking the List fonts by similarity to list arrow and then selecting the font you want to check.

7. Click the **Large Icons button** 🔲 on the Fonts toolbar, then click the **Close button** in the Fonts window

TABLE E-2: Fonts toolbar buttons

button	description
⬅	Moves you back to a previously opened folder
➡	Moves you forward to a previously opened folder
🔲	Moves to the next level up in the hierarchy of folders
🔲	Lists fonts by large icon
🔲	Lists fonts alphabetically
🔲	Lists fonts by similarity to the selected font
🔲	Lists details of fonts, including filename, font name, size, and date last modified

FIGURE E-10: Fonts window

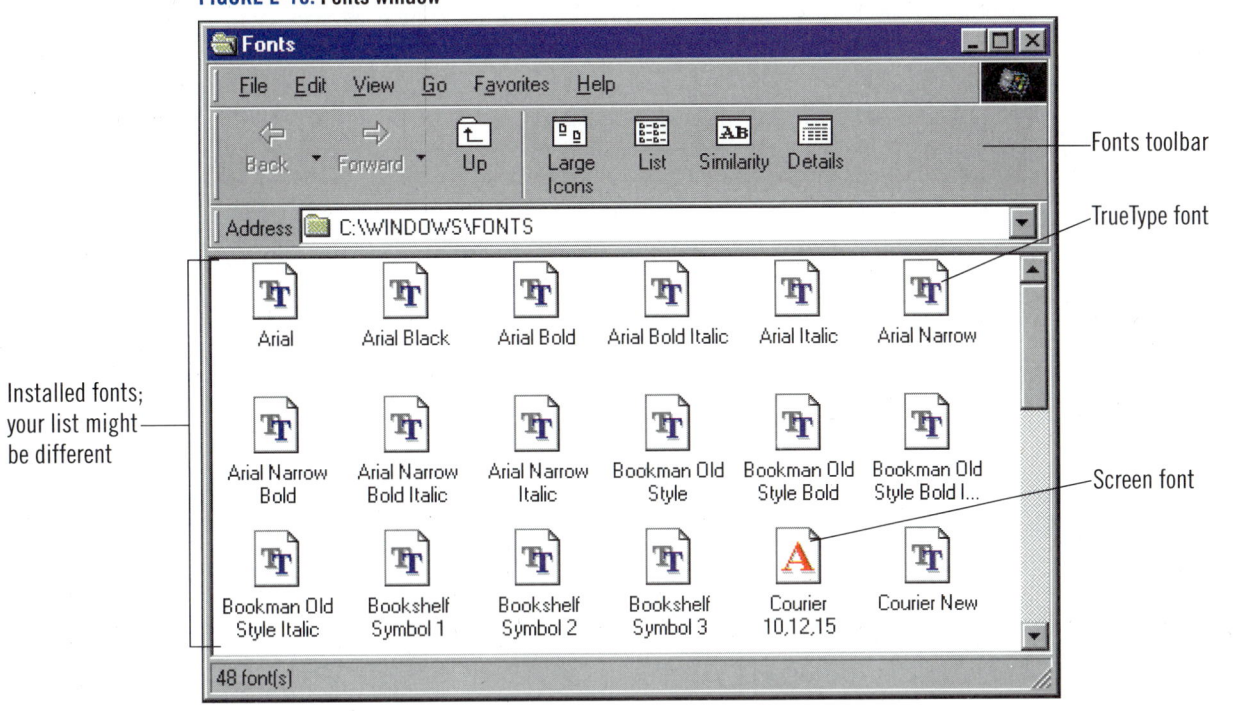

Fonts toolbar

TrueType font

Installed fonts; your list might be different

Screen font

FIGURE E-11: Selected font and how it appears in different sizes

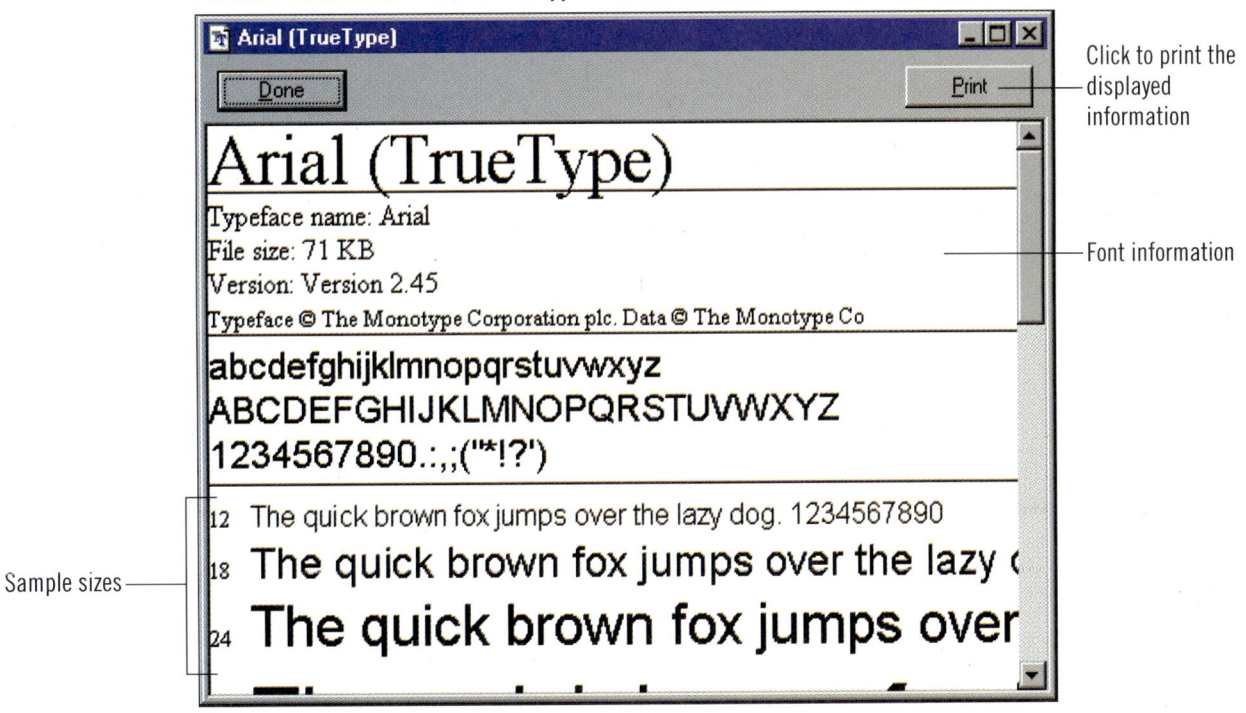

Click to print the displayed information

Font information

Sample sizes

Installing a font

Windows 98 might not come with all the fonts you need or want, but you can purchase additional fonts and easily install them. To install a new font, click Install New Font on the File menu in the Fonts window, indicate the location of the font you want to install (on the hard drive or a floppy disk drive), and then click OK. The new font will be installed and will be available in the Fonts window of the Control Panel and in all your Windows programs.

Windows 98

Customizing Mouse Operations

You can adjust the way your mouse works to suit your own habits and preferences. You can control which mouse button is the primary one (left or right), the size and appearance of the mouse pointer, and the speed at which the pointer moves across the screen. John decides to change how his mouse operates, to make it easier to maneuver. Also, to make the mouse easier to see, he adds a **pointer trail**, or shadow, to the mouse pointer.

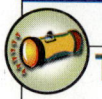
Trouble?

If you're using a mouse with a wheel, your Mouse Properties dialog box will be different. See your instructor or technical support person for assistance.

QuickTip

Restore the original mouse click speed by moving the slider back to its original position (or, if available, click Use Defaults).

1. **Double-click the Mouse icon in the Control Panel (you might have to scroll to see it), then click the Buttons tab if necessary**
   The Mouse Properties dialog box opens, as shown in Figure E-12. In the Buttons tab you can change the primary button you'll use for most actions. Right-handed users click the left mouse button most often, and vice versa. You can also set the speed that you double-click your mouse button (the time between two clicks required for Windows to recognize the action as double-clicking and not two single clicks). John will increase the double-click speed of his mouse.

2. **Drag the slider in the Double-click speed section to the right**
   The time between clicks is decreased. New mouse users should leave a relatively large amount of time between required clicks. As you become familiar with using the mouse, you can adjust this time to respond to the way you work. Next John tests the double-click speed.

3. **Double-click the test icon in the Double-click speed Test area box**
   The jack-in-the-box icon opens when you use the correct click speed. You might have to double-click the Test icon again if it doesn't change. Next John changes how the pointer appears as he drags the mouse.

4. **Click the Pointers tab**
   The Pointers tab opens, displaying different types of mouse pointers, as shown in Figure E-13. You can select from a series of schemes that will change the shape of the pointer, ranging from changing its size to adding a third dimension to it.

5. **Click the Motion tab, then click the Show pointer trails check box**
   See Figure E-14. Now when you move the mouse, the pointer displays a trail, making it easier to see. A pointer trail is especially useful on laptop computers because it allows the user to easily track where the pointer is and not "lose it" while working.

6. **Click Cancel so the settings are left unchanged**
   None of the changes you make occur unless you click OK in this dialog box. The Mouse Properties dialog box closes, and you return to the Control Panel.

FIGURE E-12: Mouse Properties dialog box

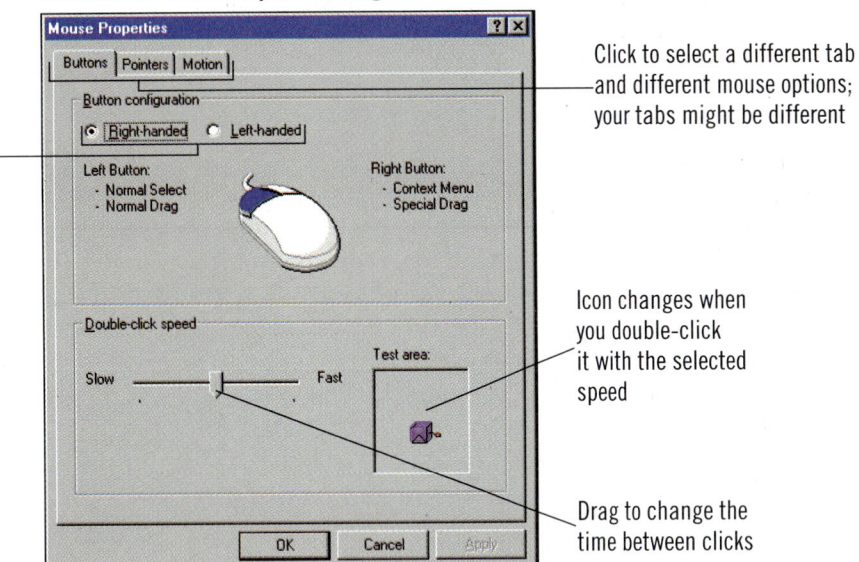

Click to configure which mouse button is primary

Click to select a different tab and different mouse options; your tabs might be different

Icon changes when you double-click it with the selected speed

Drag to change the time between clicks

FIGURE E-13: Changing the appearance of the mouse pointer

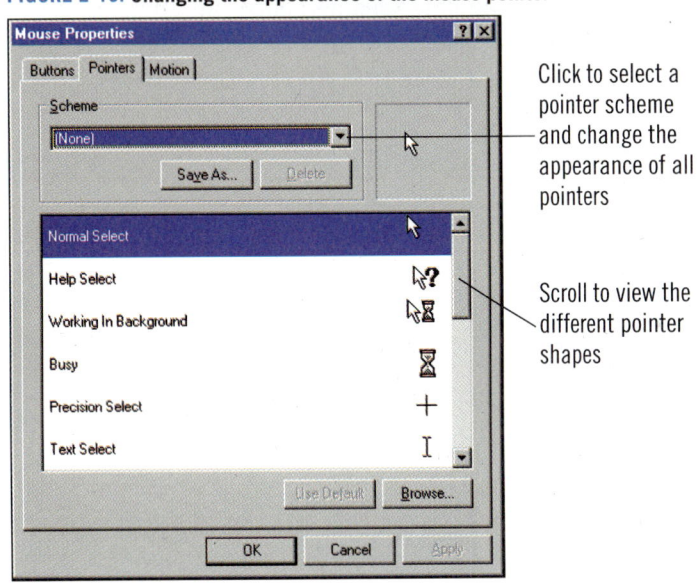

Click to select a pointer scheme and change the appearance of all pointers

Scroll to view the different pointer shapes

FIGURE E-14: Changing the motion of the mouse pointer

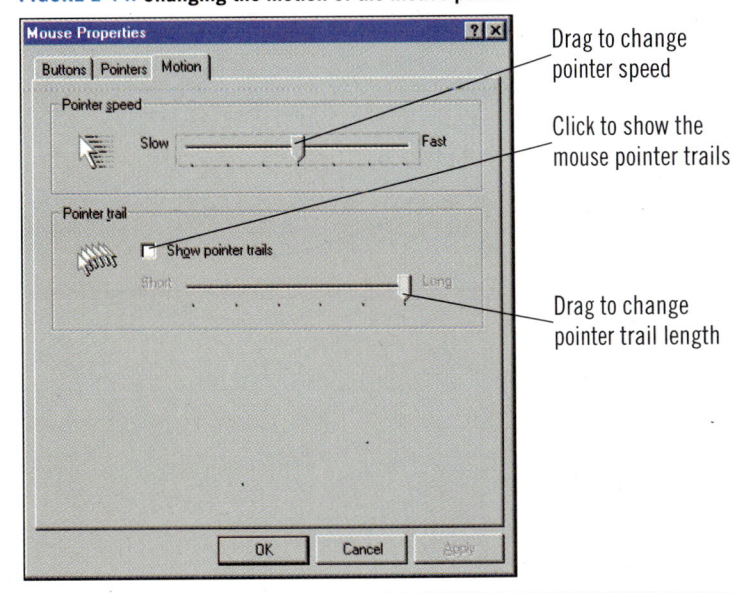

Drag to change pointer speed

Click to show the mouse pointer trails

Drag to change pointer trail length

Examining System Properties

In this lesson, you will become familiar with the System Properties dialog box (accessed from the Control Panel), where you can view and modify your computer's hardware settings. This information helps you know more about your system in general and is important should you need to describe your system's characteristics to a technical support person. John's computer has been running slow, so he decides to examine the computer's system properties to find out if any performance problems exist.

Steps

1. In the Control Panel, double-click the System icon (you might have to scroll to find it)
The System Properties dialog box opens. Table E-3 describes the options available on each of the tabs.

2. If it is not already selected, click the General tab
As Figure E-15 shows, John's computer system is running Windows 98 version 4.10.1650, and it has an Intel central processing unit and 16.0 MB of RAM.

3. Click the Performance tab
The Performance tab opens, as shown in Figure E-16. This tab provides detailed information about the computer and its performance running Windows. The most important indicator in this tab is the percent of resources that are free, which, in this case, is 73%. This number reflects how much memory and other important components of the operating system are free to perform additional tasks, such as opening new programs or documents. As this number gets smaller, your computer is being asked to do more work with less energy. When this number becomes too small, the system could halt on its own and have to be restarted. To fix the problem of low system resources, you could add more memory to your computer.

4. In the Advanced settings section, click File System
The File System Properties dialog box opens, providing you with a look at some of the features you can adjust to help make Windows perform at its maximum level of efficiency.

5. Click Cancel
The File System Properties dialog box closes.

6. Click OK, then click the Close button on the Control Panel
The Control Panel closes, and you return to the desktop.

> **QuickTip**
>
> Use the information in the System Properties dialog box to learn about your system, but don't change any settings without the advice of your instructor or technical support person.

TABLE E-3: System Properties tabs

system tab	description
General	Lists the general information about the system
Device Manager	Allows you to investigate the properties of the different hardware devices attached to your computer, such as the mouse
Hardware Profiles	Allows you to set up a particular hardware configuration you can use when you start Windows
Performance	Provides information on the computing resources that remain, the amount of memory installed, and whether disk compression is being used

FIGURE E-15: System Properties dialog box with General tab

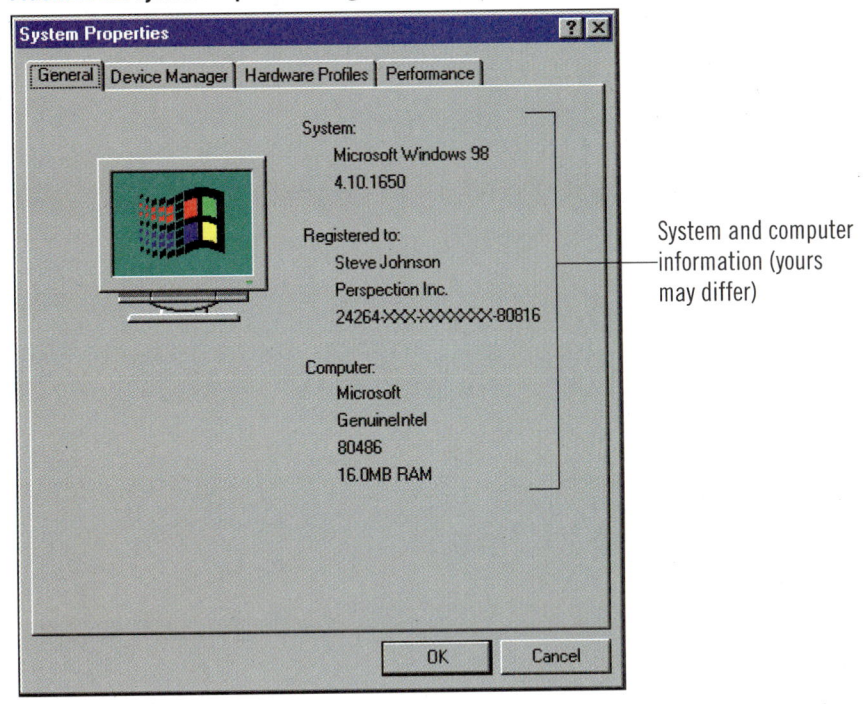

System and computer information (yours may differ)

FIGURE E-16: System Properties dialog box with Performance tab

Your properties might be different

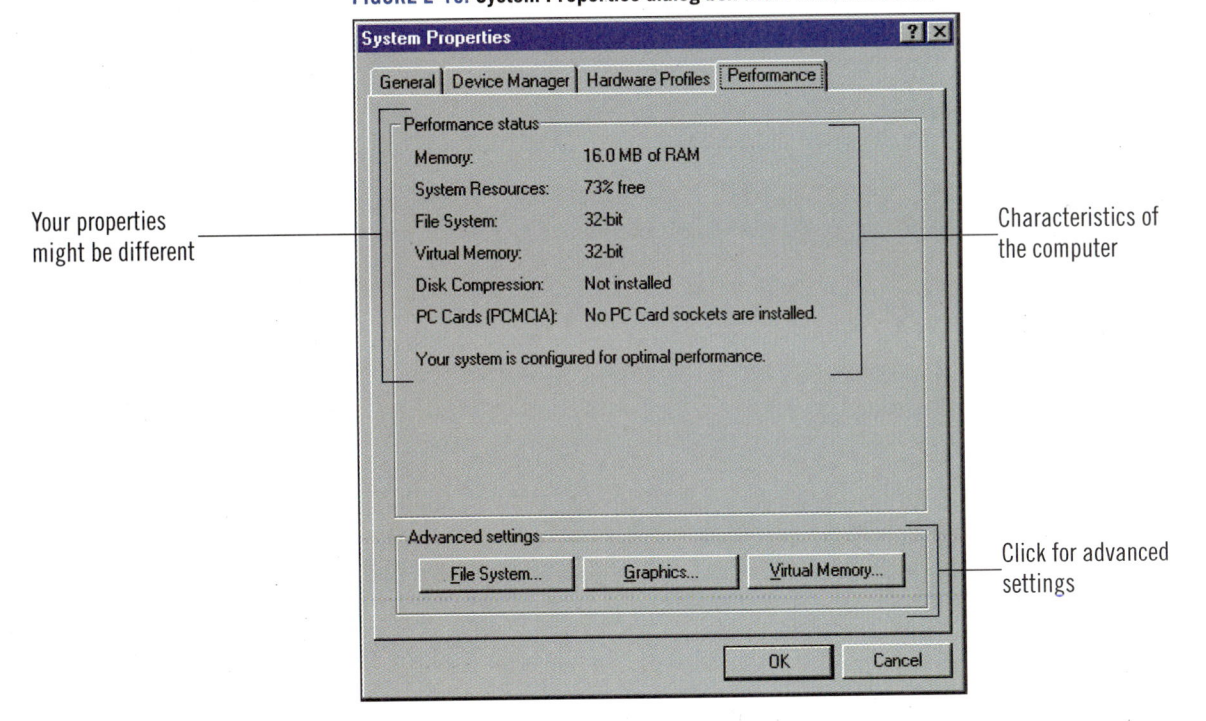

Characteristics of the computer

Click for advanced settings

CLUES TO USE

Adding new hardware and software to Windows

You can add new hardware, such as a printer, and add or remove programs by using tools on the Control Panel. The Add New Hardware and Add/Remove Programs dialog boxes walk you through the necessary steps. To start the add new hardware procedure, click the Add New Hardware icon in the Control Panel, and then click Next and follow the prompts. To add or remove a program, click the Add/Remove Program icon, click Install, and then follow the prompts. In both cases, Windows 98 should recognize that new hardware needs to be added or that an installation file needs to be executed.

Windows 98

Customizing the Taskbar

The taskbar is most often used for switching from one program to another. The taskbar is initially located at the bottom of the Windows desktop. As with other Windows elements, you can customize the taskbar; for example, you can change its size and location, or add or remove toolbars to it that help you perform the tasks you need to do. Sometimes you need more room on the screen to display a window, and it will help to hide the taskbar. You can use the **Auto hide** feature to help you automatically hide the taskbar when you don't need it. John removes and adds a toolbar to the taskbar and then learns how the Auto hide feature works.

Steps

1. Place the mouse pointer in an empty section of the taskbar, right-click the **taskbar**, then point to **Toolbars**

   The Toolbars submenu appears, as shown in Figure E-17. You can add or remove a variety of existing toolbars to the taskbar or create a new one.

2. Click **Quick Launch** to deselect it

   The Quick Launch toolbar is removed from the taskbar. Now you have more room on the taskbar for program buttons. John wants to try out the Auto hide feature.

3. Click the **Start button**, point to **Settings**, then click **Taskbar & Start Menu**

   The Taskbar Properties dialog box opens, displaying the Taskbar Options tab, as shown in Figure E-18. You can change how items (such as the clock and small icons on the Start menu) are displayed on the taskbar or how the taskbar is displayed on the screen.

4. Click the **Auto hide check box** to select it

   The taskbar in the Preview box is hidden.

5. Click **OK**

   The taskbar is hidden at the bottom of the screen.

6. Move the mouse pointer to the bottom of the screen

   While the mouse pointer is located at the bottom of the screen, the taskbar is shown. When you move the mouse pointer up, the taskbar is hidden.

7. Right-click in an empty section of the taskbar, point to **Toolbars**, then click **Quick Launch** to select it

   The Quick Launch toolbar is added to the taskbar. John prefers the taskbar not to move so he disables the Auto hide feature.

8. Click the **Start button**, point to **Settings**, then click **Taskbar & Start Menu**

   The Taskbar Properties dialog box opens.

9. Click the **Auto hide check box** to deselect it, then click **OK**

FIGURE E-17: Removing a toolbar from the taskbar

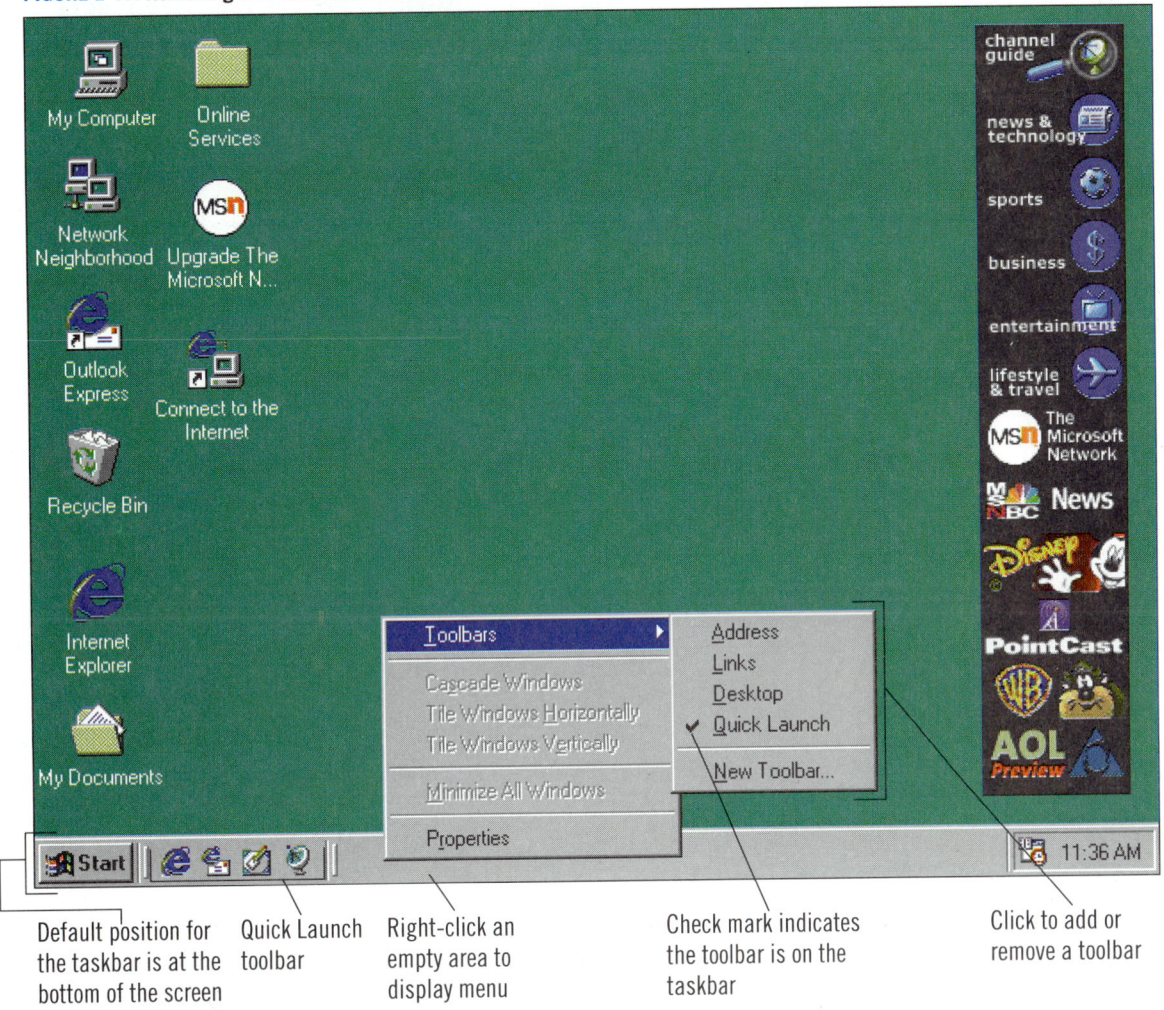

Default position for the taskbar is at the bottom of the screen

Quick Launch toolbar

Right-click an empty area to display menu

Check mark indicates the toolbar is on the taskbar

Click to add or remove a toolbar

FIGURE E-18: Taskbar Properties dialog box with Taskbar Options tab

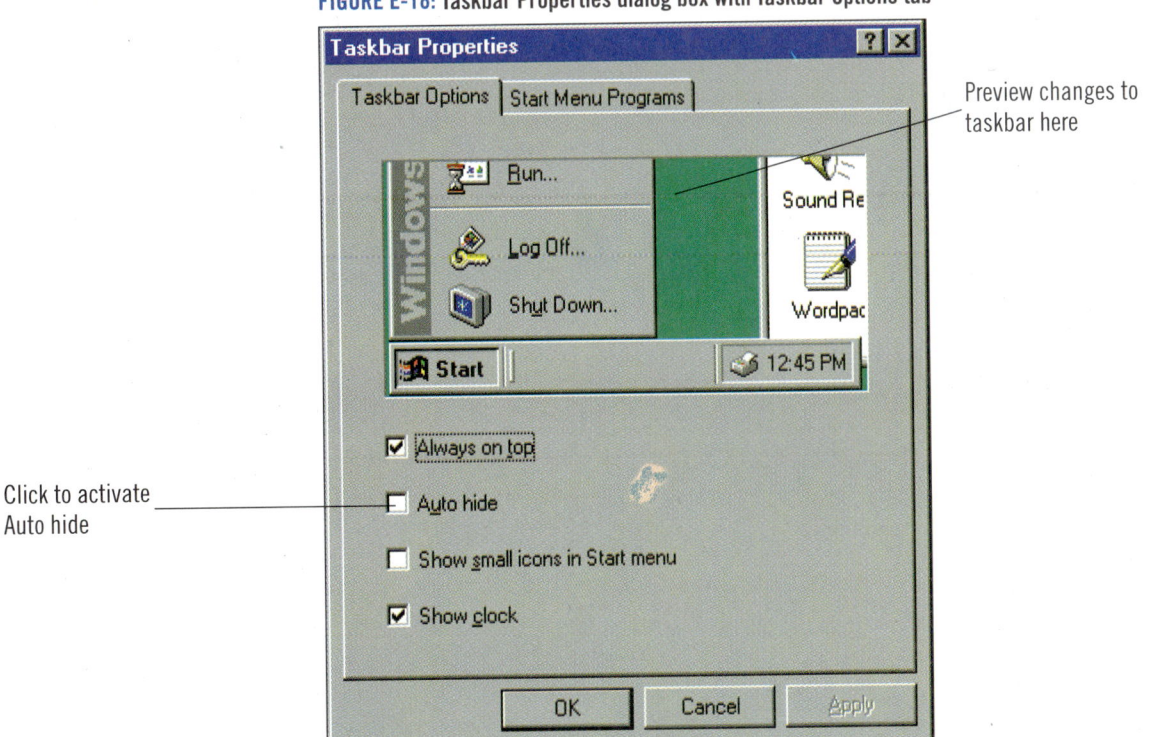

Preview changes to taskbar here

Click to activate Auto hide

Adding an Item to the Start Menu

To give you easier access to them, you can add shortcuts to programs, files, or folders to the Start menu. Instead of having to click through several levels of the Start menu to start a program or access a file, all you have to do is click the Start button and click the item you want on the Start menu. Of course, if you add too many items to the Start menu, you defeat the purpose. ✎ Because John will use the Wired Coffee logo so often in his work, he decides to add the file to the Start menu.

1. **Click the Start button, point to Settings, click Taskbar & Start Menu, then click the Start Menu Programs tab**
   The Taskbar Properties dialog box appears, as shown in Figure E-19. You can use the Start Menu Programs tab to add and delete items from the Start menu. To add the Wired Coffee Logo file to the Start menu, you need to specify where the file is located.

2. **Make sure your Student Disk is in the floppy disk drive, click Add, then click Browse**
   The Browse dialog box opens, where you can navigate to and select a file, folder, or program you want to add to the Start menu.

3. **Click the Look in list arrow, then click the drive that contains your student disk**
   You need to display all the types of files in order to view the Wired Coffee Logo file.

4. **Click the Files of type list arrow, then click All Files**
   Now you see all the files on your Student Disk.

5. **Double-click Wired Coffee Logo, then click Next**
   Once the file is located, you need to specify where to place the file on the Start menu. John wants the file on the main Start menu.

6. **Click Start Menu in the Select Program Folder dialog box, click Next, click Finish, then click OK**
   Now open the Start menu and verify that the file has been added.

7. **Click the Start button**
   The Wired Coffee Logo file now appears at the top of the Start menu, as shown in Figure E-20. To open the Wired Coffee Logo file, all you need to do is click the icon on the Start menu. Now remove this item from the Start menu to return your desktop to its original settings.

8. **Press [Esc] to close the Start menu, right-click in an empty area on the taskbar, click Properties, then click the Start Menu Programs tab**

9. **Click Remove, locate and click Wired Coffee Logo in the list, click Remove, click Close, then click OK**
   The Taskbar Properties dialog box closes, and the Wired Coffee shortcut is removed from the Start menu.

QuickTip
You can also add an item to the Start menu by creating a shortcut to it (on the desktop or in Windows Explorer, for example) and dragging the icon to the Start button.

FIGURE E-19: Taskbar Properties dialog box with Start Menu Programs tab

Click to add or remove programs to and from the Start menu

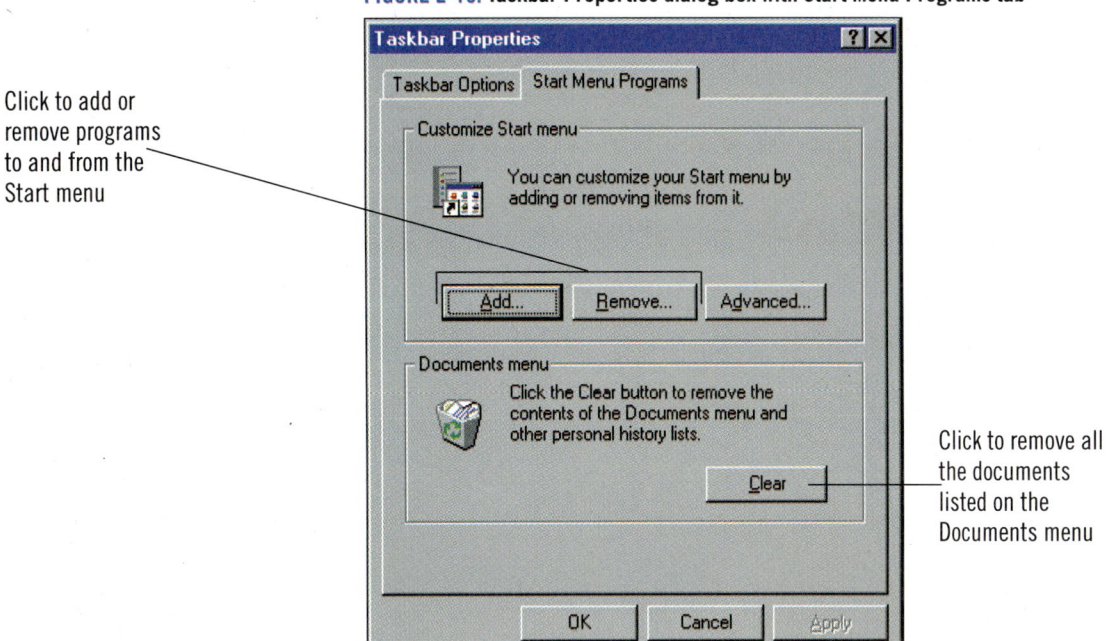

Click to remove all the documents listed on the Documents menu

If you wanted to open the file, you would click here

FIGURE E-20: File added to the Start menu

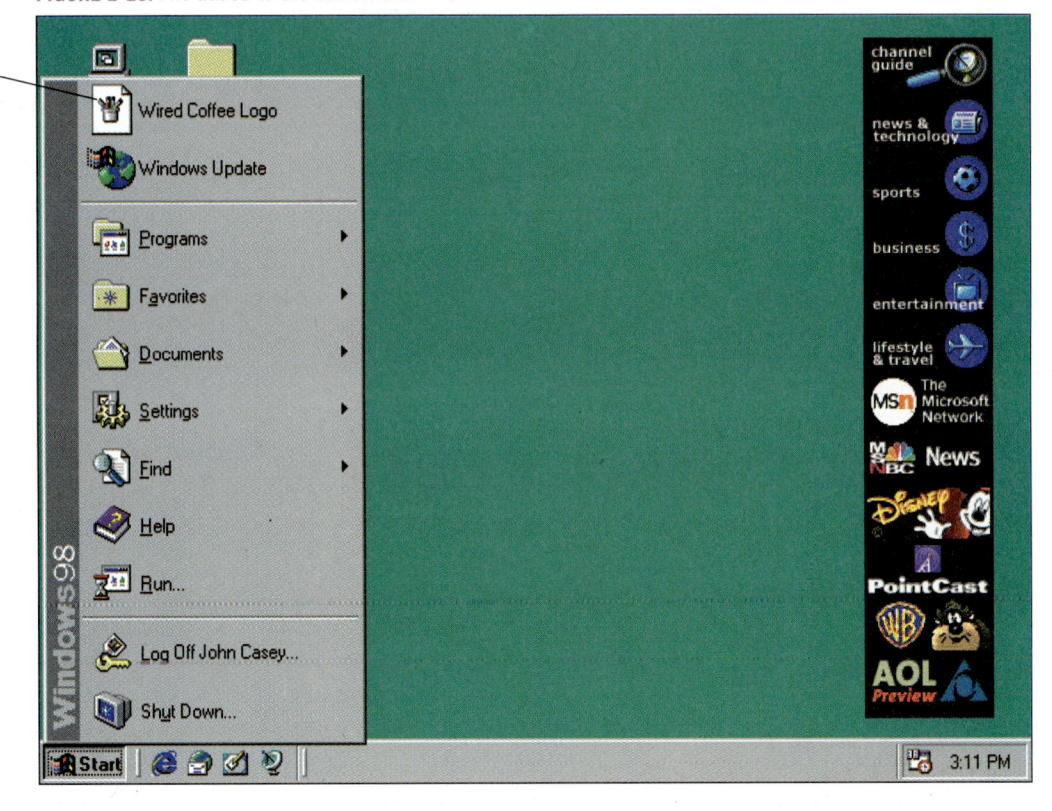

Rearranging Start menu items

If you don't like the location of an item on the Start menu, you can move the item to a different location by dragging it to the desired location. A blank line appears as you move the mouse pointer indicating the new location of the item. For example, to move the Windows Explorer menu item from the Programs submenu to the Start menu, open the Start menu, then drag the Windows Explorer item to the Start menu.

Practice

► Concepts Review

Label each of the elements of the screen shown in Figure E-21.

FIGURE E-21

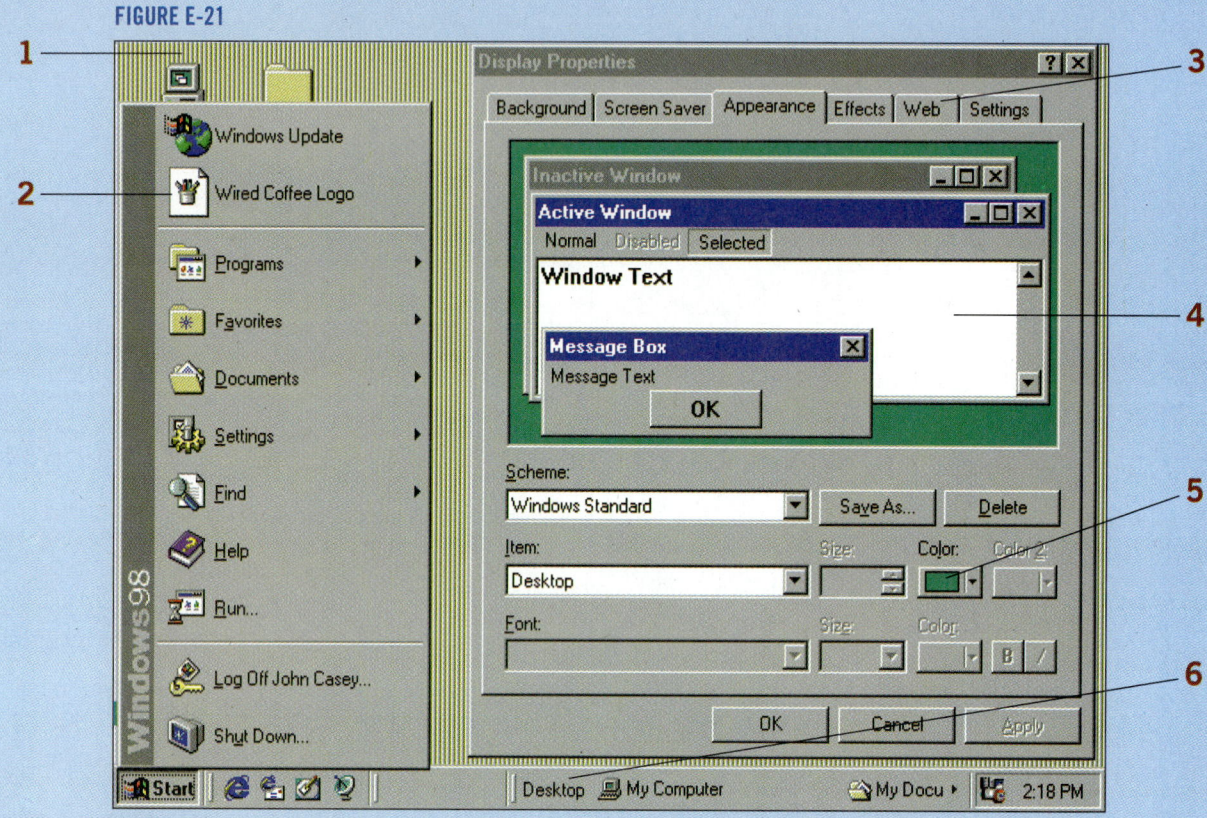

Match each of the terms with the statement that describes its function.

7. Patterns   a. Used to change properties of various elements of a computer
8. Screen saver   b. Preset combinations of desktop colors
9. Color schemes   c. Used to prevent damage to the monitor
10. Control Panel   d. Preset designs for the desktop
11. Start menu   e. Used to start programs and open documents

Select the best answer from the following list of choices.

12. To customize the Active Desktop, you need to open the
    a. Folder Options dialog box.
    b. Display Properties dialog box.
    c. Desktop Settings dialog box.
    d. Custom Desktop dialog box.

13. To change the pattern on the desktop from the Display Properties dialog box in the Control Panel, click the
    a. Background tab.
    b. Screen Saver tab.
    c. Appearance tab.
    d. Settings tab.

14. **An Internet document or Paint file used as a background is called a**
    a. Pattern.
    b. Wallpaper.
    c. Display.
    d. Shortcut.
15. **To change the scheme on the desktop from the Display Properties dialog box in the Control Panel, click the**
    a. Screen Saver tab.
    b. Appearance tab.
    c. Effects tab.
    d. Background tab.

▶ Skills Review

1. **Customize the Active Desktop**
   a. Right-click in an empty area on the desktop.
   b. Point to Active Desktop, then click Customize my Desktop.
   c. Click the Web tab, if necessary.
   d. Click Folder Options, then click Yes to close the Display Properties dialog box.
   e. Click the Classic style option button, and view the change in the Preview box at the top of the dialog box.
   f. Click the Custom, based on settings you choose option button, then click the Close button.

2. **Change the desktop background and screen saver settings.**
   a. Click the Start button, point to Settings, then click Control Panel.
   b. Double-click the Display icon.
   c. Click the Background tab, if necessary, then click Blue Rivets in the Wallpaper section.
   d. Click the Screen Saver tab, click the Screen Saver list arrow, click 3D Pipes, then click Preview.
   e. Move the mouse to end the Screen Saver preview.

3. **Change the desktop color scheme.**
   a. Click the Appearance tab.
   b. Click the Item list arrow, then click Desktop.
   c. Choose any color you want for the desktop, then click Apply.
   d. Click Save As, type "Fred," then click OK.
   e. Click Delete.
   f. Click the Scheme list arrow, then click Windows Standard, then click Apply.
   g. Click the Screen Saver tab, click the Screen Saver list arrow, then click (None).
   h. Click the Background tab, click (None) in the Wallpaper section, then click OK.

4. **Set the date and time.**
   a. Double-click the Date/Time icon.
   b. Double-click the number of minutes.
   c. Click the up arrow three times, then click Apply.
   d. Double-click the number of minutes.
   e. Click the down arrow three times, then click OK.

5. **Work with fonts.**
   a. Double-click the Fonts icon.
   b. Double-click a Times New Roman icon.
   c. Click Print, click OK, click Done, then click the Close button.

6. **Customize mouse operations.**
    a. Double-click the Mouse icon.
    b. Click the Motion tab, then click the Show pointer trails check box.
    c. Drag the slider to the middle of the Pointer trails bar, then click Apply.
    d. Change the mouse settings back to the default, then click OK.

7. **Examine system properties.**
    a. Double-click the System icon.
    b. Click the Performance tab, then write down the percent of resources available.
    c. Close the System Properties dialog box.
    d. Click the Start button, open WordPad, then click the Minimize button.
    e. Reopen the System Properties dialog box, then click the Performance tab.
    f. Write down the percent of resources available.
    g. Compare the amount of resources that are now available to what you wrote in Step c, then click OK.
    h. Close the Control Panel and WordPad.

8. **Customize the taskbar.**
    a. Right-click the taskbar, point to Toolbars, then click Quick Launch to remove that toolbar from the taskbar.
    b. Click the Start button, point to Settings, then click Taskbar & Start Menu.
    c. Click the Auto hide check box to select it, then click OK.
    d. Move the mouse pointer to the bottom of the screen.
    e. Right-click the taskbar, point to Toolbars, then click Quick Launch to add the toolbar back to the taskbar.
    f. Click the Start button, point to Settings, then click Taskbar & Start Menu.
    g. Click the Auto hide check box to deselect it, then click Apply.

9. **Add an item to the Start menu.**
    a. Click the Start Menu Programs tab, click Add, then click Browse.
    b. Double-click Program Files, then double-click Accessories, double-click WordPad, then click Next.
    c. Double-click Start Menu, then click Finish.
    d. Click Remove.
    e. Click WordPad, then click Remove, click Close, then click OK.

▶ Independent Challenges

1. You have been retained as a consultant by a large law firm that has just installed Windows 98. The firm's employees need to be taught how to customize Windows 98 to fit their needs. As you prepare your presentation, you are going to customize the display so it is easier for them to see. Make the following changes, and make sure you change them back to the default setting or setup when you are finished.

To complete this independent challenge:

1. Open the Display Properties dialog box from the Control Panel.
2. Change the background to Straw Mat.
3. Set the screen saver for 1 minute so you can show them how it works without waiting too long.
4. On the Appearance tab, set the Scheme to High contrast black (extra large).
5. Save the scheme as Demo, then apply the changes.
6. Print the screen. (Press the Print Screen key to make a copy of the screen, open Paint, click Edit on the menu bar, click Paste to paste the screen into Paint, then click Yes to paste the large image, if necessary. Click File on the menu bar, click Print, then click OK.)
7. Delete the scheme Demo, then select the Windows Standard scheme.
8. Set the screen saver for 5 minutes.

2. As the owner of a small optical laboratory, you are trying to abide by the Americans with Disabilities Act, which states that employers should make every reasonable effort to accommodate workers with disabilities. You have one worker who is visually impaired. Customize the Windows desktop for this employee so that it is easier to work in, desktop items are easier to see and read, and desktop colors are strongly contrasted with each other but still easy on the eyes. Save this custom configuration so that this employee can use it when necessary.

To complete this independent challenge:

1. Open the Display Properties dialog box from the Control Panel.
2. Change the desktop color to red.
3. Change the font size for the menu to 12.
4. Change the size and color of the text in the title bar for the Active Window to 24 and light blue (the second color in the fifth row).
5. Change the font style for the message box to bold.
6. Save the custom configuration as Visible.
7. Apply the scheme.
8. Print the screen. (See Independent Challenge 1, Step 6 for screen printing instructions.)
9. Delete the scheme Visible.
10. Select the Windows Standard scheme.

3. You've been using Windows 98 for about two weeks, and while you really like its features, it seems to be a bit sluggish. To see if you can speed it up, you need to provide certain information to your system administrator or instructor.

To complete this independent challenge:

1. Open the System Properties dialog box from the Control Panel.
2. Record what type of central processor is being used.
3. Record the percent of resources that are available.
4. Record what version of Windows you are using.
5. Record how much memory is available.
6. Print the screen. (See Independent Challenge 1, Step 6 for screen printing instructions.)

4. As the owner of Lew's Office Supply, you need to make your business computers easier for your employees to use. One way to do that is to add programs to the Start menu. Your employees use WordPad and Paint almost exclusively, and they also use the same documents quite often.

To complete this independent challenge:

1. Add a WordPad shortcut to the Start menu. (*Hint*: Select WordPad.exe located in the Accessories folder within the Program Files folder.
2. Add a Paint shortcut to the Start menu. (*Hint*: Select MSpaint.exe located in the same place as WordPad.)
3. Create a memo to employees about the upcoming company picnic using WordPad, then save the memo on your Student Disk as "Company Picnic Memo."
4. Close the memo and WordPad.
5. Add the Company Picnic Memo file to the Start menu.
6. Open the Company Picnic Memo from the Start menu.
7. Print the screen. (See Independent Challenge 1, Step 6 for screen printing instructions.)
8. Remove all the shortcuts you created.

► Visual Workshop

Re-create the screen shown in Figure E-22, which displays the Windows desktop, then print the screen. (See Independent Challenge 1, Step 6 for screen printing instructions.) You don't have to change the Log Off name on the Start menu.

FIGURE E-22

Exploring
the Internet with Microsoft Internet Explorer

Objectives

- ▶ **Understand Web browsers**
- ▶ **Start Internet Explorer**
- ▶ **Explore the browser window**
- ▶ **Open a Web page and follow links**
- ▶ **Add a Web page to the Favorites list**
- ▶ **Add an active channel to the Channels list**
- ▶ **Select a home page and add a link button**
- ▶ **Search the Web**
- ▶ **Print a Web page**

Another component of Windows 98 is Microsoft Internet Explorer, a software program that helps you access the World Wide Web. In this unit you will learn about the benefits of the World Wide Web, examine the basic features of Internet Explorer 4, and access Web pages. This unit requires a connection to the Internet. If your computer is not connected to the Internet, check with your instructor or technical support person to see if it's possible for you to connect. If not, simply read the lessons to learn about using Internet Explorer. 🖌 Wired Coffee Company is a growing business that wants to take advantage of Internet technology. John Casey, owner of the company, uses Internet Explorer to open the company Web page and find information related to the coffee business.

Understanding Web Browsers

The Internet is a collection of over 40 million computers from all over the world linked together to share information. The Internet's physical structure includes telephone lines, cables, satellites, and other telecommunications media, as depicted in Figure F-1. Using the Internet, computer users can share many types of information, including text, graphics, sounds, videos, and computer programs. The **World Wide Web** (also known as the Web or WWW) is a part of the Internet that consists of Web sites located on different computers around the world. A **Web site** contains Web pages that are linked together to make looking for information on the Internet easier. **Web pages** are documents that contain highlighted words, phrases, and graphics, called **hyperlinks** (or simply links) that open other Web pages when you click them. Figure F-2 shows a sample Web page. **Web browsers** are software programs that you use to "browse the Web," or access and display Web pages. Some Web pages contain frames. A **frame** is a separate window within a Web page. Frames give you the ability to show more than one Web page at a time. Browsers make the Web easy to navigate by providing a graphical, point-and-click environment. This unit features Internet Explorer 4, a popular browser from Microsoft that comes with Windows 98. Netscape Communicator is another popular browser. John realizes that there are many applications for Internet Explorer in his company. He notes the following applications:

 ### Display Web pages from all over the world
John can look at Web pages for business purposes, such as checking the pages of other coffee companies to see how they are marketing their products.

 ### Use links to move from one Web page to another
John can click links (which appear as either underlined text or graphics) to move from one Web page to another, investigating different sources for information. Since a Web page can contain links to any location on the Internet, you can jump to Web pages all over the world.

 ### Play audio and video clips
John can click links that play audio and video clips, such as the sound of coffee grinding or a video of workers picking coffee beans. He can also play continuous audio and video broadcasts through radio and television stations over the Internet.

 ### Search the Web for information
John can use search programs that allow him to look for information about any topic contained in Web pages on computers throughout the world.

 ### Subscribe to a favorite Web page or active channel
John can create a list of his favorite Web pages to make it easy for him to return to them at a later time. He can also subscribe to a Web page or active channel. When you **subscribe** to a Web page, you are automatically notified when the Web page changes.

 ### Print the text and graphics on Web pages
If John finds some information or images that he would like to print, he can easily print all or part of the Web page, including the graphics.

FIGURE F-1: Structure of the Internet

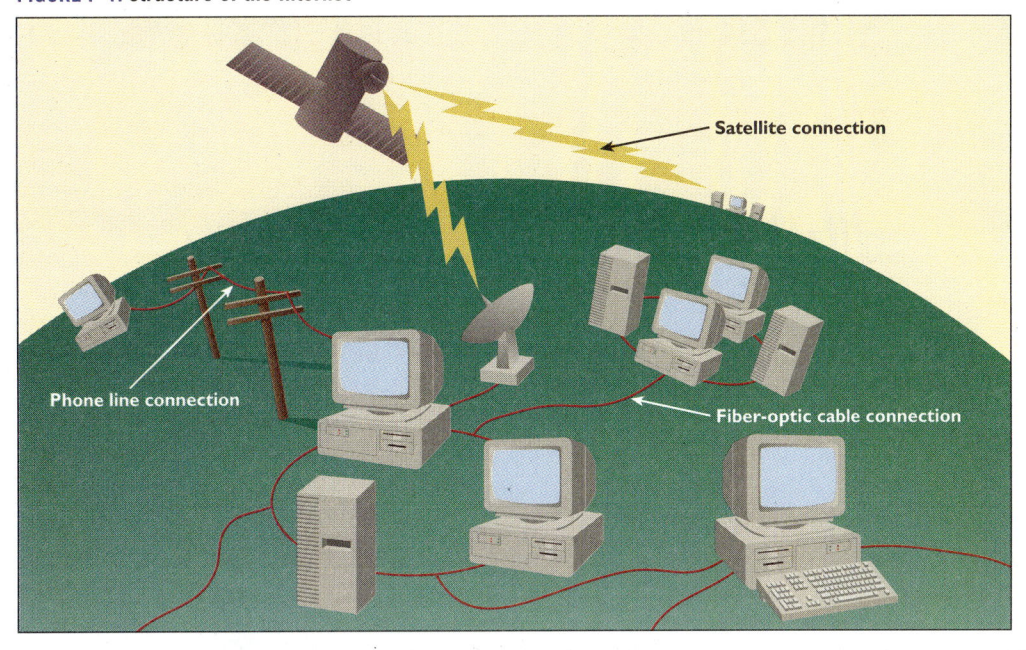

Satellite connection

Phone line connection

Fiber-optic cable connection

FIGURE F-2: World Wide Web page

Title of Web page and name of broswer

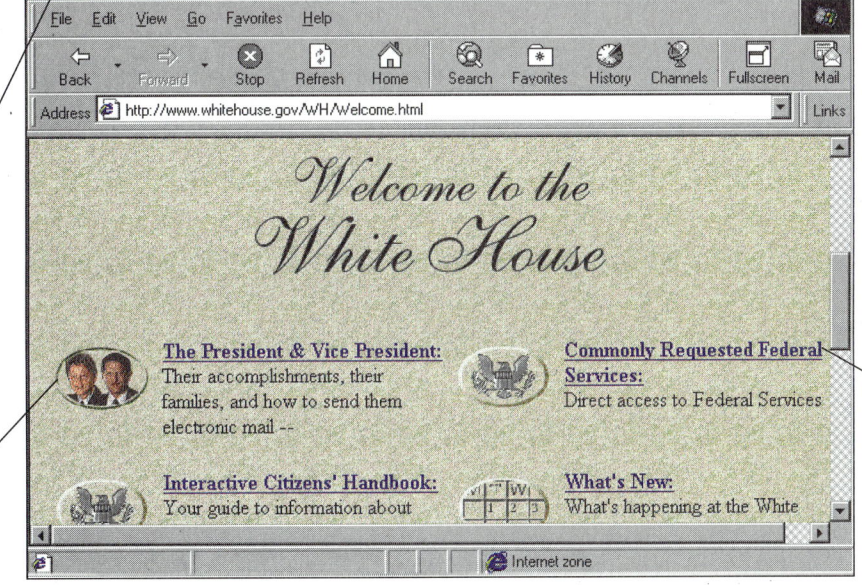

Graphic hyperlink you can click to view information on the President and Vice President

Text hyperlink you can click to view information on commonly requested federal services

CLUES TO USE

The history of the Internet and World Wide Web

The Internet has its roots in the Advanced Research Projects Agency Network (ARPANET), which the United States Department of Defense started in 1969. In 1986, the National Science Foundation formed NSFNET, which replaced ARPANET. NSFNET expanded the foundation of the U.S. portion of the Internet with high-speed, long distance data lines. In 1991, the U.S. Congress expanded the capacity and speed of the Internet further and opened it up to commercial use. The Internet is now accessible in over 200 countries. The World Wide Web was developed in Switzerland in 1991 to make finding documents on the Internet easier. Software programs designed to access the Web (Web browsers) use "point and click" interfaces. The first such Web browser, Mosaic, was introduced at the University of Illinois in 1993. Recently, Microsoft Internet Explorer and Netscape Communicator have become the two most popular Web browsers.

Starting Internet Explorer

Internet Explorer is a Web browser that you use to search the World Wide Web (you also need a physical connection to the Internet). When you install Windows 98, an icon for Internet Explorer will appear on the desktop, and a button for it will appear on the Quick Launch toolbar on the taskbar. Windows 98 also displays a Channel Bar on the desktop. The Channel Bar allows you to quickly access specialized Web pages known as active channels. An **active channel** is a specific channel on the Channel Bar, such as Disney, MSNBC, or The Microsoft Network. If you don't see the active channel you want to open, you can use the View Channels button on the Quick Launch toolbar to view an available list. If your computer is not connected to the Internet, check with your instructor or technical support person to see if it's possible for you to connect. Before John can take advantage of the many features of the World Wide Web, he must start Internet Explorer.

1. **Establish a connection to the Internet via the network or telephone**

   If you connect to the Internet through a network, follow your instructor's directions to establish your connection. If you connect by telephone, use an existing Dial-Up Networking connection, or create a new connection using the Connection Wizard to establish your connection.

2. **Locate the Internet Explorer icon on your desktop**

   The icon will probably appear on the left side of your screen, as shown in Figure F-3, but it doesn't matter where it is or even if it is not on your desktop. There are several different ways to start Internet Explorer, depending on your circumstances. See Table F-1 for a description of different ways to start Internet Explorer.

3. **Double-click the Internet Explorer icon**

   Internet Explorer opens and displays a Web page, as shown in Figure F-4. It's okay if the Web page on your screen is not the same as the one shown in Figure F-4. Later in this unit you will learn how to change the Web page that is displayed when you first start Internet Explorer. Continue with the next lesson to view the various elements of the browser window.

Trouble?

If the Internet Explorer icon isn't on your desktop, click the Start button, point to Programs, point to Internet Explorer, then click Internet Explorer.

TABLE F-1: Ways to start Internet Explorer

method	results
Double-click the Internet Explorer icon on the desktop	Starts Internet Explorer and displays the home page
Click the Launch Internet Explorer Browser button on the Quick Launch toolbar	Starts Internet Explorer and displays the home page
Click the Start button, point to Programs, point to Internet Explorer, then click Internet Explorer	Starts Internet Explorer and displays the home page
Click an active channel on the Channel Bar	Starts Internet Explorer and displays the active channel you selected
Click the View Channels button on the Quick Launch toolbar	Starts Internet Explorer and displays a list of available active channels

FIGURE F-3: Windows desktop

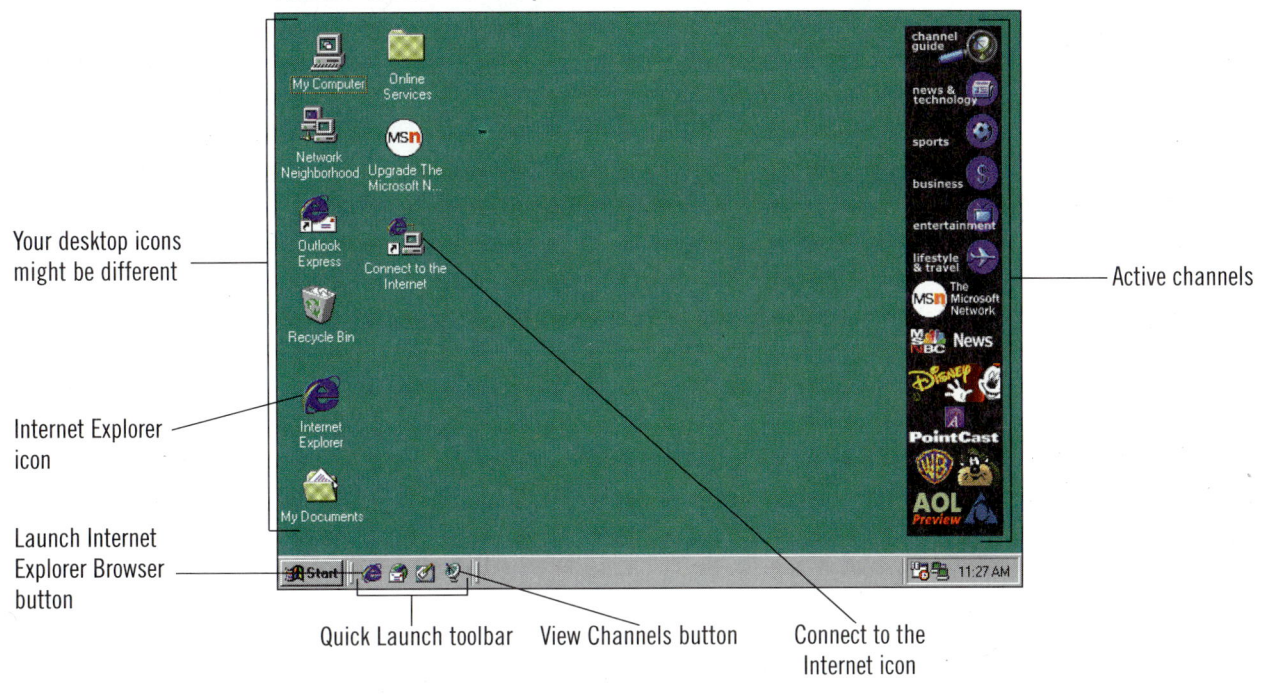

Your desktop icons might be different

Internet Explorer icon

Launch Internet Explorer Browser button

Active channels

Quick Launch toolbar   View Channels button   Connect to the Internet icon

FIGURE F-4: Web page featuring the Microsoft Corporation

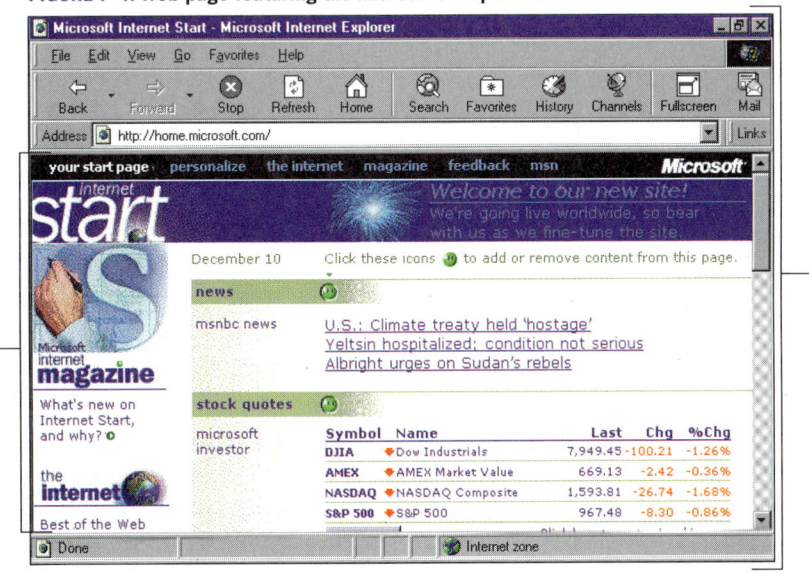

Current Web page displayed (yours might be different)

Internet Explorer window

Connecting to the Internet

Sometimes connecting your computer to the Internet can be the most difficult part of getting started. The Connection Wizard simplifies the process, whether you want to set up a new connection using an existing account or you want to select an **Internet service provider (ISP)**—a company that provides access to the Internet for a fee—and set up a new account. You might need to obtain connection information from your ISP or your system administrator. To get connected to the Internet using the Connection Wizard, double-click the Connect to the Internet icon on the desktop, then follow the step-by-step instructions. If you are on a network, you might need to use a **proxy server**, which provides a secure barrier between your network and the Internet and prevents other people from seeing confidential information on your network. To configure your computer to use a proxy server, click View on the Internet Explorer menu bar, click Internet Options, then click the Connection tab. See your system administrator for getting details to connect to your network.

Exploring the Browser Window

The elements of the Internet Explorer program window, shown in Figure F-5, allow you to view, print, and search for information on the Internet. Before exploring the Web, John decides to familiarize himself with the components of the browser window.

Details

He notes the following features:

 The **title bar** at the top of the page displays the name of the Web page and the name of the browser you are using.

 The **menu bar** provides access to a variety of commands, much like other Windows programs.

 The **toolbar** provides buttons for easy access to the most commonly used commands with Internet Explorer. See Table F-2 for a description of each toolbar button. These button commands are also available on the menus.

 The **Address bar** displays the address of the current Web page or the contents of a local or network computer drive. The **Web address**, like a postal address, is a unique place on the Internet where you can locate a Web page. The Web address is also referred to as the **URL**, which stands for Uniform Resource Locator.

 The **Links bar** displays link buttons to Web pages on the Internet or to documents on a local or network drive.

 The **status indicator** (the Windows logo) will animate while a new Web page is loading.

 The **document window** displays the current Web page or the contents of a local or network computer drive. You might need to scroll down the page to view the entire contents.

 The **vertical scroll bar** allows you to move up or down the current Web page. The **scroll box** indicates your relative position within the Web page.

 The **status bar** displays information about your connection progress with new Web pages that you open, including notification that you have connected to another site and the percentage of information that has been transferred. This bar also displays the function of the links in the document window as you move your mouse pointer over them.

FIGURE F-5: Elements of the Internet Explorer program window

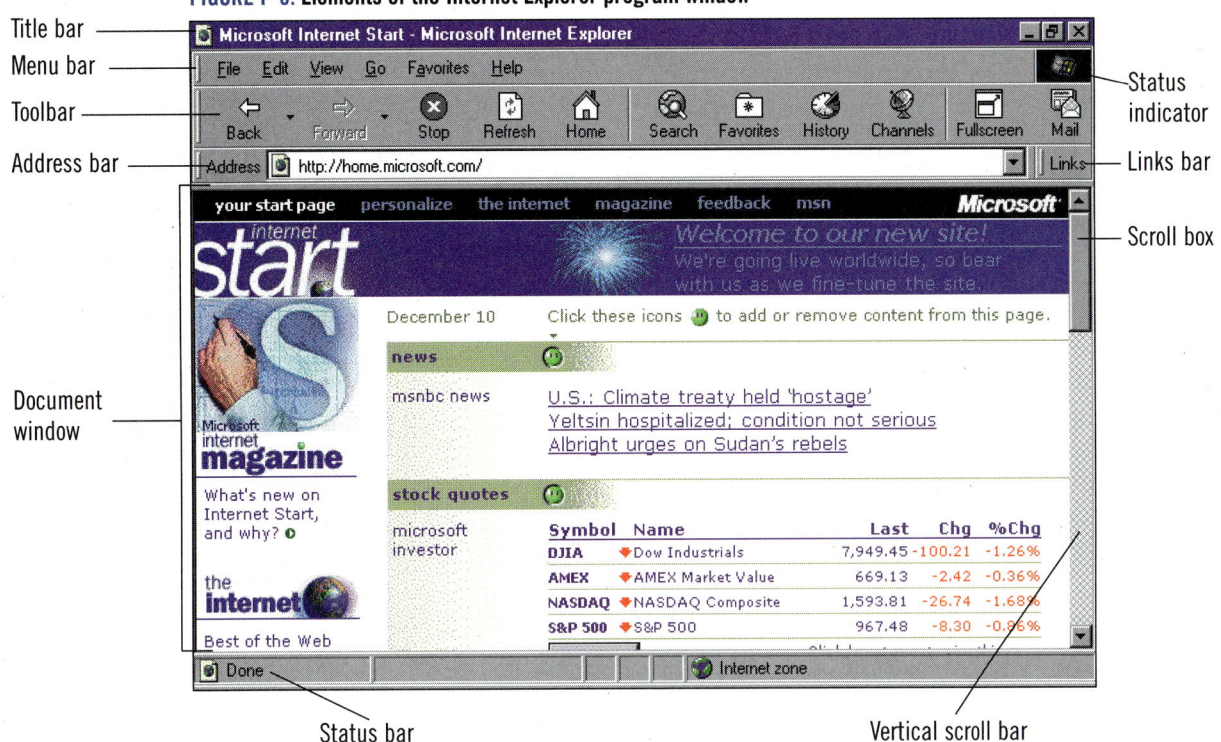

Title bar — Menu bar — Toolbar — Address bar — Document window — Status indicator — Links bar — Scroll box — Status bar — Vertical scroll bar

Displaying the entire Internet Explorer toolbar

On monitors set to a small screen size, such as 640 × 480, the Internet Explorer toolbar does not have enough room to display the Print and Edit buttons on the screen. To display all the buttons on the toolbar, you can either remove the text labels from the buttons to make them smaller or increase the screen size. To remove the text labels from the buttons, click the View menu, point to Toolbars, then click Text Labels. To increase the screen size, right-click a blank area of the desktop, click Properties, click the Settings tab, drag the Screen Area slider to 800 × 600 or higher, then click OK. (If you are working in a lab, check with your instructor or technical support person before changing the screen size.)

TABLE F-2: Internet Explorer toolbar buttons

button	description	button	description
Back	Opens the previous page	History	Opens the History list
Forward	Opens the next page; only available after you have gone back in the list of previously visited locations	Channels	Opens the Channels list
		Fullscreen	Displays the Internet Explorer window using the full screen
Stop	Stops loading a page		
Refresh	Refreshes the contents of the current page	Mail	Displays options for working with Mail and News
Home	Opens the home page	Print	Prints the page using current print options
Search	Opens the Search list	Edit	Opens the page in a Web page editor (only if a Web page editor is installed and selected in the Options dialog box)
Favorites	Opens the Favorites list		

Opening a Web Page and Following Links

You can open a Web page quickly and easily using the Address bar. To open a Web page, you select the current address in the Address bar, type the Web address, or URL, for the Web page you want to open, and then press [Enter]. If you change your mind or the Web page takes too long to **download**, to open and display on the screen, you can click the Stop button on the toolbar. If you stop a Web page while it is downloading and the page doesn't completely display, you can click the Refresh button on the toolbar to update the screen. Web pages can be connected to each other through links which you can follow to obtain more information about a topic, as shown in Figure F-6. A link can move you to another location on the same Web page, or it can open a different Web page altogether. To follow a link, simply click the highlighted word, phrase, or graphic (the mouse pointer changes to the hand pointer when it is over a link). ◄━━ John contracted a Web development company to create a Web site for Wired Coffee. He wants to access the new Web site and follow some of the links in order to give feedback to the developer. John knows that the URL for the Web page is http://www.course.com/illustrated/wired/.

Trouble?

If you receive an error message, type one of the URLs listed in Table F-3 in the Address bar instead.

1. **Click anywhere in the Address bar**
   The current address is highlighted and any text you type will replace the current address. If the current address isn't highlighted, select the entire address.

2. **Type http://www.course.com/illustrated/wired/, then press [Enter]**
   Be sure to type the address exactly as it appears. The status bar displays the connection process. After downloading for a few seconds, the Web page appears in the document window.

3. **Locate the link menu, and move the mouse pointer over the link**
   When you move the mouse pointer over a link, the mouse pointer changes to 🖑, as shown in Figure F-7. This indicates that the text or graphic is a link. The address of the link appears in the status bar.

4. **Click the link menu**
   The status indicator animates as the new Web page is accessed and displayed. The Web page called "menu.htm" appears in the document window.

5. **Move the mouse pointer over the Wired Coffee logo (the image in the upper-left corner), then click the graphic link**
   The Web page called "company.htm" appears in the document window. You can click the Back button on the toolbar to quickly return to the previous Web page.

6. **Click the Back button [⇐ Back] on the toolbar**
   The previous Web page appears in the document window. If you want to return to the Web page called company.htm you visited in Step 5, you can click the link Wired Coffee logo again or click the Forward button on the toolbar.

7. **Click the Forward button [⇒ Forward] on the toolbar**
   The next Web page appears in the document window. If you want to go back more than one Web page, you can click the Back button list arrow, then click the Web page you want to display.

8. **Click the Back button list arrow [⇐ Back] on the toolbar, then click Home Page**
   The Web page called "wired_main.htm" appears in the document window. Notice that the link menu color appears in blue (your color might be different) instead of teal. When you have already visited a link, the color of the link changes.

FIGURE F-6: Web pages connected by a hyperlink

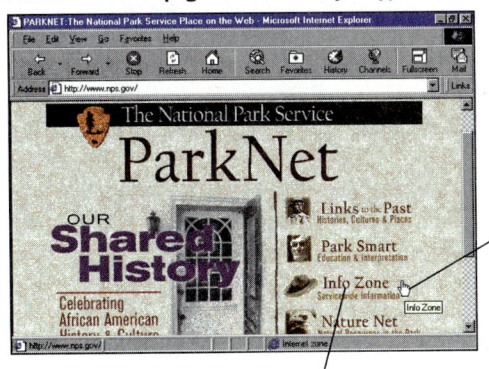 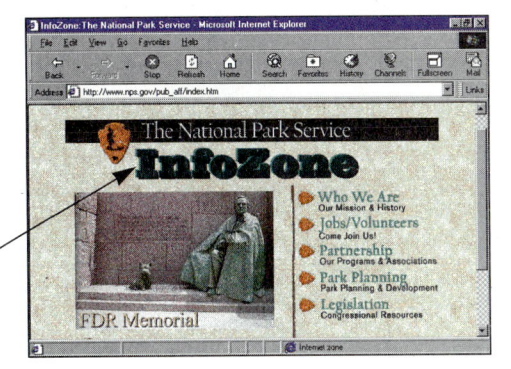

Graphic hyperlink; click to
jump to the InfoZone Web page

FIGURE F-7: Wired Coffee Company Web page

Web page address

Graphic hyperlinks
appear without
any distinguishing
marks

Mouse pointer
changes to a hand
when positioned
over a link

Text hyperlinks
appear in color
with an underline
(your color might
be different)

TABLE F-3: URLs of Web sites dealing with coffee

name of company	url
Peet's Coffee & Tea	http://www.peets.com
Seattle's Best Coffee	http://www.seabest.com
Starbucks Coffee	http://www.starbucks.com

CLUES TO USE

Understanding a Web address

The address for a Web page is referred to as a URL. Each Web page has a unique URL that begins with "http" (HyperText Transfer Protocol) followed by a colon, two slashes, and the name of the Web site. The Web site is the computer where the Web pages are located. At the end of the Web site name, another slash might appear, followed by one or more folders and a filename. For example, in the address, http://www.course.com/illustrated/wired/wired_main.htm, the name of the Web site is *www.course.com*; a folder at that site is called */illustrated/wired*; and within the wired folder is a file called *wired_main.htm*.

Adding a Web Page to the Favorites List

Rather than memorizing the URLs or keeping a handwritten list of Web pages you want to return to, you can use a feature called **Favorites** to store and organize the addresses. Once you add a Web page to the Favorites list, you can return to the page by opening the Favorites folder and selecting the address you want. To add a Web page to your Favorites list, display the Web page in your document window, click Favorites on the menu bar, then click Add to Favorites. You have the option to simply add the Web page to your Favorites list or to subscribe to the page. When you subscribe to a Web page, you are automatically notified when the Web page changes. John decides to subscribe to the Wired Coffee Company Web page so that he will be notified when changes are made to the Web site.

QuickTip

To view Web pages offline, click File on the menu bar, then click Work Offline. If you want to access other Web pages, you'll need to reconnect to the Internet.

1. **Click Favorites on the menu bar, then click Add to Favorites**
   The Add Favorite dialog box opens, as shown in Figure F-8. You can add the page to your Favorites list, you can subscribe to the page, or you can subscribe to the page and download it for offline viewing. When you download a Web page for **offline** viewing, the page is copied to your computer and your Internet connection is disconnected. This is helpful when you want to read a Web page without having to worry about your connect time.

2. **Click the Yes, but only tell me when this page is updated option button**
   The name of the Web page as it will appear in your Favorites list appears in the Name text box at the bottom of the Add Favorite dialog box. To change the Web page name, select the text, and type a new name. John decides to change the name to reflect the entire company name.

3. **In the Name text box, select the current text, type Wired Coffee Company, then click OK**
   The Web page is added to your Favorites list, and the subscription takes effect. When the Web page is changed, you'll be notified.

4. **Click anywhere in the Address bar, type http://www.course.com, then press [Enter]**
   Next you'll visit the Wired Coffee Company Web page using your Favorites list.

Trouble?

URLs can be case-sensitive, meaning that you must type them exactly as they appear, using uppercase and lower-case letters.

5. **Click the Favorites button on the toolbar**
   The Explorer Bar opens on the left side of the document window and displays the Favorites list. The Favorites list contains several folders, including a Channels folder, a Links folder, the Software Updates folder, and individual favorite Web pages.

6. **Click Wired Coffee Company in the Favorites list**
   The Wired Coffee Company Web page appears in the document window, as shown in Figure F-9. The Favorites list also includes folders to help you organize your Favorites list. You can click a folder icon in the Favorites list to display its contents.

7. **Click the Links folder in the Favorites list**
   The Favorites in the Links folder expand and appear in the Explorer Bar, as shown in Figure F-10. To open a Favorite in the Links folder, position the mouse pointer over the Favorite you want to open (the mouse pointer changes to a hand and the Favorite appears underlined), then click the mouse button.

8. **Click the Links folder in the Favorites list again**
   The Favorites in the Links folder collapse to display only the Links folder icon. If you no longer use a favorite, you can delete it from the Favorites list.

9. **Right-click Wired Coffee Company in the Favorites list, click Delete, click Yes, then click the Close button in the Explorer Bar**
   The Explorer Bar with the Favorites list closes.

FIGURE F-8: Add Favorite dialog box

Subscribe options

Displays the name of the Web page as it will appear in your Favorites list

Click to change how and when you are notified of changes to the Web page

Click to save the current page in another folder

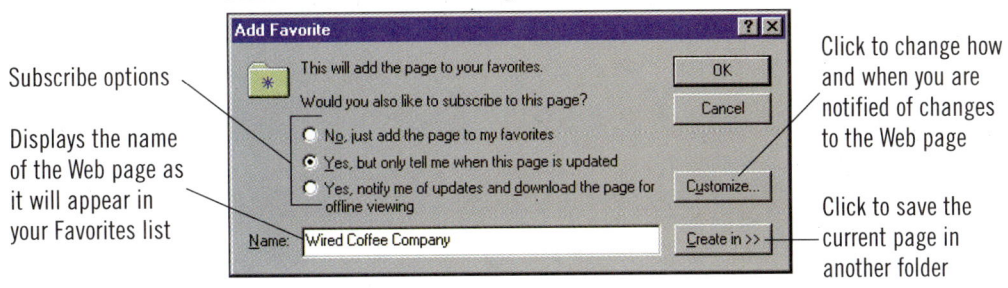

FIGURE F-9: Internet Explorer window with the Favorites list

Click to close Explorer bar

Explorer Bar displaying the Favorites list

Folders to help you organize your Favorites list

Individual Favorite Web pages

Your Favorites list might be different

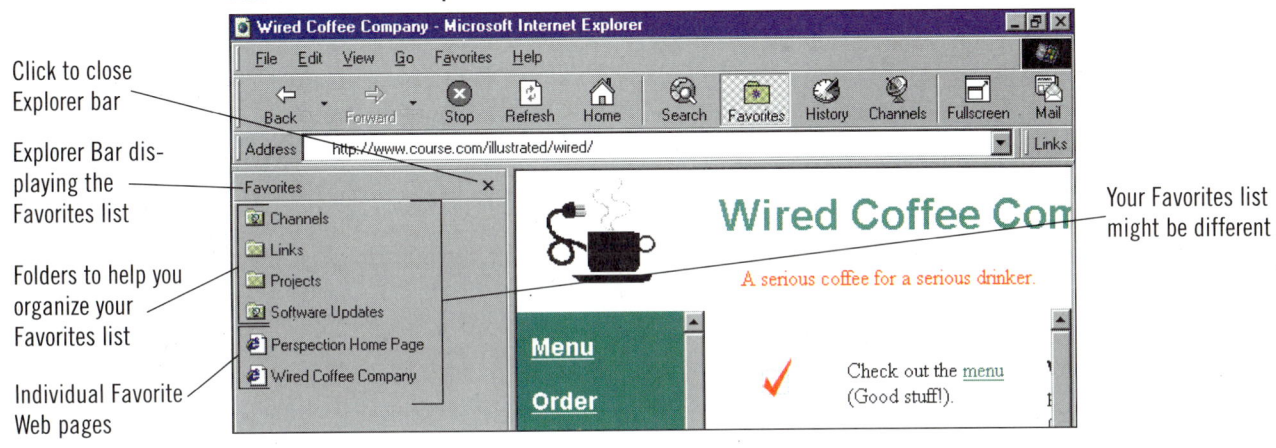

FIGURE F-10: Links folder with Favorites displayed

Click to display or collapse the list of Favorites in the Links folder

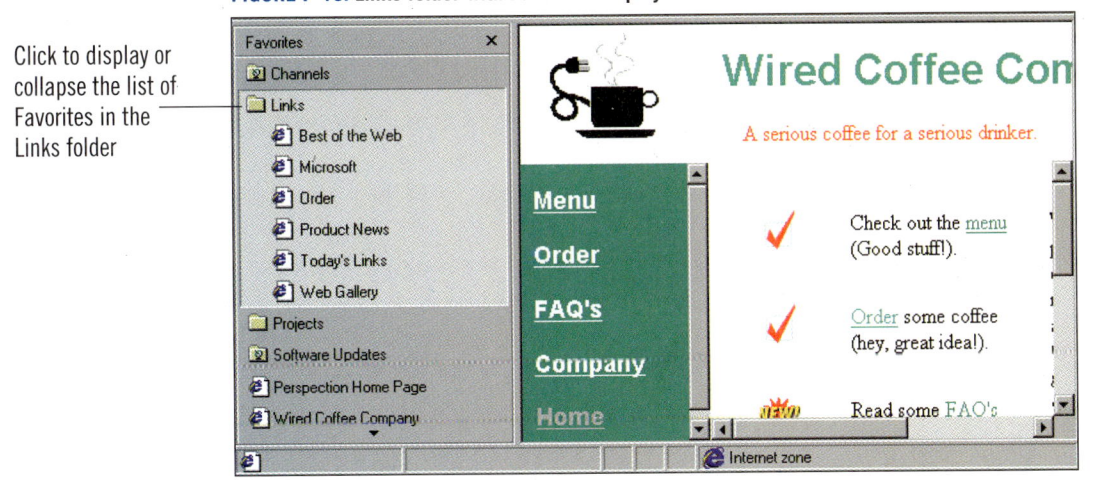

CLUES TO USE

Organizing your favorites

If your list of favorites gets too long, you can delete favorites you don't want anymore or move them into folders. To delete and move your favorites, click Favorites on the menu bar, click Organize Favorites, select one or more files from the Favorites list, then click Delete or Move. If you want to add a new folder to your Favorites list, click the Create New Folder button, type the new folder name, then press [Enter]. If you prefer to use another name for a favorite, you can select the one you want to rename, click Rename, type the new name, then press [Enter]. When you're finished making changes, click Close to exit.

Adding an Active Channel to the Channels List

Active channels are Web sites that deliver information to your computer in a variety of ways: through a Web page, via e-mail, as a screen saver, or directly to your desktop. Unlike cable channels on television, there are no costs involved in subscribing to Internet Explorer channels. There are hundreds of channel partners ready to deliver content to your desktop, including MSNBC, Computer Weekly, Better Homes & Gardens, Disney, and CBS Sportsline, to name a few. To view and subscribe to an active channel, click the Channels button on the Internet Explorer toolbar, click the channel you want to subscribe to, click the Add Active Channel button found on the Web site, then click the subscription option you want or click Customize to select specialized delivery options. ◆ John wants to stay abreast of the latest U.S. government policies. He decides to add the C-Span active channel to his Channels list.

Steps 1234

1. Click the **Channels button** ☐ on the toolbar

   The Explorer Bar opens on the left side of the document window and displays the Channels list. The Channels list contains active channels you can view and subscribe to. To view a channel, click the active channel you want in the Channels list. If you can't find the active channel you want, select the Channel Guide to view a more extensive list of active channels. John decides to view the channel guide to find C-Span.

2. Click **Microsoft active channel guide** in the Channels list

   The Microsoft active channel guide Web page appears in the document window, as shown in Figure F-11. Active channels on the Web continually change, so your active channel Web pages might look different. The Web page can be hard to read in the small window. You can use Internet Explorer's full screen button to view the page using the entire screen.

QuickTip

To hold the Channels list in place, move the mouse pointer to the left edge of the screen to display the Channels list, then click the Pin button ⊞.

3. Click the **Fullscreen button** ☐ on the toolbar

   The Microsoft active channel guide Web page appears using the full screen. The Channels list hides to the left side of the screen in the same way the taskbar hides to the bottom of the screen. To display the Channels list or the taskbar, move the mouse pointer to the left or bottom edge of the screen.

4. Click the **Search button** on the active channel guide Web page

   The Microsoft active channel guide search page appears, as shown in Figure F-12. You can specify a general category or enter a specific type of channel in the Keywords text box, then click the Search button to search for the active channel. John decides to search for the C-Span active channel.

QuickTip

Instead of adding an active channel to the channels list, you can click the Visit Active Channel button to preview the site first.

5. In the Keywords text box, type **C-Span**, then click the **Search button**

6. Click the link **C-Span**, then click **Add Active Channel** ┌Add Active Channel 🔵┐

   The C-Span Web page displays a preview of the active channel. When you click Add Active Channel, the Add Active Channels dialog box opens, asking how you want to add the channel to the Channels list.

7. Click the **Yes, but only tell me when updates occur option button**, then click **OK**

   The C-Span active channel Web page is added to the Channels list.

8. Click the **Fullscreen button** ☐ on the toolbar

   After viewing C-Span for awhile, John decides to remove it from the Channels list.

9. Right-click **C-Span** in the Channels list, click **Delete**, then click **Yes**

   The C-Span active channel is deleted from the Channels list.

10. Click the **Close button** in the Explorer Bar

FIGURE F-11: Explorer Bar with the Channels list

Click to view the channel guide

Your active channel page may differ

Click to scroll the Channels list

Click to view Internet Explorer window in full screen

Click to view the Channels list

Click to go to the active channel guide search page

FIGURE F-12: The active channel guide in full screen

Your active channel page may differ

Toolbar in the full screen window

Enter key words for channels you want ot find here

Click to search for an active channel

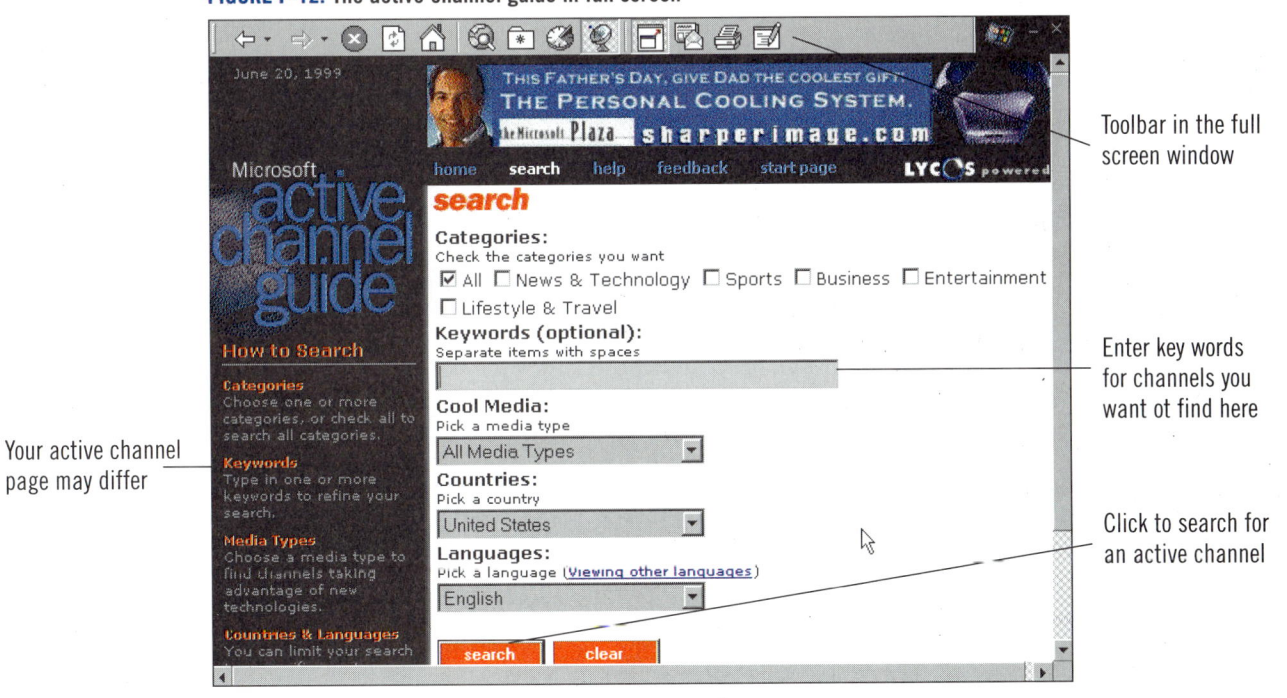

![CLUES TO USE icon]

Managing and updating subscriptions

After you have subscribed to a Web page or an active channel, you can update your subscriptions or change the way the subscription is updated. To quickly update all your subscriptions at once, click Favorites on the menu bar, then click Update All Subscriptions. To update individual subscriptions or change the way

the subscription is updated, click Favorites on the menu bar, then click Manage Subscriptions. Right-click the subscription you want to change, click Properties, click the Subscription or Receiving tab, then make the update changes you want.

98
Windows 98

Selecting a Home Page and Adding a Link Button

A **home page** is the page that opens when you start Internet Explorer. When you first install Internet Explorer, the default home page is the Microsoft Corporation Home Web site. If you want a different page to appear when you start Internet Explorer (and whenever you click the Home button), you can click View on the menu bar, then click Internet Options. You can choose one of the millions of Web pages available through the Internet, or you can select a particular file on your hard drive. You can also change the Web pages associated with the buttons on the Links bar. John decides to change his home page to the Wired Coffee Company Web page and to add a link button to the Links bar.

1. Click the **Back button list arrow** on the toolbar, then click **Home Page**
   John returns to the Wired Coffee Company home page. He wants to select this page as Internet Explorer's home page.

QuickTip

You will change your home page back to http://home.microsoft.com in the Skills Review exercise at the end of this unit. If you want to change it back at any other time, type "http://home.microsoft.com" in the Address bar, press [Enter], then complete Steps 1 through 3 from this lesson.

2. Click **View** on the menu bar, then click **Internet Options**
   The Internet Options dialog box opens, as shown in Figure F-13. The Internet Options dialog box allows you to change a variety of Internet Explorer settings and preferences. See Table F-4 for a description of each tab.

3. Click the **General tab** (if necessary), then click **Use Current**
   The address of the Wired Coffee Company Web page appears in the Address text box.

4. Click **OK**
   The Home button on the toolbar is now associated with the current Web page, Wired Coffee Company. John tests the change using the Home button.

5. Click the link **FAQ's**, then click the **Home button** on the toolbar
   The home page appears in the document window. Now John wants to add a link button.

QuickTip

You can move the Links bar by dragging it to a new location.

6. Double-click the **Links bar** (position the mouse pointer over the word "Links")
   The Links bar opens and hides the Address bar. The Links bar contains buttons with links to Web pages. You can drag a link on a page or a Web site address in the Address bar to a blank area on the Links bar to create a new Links button.

7. Drag the link **Order** to the left of the first button on the Links bar (the mouse pointer changes to a black bar to indicate the placement of the button), then release the mouse button
   A new link button appears on the Links bar labeled with the name associated with the Web site, as shown in Figure F-14. You can delete or change the properties of a link button. Simply right-click the link button you want to change, then click the Delete or Properties command on the shortcut menu.

8. Right-click the **Order button** on the Links bar, click **Delete**, then click **Yes**
   The home page appears in the document window. John closes the Links bar and displays the Address bar.

9. Double-click the **Links bar** to hide it

FIGURE F-13: Internet Options dialog box

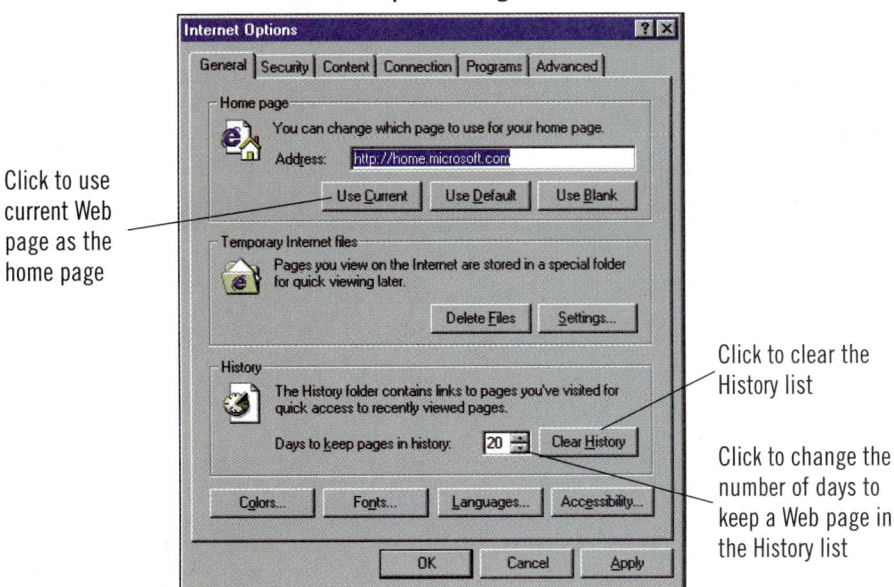

Click to use current Web page as the home page

Click to clear the History list

Click to change the number of days to keep a Web page in the History list

FIGURE F-14: New button on the Links bar

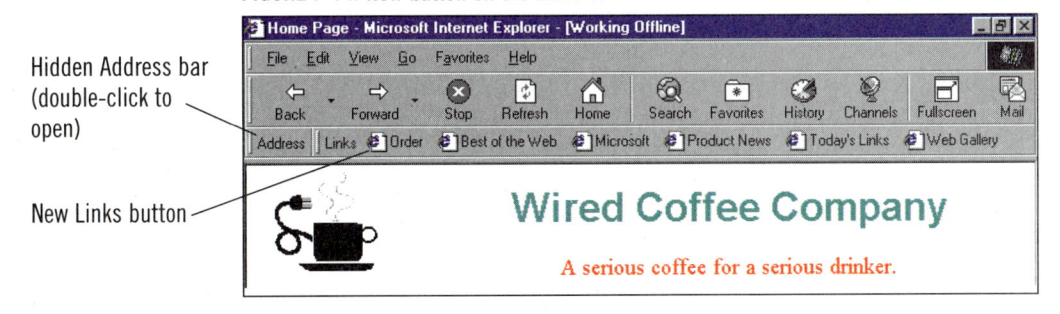

Hidden Address bar (double-click to open)

New Links button

Wired Coffee Company

A serious coffee for a serious drinker.

TABLE F-4: Internet Options dialog box tabs

tab	allows you to
General	Change your home page, temporary file settings, and history settings
Security	Select security levels for different parts of the Internet
Content	Set up a rating system for Internet content and information for buying items over the Internet
Connection	Change connection settings (phone and network)
Programs	Choose which programs (Mail, News, and Internet call) you want to use with Internet Explorer
Advanced	Change individual settings for browsing, multimedia, security, printing, and searching

CLUES TO USE

Viewing and maintaining a History list

Sometimes you run across a great Web site and simply forget to add it to your Favorites list. With Internet Explorer there's no need to try to remember all the sites you've visited. The History feature keeps track of where you've been for days, weeks, or even months at a time. To view the History list, click the History button on the toolbar, then click a day or week in the Explorer Bar to expand the list of Web sites visited. Because the History list can grow to occupy a large amount of space on your hard drive, it's important that you control the length of time Web sites are retained in the list. Internet Explorer will delete the History list periodically based on the settings you specify in the General tab of the Internet Options dialog box, shown in Figure F-13.

Searching the Web

You can find all kinds of information on the Web. The best way to find information is to use a search engine. A **search engine** is a program found on a Web site that allows you to search through a collection of information found on the Internet to find what you are looking for. There are many search engines available on the Web, such as Yahoo! and Excite. When performing a search, the search engine compares the words or phrases, known as **keywords,** you submit with words that have been found on various Web sites on the Internet. If it finds your keywords in the stored database, the matched sites are listed on a Web page (these matched sites are sometimes called **hits**). The company who manages the search engine determines what information is stored in their database, so search results for different search engines will vary. John wants to search for other coffee-related Web sites to check out the competition.

1. **Click the Search button ⊕ on the toolbar**
   A search engine appears in the Explorer Bar. If you prefer another search engine, you can choose the search engine you want using the Choose provider list arrow. John likes to use the search engine Excite.

   Trouble?
   If Excite is not in the list, click List of all search engines, click Excite to add the item to the list, then repeat step 2.

2. **Click the Choose a Search Engine list arrow, then click Excite**
   The Excite search engine appears in the Explorer Bar, as shown in Figure F-15. To search for the information you are looking for, you need to enter keywords, usually the word or phrase that best describes what you want to retrieve, in the search text box. The more specific you are with your search criteria, the better list of matches you'll receive from the search engine. John wants to search for coffee imports on the Internet.

3. **In the search text box, type coffee imports**
   Now John is ready to start the search.

4. **Click Search in the Explorer Bar**
   The search engine retrieves and displays a list of Web sites that match your criteria, as shown in Figure F-16. The total number of Web sites found is listed at the top. The search results appear in decreasing order of relevance. The percentage next to the Web sites found indicates the degree of relevance. If the search results return too many hits, you should narrow the search criteria by adding more keywords. As you add more keywords, the search engine will find fewer Web pages that contain all of those words. See Table F-5 for other techniques to narrow a search.

5. **Click a link to a Web site in the list of matches**
   The Web site that you opened appears in the right pane of the document window. You can follow links to other pages on this Web site or jump to other Web sites. Once you are finished, close the Explorer Bar.

6. **Click the Close button in the Explorer Bar**
   The Explorer Bar closes. John returns to the Wired Coffee Company home page.

7. **Click the Back button list arrow ⇐ on the toolbar, then click Home Page**

CLUES TO USE

Finding people on the Web

Internet Explorer provides several directory services to help you find people who may have access to the Internet (one service, Bigfoot, is shown in Figure F-17). To find a person on the Internet, click the Start button, point to Find, click People, select the directory service you want to use, type the person's name, then click Find Now. Each directory service accesses different databases on the Internet, so if you don't find the person you want using the first service you use, try looking with a different service.

FIGURE F-15: Explorer Bar with a search engine

Click to change search engine

Your search engine might be different

Type search criteria here

Click to retrieve Web site matches

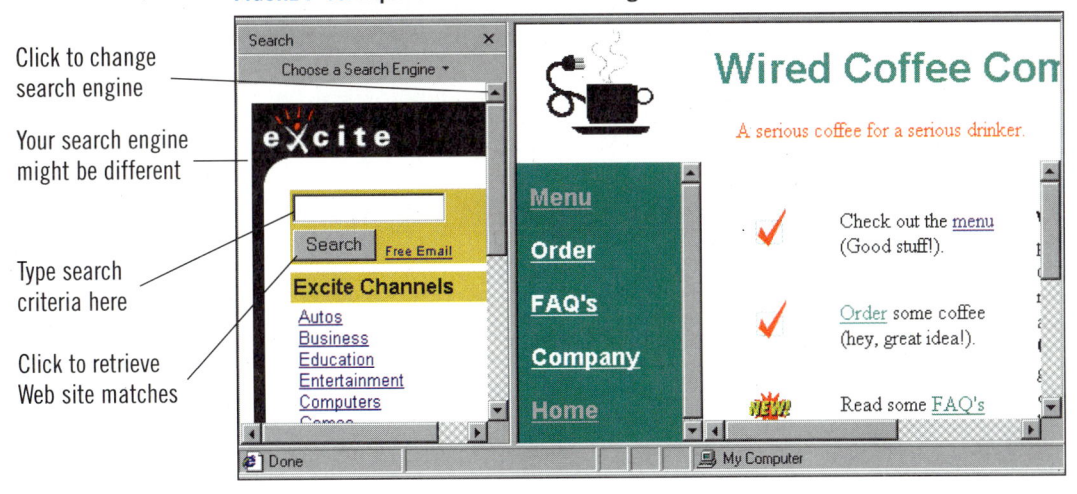

FIGURE F-16: Search engine results

Search results; your list might be different (scroll down to see entire list)

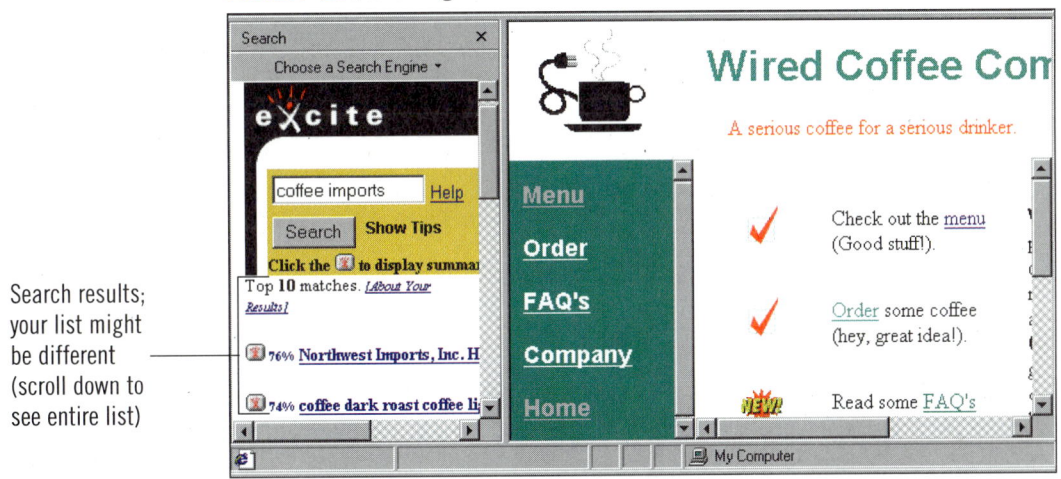

FIGURE F-17: Find People dialog box

Click to choose a different directory service

Enter the name or e-mail address of person you want to find here

Click to open the Web site for the selected directory service

TABLE F-5: Techniques to narrow a search

technique	example
Use descriptive, specific words	beaches surfing Pacific
Use plain English phrases	Surfing beaches on the Pacific ocean
Place exact phrases and proper names in quotation marks	"Sunset Beach"
Use the plus sign (+) for words your results *must* contain	surf + beach
Use the minus sign (−) for words your results should *not* contain	surf + beach − Atlantic
Use AND to find results with all words	surf AND sea AND sand
Use OR to find results with at least one word	surf OR beach

Printing a Web Page

Web pages are designed to be viewed on a computer screen, but you can also print all or part of one. Internet Explorer provides many options for printing Web pages. For Web pages with frames, you can print the page just as you see it, or you can elect to print a particular frame or all frames. You can even use special Page Setup options to include the date, time, or window title on the printed page. You can also choose to print the Web addresses for the links contained in a Web page. To print a Web page, click File on the menu bar, then click Print to open the Print dialog box, then choose the appropriate print options or click the Print button on the toolbar. When you are ready to exit Internet Explorer, click the Close button in the upper-right corner of the Internet Explorer window or click File on the menu bar, then click Exit. There is no need to save before you exit, because you only view documents with Internet Explorer; you do not create or change documents. ✎ John prints a Web page and then exits Internet Explorer.

Steps 1 2 3 4

1. **Click File on the menu bar, then click Print**
   The Print dialog box opens, as shown in Figure F-18. John makes sure the printer he wants to use is selected. Make sure the printer you want to use is connected to your computer.

2. **Click the Name list arrow, then select the printer you want to use**
   When a Web page contains one or more frames, the Print dialog box gives you several options for printing the frames. You can print the Web page as it is laid out on the screen, only the selected frame, or all the frames included in the Web page individually. John decides to print all the frames of the Web page individually.

3. **Click the All frames individually option button**
   Instead of writing down the links included in a Web page, you can also automatically print the Web site addresses for each link. John wants to print the addresses of the links.

4. **Click the Print table of links check box to select the option**
   John is ready to print the frames and a table of the associated links.

5. **Click OK**
   The Web frames and a table of the links print on the selected printer.

6. **Click the Close button in the Internet Explorer window**
   Internet Explorer closes. If you connected to the Internet by telephone, a disconnect dialog box appears. If you are connected to the Internet through a network, follow your instructor's directions to close your connection.

7. **If the disconnect dialog box appears, click Yes**

Trouble?

If the disconnect dialog box doesn't appear, right-click the Connect Icon 🖳 on the right side of the taskbar, then click Disconnect.

FIGURE F-18: Printing a Web page

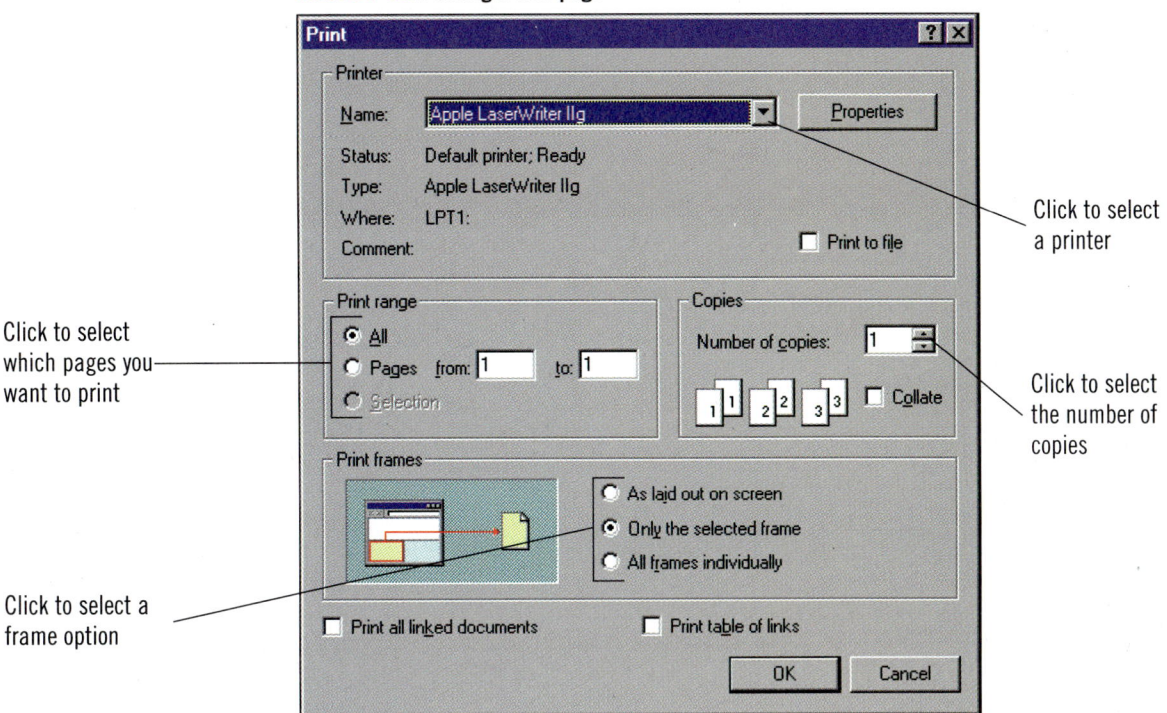

Click to select a printer

Click to select which pages you want to print

Click to select the number of copies

Click to select a frame option

Setting the page format

When you print a Web page, you can use the Page Setup dialog box to control the way text and graphics are printed on a page. The Page Setup dialog box, shown in Figure F-19, specifies the printer properties for page size, orientation, and paper source; in most cases, you won't want to change them. From the Page Setup dialog box, you can also change header and footer information. In the Header and Footer text boxes, you can type text that will appear as a header or footer of the Web page you print. In these text boxes, you can also use variables to substitute for information about the current page, and you can combine text and codes. For example, if you type "Page &p of &P" in the Header text box, the current page number and the total number of pages will be printed at the top of each page. Check Internet Explorer Help for a complete list of header and footer codes.

FIGURE F-19: Page Setup dialog box

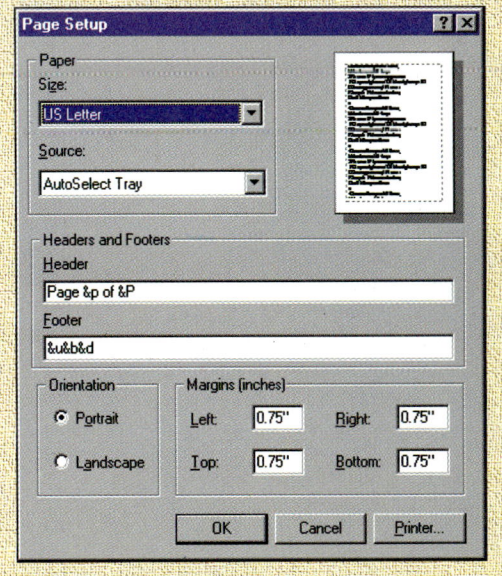

Practice

▶ Concepts Review

Label each of the elements of the screen shown in Figure F-20.

FIGURE F-20

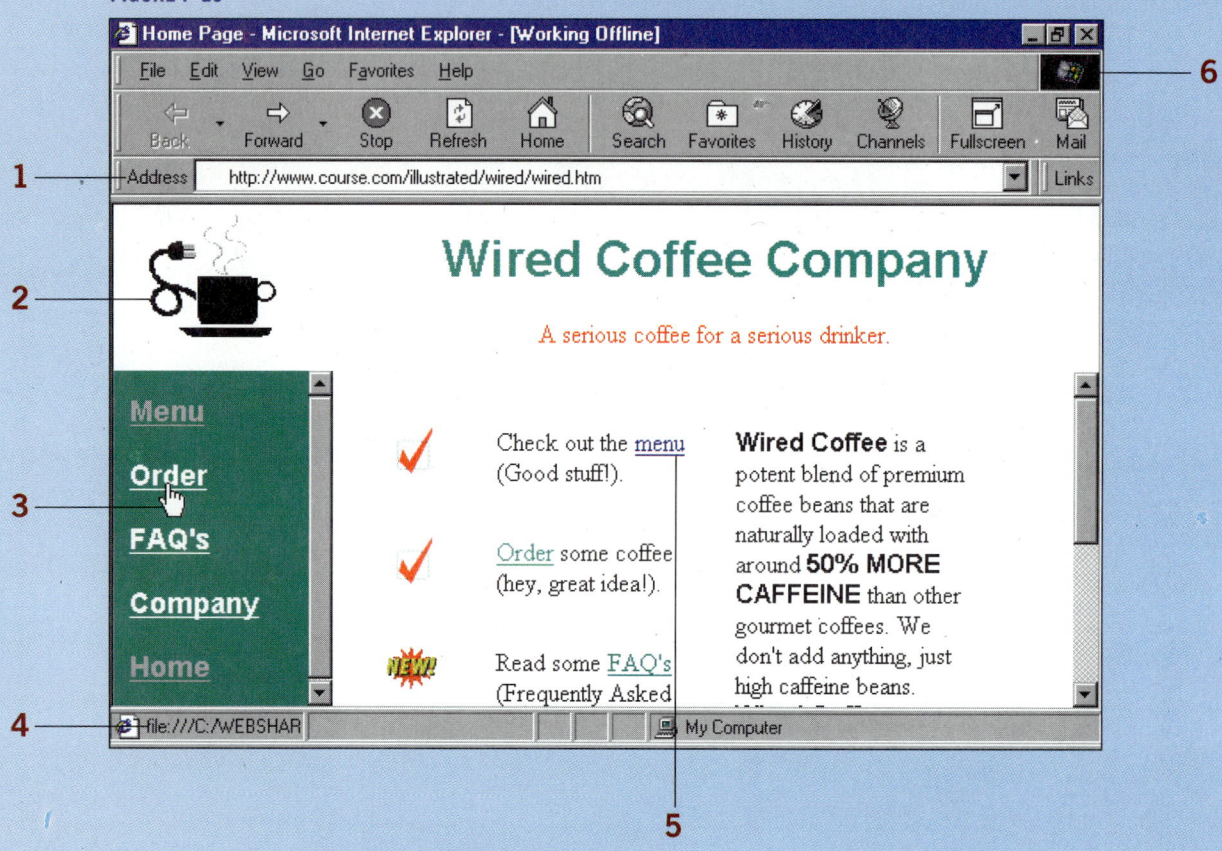

Match each of the terms with the statement that describes its function.

7. Address bar	a. Animates when Internet Explorer is loading a page
8. Toolbar	b. Displays the URL for the current page
9. Favorites button	c. Provides shortcuts for options on the menu bar
10. Status indicator	d. Displays a list of selected Web pages and folders to organize them
11. Back button	e. Displays the previously viewed page

Select the best answer from the following list of choices.

12. Software programs that are used to access and display Web pages are called
   a. Web sites.
   b. Search engines.
   c. Web utilities.
   d. Web browsers.

13. If you want to save the name and URL of a Web page in Internet Explorer and return to it later, you can add it to a list called
    a. Favorites.
    b. Bookmarks.
    c. Home pages.
    d. Preferences.

14. An international telecommunications network that consists of linked documents is called the
    a. NSFNET.
    b. Netscape Communicator.
    c. Internet Explorer.
    d. World Wide Web.

15. In Internet Explorer, where are the buttons located that perform common functions such as moving to a previous Web page?
    a. Address bar
    b. Toolbar
    c. Status bar
    d. Menu bar

16. Which of the following is a valid URL?
    a. http:/www.usf.edu/
    b. http://www.usf.edu/
    c. htp:/ww.usf.edu/
    d. http//www.usf.edu/

17. Underlined words that you click to jump to another Web page are called
    a. Explorers.
    b. Favorites.
    c. Web browsers.
    d. Hyperlinks.

18. The URL of the current Web page is displayed in the
    a. Title bar.
    b. Document window.
    c. Address bar.
    d. Status bar.

 ## Skills Review

1. Start Internet Explorer and explore the browser window.
   a. Connect to the Internet.
   b. Start Internet Explorer.
   c. Identify the toolbar, menu bar, Address bar, Links bar, status bar, status indicator, URL, document window, and scroll bars.
   d. In the toolbar, identify icons for searching, viewing favorites, viewing history, viewing Internet Explorer in full screen, and moving to the previous page.

2. **Open a Web page and follow links.**
   a. Click in the Address bar, then type "http://www.course.com".
   b. Press [Enter].
   c. Explore the Web site by using the scroll bars, toolbar, and hyperlinks.
   d. Click in the Address bar, then type "http://www.sportsline.com/".
   e. Press [Enter].
   f. Follow the links to investigate the content.

3. **Add a Web page to the Favorites list.**
   a. Click in the Address bar, type "http://www.loc.gov/", then press [Enter].
   b. Click Favorites on the menu bar, then click Add to Favorites.
   c. Click OK.
   d. Click the Favorites button.
   e. Click the Home button.
   f. Click Library of Congress Home Page in the Favorites list.
   g. Right-click Library of Congress Home, click Delete, then click Yes.
   h. Click the Close button in the Favorites list.

4. **Add an active channel to the Channels list.**
   a. Click the Channels button.
   b. Click Microsoft active channel guide.
   c. Click the Fullscreen button.
   d. Click the Search button, click the Sports checkbox, then click the Search button.
   e. Click the link ESPN SportsZone, then click Add Active Channel.
   f. Click the Yes, but only tell me when updates occur option button, then click OK.
   g. Click the Fullscreen button.
   h. Right-click the ESPN SportsZone in the Channels list, click Delete, then click Yes.
   i. Click the Close button in the Explorer Bar.

5. **Select a home page and add a link button.**
   a. Click in the Address bar, then type "http://home.microsoft.com/".
   b. Press [Enter].
   c. Click View on the menu bar, then click Internet Options.
   d. Click the General tab.
   e. Click Use Current.
   f. Click OK.
   g. Click the Back button.
   h. Click the Home button.

6. **Search the Web.**
   a. Click the Search button.
   b. Click the Choose a Search Engine list arrow, then click Yahoo.
   c. Enter "job computer training" in the Search text box.
   d. Click Search.
   e. Click a link to a Web site in the list of matches.
   f. Click the Close button in the Explorer Bar.
   g. Click the Home button.

7. Print a Web page and exit Internet Explorer.
   a. Click File on the menu bar, then click Print.
   b. Click the Name list arrow, then select a printer.
   c. Click the Pages option button (use the range 1 to 1).
   d. Click the As laid out on screen option button.
   e. Click OK.
   f. Click the Close button to exit Internet Explorer.
   g. Click Yes to disconnect, if necessary.

▶ Independent Challenges

1. You will soon graduate from college with a degree in business management. Before entering the workforce, you want to make sure that you are up-to-date on all of the advances in the field. You decide that the Web would provide the most current information. In addition, you can look for companies with employment opportunities. Use Internet Explorer to investigate the All Business Network at http://www.all-biz.com/. Follow the links, and when you find a promising site, print the page.

2. You are leaving tomorrow for a business trip in France. You want to make sure that you take the right clothes for the season, and decide that the best place to check France's weather might be the Web. Access one or two of the following weather sites and print at least two reports on the weather in Paris. (*Hint:* Web addresses are case sensitive so be sure to type capital letters where indicated.)

The Weather Channel	http://www.weather.com/
World Weather Guide	http://www.world-travel-net.co.uk./weather/
CNN Weather	http://www.cnn.com/WEATHER/

3. Your boss wants to buy a new desktop computer (as opposed to a laptop). He assigns you the task of investigating the options. You decide that it would be more expedient to look on the Web than to visit the computer stores in the area. Visit the following Web sites, and print a page from the two that you think offer the best deal.

IBM	http://www.ibm.com/
Apple	http://www.apple.com/
Dell	http://www.dell.com/

4. During the summer, you want to travel to national parks in the United States. Use one of the Internet's search engines to find Web sites with maps of the national parks. Visit four or five Web sites from the match list and print a page from the three sites that you think offer the best maps and related information for park visitors.

▶ Visual Workshop

Recreate the screen shown in Figure F-21, which displays the document window with a search engine and a Web site. Print the Web page and print the screen. (To print the screen, press the PrintScreen key to make a copy of the screen, open Paint, click Edit on the menu bar, click Paste to paste the screen into Paint, then click Yes to paste the larger image if necessary. Click File on the menu bar, click Print, then click OK.)

FIGURE F-21

Exchanging
Mail and News

Objectives

► **Start Outlook Express**
► **Explore the Outlook Express window**
► **Add a contact to the Address Book**
► **Compose and send e-mail**
► **Retrieve, read, and respond to e-mail**
► **Manage e-mail messages**
► **Select a news service**
► **View and subscribe to a newsgroup**
► **Read and post news articles**

Windows 98 includes Microsoft Outlook Express, a powerful program for managing electronic mail (known as e-mail). With an Internet connection and Microsoft Outlook Express, you can exchange e-mail messages with anyone on the Internet and join any number of **newsgroups**, collections of e-mail messages on related topics posted by individuals to specified locations on the Internet. If you are not connected to the Internet, you will not be able to work the steps in this unit; however, you can read the lessons without completing the steps to learn what you can accomplish using Outlook Express. In this unit John Casey, owner of Wired Coffee Company, will use Outlook Express to send and receive e-mail messages and join a newsgroup about the coffee industry.

Starting Outlook Express

Outlook Express puts the world of online communication on your desktop. Whether you want to exchange e-mail with colleagues and friends or join newsgroups to trade ideas and information, the tools you need are here. When you install Windows 98, an icon for Outlook Express will automatically appear on the desktop, and a button will appear on the Quick Launch toolbar on the taskbar. If your computer is not connected to the Internet, check with your instructor or technical support person to see if it's possible for you to connect. ✒ John realizes that e-mail is a powerful way to communicate. He wants to use Outlook Express to communicate more effectively with his employees.

Steps 1 2 3 4

1. **If necessary, establish a connection to the Internet via the network or telephone**
   If you connect to the Internet through a network, follow your instructor's directions to establish your connection. If you connect by telephone, use an existing Dial-Up Networking connection, or create a new connection using the Connection Wizard to establish your connection. Once you have established a connection, you can start Outlook Express.

2. **Locate the Outlook Express icon on your desktop**
   The icon should appear on the left side of your screen, as shown in Figure G-1.
   You can also click the Launch Outlook Express button ⬚ on the Quick Launch toolbar to start Outlook Express.

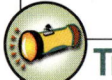

Trouble?

If a Browse For Folder dialog box appears, click OK to accept the default folder where Outlook Express should store your messages, then continue.

3. **Double-click the Outlook Express icon on your desktop**
   The Outlook Express window opens and displays the Outlook Express Start Page, as shown in Figure G-2. Continue with the next lesson to view the various elements of the Outlook Express window.

4. **If necessary, click the Maximize button to maximize the Outlook Express window**
   If you connect to the Internet through a network, follow your instructor's directions to log on. If you connect to the Internet by telephone using a Dial-Up Networking connection, continue with the following steps as necessary.

QuickTip

You can set up Outlook Express to automatically start your Dial-Up Networking connection when the program starts. In Outlook Express, click Tools on the menu bar, click Options, click the Dial Up tab, click the Dial this connection option button, then select a connection from the list box.

5. **If necessary, click the Connect button ⬚ on the toolbar to start your Dial-Up Networking connection**
   The Logon Microsoft Outlook Express dialog box opens. You need to enter your username and password to connect to the Internet. See your instructor or technical support person for this information.

6. **If necessary, enter your user name, press [Tab], enter your password, then click OK**
   A Connection dialog box opens, displaying dial-up connection status information. Upon completion of the dial-up connection, you are connected to the Internet (unless an error message appears).

FIGURE G-1: Windows desktop

Outlook Express icon

Your desktop might be different

Launch Outlook Express button

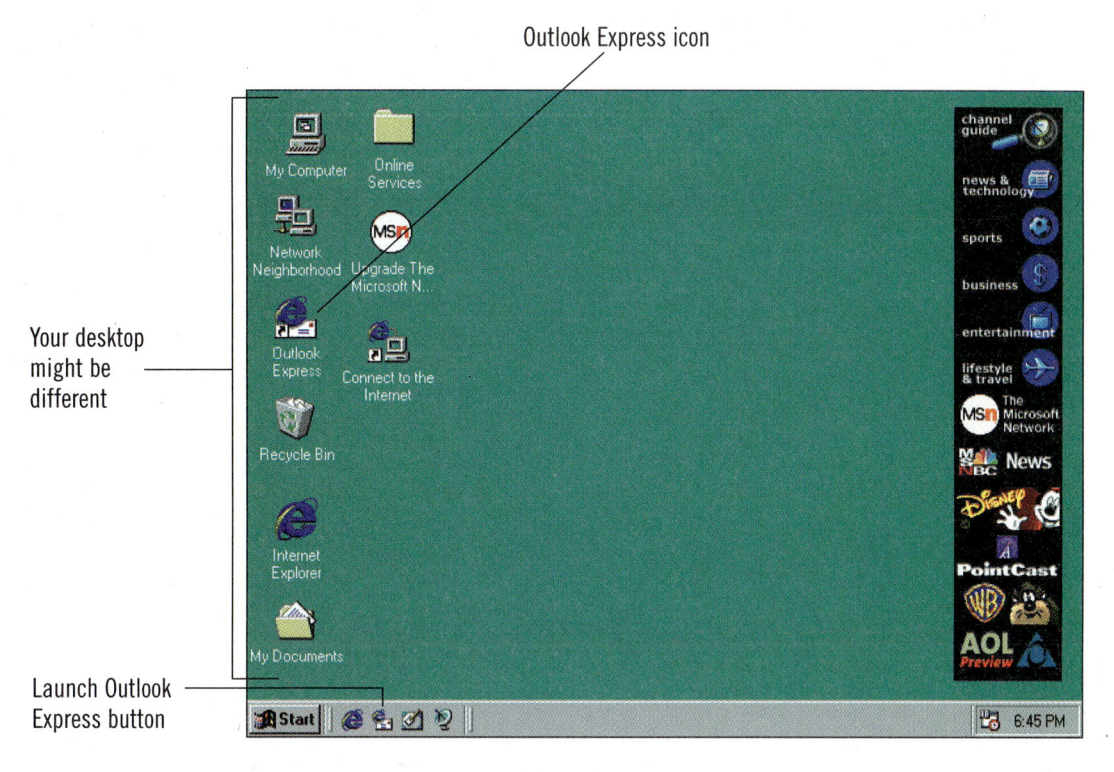

FIGURE G-2: Outlook Express window

Outlook Express Start Page

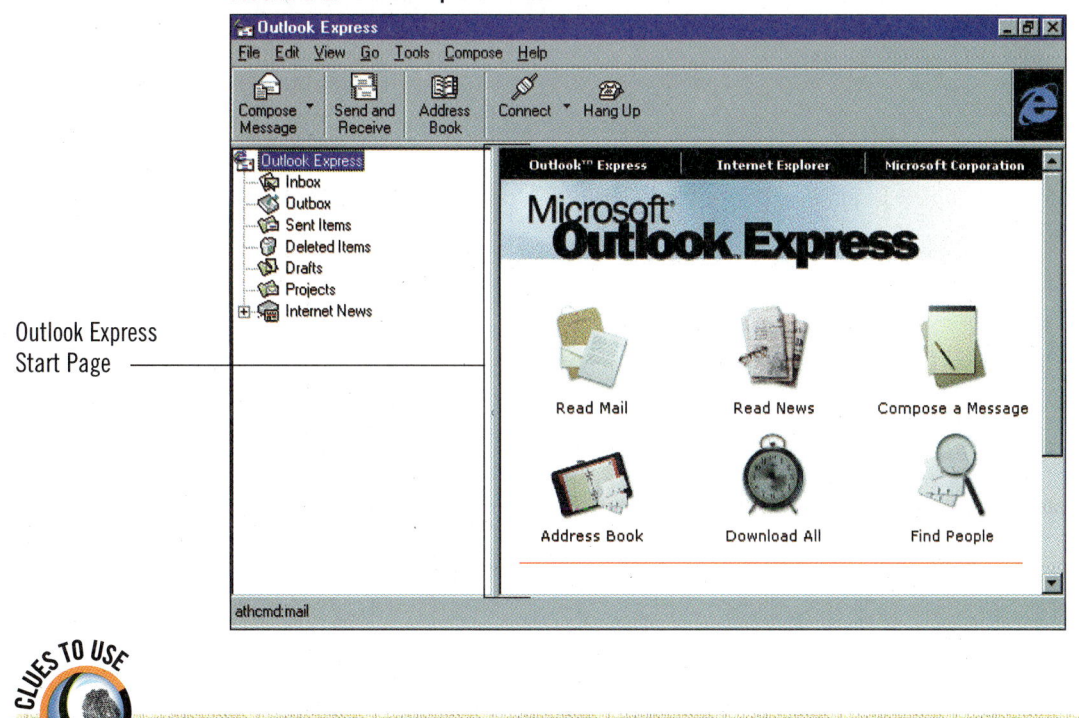

CLUES TO USE

Starting Outlook Express from your Web browser

You can set Outlook Express to be your default e-mail program, so that whenever you click an e-mail link on a Web page or choose the mail command in your Web browser, Outlook Express opens. Likewise, you can set Outlook Express to be your default news reader, so that when you click a newsgroup link on a Web page or choose the news reader command in your Web browser, Outlook Express opens. To set Outlook Express to be your default e-mail or newsgroup program, start Internet Explorer, click Tools on the menu bar, click Options, click the General tab, then select the following check box(es): Make Outlook Express my default e-mail program, or Make Outlook Express my default news reader, or both.

Exploring the Outlook Express Window

After you start Outlook Express, the Outlook Express window displays the Outlook Express Start Page, shown in Figure G-3. The **Outlook Express Start Page** displays tools that you can use to read e-mail, download the latest newsgroup messages, read newsgroup messages, compose e-mail messages, enter and edit Address Book information, and find people on the Internet. Before reading his e-mail, John decides to familiarize himself with the components of the Outlook Express window.

He notes the following features:

 The **title bar** at the top of the window displays the name of the program.

 The **menu bar** provides access to a variety of commands, much like other Windows programs.

 The **toolbar** provides icons, or buttons, for easy access to the most commonly used commands. See Table G-1 for a description of each toolbar button. These button commands are also available on menus.

 The **Internet Explorer link** opens Microsoft Internet Explorer.

 The **folder list** displays folders where Outlook Express stores e-mail messages. You can also use folders to organize your e-mail messages.

 The **Read Mail link** jumps to the Inbox where you can read and reply to incoming e-mail messages.

 The **Read News link** connects to newsgroups that you can view and subscribe to.

 The **Compose a Message link** opens the New Message dialog box where you can compose and send e-mail messages.

 The **Address Book link** opens the Windows Address Book where you can enter and edit your Contact list.

 The **Download All link** downloads all the latest newsgroup messages.

 The **Find People link** opens the Find People dialog box where you can search for people on the Internet or in your Address Book.

 The **status bar** displays information about your Internet connection with a mail or newsgroup server.

FIGURE G-3: Outlook Express window with the Start Page

Title bar

Menu bar

Toolbar

Internet Explorer link

Folder list; your list might be different

Outlook Express Start Page links

Status bar

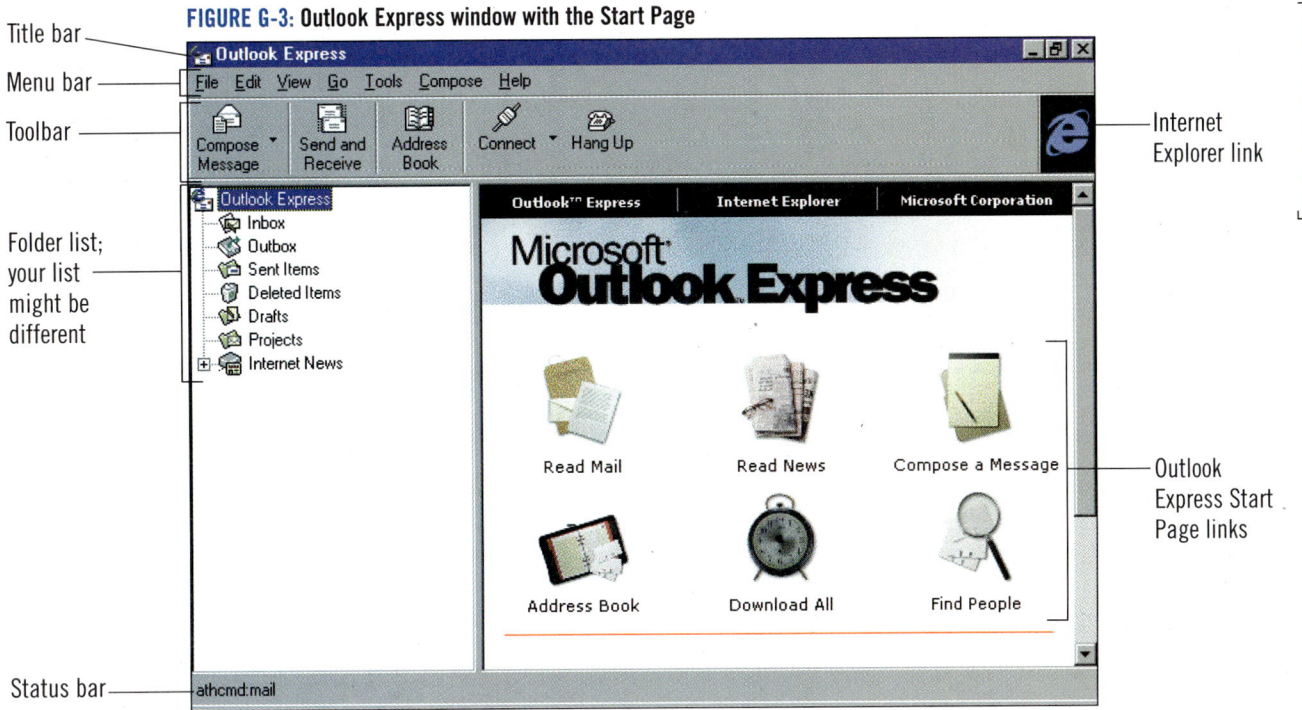

TABLE G-1: Outlook Express Start Page toolbar buttons

button	description
Compose Message	Opens the e-mail message composition window
Send and Receive	Sends e-mail messages and checks for new messages
Address Book	Opens the Address Book
Connect	Connects to the mail or newsgroup server on the Internet
Hang Up	Hangs up the Internet connection

CLUES TO USE

Getting help in Outlook Express

If you need help connecting to the Internet to get mail or learning how to use Outlook Express features, you can get help from several different sources. To get Outlook Express Help, you can use the online Help system that comes with the program or view Outlook Express Web sites on the Internet. To open Outlook Express online Help, click Help on the menu bar, then click Contents and Index. To learn about Outlook Express from Web sites on the Internet, click the Outlook Express link at the top of the Outlook Express Start Page, or click Help on the menu bar, then click Learn About Microsoft Outlook. Internet Explorer starts and displays the Outlook Express Web sites.

Adding a Contact to the Address Book

A **contact** is a person or company that you communicate with. One contact can have several mailing addresses, phone numbers, e-mail addresses, or Web sites. You can store this information in the **Address Book** along with other detailed information, such as the contact's job title, cellular phone number, and personal Web page addresses. When you want to create a new contact or edit an existing one, you use the Properties dialog box to enter or change contact information. You can organize your contacts into **contact groups**, which are groups of related people you communicate with on a regular basis. One contact group might be your family members or people at work. ◢ John wants to add a new employee to his Address Book.

QuickTip

You can also click the Address Book button on the toolbar to open the Address Book.

1. **Click the Address Book link on the Outlook Express Start Page**
   The Address Book window opens, as shown in Figure G-4, displaying the current contacts in the Address Book. Your list of contacts might be different or empty. Above the list of contacts is the Address Book toolbar. See Table G-2 for a description of each toolbar button. These button commands are also available on the menus.

2. **Click the New Contact button on the Address Book toolbar**
   The Properties dialog box opens, displaying the Personal tab with empty text boxes. See Table G-3 for a description of each tab in the Properties dialog box. John types the name and e-mail address for the new employee.

3. **Type Shawn, press [Tab] twice to move to the Last name text box, then type Brooks**
   Now you can enter Shawn's e-mail address.

4. **Click the Add New text box, type shawnbrooks@course.com, then click Add**
   The e-mail address appears in the box below the Add New text box, as shown in Figure G-5. E-mail addresses are not case-sensitive (capitalization doesn't matter) and cannot contain spaces. To modify an e-mail address, select it, then click Edit. To delete an e-mail address no longer in use, select it, then click Remove.

5. **Click OK**
   The Properties dialog box closes and you return to the Address Book. Instead of opening the Properties dialog box every time you want to see a more complete listing of a contact's information, you can position the mouse pointer over a contact in the Address Book to display a ToolTip summary of the contact's information.

6. **Position the mouse pointer over Shawn Brooks in the Address Book**
   A ScreenTip summary appears on the screen. You can move the mouse pointer to remove the ScreenTip or wait. To edit a contact, simply double-click anywhere on the contact entry in the Address Book.

7. **Double-click Shawn Brooks**
   The Shawn Brooks Properties dialog box opens and displays the selected contact's information. You can use any of the tabs in this dialog box to add to or change the contact information. John adds Shawn's business phone number.

8. **Click the Business tab, click the Phone text box, type 925-555-3084, then click OK**
   Shawn's business phone number appears in the Address book. Finished making changes, John closes the Address Book.

9. **Click the Close button in the Address Book window**

FIGURE G-4: Address Book window

Address Book toolbar —

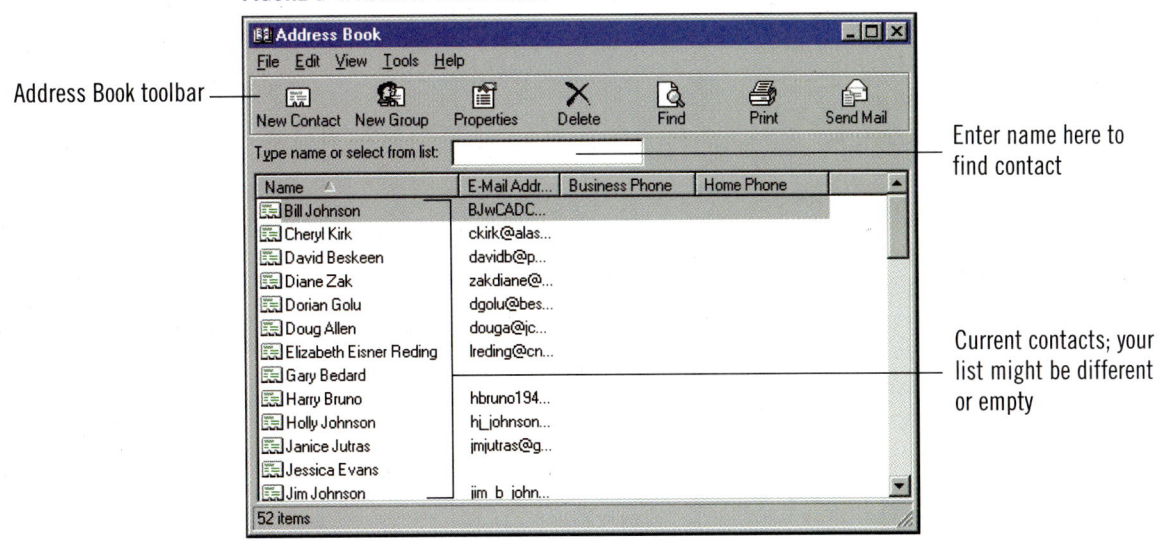

Enter name here to find contact

Current contacts; your list might be different or empty

FIGURE G-5: Properties dialog box with a new contact

Enter e-mail address here

E-mail address added here

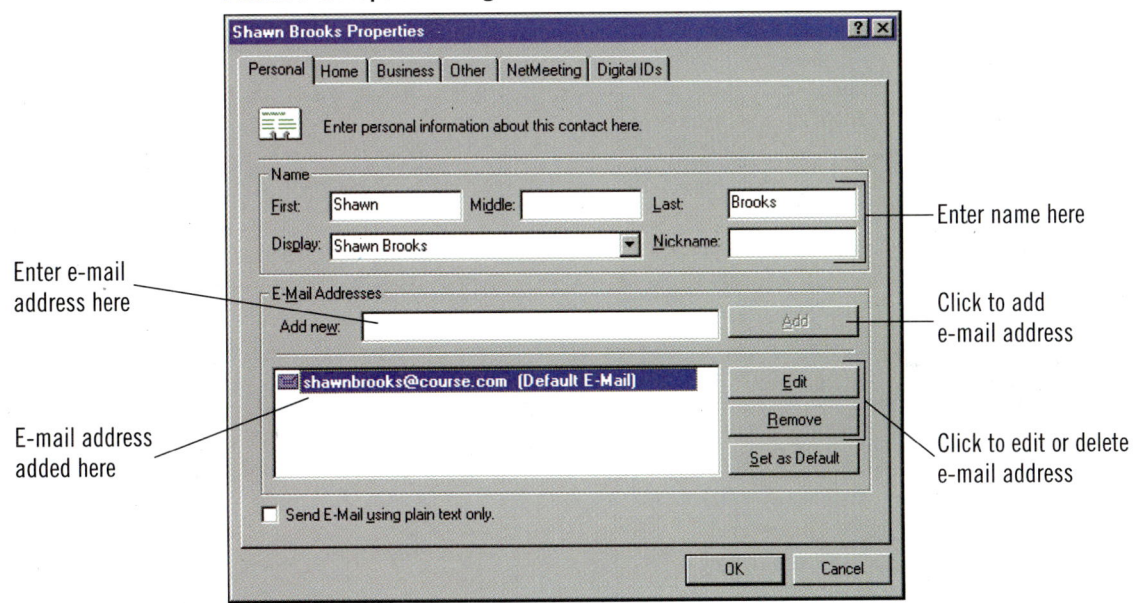

Enter name here

Click to add e-mail address

Click to edit or delete e-mail address

TABLE G-2: Address Book toolbar buttons

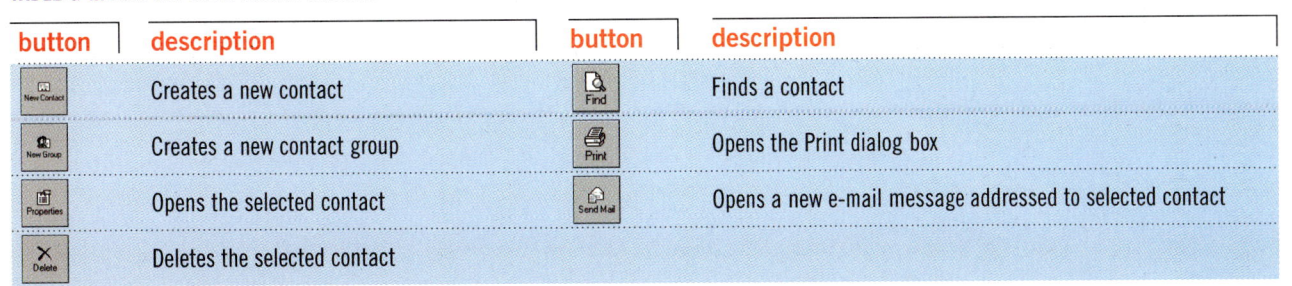

button	description	button	description
New Contact	Creates a new contact	Find	Finds a contact
New Group	Creates a new contact group	Print	Opens the Print dialog box
Properties	Opens the selected contact	Send Mail	Opens a new e-mail message addressed to selected contact
Delete	Deletes the selected contact		

TABLE G-3: New contact Properties dialog box tabs

tab	description	tab	description
Personal	Enter personal information	Other	Enter notes about contact
Home	Enter information related to the contact's home	NetMeeting	Add and modify e-mail conferencing addresses and servers
Business	Enter business related information	Digital IDs	Add, remove, and view security identification numbers for the contact

Composing and Sending E-mail

Windows 98

E-mail is quickly becoming the primary form of written communication for many people. E-mail messages follow a standard memo format with fields for the sender, recipient, date, and subject of the message. To send an e-mail message, you need to enter the recipient's e-mail address, type a subject, and then type the message itself. You can send the same message to more than one individual, or to a contact group, or a combination of individuals and groups. You can personalize your e-mail messages (and newsgroup messages) with built-in stationery, or you can design your own. John wants to send an e-mail message to the new employee whose name he entered into the Address Book in the previous lesson.

Steps 1234

QuickTip

You can also click Compose on the menu bar, then click New Message, or click the Compose a Message link to open the New Message window.

1. Click the **Compose Message button list arrow** on the toolbar, then click **Ivy**
The New Message window opens, as shown in Figure G-6, displaying the Ivy stationery in the message box. You can click the Compose Message button to create a new message without stationery.

2. Click the **Select recipients from a list icon** next to the To text box
The Select Recipients dialog box opens, as shown in Figure G-7, displaying the contacts from the Address Book.

3. In the list of contacts, click the **down scroll arrow** if necessary, then click **Shawn Brooks**

4. Click the **To button**
The contact, Shawn Brooks, appears in the Message recipients list box. You can also add additional recipients to this list, select another recipient and click the Cc (carbon copy) button to send a copy of your e-mail message to that person, or click the Bcc (blind carbon copy) button to send a copy of your e-mail message to another person without displaying the names of the blind copy recipients in the e-mail message.

QuickTip

To remove a name from the Message recipients list, click the person's name in the Message recipients list box, then press [Delete].

5. Click **OK**
Shawn Brooks's name appears in the To text box. Shawn's e-mail address is associated with the name selected even though it is not displayed. John includes a subject title.

6. Click **<click here to enter the subject>**, then type **Welcome aboard!**
The message title bar changes from New Message to the subject text, Welcome aboard! Now you can type your message.

7. Click the text box at the bottom of the message window
The Formatting toolbar, just below the Subject box, is activated. The Formatting toolbar works just like the Formatting toolbar in WordPad or other Windows programs. You can use it to change the format of your message text at any time.

8. Type **Dear Shawn:**, press **[Enter]** twice, type **I would like to welcome you to the Wired Coffee Company. We are excited that you have joined our team. Wired Coffee is a growing company, and I believe your contributions will make a big difference. Please come to a luncheon for new employees this Thursday at 12:30 in the company cafe.**, press **[Enter]** twice, then type **John**

QuickTip

If you don't want to send the e-mail message right now, click File on the menu bar, then click Send Later. The e-mail message is placed in the Outbox but not sent.

9. Click the **Send button** on the toolbar
The New Message window closes, and the e-mail message is placed in the Outbox, a folder where outgoing messages are stored, and then automatically sent to the recipient.

FIGURE G-6: New Message window with Ivy stationery

Click to select a recipient from the Address Book

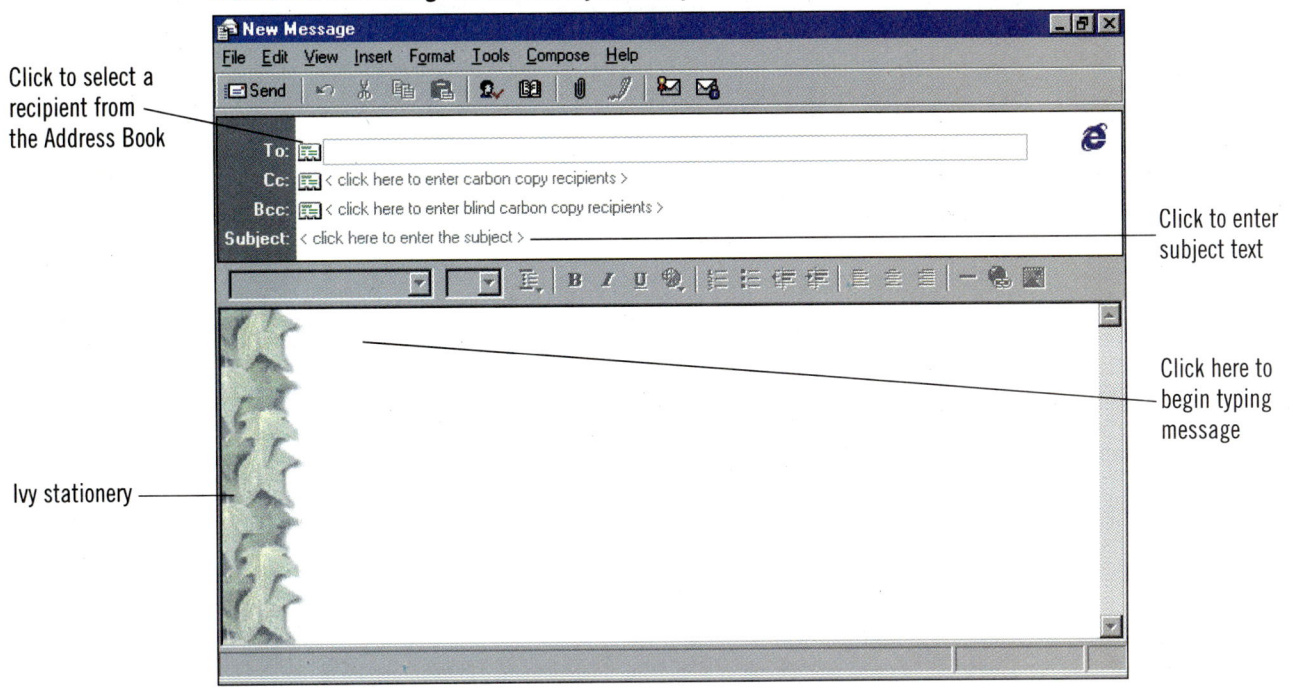

Click to enter subject text

Click here to begin typing message

Ivy stationery

FIGURE G-7: Selecting recipients for an e-mail message

Enter name here to find a recipient, or click the Find button

Select a contact from this list, then click the To button (your list will differ)

Click to add a new contact

Click to choose the selected contact as a recipient for this message

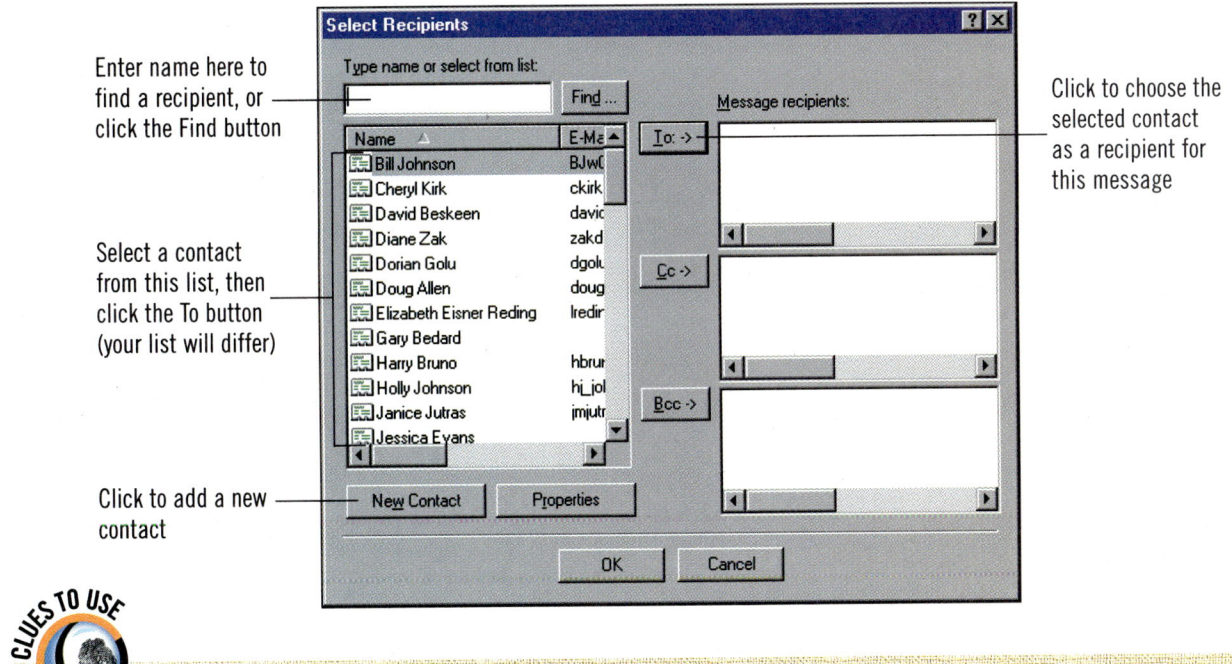

Attaching a file to an e-mail message

In addition to exchanging messages, another powerful feature of e-mail is the ability to easily share files. You can send a file, such as a picture or a document by attaching it to an e-mail message. When the e-mail is received, the recipient can open the file in the program in which it was created. For example, suppose you are working on a report that you created using WordPad and that a colleague working in another part of the country needs to present today. After you finish the report, you can attach the report file to an e-mail message and send the message to your colleague, who can then open, edit, and print the report. To attach a file to an e-mail message, create the message, click the Insert File button 📎 on the toolbar, select the file you want to attach, then click Attach. The attached file appears at the bottom of the message window as an icon that the message recipient can double-click to open the file.

Retrieving, Reading, and Responding to E-mail

To retrieve your e-mail, you can manually connect to the Internet or set Outlook Express to automatically retrieve your messages. New messages appear in the Inbox along with any messages you haven't yet stored elsewhere or deleted. A **message flag** appears next to any message that has a certain priority or a file attached to it and helps you determine the content of a message and its status, or whether or not the message has been read, if it has an attachment, and its priority. See Table G-4 for a description of the message flags. ✎ John forwards an e-mail message he received from Shawn Brooks to another person at the company..

Steps

1. Click the **Send and Receive button** 📧 on the toolbar
   A dialog box displays the progress of the e-mail messages you are sending and receiving. After your e-mail messages have been sent or received, the dialog box closes. When you receive new e-mail, the Inbox folder in the Folder list is bold, indicating that it contains unread messages, and a number in parenthesis indicates the number of new e-mail messages you have received.

2. In the Folder list, click **Inbox**
   The Inbox folder opens as shown in Figure G-8. The **preview pane** displays the messages in your Inbox. The **display pane** displays the e-mail message that is selected in the preview pane. E-mail messages in the preview pane with the subject or heading text in bold are messages that have not been opened.

3. Click the **message** you received from Shawn Brooks
   When a message you receive is short, you can quickly read the message text in the display pane. Longer messages, like the one from Shawn Brooks, are easier to open and read in a full window.

Trouble?

If you didn't receive a message from Shawn Brooks, click the Send and Receive button on the toolbar again. It may take a few minutes for the message to arrive.

4. Double-click the **message** you received from Shawn Brooks in the preview pane, then click the **Maximize button** in the message window
   After reading a message, you can reply to the author, reply to all of the recipients, forward the message to another person, or simply close or delete the message. John forwards the message to his human resources administrator to ask her to add Shawn Brooks to the list of luncheon attendees. You will forward the message to your instructor or to someone else whose e-mail address you know.

5. Click the **Forward Message button** 🔲 on the message toolbar
   The Forward Message window opens, as shown in Figure G-9, displaying the original e-mail message you sent. At the top of the message box, you can add additional text to the message.

Trouble?

If you don't know an e-mail address to send the forwarded message to, click the Close button in the message window, then continue with the next lesson.

6. Click in the upper-left corner of the message box, then type **Please add Shawn Brooks to Thursday's luncheon guest list.**
   Next enter the e-mail address of someone you know who won't mind receiving this message, possibly your instructor.

7. Click **<click here to enter recipients>**, type the e-mail address of your instructor or someone else you know, then click the **Send button** 📧 Send on the toolbar
   The e-mail message is sent. John deletes Shawn from his Address Book.

8. Click the **Address Book button** 📖 on the toolbar, click **Shawn Brooks**, click the **Delete button** ❌, click **Yes**, then click the **Close button**

FIGURE G-8: Outlook Express window with the Inbox

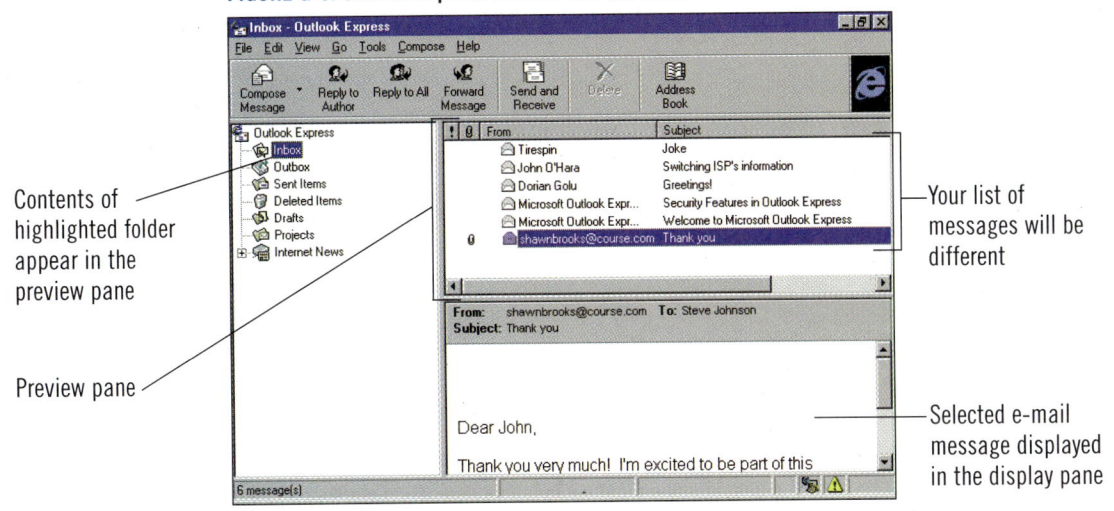

Contents of highlighted folder appear in the preview pane

Preview pane

Your list of messages will be different

Selected e-mail message displayed in the display pane

FIGURE G-9: Forward Message window

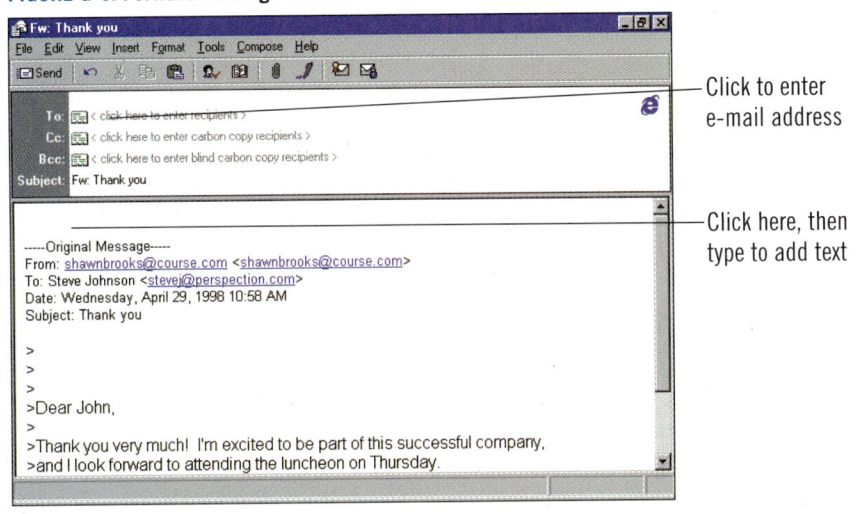

Click to enter e-mail address

Click here, then type to add text

TABLE G-4: Mail message flag icons

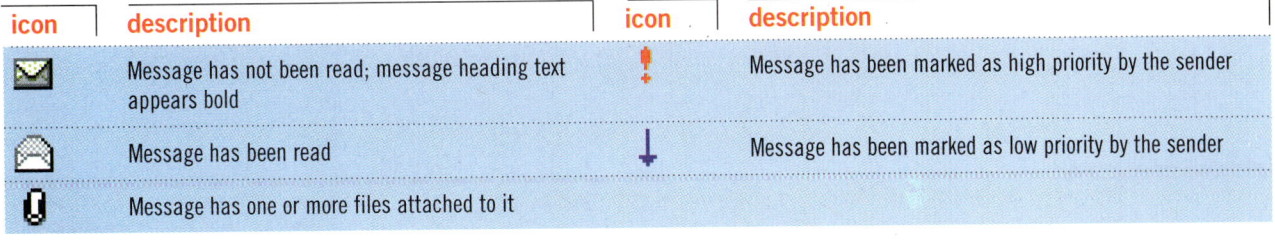

icon	description	icon	description
✉	Message has not been read; message heading text appears bold	!	Message has been marked as high priority by the sender
✉	Message has been read	↓	Message has been marked as low priority by the sender
📎	Message has one or more files attached to it		

Diverting incoming e-mail to folders

Outlook Express can direct incoming messages that meet criteria that you specify to folders you specify, rather than to your Inbox. Let's say that you have a friend who loves sending you funny e-mail, but you often don't have time to read it right away. You can set the Inbox Assistant to store any messages you receive from your friend in a different folder so they won't clutter your Inbox. When you are ready to read the messages, you simply open the folder and access the messages just as you would in the Inbox. To set criteria for incoming messages, click Tools on the menu bar, click Inbox Assistant to open the Inbox Assistant dialog box, click Add to open the Properties dialog box, click the From button, select your friend's e-mail address from the Select Recipients dialog box, click the Move To check box, click Folder, and then select or create a folder where you would like your friend's messages to be stored.

Managing E-mail Messages

A common problem with using e-mail is an overcrowded Inbox. To help you keep your Inbox organized, you should move messages you want to keep to other folders and subfolders, delete messages you no longer want, and create new folders as you need them. Storing incoming messages in other folders and deleting unwanted messages make it easier to see the new messages you receive and to keep track of messages to which you have already responded. John wants to create a new folder for his important messages, move a message from the Inbox to the new folder, and then delete the messages he no longer needs.

Steps

1. Click **File** on the menu bar, point to **Folder**, then click **New Folder**
   The Create Folder dialog box opens, displaying the list of folders contained in the Outlook Express folder, as shown in Figure G-10. John will name the new folder Important.

2. Type **Important**
   Now you need to select where you want to store the new folder. John wants the new Important folder to be in the Outlook Express folder.

3. Click **Outlook Express** at the top of the Folder list
   The new folder will appear in the Folder list under Outlook Express. To create a **subfolder** (a folder in a folder), you would select one of the folders in the Folder list under Outlook Express. The Folder list works like the left pane of Windows Explorer. When a subfolder is created, a plus sign (+) is displayed next to the folder which contains the subfolder.

4. Click **OK**
   The new folder, Important, appears in the Folder list under Outlook Express.

5. In the preview pane of the Inbox, right-click the **message** you received from Shawn Brooks
   A pop-up menu appears, displaying commands, such as move, copy, delete, and print, to help you manage your e-mail messages.

6. Click **Move To** on the pop-up menu
   The Move To dialog box opens, asking you to select the folder where you want the selected message to be stored.

7. Click the **Important folder**, then click **OK**

8. In the Folder list, click the **Important folder**
   The e-mail message you just moved appears in the preview and display panes, as shown in Figure G-11. Next John deletes the Important folder.

9. In the Folder list, right-click the **Important folder**, click **Delete**, then click **Yes**
   The Important folder and all of its contents are deleted.

FIGURE G-10: Create Folder dialog box

Enter new folder name here —

Select the folder in which you want to create a new folder (your list might be different)

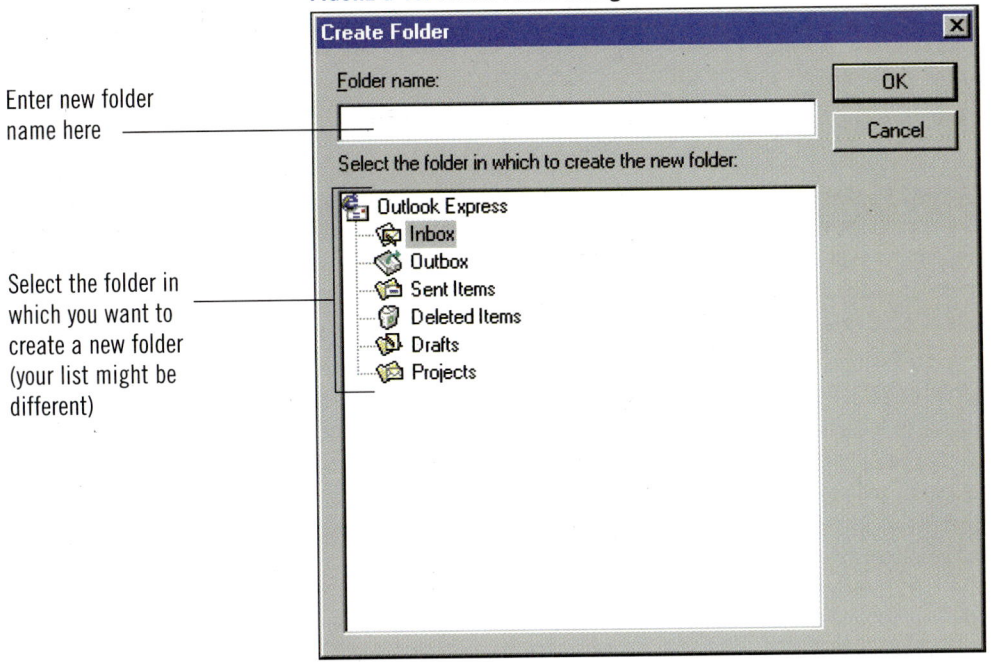

FIGURE G-11: Important folder

Click to display the contents of the folder

Right-click to display a pop-up menu of file management commands

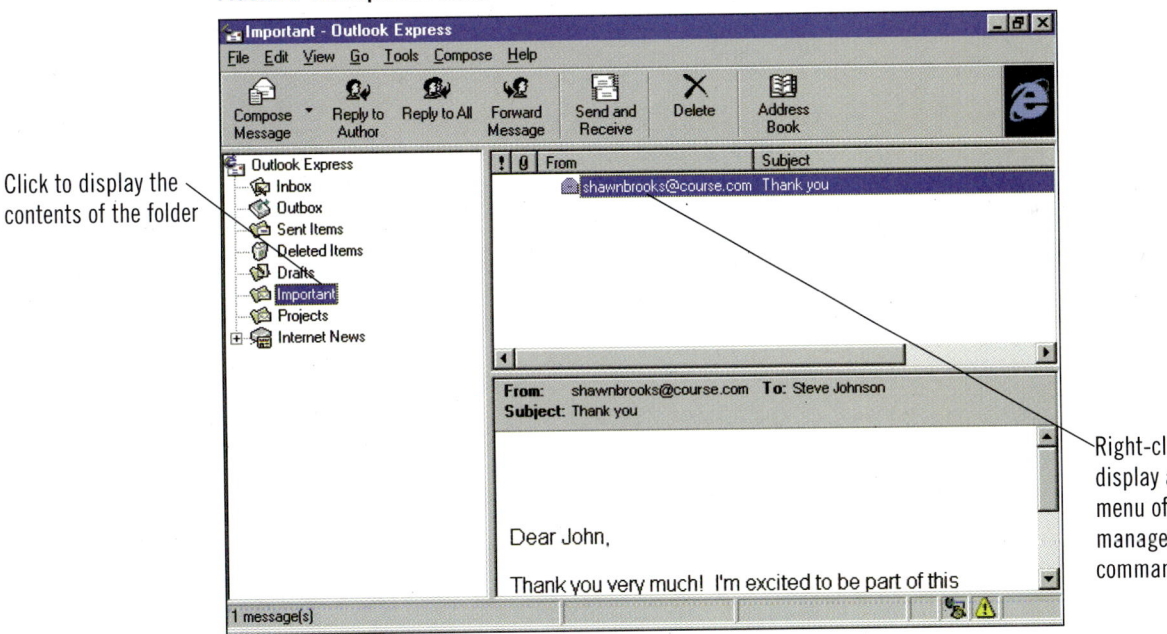

CLUES TO USE

Printing e-mail messages and contacts

You can print your e-mail messages from any folder at any time using Outlook Express. To print an e-mail message, open the message, then click the Print button 🖨 on the toolbar. You can also open the Address Book and print contact information in a variety of formats, such as Memo, Business Card, and Phone List. The Memo style prints all the information you have for a contact with descriptive titles. The Business Card style prints the contact information without descriptive titles. The Phone List style prints all the phone numbers for a contact or for all your contacts. To print contact information, open the Address Book, select a specific contact (if desired), click the Print button 🖨 on the toolbar, then select a print range, print style, and the number of copies you want to print.

Selecting a News Service

A newsgroup is an electronic forum where people from around the world with a common interest can share ideas, ask and answer questions, and comment on and discuss any subject. You can find newsgroups on almost any topic, from the serious to the lighthearted, from educational to controversial, from business to social. Before you can participate in a newsgroup, you must select a news server. A **news server** is a computer located on the Internet where newsgroup messages, called **articles**, on different topics are stored. Each news server contains several newsgroups from which to choose. The Internet Connection Wizard walks you through the process of selecting a news server. This wizard also appears the first time you use Outlook Express News. To complete the wizard and the steps in this lesson, you'll need to get the name of the news server you want to use from your instructor, network administrator, or Internet service provider (ISP), and possibly an account name and password. John wants to add a news server account so he can access coffee-related newsgroups.

Steps 1234

Trouble?

If you do not already have a news server selected, the Internet Connection Wizard will appear, and you should skip to Step 4 to complete the wizard. If you already have a news server, continue with the next step.

1. In the Folder list, click **Outlook Express**, then click the **Read News link**

2. Click **Tools** on the menu bar, then click **Accounts**
   The Internet Accounts dialog box opens, as shown in Figure G-12, displaying the News tab with your list of available news servers. Using the Internet Accounts dialog box, you can add, remove, and view properties for news servers, mail servers, and directory services.

3. Click **Add**, then click **News**
   The Internet Connection Wizard dialog box opens.

4. Type your **name**, then click **Next**
   Individuals participating in the newsgroup need to know your e-mail address so they can reply to your news messages either by posting another news message or by sending you an e-mail message.

5. Type your **e-mail address**, then click **Next**

6. Type the name of the news server provided by your instructor, network administrator, or ISP, as shown in Figure G-13, then click **Next**
   To make it easier to identify, give the news server a more friendly name.

7. Type **General News**, then click **Next**
   You need to select which method you want to use to connect to the Internet. You can connect to the Internet using a phone line or a local area network (LAN), or by establishing a manual connection.

8. Click the appropriate connection type option button, then click **Next**
   Some connection types require additional information. If so, see your instructor or network administrator for instructions, and then click Next to continue.

9. Click **Finish**, click **Close** if necessary, then click **No**
   If the Internet Accounts dialog box is open, you'll need to close it. The news server name appears in the Folder list, as shown in Figure G-14. At this time, you'll click No to view a list of available newsgroups. In the next lesson, you'll view the list.

FIGURE G-12: Internet Accounts dialog box

Click to select server type

Click to add a server

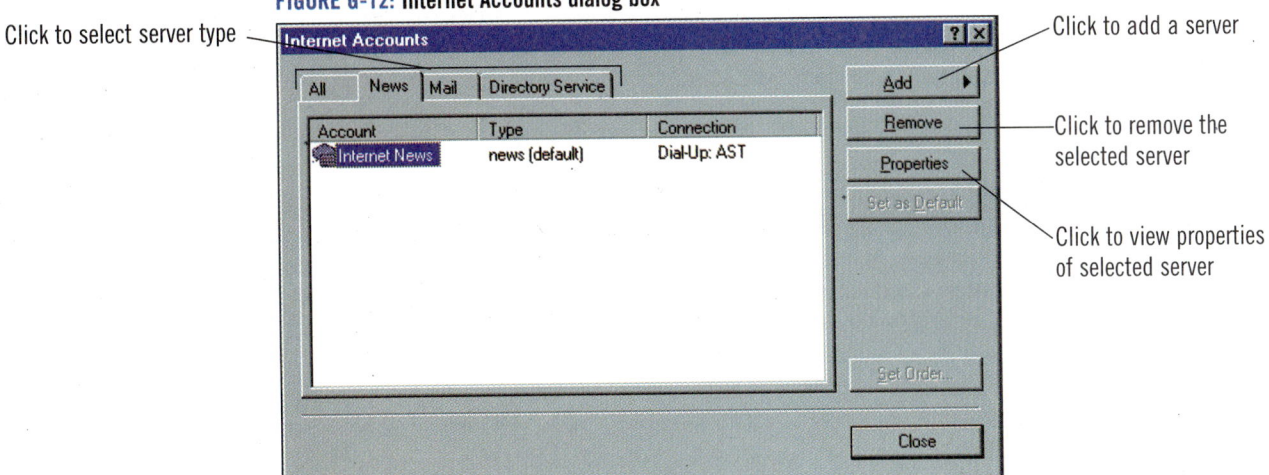

Click to remove the selected server

Click to view properties of selected server

FIGURE G-13: Internet Connection Wizard dialog box

Enter news server name here

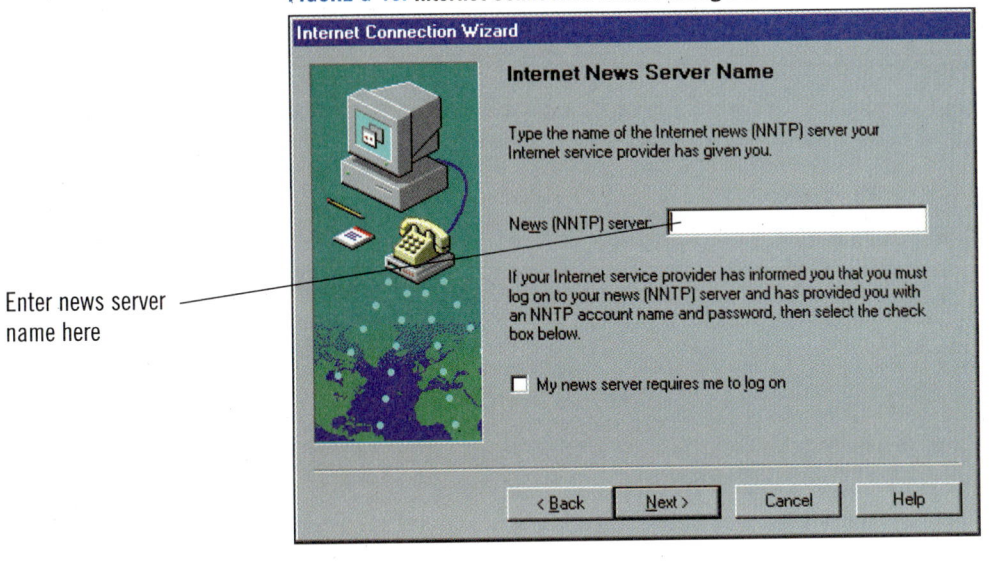

FIGURE G-14: Outlook Express window with news servers

News servers

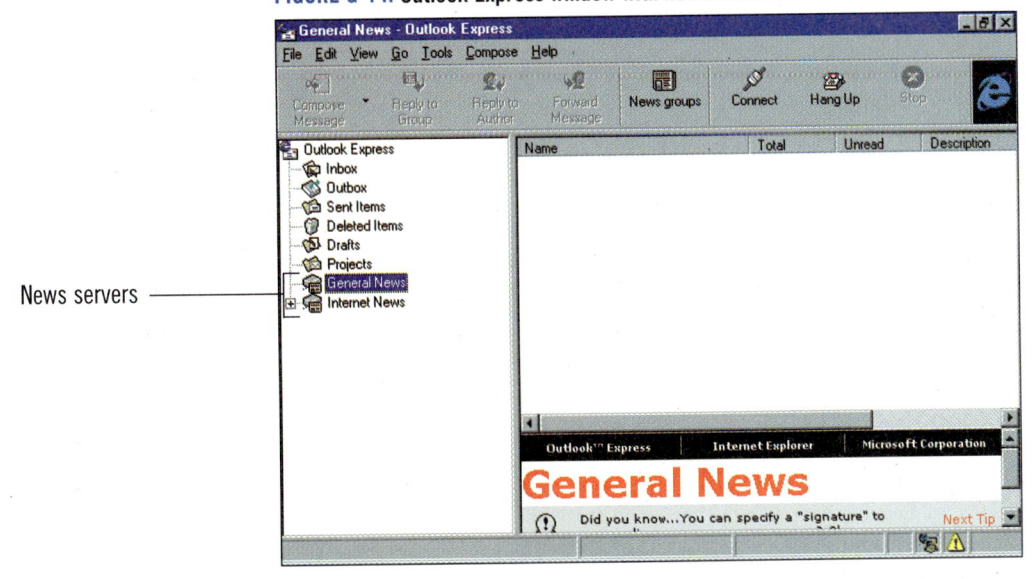

Viewing and Subscribing to a Newsgroup

When you add a news server account to Outlook Express, it retrieves a list of newsgroups available on that server. Often this list is quite lengthy. Rather than scroll through the entire list looking for a particular topic, you can have Outlook Express search the list for that topic. Similarly, you can search a newsgroup for a particular message from all the messages you retrieve from a newsgroup. Once you select a newsgroup, you can merely view its contents, or, if you expect to come back to the newsgroup often, you can subscribe to it. Subscribing to a newsgroup places a link to the group in the news server folder in your Outlook Express Folder list, providing easy access to the newsgroup. John wants to find and subscribe to a newsgroup for coffee drinkers, so he can keep track of what people want from a coffee company.

Trouble?

The news server list on the left in the dialog box will not appear if you have only one news server account.

1. Click the **News groups button** ![icon] on the toolbar
   The Newsgroups dialog box opens, as shown in Figure G-15, displaying news servers on the left (if more than one exists) and related newsgroups on the right.

2. In the News server list, click **General News** (the news server you added in the previous lesson) if available
   A list of the newsgroups you have subscribed to appears in the preview pane. Your list might be empty.

3. Type **coffee** in the text box
   Newsgroups related to coffee appear in the News groups list box.

4. Scroll if necessary, click the newsgroup **rec.food.drink.coffee** (if available), or click a different newsgroup from your list, then click **Go To**
   The newsgroup name you have chosen appears selected in the Folder list and the newsgroup messages appear in the preview pane of the Outlook Express window, as shown in Figure G-16. John thinks this newsgroup looks promising, so he decides to subscribe to it.

QuickTip

To subscribe or unsubscribe to a newsgroup, you can also click the News groups button on the toolbar, select a newsgroup, then click Subscribe or Unsubscribe.

5. Right-click the **newsgroup name** in the Folder list, then click **Subscribe to this newsgroup**
   The number of newsgroup messages appears next to the newsgroup name in the folder list.

CLUES TO USE

Filtering unwanted newsgroup messages

After you become familiar with a newsgroup, you might decide that you don't want to retrieve messages from a particular person, about a specific subject, of a certain length, older than a number of days. This is called **filtering** newsgroup messages. To filter unwanted messages, click Tools on the menu bar, click Newsgroup Filters, click Add, click News, select the newsgroup or new server you want to filter, then set your criteria.

FIGURE G-15: Newsgroup dialog box

Click to
select a news
server

News server
list may not
appear if you
have only one
news server
account

Click to
subscribe to
the selected
newsgroup

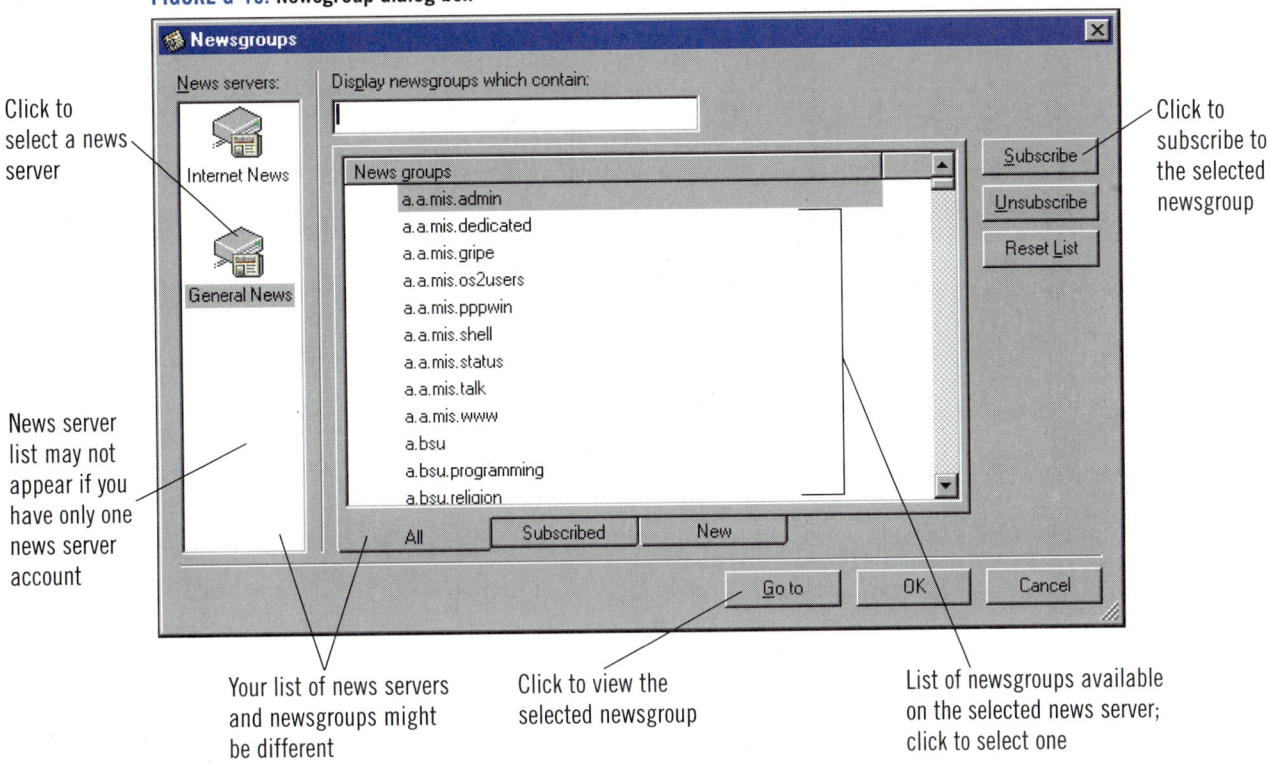

Your list of news servers
and newsgroups might
be different

Click to view the
selected newsgroup

List of newsgroups available
on the selected news server;
click to select one

FIGURE G-16: Outlook Express window with a newsgroup

Newsgroup

Messages
in selected
newsgroup

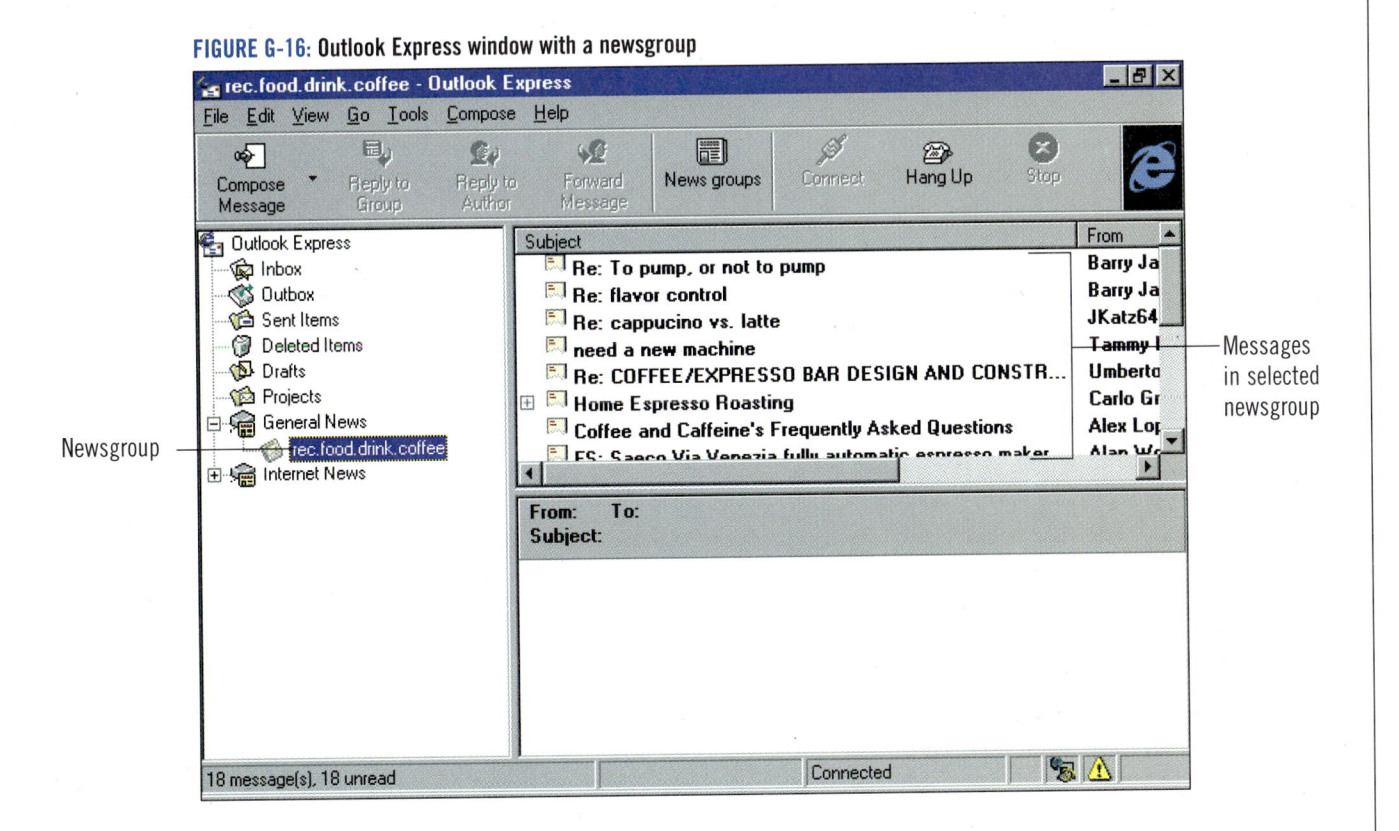

Reading and Posting News Articles

After retrieving new newsgroup messages, you can read them. Newsgroup messages appear in the preview pane, just as e-mail messages do. To view a newsgroup message in the display pane, click the title of the message in the preview pane. If a plus sign (+) in a box appears to the left of a newsgroup message, then the message contains a conversational thread. A **thread** consists of the original message on a particular topic along with any responses that include the original message. To read the responses, click the + to display the message titles, and then click the title of the message you want to read. ✏️ John decides to read some of the messages in the newsgroup.

Steps 1234

Trouble?

If a newsgroup message doesn't have a +, click a message without a +, then skip to Step 3.

1. Click a **newsgroup message** in the preview pane with a + to the left of the title, then read the message in the display pane
   The newsgroup message appears in the display pane.

2. Click the **+** next to the newsgroup message
   The titles of the responses to the original message appear under the original newsgroup message, as shown in Figure G-17.

3. Click each reply message under the original message, and read the reply
   As you read each message, you have the choice to compose a new message, send a reply message to everyone viewing the newsgroup (known as **posting**), send a reply message to the author's private e-mail address (rather than posting it on the newsgroup), or forward the message you are reading to another person. John wants to post a message about the coffee business.

4. After reading the last reply message, click the **Reply To Group button** [Reply to Group] on the toolbar
   John types his reply.

5. Type a response to the newsgroup message
   Once you've entered your response, as shown in Figure G-18, you're ready to post the message to the news server for everyone viewing the newsgroup to download and read.

6. Click the **Post button** [Post] on the toolbar, then click **OK**
   Your reply message appears in the preview pane along with the other replies to the original message. Next John unsubscribes from this newsgroup and removes the news server from the Folder list.

7. Right-click the **newsgroup** in the Folder list, click **Unsubcribe from this newsgroup**, then click **Yes**

8. Right-click **General News** in the Folder list, click **Remove Server**, then click **Yes**

9. Click **File** on the menu bar, click **Exit**, then click **Yes** if necessary to disconnect from the Internet

FIGURE G-17: Reading a newsgroup message

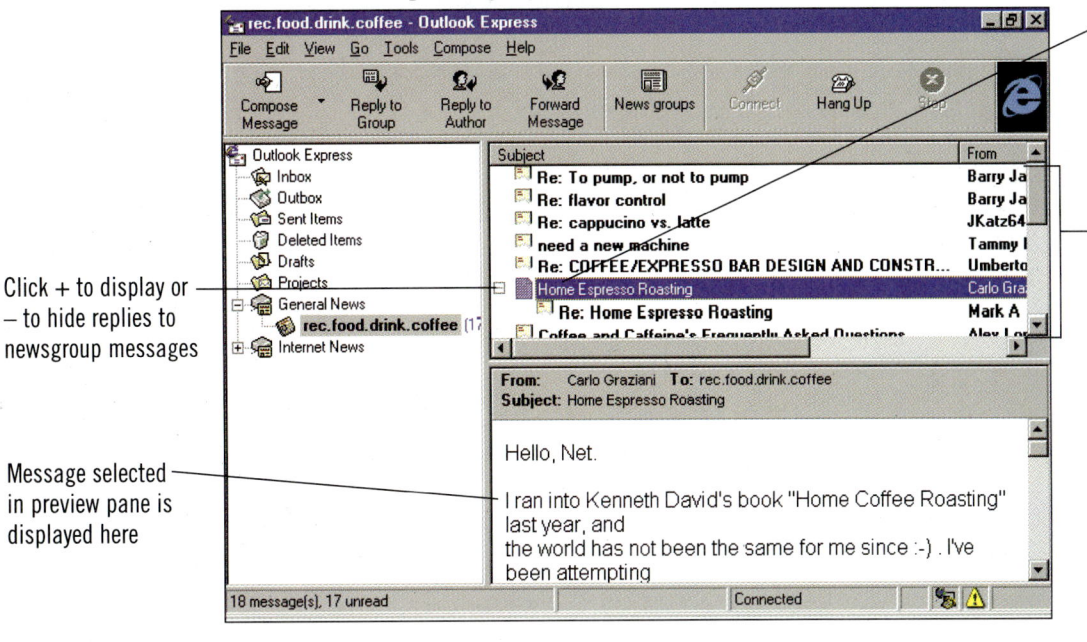

Click a message
to display it in
the display pane

Your list of
messages might
be different

Click + to display or
– to hide replies to
newsgroup messages

Message selected
in preview pane is
displayed here

FIGURE G-18: Posting a newsgroup message

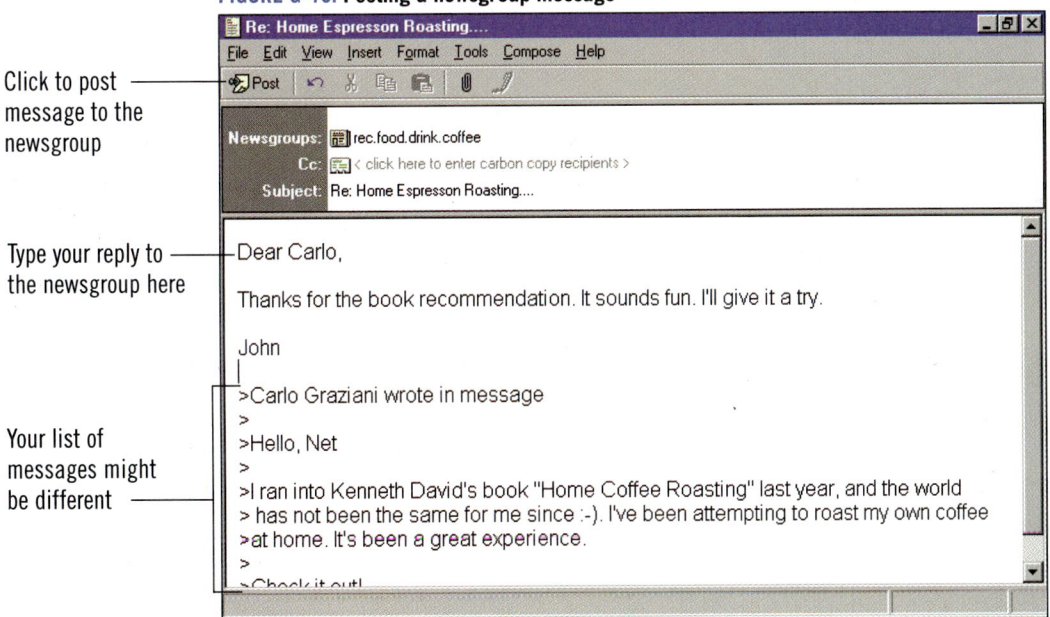

Click to post
message to the
newsgroup

Type your reply to
the newsgroup here

Your list of
messages might
be different

Deleting old news articles

Newsgroup messages are stored on your hard drive. This means you should delete messages you don't need to free up disk space. Outlook Express gives several clean up options to help you optimize your hard drive space. You can delete entire messages (titles and bodies), compress messages, remove just the message bodies (leaving the title headers), or reset the information stored for selected messages, which allows you to re-download messages. To clean up files on your local hard drive, select a news server in the Folder list, click File on the menu bar, click Clean Up Files, select the news server or newsgroup that you want to clean up, click the button for the clean up option you want, then click Close.

Practice

► Concepts Review

Label each of the elements of the screen shown in Figure G-19.

FIGURE G-19

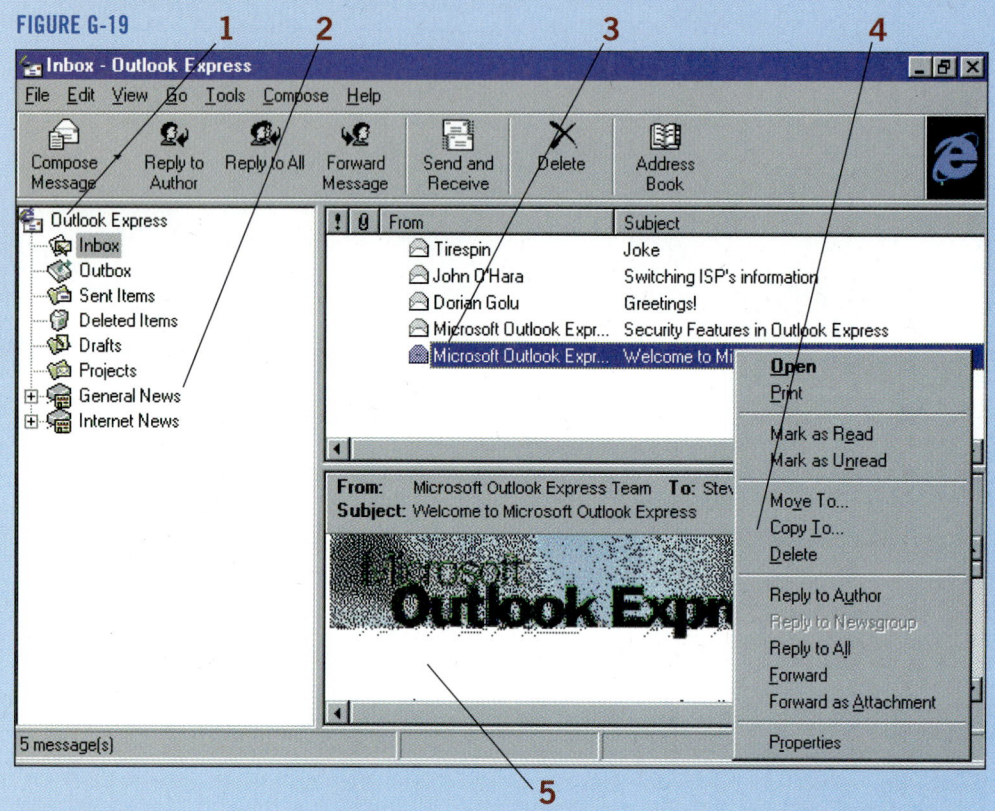

Match each of the terms with the statement that describes its function.

6. **Message flag**
7. **Outlook Express Start Page**
8. **Inbox Assistant**
9. **Outlook Express window**
10. **News server**

a. A computer on the Internet where articles are stored
b. Displays e-mail and newsgroups
c. An icon that indicates e-mail status
d. Diverts selected incoming e-mail to folders
e. Jumps to folders and opens tools

Select the best answer from the following list of choices.

11. The location that allows you to jump to folders and open tools is called
   a. Outlook Express window.
   b. Outlook Express Start Page.
   c. Folder list.
   d. Outlook Express Link Page.

12. To compose a message, you can
   a. Click the Compose a Message link.
   b. Click Compose Message button on the toolbar.
   c. Click Compose on the menu bar, then click New Message.
   d. All of the above.

13. A contact is a
   a. Person you communicate with.
   b. Mailing address.
   c. Newsgroup.
   d. Group you communicate with.

14. When you click the Send button, an e-mail message is sent first to the
   a. E-mail address.
   b. Outbox.
   c. Internet.
   d. Cc and Bcc addresses.

15. ✉ indicates that the message has
    a. Not been read.
    b. Been read.
    c. One or more files attached to it.
    d. Been marked as low priority by sender.

16. Printing styles in the Address Book include
    a. Memo.
    b. Business Card.
    c. Phone List.
    d. All of the above.

17. A location on the Internet where articles are stored is called a
    a. Newsgroup.
    b. News service.
    c. News server.
    d. News article.

18. When you subscribe to a newsgroup, you are
    a. Purchasing newsgroup messages.
    b. Linking to a newsgroup.
    c. Selecting a newsgroup.
    d. Viewing a newsgroup.

▶ Skills Review

1. **Start Outlook Express and explore the window.**
    a. Connect to the Internet.
    b. Double-click the Outlook Express icon.
    c. Identify the title bar, menu bar, toolbar, Internet Explorer link, Folder list, Read Mail link, Read News link, Compose a Message link, Address Book link, Download All link, Find People link, and status bar.
    d. On the toolbar, identify icons for opening the Address Book, sending and receiving e-mail messages, composing a message, connecting to the mail or news server, and hanging up the Internet connection.
    e. If necessary, click the Connect button on the toolbar, enter your username and password, then click OK.

2. **Add a contact to the Address Book.**
    a. Click the Address Book button.
    b. Click the New Contact button.
    c. Type "John", press [Tab] twice, then type "Asher".
    d. Click in the Add New box, type "JohnA@course.com".
    e. Click Add.
    f. Click OK.
    g. Click the Close button.

3. **Compose and send e-mail.**
    a. Click the Compose Message button.
    b. Click the Select recipients from a list icon.
    c. Click "John Asher".
    d. Click the To button.
    e. Click OK.
    f. Click <click here to enter the subject>.
    g. Type "Financial Update Request".
    h. Press [Tab] to move to the message window.
    i. Type "John: Please send 1998 year-end financial report ASAP. Thanks".
    j. Click the Send button.

4. **Retrieve, read, and respond to e-mail.**
    a. Click the Send and Receive button. It may take a few minutes before you receive a message from John Asher.
    b. In the Folder list, click Inbox.
    c. Click the message you just received from John Asher.
    d. Click the Forward Message button.
    e. Click <click here to enter recipients>.
    f. Enter your e-mail address.
    g. Click the Send button.

5. **Manage e-mail messages.**
    a. Click File on the menu bar, point to Folder, then click New Folder.
    b. Type "Archive".

    c. Click Outlook Express in the Folder list.

    d. Click OK.

    e. Right-click the message received from John Asher.

    f. Click Move To on the pop-up menu.

    g. Click Archive, then click OK.

    h. In the Folder list, click the Archive folder.

    i. Right-click the message received from John Asher.

    j. Click Delete on the pop-up menu.

    k. Right-click the Archive folder, click Delete, then click Yes.

    l. Click the Address Book button.

    m. Click John Asher, click the Delete button, then click Yes.

    n. Click the Close button.

6. Select a news server.

    a. In the Folder list, click Outlook Express.

    b. Click Read News link.

    c. If the Internet Connection Wizard appears, skip to Step e. Otherwise, click Tools on the menu bar, then click Accounts.

    d. Click Add, then click News.

    e. Type your name, then click Next.

    f. Type your e-mail address, then click Next.

    g. Type the name of a news server (see your instructor, technical support person, or ISP for a name), then click Next.

    h. Type another name for the news server, then click Next.

    i. Click a connection type option button, then click Next.

    j. Click Finish, click Close (if necessary), then click No.

7. View and subscribe to a newsgroup.

    a. Click the News groups button.

    b. In the News server list, click the news server you just added (if available).

    c. Type "Caffeine".

    d. Click a newsgroup.

    e. Click Go To.

    f. Right-click the newsgroup in the Folder list, then click Subscribe to this newsgroup.

8. Read and post news articles.

    a. Click a newsgroup with a +.

    b. Click the + next to the newsgroup.

    c. Click each reply and read it.

    d. Click the Reply To Group button.

    e. Type a response.

    f. Click the Post button, then click OK.

    g. Right-click the newsgroup in the Folder list.

    h. Click Unsubscribe from this newsgroup on the pop-up menu, then click Yes.

    i. Right-click the news server in the Folder list.

    j. Click Remove Server.

    k. Click Yes.

    l. Click File on the menu bar, then click Exit.

    m. Click Yes if necessary to disconnect.

▶ Independent Challenges

1. You are a new lawyer at Bellig & Associates. You have a computer with Windows 98 and Outlook Express. Since e-mail is an important method of communication at the law firm, you want to start Outlook Express, open the Address Book, and enter colleagues' e-mail addresses.

    To complete this independent challenge:

    1. Start Outlook Express.

    2. Open the Address Book.

3. Enter the following names and e-mail addresses:

Gary Bellig	garyb@bellig_law.com
Greg Bellig	gregb@bellig_law.com
Jacob Bellig	jacobb@bellig_law.com
Jarod Higgins	jarodh@bellig_law.com

4. Print the Address Book in the Business Card and Memo styles.
5. Delete the names and e-mail addresses you just entered in the Address Book.

2. You are the president of Auto Metals, a manufacturing company. You have just negotiated a deal to export metal auto parts to an assembly plant in China. To complete the deal, you need to draw up contracts for each party to sign. Your lawyer is Josh Higgins at Higgins Associates. He has already worked up a preliminary contract. You want to send Josh an e-mail indicating the terms of the deal so he can finish the contract. When Josh responds, move the e-mail into the Legal folder. (*Note:* If you do not have a connection to the Internet, ask your instructor or technical support person for help in completing this challenge.)

To complete this independent challenge:

1. Open a New Message window using the stationery called Technical (*Hint:* Use More Stationery command, then select Technical.htm).
2. Type "jhiggins@course.com" in the To text box in the message window.
3. Type "China Deal Contract" in the Subject text box.
4. Type the following text in the message box:
   Dear Josh,
   I have completed the negotiations for exporting metal auto parts to an assembly plant in China. Please modify the following terms to the contract:
   1. All parts shall be inspected before shipping.
   2. Ship 10,000 units a month for 3 years with an option for 2 more years.
   Sincerely yours,
   [your name here]
5. Send the e-mail.
6. Print the e-mail you receive from Josh Higgins.
7. Create a new folder called "Legal".
8. Move the e-mail message you received from Josh Higgins to the new folder.
9. Delete the Contracts folder.

3. You are a legal assistant at Blazer, Jarvis, and Whitefield, a law firm specializing in international law. You received an e-mail message from your boss asking you to research international contracts with China. You decide to start your research with newsgroups on the Internet.

To complete this independent challenge:

1. Select a news server (see your instructor, technical support person, or ISP to provide you with a news server).
2. Subscribe to a newsgroup about China.
3. Read several newsgroup messages and replies.
4. Reply to a message.
5. Post a new message.
6. Print the newsgroup messages including the original message and replies.

4. You like all types of sports, from hockey to football, from basketball to baseball, from soccer to volleyball. You like to play sports, watch sports, read about sports, and talk about sports all the time, so you join a sports newsgroup.

To complete this independent challenge:

1. Select a news server (see your instructor or network administrator to provide you with a news server).
2. Subscribe to a newsgroup about sports.
3. Read several newsgroup messages and replies.
4. Reply to the message.
5. Post a new message.
6. Print the newsgroup messages including the original message and replies.

► **Visual Workshop**

Re-create the screen shown in Figure G-20, which displays the Outlook Express window with a message that has been sent. Print the Outlook Express window. (To print the screen, press the Print Screen key, open Paint, click File on the menu bar, click Paste to paste the screen into Paint, then click Yes to paste the large image if necessary. Click File on the menu bar, click Print, then click OK.)

FIGURE G-20

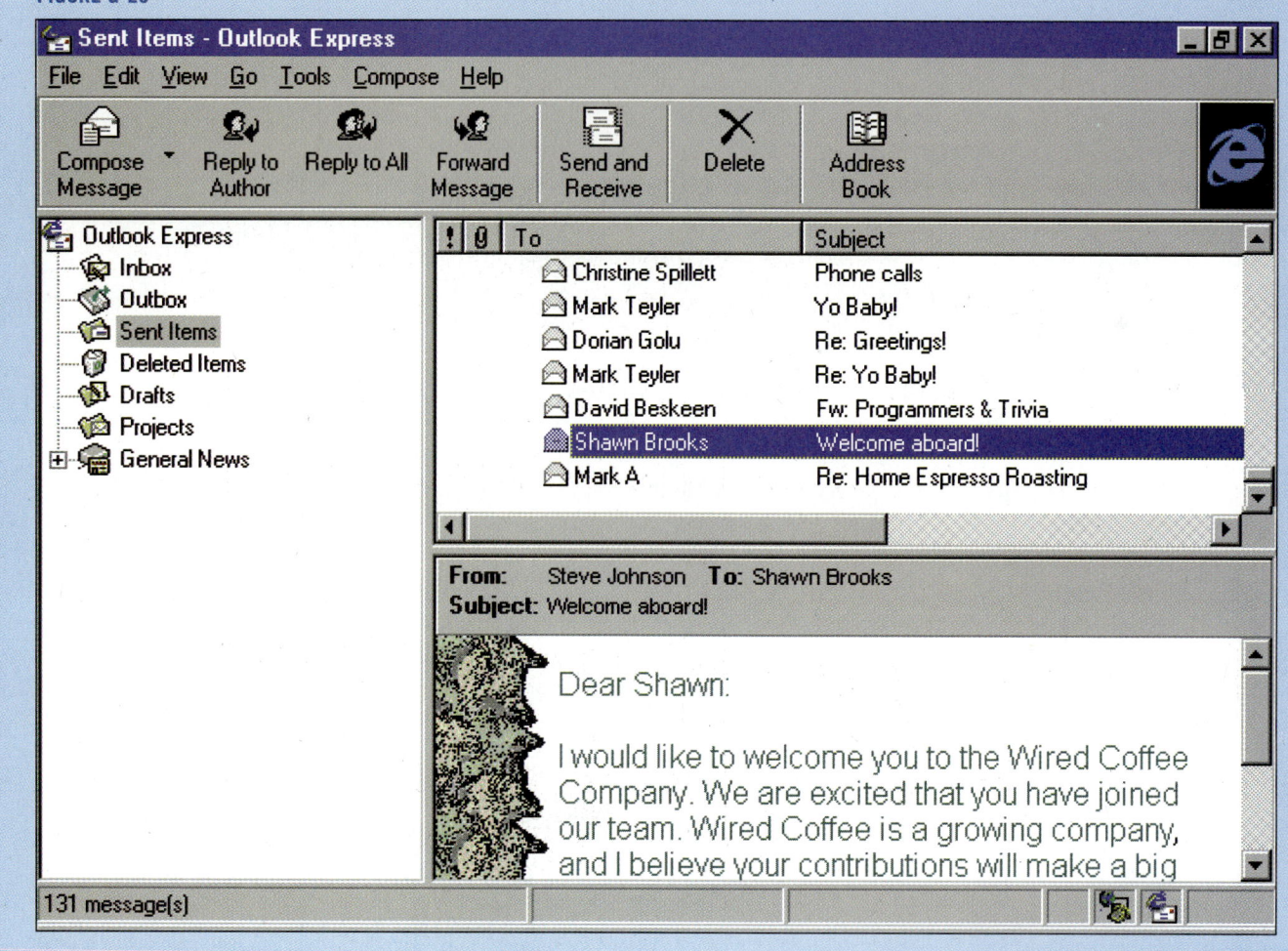

Managing

Shared Files Using Network Neighborhood

Objectives

- ► Understand network services
- ► Open and view Network Neighborhood
- ► Examine network drive properties
- ► Create a shared folder
- ► Map a network drive
- ► Copy and move shared files
- ► Open and edit a shared file
- ► Disconnect a network drive

Windows 98 includes Network Neighborhood, a powerful tool for managing files and folders across a network. A **network** is a system of two or more computers connected together to share resources. **Network Neighborhood** is integrated with Windows Explorer, allowing you to view the entire network and to share files and folders with people from other parts of the network. If you are not connected to a network, you will not be able to work the steps in this unit; however, you can read the lessons without completing the steps to learn what is possible in a network environment. ✎ In this unit John Casey will use Network Neighborhood to manage files and folders that will be used by multiple users on the Wired Coffee Company network.

Windows 98

Understanding Network Services

Windows 98 is a secure, reliable network operating system that allows people using many different computers to share programs, files, and folders that are stored on computers other than their own. A single computer, called a **server**, can be designated to store these resources. Other computers on the network, called **clients**, can access the resources on the server instead of having to store them. You can also share resources using two or more client computers. This sort of configuration is called peer-to-peer networking. Figure H-1 is an example of a typical network configuration. **File sharing** allows many people to work on the same files without the need for creating or storing multiple copies. In this unit you will integrate the essential Windows file management skills you have already acquired with the specific methods required to take full advantage of the Windows networking capabilities. ◀ John realizes there are many benefits to using the Wired Coffee network to manage files and folders.

Share central resources through client/server networking

Windows 98 provides the option of using a setup called **client/server networking**. Under this arrangement, a single computer is designated as a server, allowing access to resources for any qualified user. Client/server networking provides all users on a network a central location for accessing shared files.

Share resources through peer-to-peer networking

The Windows 98 network operating system also offers a network configuration called peer-to-peer networking. **Peer-to-peer networking** enables two or more computers to link together without designating a central server. In this configuration, any computer user can access resources stored on any other computer, as long as those resources aren't restricted. Peer-to-peer networking allows individual computer users to share files and other resources, such as a printer, with other users on the network. Using peer-to-peer networking you can transfer files from one computer directly to another without having to access a server.

Grant permission to share designated files and folders on your machine with other users

Windows 98 provides support for security, so that even though your computer is connected to a network, you can designate which resources on your computer you want to share with others on the network. Before being able to take advantage of any resources on your computer, other users must be granted the required permission.

Map drives on your machine that let you share the resources of another client or server

If you have rights to share resources on another computer, Windows 98 includes a method for connecting automatically to the other computer. You can add a drive letter to your computer that is automatically linked to the shared folder on the other computer every time you log on.

FIGURE H-1: A typical client/server network

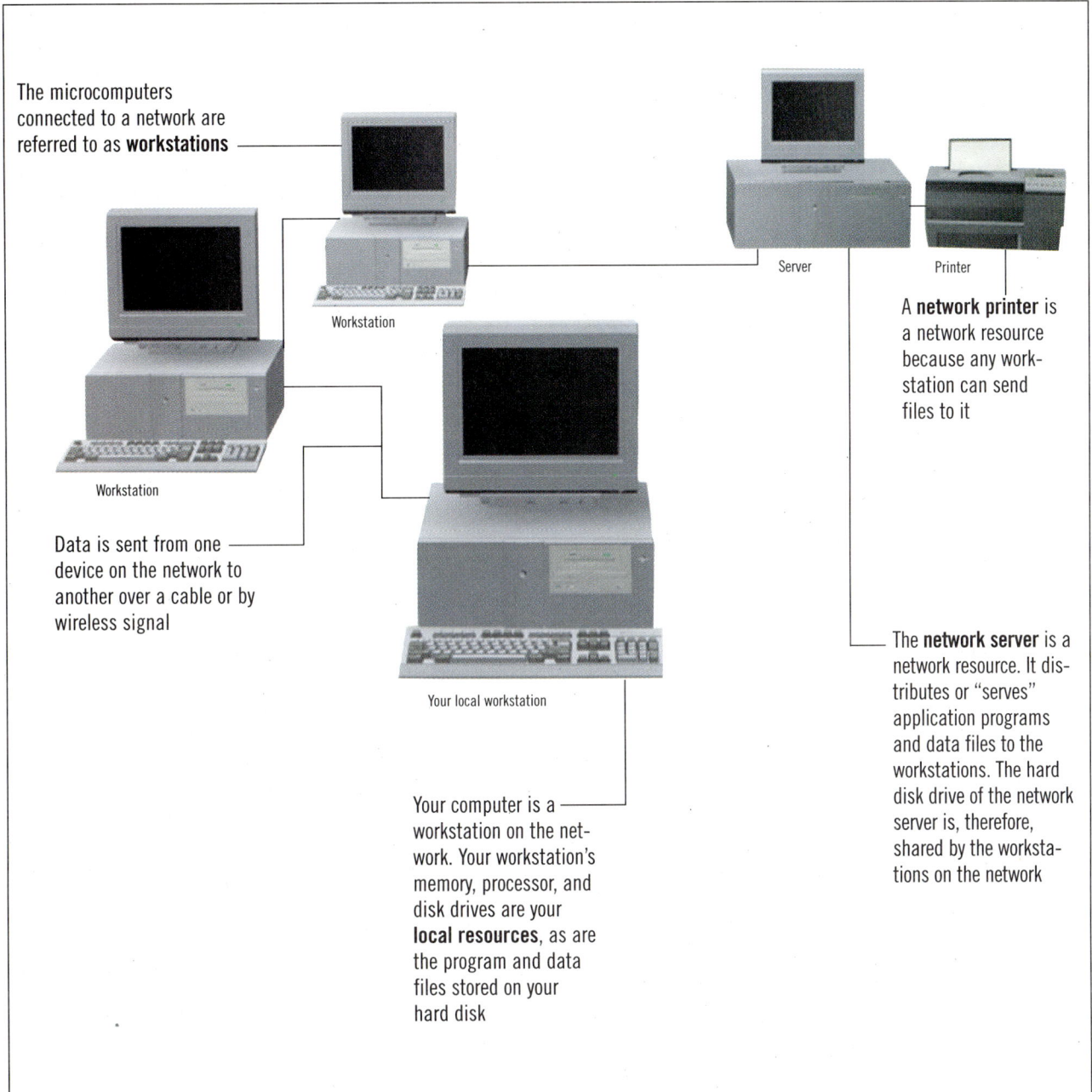

The microcomputers connected to a network are referred to as **workstations**

Workstation

Workstation

Your local workstation

Server

Printer

A **network printer** is a network resource because any work-station can send files to it

Data is sent from one device on the network to another over a cable or by wireless signal

The **network server** is a network resource. It dis-tributes or "serves" application programs and data files to the workstations. The hard disk drive of the network server is, therefore, shared by the worksta-tions on the network

Your computer is a workstation on the net-work. Your workstation's memory, processor, and disk drives are your **local resources**, as are the program and data files stored on your hard disk

File permission properties

Every file in the Windows 98 file system includes **permissions** for each user, or settings that designate what each user can and cannot do to each file. Two basic types of file permissions are available for users: read and full. **Read** permission allows the user to view the file, but not to make changes that can be saved to the file. **Full** permission allows the user to edit and save changes to the file (or "write") and execute programs on server or client computers. Qualified users or system administrators use file permissions to control who has access to any specific area of the network by using passwords. In this way, the network remains secure against unauthorized use.

98
Windows 98

Opening and Viewing Network Neighborhood

The key to managing files and folders in a network environment is understanding the structure of your particular network. Most networks are comprised of multiple types of computers and operating systems. Network Neighborhood lets you view the entire network or just your part of the network at a glance. John uses Network Neighborhood to see where his computer fits in with all the others on his network.

1. **Double-click the Network Neighborhood icon on the desktop, then click the Maximize button in the Network Neighborhood window if necessary**
   The icon is usually located right below the My Computer icon on the desktop. Network Neighborhood opens, as shown in Figure H-2, and displays icons for all of the active computers in John's immediate network (including an icon for his own computer) and an icon for the Entire Network. John's immediate network, also known as the **neighborhood**, is currently running server and client computers.

2. **Double-click the Entire Network icon 🖳 if available (if not, skip to Step 4)**
   Network Neighborhood displays the various segments and computers connected to John's network, as shown in Figure H-3. If you are on a large network, you might have other choices that will display more segments of the network.

3. **Click the Back button ⇦ on the toolbar**
   The Network Neighborhood window again displays the active computers in John's immediate neighborhood. John decides to view the contents of a computer connected to his network.

4. **Double-click a network computer icon 🖳 in your immediate network**
   The computer connected to your network opens and displays the contents of the drive or folder.

5. **Click ⇦ on the toolbar**
   The Network Neighborhood window again displays the active computers in John's immediate neighborhood.

QuickTip

To check the status of your logon credentials and all current connections, right-click the Network Neighborhood icon, click Properties, then click the Identification tab.

CLUES TO USE

Setting up your computer for networking

Before you can use your computer on the network, you need to make sure the file and print sharing option is selected. To set up your computer for networking, right-click the Network Neighborhood icon, click Properties, click File and Print Sharing, click the I want to be able to give others access to my files checkbox, click OK (insert the Windows 98 installation CD if necessary and click Continue), then click OK. Now you can share files on your computer with other users on the network. If you are working in a lab, check with your administrator before setting up your computer for networking.

FIGURE H-2: Network Neighborhood window

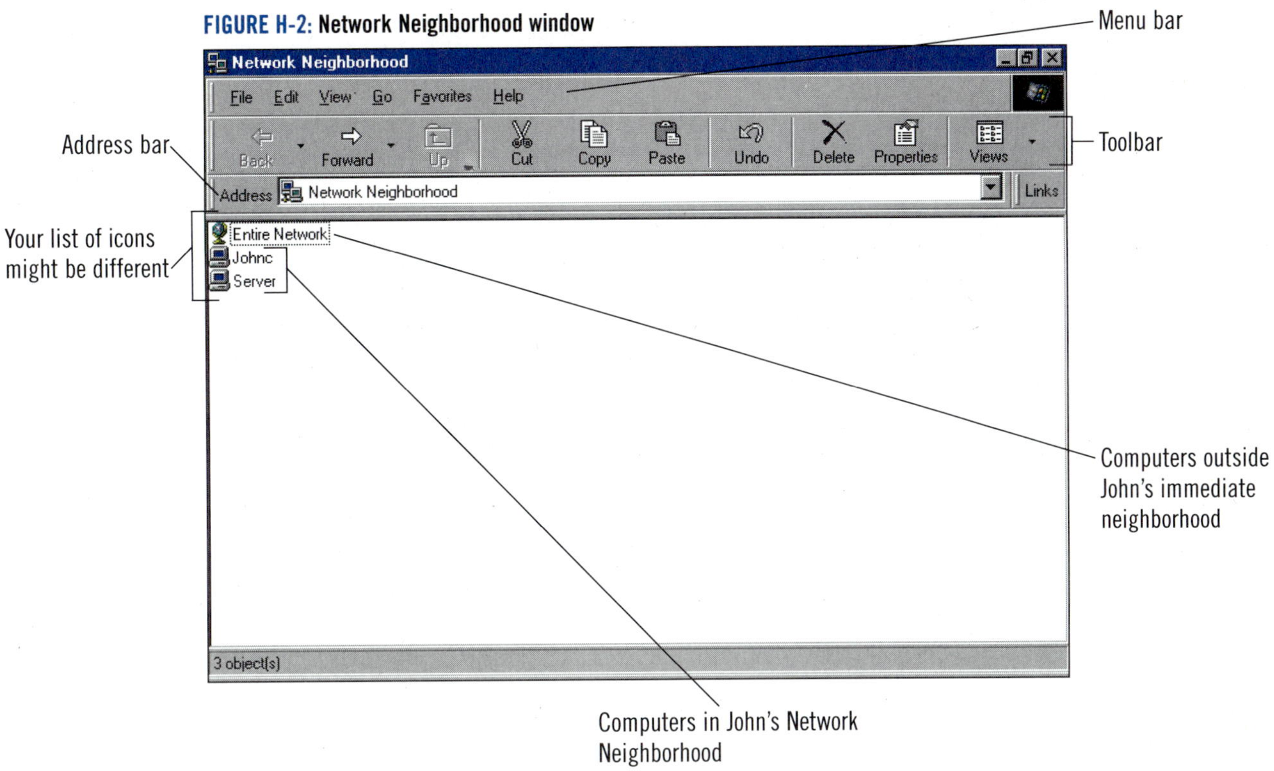

Menu bar

Address bar

Your list of icons
might be different

Toolbar

Computers outside
John's immediate
neighborhood

Computers in John's Network
Neighborhood

FIGURE H-3: Entire Network window

Your list of network components
might be different

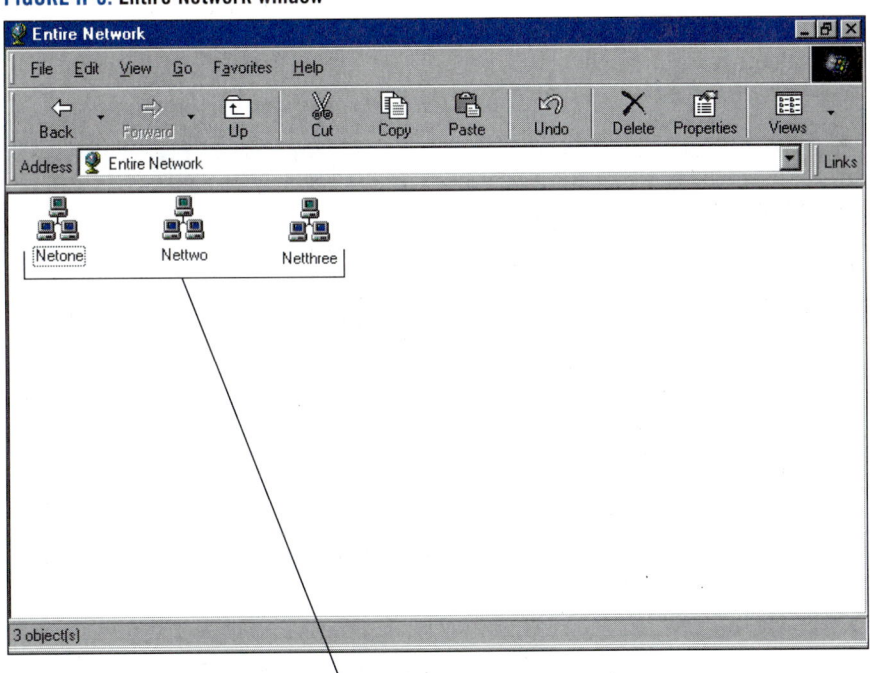

Examining Network Drive Properties

Computers are identified on networks by names and workgroups. The computer's name refers to the individual machine. Individual machines are then organized into larger **workgroups**, which are specific computers that share a lot of information, also given a name. Workgroups are then organized into a larger group of related computer networks called a **domain**. In this way, computers anywhere in the network can be located easily through this naming hierarchy and can be addressed individually by name. You can find out the name, workgroup, and domain of a computer on the network by examining the network computer properties. John decides to check the properties of his network computer.

Steps

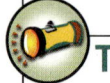
QuickTip

To identify your network computer name, double-click the Network icon in the Control Panel, then click the Identification tab.

1. **Right-click the icon for your network computer**
   John opens the networked computer called johnc. The icon representing the network computer is highlighted, and a pop-up menu opens.

2. **Click Properties on the pop-up menu**
   The Properties dialog box for the selected network computer opens with the General tab in front, as shown in Figure H-4. In Figure H-4, the network computer name appears at the top of the General tab. Below the network computer name appears a comment (generally the user name), the workgroup name, the name of the user logged on, and the name of the logon domain. In this case, the network computer name is Johnc; the workgroup and domain name is NETONE; and the user logged on is John Casey.

Trouble?

If a button to a utility program is grayed out, the utility is not installed on your computer. If necessary, see your instructor or technical support person for installation details.

3. **Click the Tools tab**
   The Tools tab appears, as shown in Figure H-5, displaying three utilities that can make working with networks easier: Net Watcher, System Monitor, and Administer. These tools are mostly used for monitoring and administering a network. Table H-1 describes the function of each utility.

4. **Click OK**
   The Properties dialog box closes.

CLUES TO USE

Viewing network properties

A computer that uses the Windows 98 network must be configured so that other machines on the network recognize it. On a small network, you might be responsible for configuring your computer or that responsibility might fall to the network administrator. You can view and modify some of the network settings for your computer using the Control Panel. In the Control Panel, double-click the Network icon to display the network settings. The Network dialog box opens displaying the Configuration tab. The network configuration consists of four components: client, adapter, protocol, and service. The client allows you to access resources such as files and printers that are available on computers on your network. The **adapter** is a device that connects your computer to the network. The **protocol** is the language that the computer uses to communicate with other computers on the network. The **service** allows you to share your computer resources, such as files and printers, with other networked computers. You can also click the Identification tab to change your network computer name, workgroup name, or computer description. This information is displayed over the network to identify your computer and appears in your network drive properties.

FIGURE H-4: Properties dialog box for a network computer

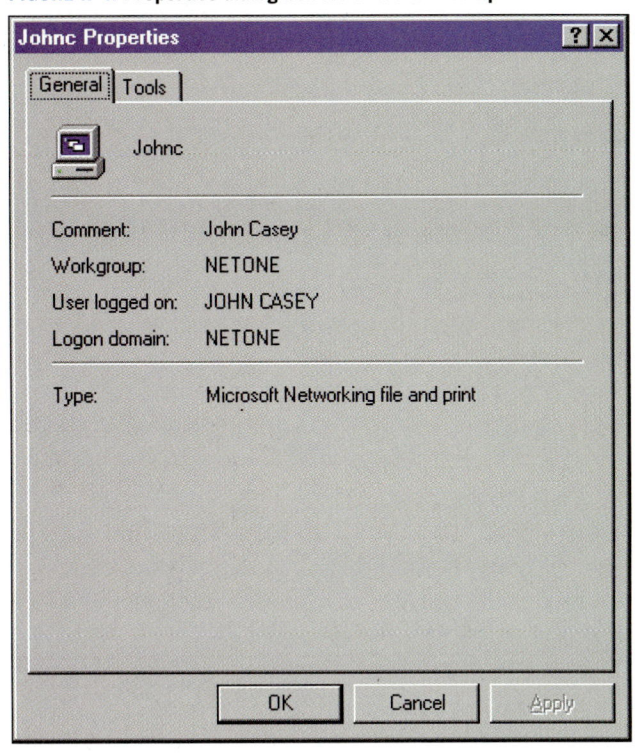

FIGURE H-5: Tools tab in the network computer Properties dialog box

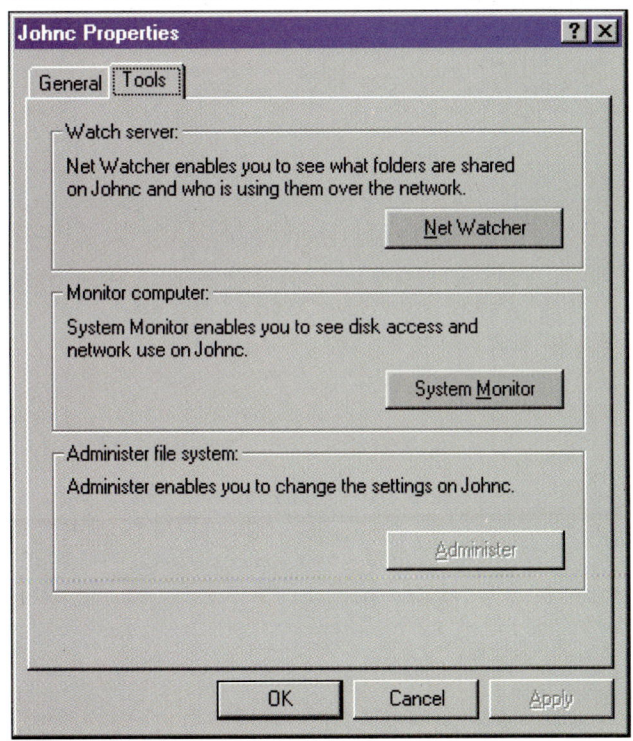

TABLE H-1: Network utilities

tool	function
Net Watcher	Allows you to see what folders are shared on the network computer and who is using them
System Monitor	Allows you to see disk access and network use on the network computer
Administer	Allows you to change the settings on the network computer

Windows 98

Creating a Shared Folder

To create a shared folder in Network Neighborhood, you use many of the file management skills you learned with Windows Explorer. You must first decide where you will put the new folder. If you are working at your own computer, you might create the shared folder in a subfolder within your My Documents folder. Otherwise, you may have to ask your instructor or technical support person for permission to create a folder in another location, or you can simply follow the steps without actually creating a folder. If you are not working in a network environment, you may not be able to complete these steps. In this case, simply read the steps without completing them. ➤ John has decided to create a shared folder called Sales on his computer that will allow employees from anywhere on the network to add information to Sales files.

1. **Click the Address list arrow on the Address bar**
   Network Neighborhood displays the desktop and drives of your computer. You can now work with the files and folders from your computer and still have the option of connecting to various other parts of the network.

2. **Click Hard Disk (C:)** (or the name and drive letter assigned to your hard drive), then double-click the **My Documents folder**
   Network Neighborhood displays the contents of the My Documents folder on your hard drive.

3. **Right-click** anywhere in the Network Neighborhood window (except on a file or folder), point to **New**, then click **Folder**
   A new folder, named New Folder, appears in the window.

4. Type **Sales**, then press **[Enter]**
   The folder is now named Sales.

5. Click **File** on the menu bar, then click **Sharing**
   The Sales Properties dialog box opens. The Sales Properties dialog box is where you adjust the settings to allow other users access to the files in your shared folder. The Sharing tab allows you to designate the kind of access you want other users to have for the folder you just created.

Trouble?

If the Sharing command is not available, double-click the Network icon in the Control Panel, click File and Print Sharing, then click the I want to be able to give others access to my files check box.

6. Click the **Shared As option button**
   The sharing information about the Sales folder is shown in Figure H-6. This tab includes a text box for entering the shared name of the folder. Unless you have a very good reason for naming it differently, it's best to make the shared name the same as the folder name. Keeping the names consistent will help to avoid confusion. By default, Windows automatically enters the name of the folder as the shared name and sets the file permission to Read-Only. John wants to give full access to other users with some password protection.

7. Click the **Full option button**
   John wants to add password protection to the Sales folder.

8. Click the **Full Access Password text box**, then type **Beans**

9. Click **OK** to close the Sales Properties dialog box
   The Password Confirmation dialog box opens, asking you to retype the password.

10. Type **Beans**, then click **OK**
    The Sales folder, shown in Figure H-7, is now accessible by anyone with the right password from anywhere on the network. The 🖐 icon, a folder with a hand underneath, indicates the folder is a shared folder.

FIGURE H-6: Sharing tab of Sales Properties dialog box

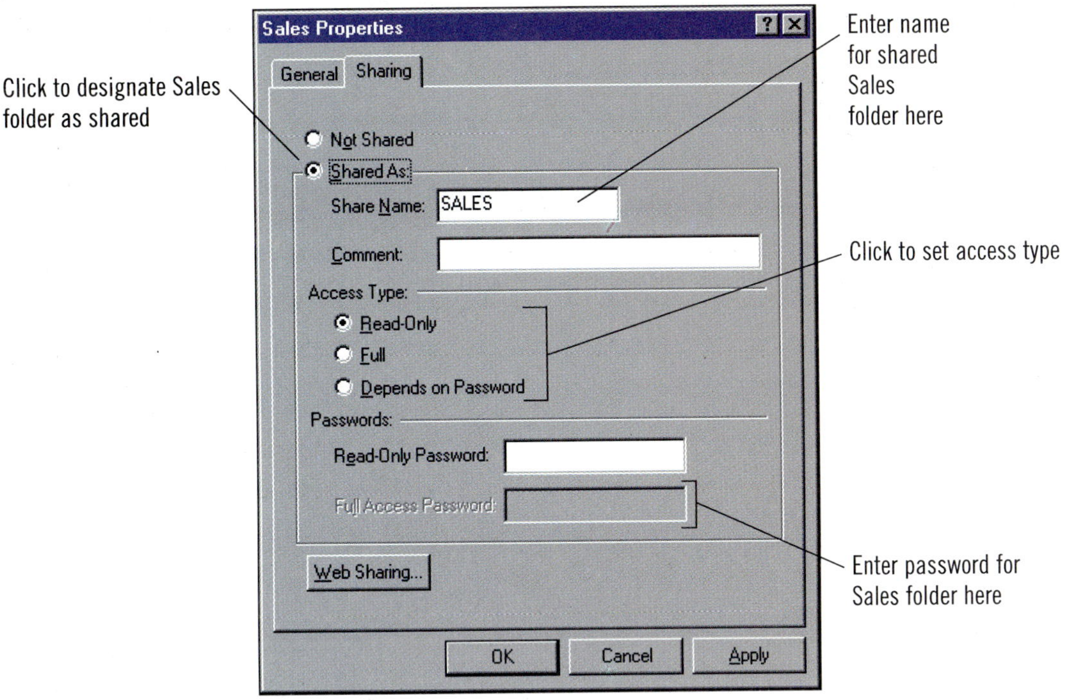

Click to designate Sales folder as shared

Enter name for shared Sales folder here

Click to set access type

Enter password for Sales folder here

FIGURE H-7: Shared folder within the My Documents folder

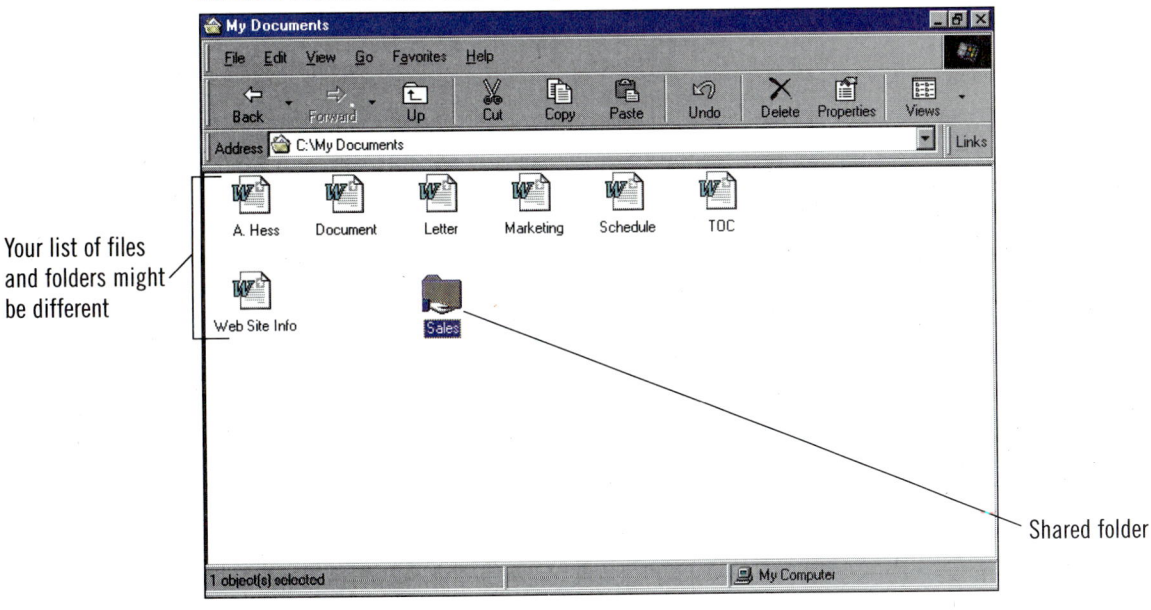

Your list of files and folders might be different

Shared folder

Password protection

With Windows 98, you can use passwords to control access to your computer, the network, and specific files and folders. You can set different passwords and varying degrees of access for the different drives, folders, and files. You can also manage your files and printers from a remote computer and set password protection to limit access. To set or change password protection in Windows 98, open the Control Panel and double-click the Passwords icon. You can also use the Power Management utility in the Control Panel to password protect your computer when it's in Sleep mode or use the Display utility to password protect files when in screen saver mode.

Mapping a Network Drive

Network Neighborhood enables you to connect your computer to other computers on the network quite easily. If you connect to a network location frequently, you might want to designate a drive letter on your computer as a direct connection to a shared drive or folder on another computer. Instead of spending unnecessary time opening Network Neighborhood and the shared drive or folder each time you want to access it, you can create a direct connection, called **mapping** a drive, to the network location for quick and easy access. At John's request, the network administrator created a shared folder called "wired coffee" on the computer named Server. Now John will use Network Neighborhood to map a drive letter from his computer to that folder so that he can easily move files to this central location for others to share. To complete these steps, you will need to map to a network computer and a folder specified by your instructor or technical support person.

Trouble?

Before beginning, ask your instructor which networked computer you can map onto your computer. If you do not have a networked computer available, read the steps without completing them.

QuickTip

If you already know the network path for the drive you want to map, right-click the Network Neighborhood icon, click Map Network Drive, enter the network path in the Path text box, then click OK.

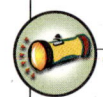

Trouble?

If your mapped drives are not automatically reconnecting when you log on, make sure your user name and password are the same for all the networks to which you connect.

1. Click the **Address list arrow**, then click **Network Neighborhood** (scroll down if necessary)
   Network Neighborhood shows all the active computers in your immediate neighborhood.

2. Double-click the **networked computer icon** supplied by your instructor or technical support person
   John opens the networked computer called Server. The window for the networked computer opens and displays the folders that are available for file sharing, as shown in Figure H-8. Your available folders might differ from those shown in Figure H-8.

3. Click the shared **wired coffee folder** (or the folder specified by your instructor or technical support person) to select it, click **File** on the menu bar, then click **Map Network Drive**
   The Map Network Drive dialog box opens, as shown in Figure H-9. By default the Map Network Drive dialog box highlights the next available drive letter. The network path is automatically entered by Network Neighborhood.

4. If you want to use a different drive letter, click the **Drive list arrow**, then click the **drive letter** you want to use
   John decides that the default choice is okay, but he would also like the drive to be reconnected every time he logs on.

5. If not already checked, click the **Reconnect at logon** check box, then click **OK**
   The Map Network Drive dialog box closes, and Network Neighborhood maps a drive connecting your computer to the shared wired coffee folder (or to the shared folder specified by your instructor or technical support person). When the connection is complete, a window appears for the newly mapped drive, allowing you to view the files within the mapped drive, as shown in Figure H-10. John can now easily copy folders and files from his floppy disk into the shared folder.

6. Click the **Close button** in the mapped drive window

7. Click the **Back button list arrow** ⬅ ▾ on the toolbar, then click **Network Neighborhood**
   The Network Neighborhood window displays the active computers in your immediate neighborhood.

FIGURE H-8: Server computer icon window

Shared folder on networked computer

Your list of folders might be different

Networked computer

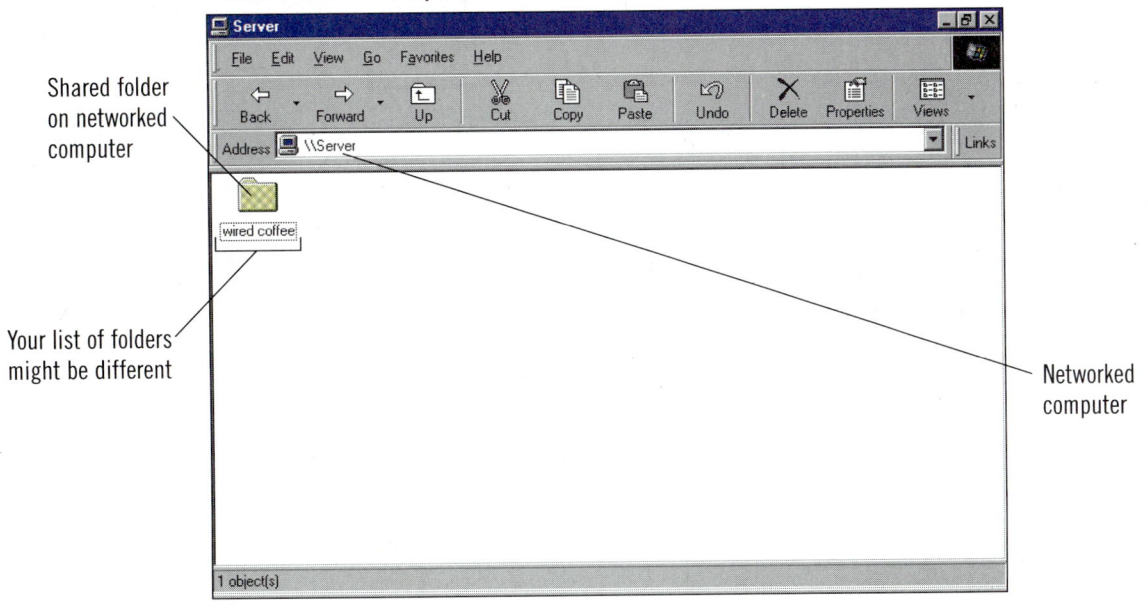

FIGURE H-9: Map Network Drive dialog box

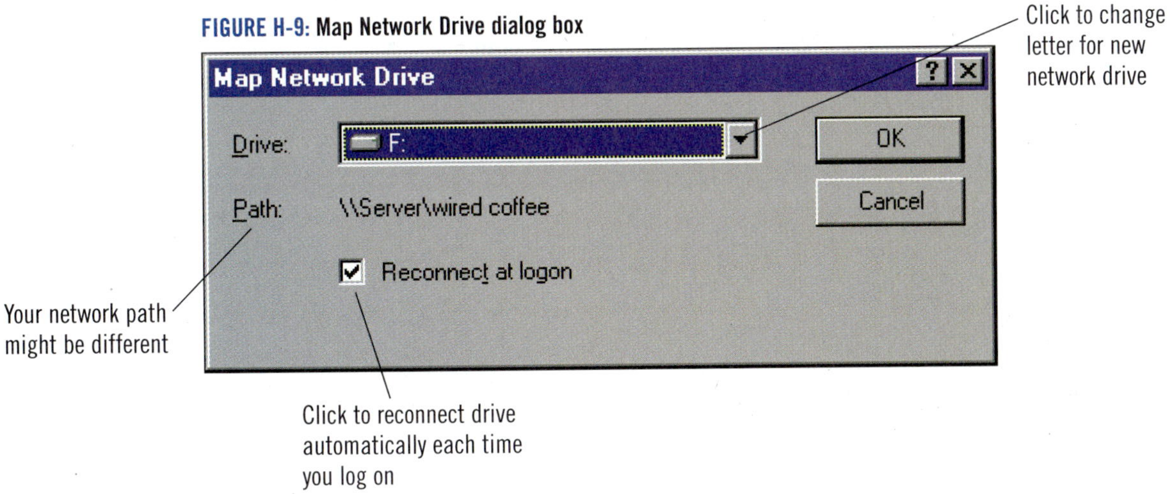

Click to change letter for new network drive

Your network path might be different

Click to reconnect drive automatically each time you log on

FIGURE H-10: Wired coffee folder window

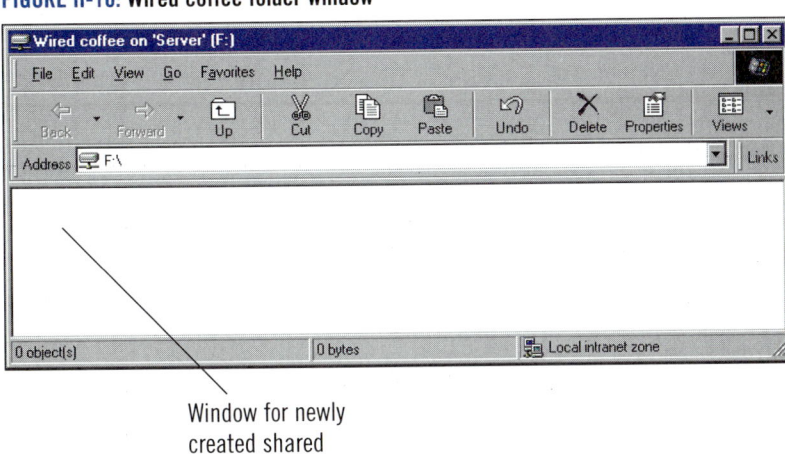

Window for newly created shared folder

Copying and Moving Shared Files

Once you have created shared folders and mapped your network drives, copying and moving shared files and folders in Windows is as easy as managing files on your own computer. The only difference is data transfer can take longer over a network than it does on your local computer. You can copy and move files using any of the Windows 98 file management tools: Network Neighborhood, My Computer, or Windows Explorer. Network Neighborhood works just like My Computer. ◤━━ John wants to copy files from his floppy disk into the shared Sales folder on his hard drive to make them accessible to the other users on his network. He also needs to move a file from the shared Sales folder to the wired coffee folder on the network drive (F:) to make it accessible to another department. Since he's copying files to several locations, John uses Windows Explorer to drag and drop the files.

Steps 1 2 3 4

1. Make sure your Student Disk is inserted in the appropriate disk drive

2. In the Network Neighborhood window, click the **Address list arrow**, then click **3½ Floppy (A:)** or **(B:)** (whichever drive holds your Student disk)
   Network Neighborhood displays the contents of the 3½ floppy drive.

3. Right-click the **Wired Coffee folder**, click **Explore**, then click the **Sales folder** in the Explorer Bar
   Windows Explorer opens, displaying the available folders and drives in the left pane, as shown in Figure H-11. You can now copy or move files easily from your computer to anywhere on the network. John will copy the files named Coffee Prices, Customer Profile, and Suppliers to the shared Sales folder he created on the (C:) hard drive.

Trouble?

If you click the shared Sales folder by mistake, click the Sales folder on the floppy disk then go to Step 5.

4. In the Explorer Bar, click the **+** next to the hard drive (C:) or the drive where you created your shared Sales folder, then click the **+** next to the My Documents folder to display the shared Sales folder (the one with a hand), as shown in Figure H-12, but *do not click the folder*

5. Click **Edit** on the menu bar, click **Select All**, then drag the files from the right pane to the shared **Sales folder** in the Explorer Bar
   The files are copied to the shared Sales folder on the hard drive. The employees who have access to John's computer can now share the files. Now John wants to move the Suppliers file to the network drive where the Supply Department can use it without any file permissions.

6. In the Explorer Bar, click the shared **Sales folder**, then click the **down scroll arrow** in the Explorer Bar until you can see the icon representing the mapped network folder
   See Figure H-12.

7. Right-click and drag the **Suppliers file** to the mapped networked folder in the Explorer Bar, then click **Move Here**
   The Suppliers file is moved to the networked folder.

8. Click the **mapped network folder** in the Explorer Bar to view the Suppliers file, then click the **Close buttons** in the Exploring and 3½ Floppy (A:) windows

FIGURE H-11: Exploring the Sales folder

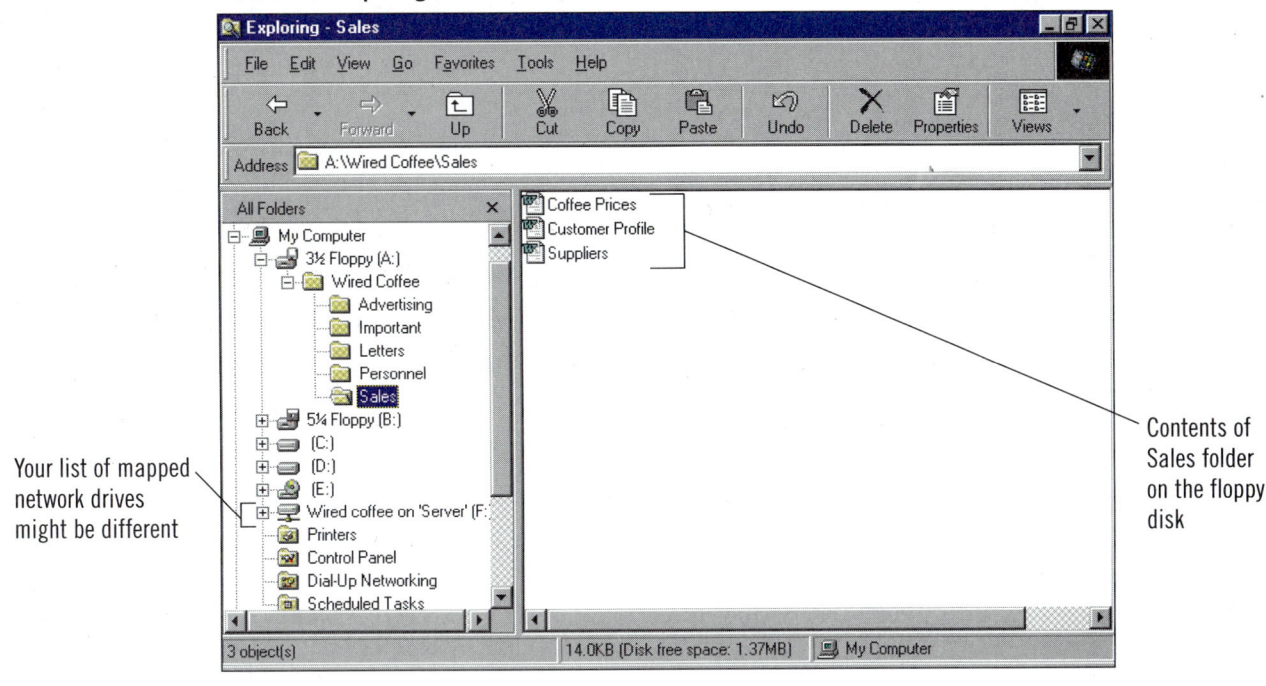

Your list of mapped network drives might be different

Contents of Sales folder on the floppy disk

FIGURE H-12: Location of the wired coffee folder on the mapped network drive (F:)

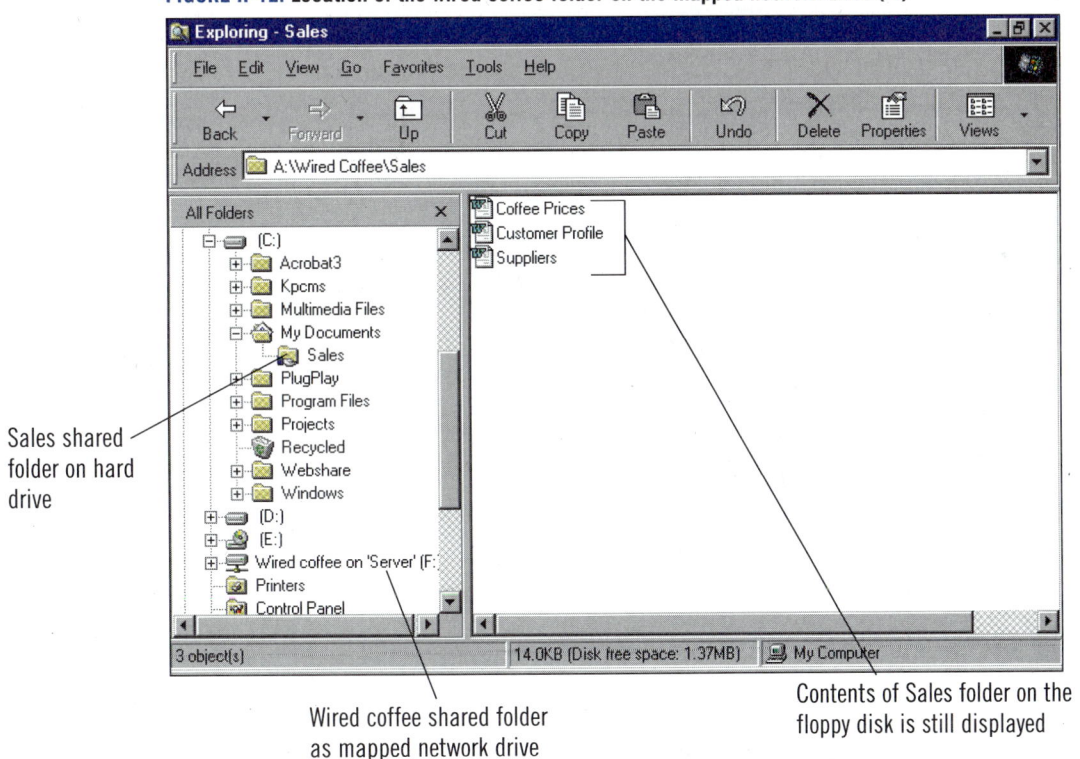

Sales shared folder on hard drive

Wired coffee shared folder as mapped network drive

Contents of Sales folder on the floppy disk is still displayed

CLUES TO USE

Network traffic

Large networks can serve hundreds of users simultaneously. Like water flowing through pipes, only a certain amount of data can pass through the wires connecting the individual computers at any given time. If the amount of network traffic is of sufficient volume, then the flow of data might slow considerably, causing file operations such as opening, saving, and copying to take longer to complete.

Opening and Editing a Shared File

Working with shared files on a network is a simple task with Windows. Once you have mapped all the necessary drives to your network folders, you can use network files in any program from your computer. For example, you can use WordPad to edit text files or Paint to create a graphic. You might also be able to use programs installed on the server specifically for the use of individual clients (ask your system administrator about available options). John will use WordPad to make corrections in the Suppliers file that he placed in the wired coffee folder on the Server.

Steps

1. Click the **Start button** on the taskbar, point to **Programs**, point to **Accessories**, then click **WordPad**
   The WordPad window opens.

2. Click **File** on the menu bar, click **Open**, then click the **Look in list arrow**
   The Open dialog box opens, as shown in Figure H-13, displaying the Look in list with local and networked drives. From here you can open files located on all drives and folders, including the drives mapped to the network.

3. Click the **icon** for the mapped network drive to the wired coffee shared folder
   A list of files stored in the networked folder appears in the Open dialog box, as shown in Figure H-14.

4. Click **Suppliers**, then click **Open**
   The file named Suppliers opens. John wants to add another supplier to the list.

5. Click the bottom of the list, then type **Homegrown USA Coffee**

6. Click the **Save button** 🖫 on the toolbar
   WordPad saves the changes to the file Suppliers.

7. Click the **Close button** in the WordPad window

FIGURE H-13: Open dialog box

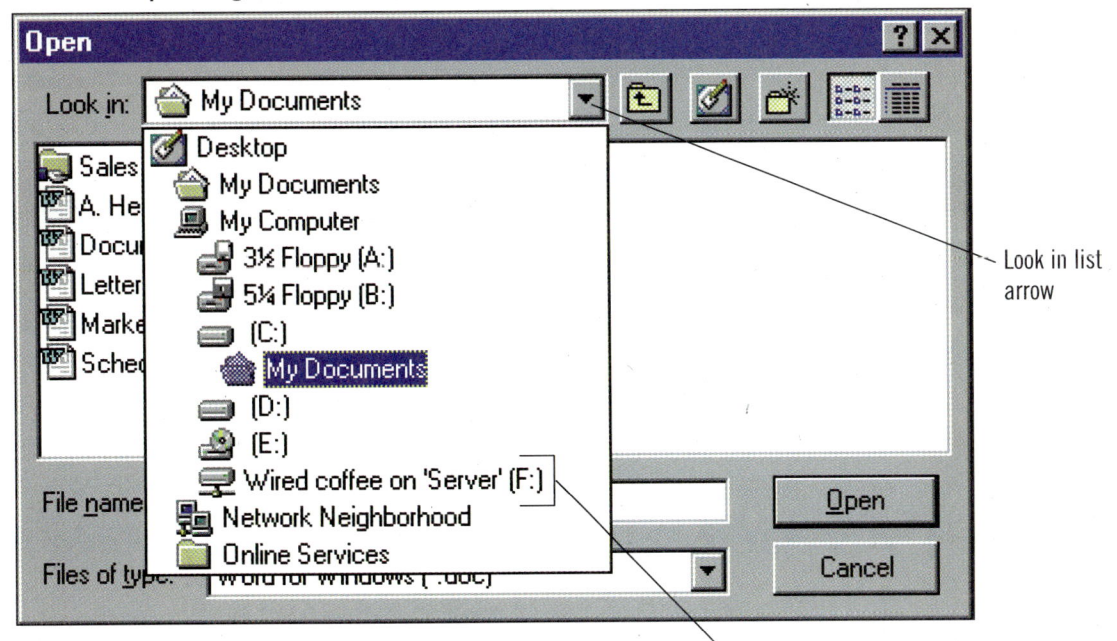

Look in list arrow

Your list of mapped drives might be different

FIGURE H-14: Files in shared wired coffee folder

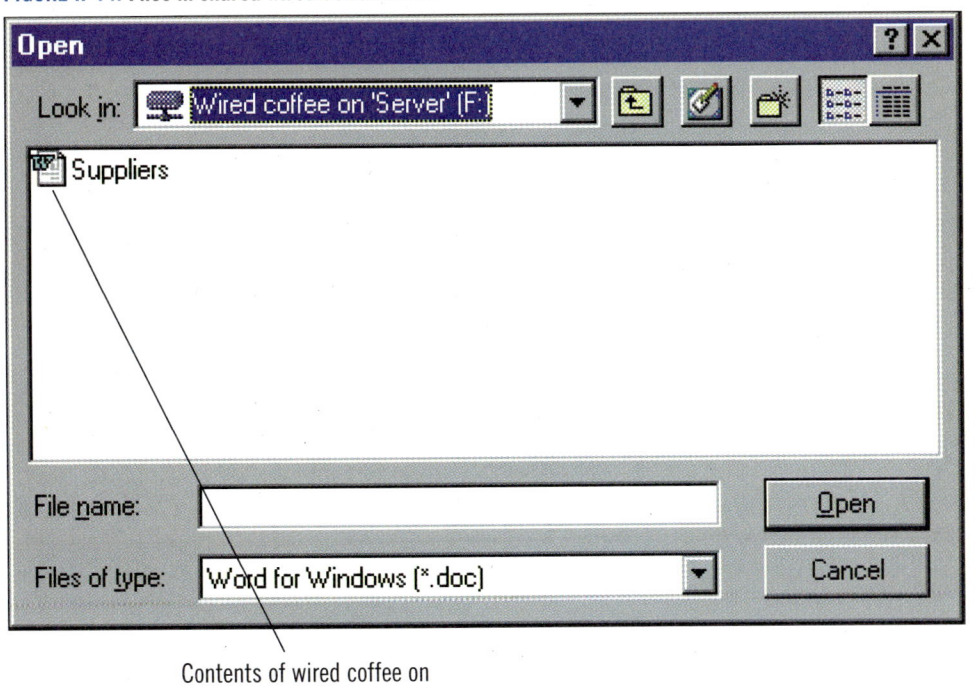

Contents of wired coffee on the 'Server' (F:) drive

Opening read-only files

If you have read-only access to a folder, you can open a file from the folder, but you cannot make any changes to the file. When you open a read-only file, the words "Read Only" appear in the title bar. You can makes changes to the file, but an error message appears when you try to save it. However, if you like, you can save the file with a new name in a different location (one you have full access to).

Disconnecting a Network Drive

Usually, you map a network drive to automatically reconnect every time you log on. However, sometimes you might find it necessary to manually disconnect a mapped drive. Your system administrator might have added new hard drives to the server, or she might have reorganized the directory structure of the network, in which case the network path for the mapped drive might now be incorrect. Windows makes the process of disconnecting a mapped drive very easy in the case of such an event. ◆ John was informed by the system administrator of a network reorganization that will take place over the weekend. He will disconnect the drive mapped to (F:) until he finds out what changes have been made. Before disconnecting the mapped drive, John cleans up his hard drive and the mapped drive.

1. Double-click the **My Computer icon** on the desktop, then double-click the **mapped drive**

   The contents of the mapped drive appear. John wants to delete the Suppliers file.

2. Right-click the **Suppliers file**, click **Delete**, then click **Yes** to confirm the deletion

3. Click the **Back button** ⇐ on the toolbar

4. Double-click the **hard drive** with the shared Sales folder, then double-click the **My Documents folder**

   John wants to delete the shared folder.

5. Right-click the shared **Sales folder**, then click **Delete**

   The Confirm Folder Delete dialog box appears. John confirms the deletion.

6. Click **Yes**, click **Yes**, then click the **Close button** in the My Documents window

   After cleaning up his hard drive and the mapped drive, John disconnects the mapped drive.

7. Right-click the **Network Neighborhood icon** on the desktop

   A pop-up menu appears for Network Neighborhood, as shown in Figure H-15. This menu provides several options for working in a network environment. See Table H-2 for a description of the options available through this menu.

QuickTip

To disconnect a network drive in Windows Explorer, right-click the mapped network drive in the left pane, then click Disconnect.

8. Click **Disconnect Network Drive** on the pop-up menu

   The Disconnect Network Drive dialog box appears, as shown in Figure H-16. The dialog box displays a list of all the network drives that you have mapped from your computer. You should check with your system administrator or instructor before actually disconnecting a drive. To quit without actually disconnecting a drive, click Cancel. John wants to disconnect the drive he mapped.

9. To disconnect the drive you mapped, click the **mapped drive** with the wired coffee folder, click **OK**, then click **Yes**, if necessary, to the warning message

   Windows disconnects the drive you have selected and closes the Disconnect Network Drive dialog box.

CLUES TO USE

Network paths

The path to a shared network directory is like the path to a file on a hard or floppy disk. For example, the path to the Suppliers file on your Student Disk is A:\Wired Coffee\Sales\Suppliers. Network paths replace the drive designation with the host computer name, as in \\Server\Wired Coffee. In either example, the path tells the computer where to go look for the files you need.

FIGURE H-15: Pop-up menu for Network Neighborhood

Pop-up menu options

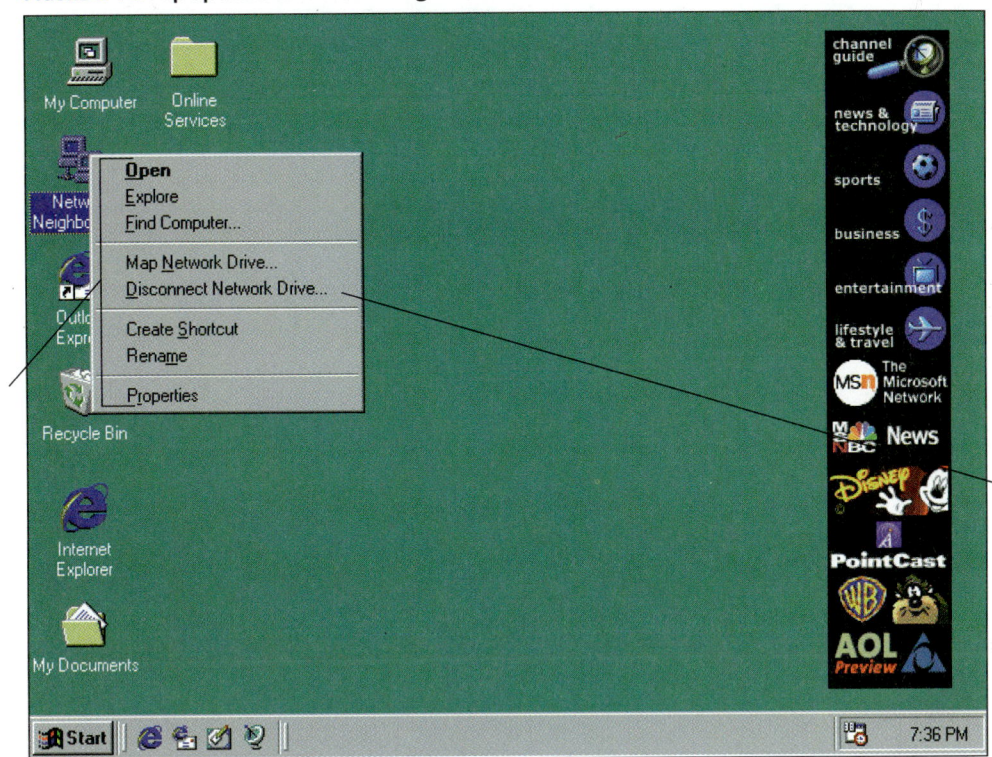

Click to disconnect network drive

FIGURE H-16: Disconnect Network Drive dialog box

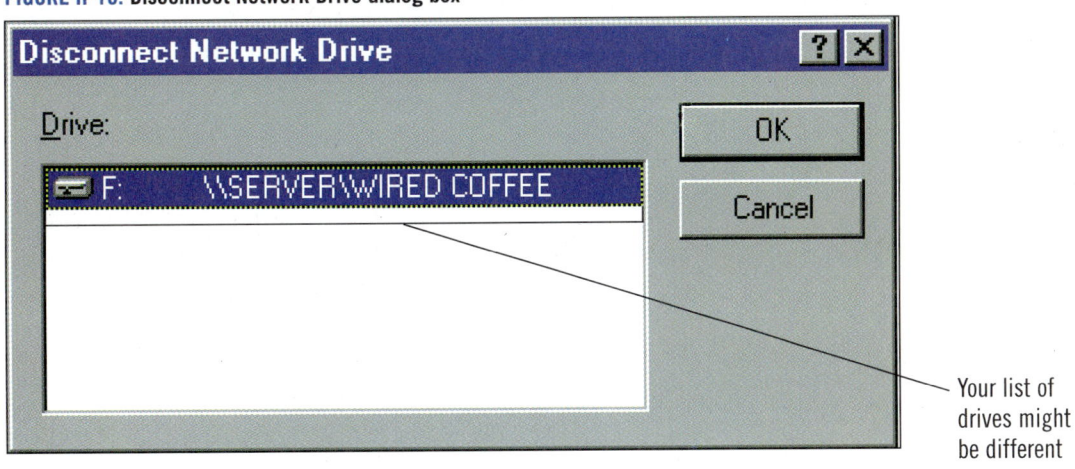

Your list of drives might be different

TABLE H-2: Pop-up menu commands for Network Neighborhood

option	function
Open	Starts Network Neighborhood
Explore	Opens Windows Explorer in order to copy and move files or folders from one folder to another, whether on your local computer or the network
Find Computer	Finds a computer whose name you know but not its location
Map Network Drive	Maps a drive from your computer to a shared directory on another computer
Disconnect Network Drive	Disconnects a drive on your computer from a shared directory on another computer
Create Shortcut	Creates a shortcut to Network Neighborhood
Rename	Renames the Network Neighborhood icon
Properties	Views the properties of your network

Practice

▶ Concepts Review

Label each of the elements of the screen shown in Figure H-17.

FIGURE H-17

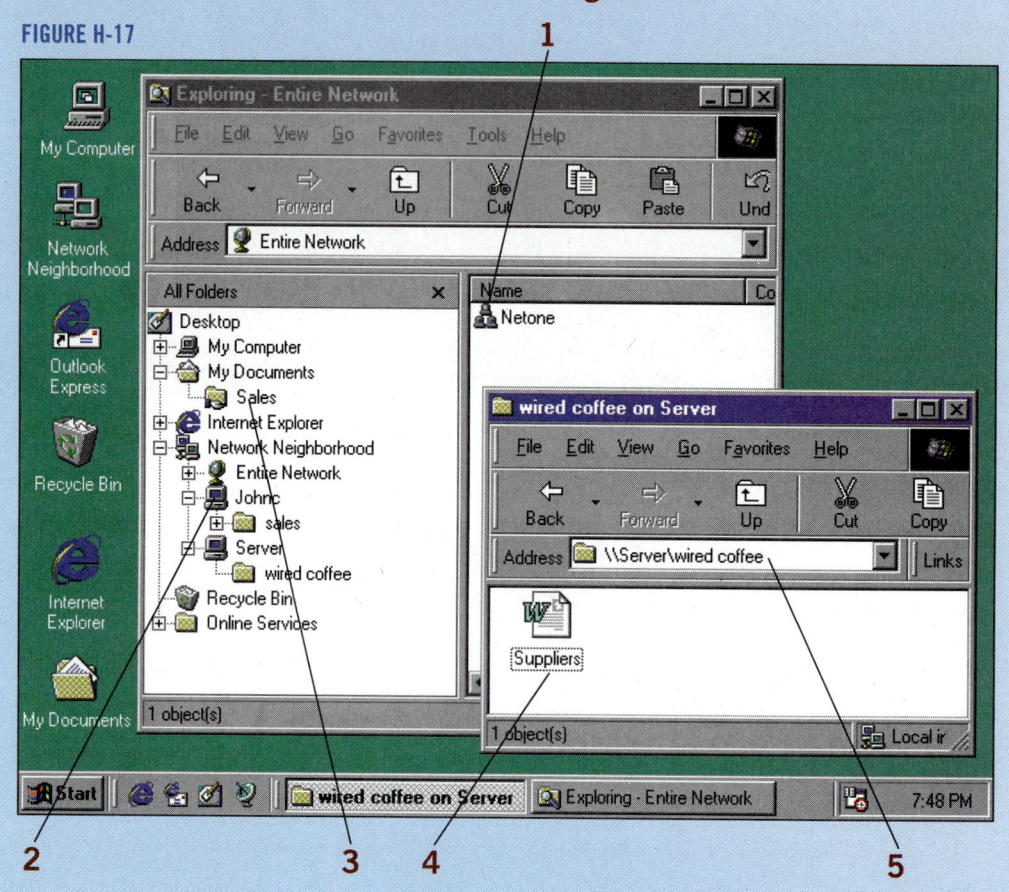

Match each of the terms with the statement that describes its function.

6. Shared folder
7. File permissions
8. Entire Network icon
9. Network path
10. Disconnect Network Drive command

a. Displays all workgroups and computers attached to a network
b. The address for an individual computer on a network
c. Determines who can read, write, or execute files
d. A location where multiple users can access the same files
e. Removes a mapped drive from the local computer

Select the best answer from the following list of choices.

11. The windows network management tool that allows you to inspect the configuration of your network is called
    a. Windows Explorer.
    b. My Computer.
    c. Network Neighborhood.
    d. File Manager.

12. **To disconnect a network drive**
    a. Double-click the drive letter in Network Neighborhood.
    b. Highlight the drive letter, click File on the menu bar, then click Delete.
    c. Click the drive letter, then drag it to the Recycle bin.
    d. Right-click the Network Neighborhood icon, then click Disconnect Network Drive.

13. **When you highlight a drive letter in Network Neighborhood, click File on the menu bar, then click Explore**
    a. My Computer starts allowing you to manage files and folders.
    b. Network Neighborhood displays the entire network.
    c. Windows Explorer starts allowing you to manage files and folders.
    d. File Manager starts allowing you to manage files and folders.

14. **When you map a networked drive**
    a. Network Neighborhood displays a graphic showing the entire structure of the network.
    b. You can use the shared files and folders of another computer on the network.
    c. The computer you are using is attached to the network.
    d. Network Neighborhood adds your computer to the network path.

15. **If the file permissions for a shared folder are set to read-only**
    a. No one can read the files in the folder.
    b. You can edit the file and save your changes.
    c. Everyone can read the files but not write to the files.
    d. Everyone can execute files but not write to the files.

▶ Skills Review

1. **Open and view Network Neighborhood.**
    a. Double-click the Network Neighborhood icon.
    b. Double-click the Entire Network icon.
    c. Click the Back button.
    d. Double-click the network icon in your immediate network.
    e. Click the Back button.

2. **Examine network drive properties.**
    a. Right-click your network computer icon.
    b. Click Properties.
    c. View the network properties.
    d. Click OK.

3. **Create a shared folder.**
    a. Click the Address list arrow, click your computer's hard drive, then double-click the My Documents folder.
    b. Right-click in the My Documents window, point to New, then click Folder.
    c. Name the new folder Memos, then press Enter.
    d. Click File on the menu bar, then click Sharing.
    e. Click the Shared As option button.
    f. Click OK.

4. Map a network drive.
   a. Click the Address list arrow, then click Network Neighborhood.
   b. Double-click the icon for the computer to which you want to map.
   c. Click the shared folder to which you want to map.
   d. Click File on the menu bar, then click Map Network Drive.
   e. Click the Reconnect at logon check box.
   f. Click OK.
   g. Click the Close button.

5. Copy shared files.
   a. Insert your Student Disk in the appropriate disk drive.
   b. Click the Address list arrow, then click 3½ Floppy (A:) or (B:).
   c. Click the Wired Coffee folder.
   d. Click File on the menu bar, then click Explore.
   e. Click the Letters folder in the Explorer Bar.
   f. Click the + next to the hard drive with the Memos folder.
   g. Click the + next to the My Documents folder.
   h. Click Edit on the menu bar, then click Select All.
   i. Drag all the files to the shared Memos folder you created on your hard drive.
   j. Click the Close buttons in the Explorer and 3½ Floppy (A:) windows.

6. Open and edit a shared file.
   a. Start WordPad.
   b. Open the IRS Letter file from the shared Memos folder on your hard drive.
   c. Change the month in the body of the letter from "July" to "August".
   d. Save the file, print it, then close the file and WordPad.

7. Disconnect a network drive.
   a. Double-click the My Computer icon.
   b. Double-click the hard drive with the shared Memos folder.
   c. Double-click the My Documents folder.
   d. Right-click the shared Memos folder, then click Delete.
   e. Click Yes, then click Yes again.
   f. Click the Close button.
   g. Right-click the Network Neighborhood icon.
   h. Click Disconnect Network Drive.
   i. Select the drive you mapped in Step 4.
   j. Click OK.

► Independent Challenges

1. As the new clerk at Holly (a craft store), you have been asked to create a list of suppliers' names. Your task is to enter the supplier information into a new file and place that file in two places for others to use. You must create a shared folder on your computer that will store the file, then map a drive to a network folder that will also contain the file. (Note: If you are not connected to a network, ask your instructor or technical support person for help in completing this independent challenge. If you are working in a lab environment, you may not be able to create a shared folder. If so, do not create a shared folder, and use the folder supplied by your instructor.)

To complete this independent challenge:

1. Open Network Neighborhood and select the icon for your computer.
2. Right-click your computer icon, then click Explorer.
3. Select a place on your hard drive to create a folder.
4. Create a shared folder called Suppliers.
5. Open WordPad and enter the following information in a new document:

Name	Address	City & State
Baskets & Things	101 Hopyard Road	Chicago, IL
Frames R Us	1934 Hummingbird Lane	Los Angeles, CA
Season's	125 34th Street	New York, NY

6. Save the file as "Supplier List" in the newly created Suppliers folder.
7. Print the Supplier List file.
8. Map a drive to a shared folder on another computer to which you have permission.
9. Create a US Suppliers folder on that drive.
10. Copy the Supplier List file from the Suppliers folder on the local computer to the US Suppliers folder on the mapped drive.
11. Print the Screen. (Press the Print Screen key to make a copy of the screen, open Paint, click Edit on the menu bar, click Paste to paste the screen into Paint, then click Yes to paste the large image if necessary. Click File on the menu bar, click Print, then click OK.)
12. Disconnect the network drive you mapped, and delete the shared folder you created.

2. As the president of your company, you have decided to increase the pay rates for two of your employees, Jessica Thielen and Debbie Cabral. You will use WordPad to write a memo that you can edit and use for both employees. After completing the memos, you will print the documents for the employees. You also want to copy the documents to the company server so they can be stored in their employee folders.

To complete this independent challenge:

1. Create a Memos folder on your Student Disk.
2. Open WordPad and type the following memo in a new document:
   Dear Jessica,
   Your service to this company is greatly appreciated. To show my appreciation to such an outstanding employee as yourself, I have decided to give you a 10% raise in salary. The raise will go into effect with the next pay period.
   Sincerely yours,
   [your name here]
3. Use the Save As command to name the document "Thielen Raise" and save it in the Memos folder, then print the document.
4. Change "Dear Jessica" to "Dear Debbie" in the Thielen Raise memo.
5. Save the file as "Cabral Raise" in the Memos folder and print the document.
6. Close the file and close WordPad.
7. Map a drive to a shared folder on another computer to which you have permission. Create a folder on that mapped drive called Thielen and copy the Thielen Raise file from your Student Disk into the Thielen folder.
8. Create a shared folder called Cabral on the mapped drive, and copy the Cabral Raise file into the Cabral folder.
9. Print the screen. (See Independent Challenge 1, Step 10 for screen printing instructions.)
10. Delete the Thielen and Cabral shared folders on the mapped drive.
11. Disconnect the network drive you mapped.

3. You are the system administrator for your company's computer network. During peak usage of the network, you want to monitor who is on the network. You will use the Properties command in the Network Neighborhood to find out who is connected to the network.

1. Using Network Neighborhood, display the properties of two or three mapped drives connected to your computer.
2. Print the screen. (See Independent Challenge 1, Step 10 for screen printing instructions.)

4. The system administrator for your network calls and informs you that he needs to make some changes to the directory structure. He advises you to move any files you have put on the server recently and to disconnect any mapped drives.

1. Map a drive to a shared folder on another computer to which you have permission, and copy two files from your Student Disk to this mapped drive.
2. Using Network Neighborhood, create a shared folder on your local hard disk called Network Files.
3. Move the files from the folder on the network drive to the shared Network Files folder on the local hard disk.
4. Print the screen. (See Independent Challenge 1, Step 10 for screen printing instructions.)
5. Disconnect the mapped drive from the network.
6. Delete the shared folder on your local hard drive.

▶ Visual Workshop

Re-create the screen shown in Figure H-18, which displays the Network Neighborhood. Print the screen. (See Independent Challenge 1, Step 10 for screen printing instructions.)

FIGURE H-18

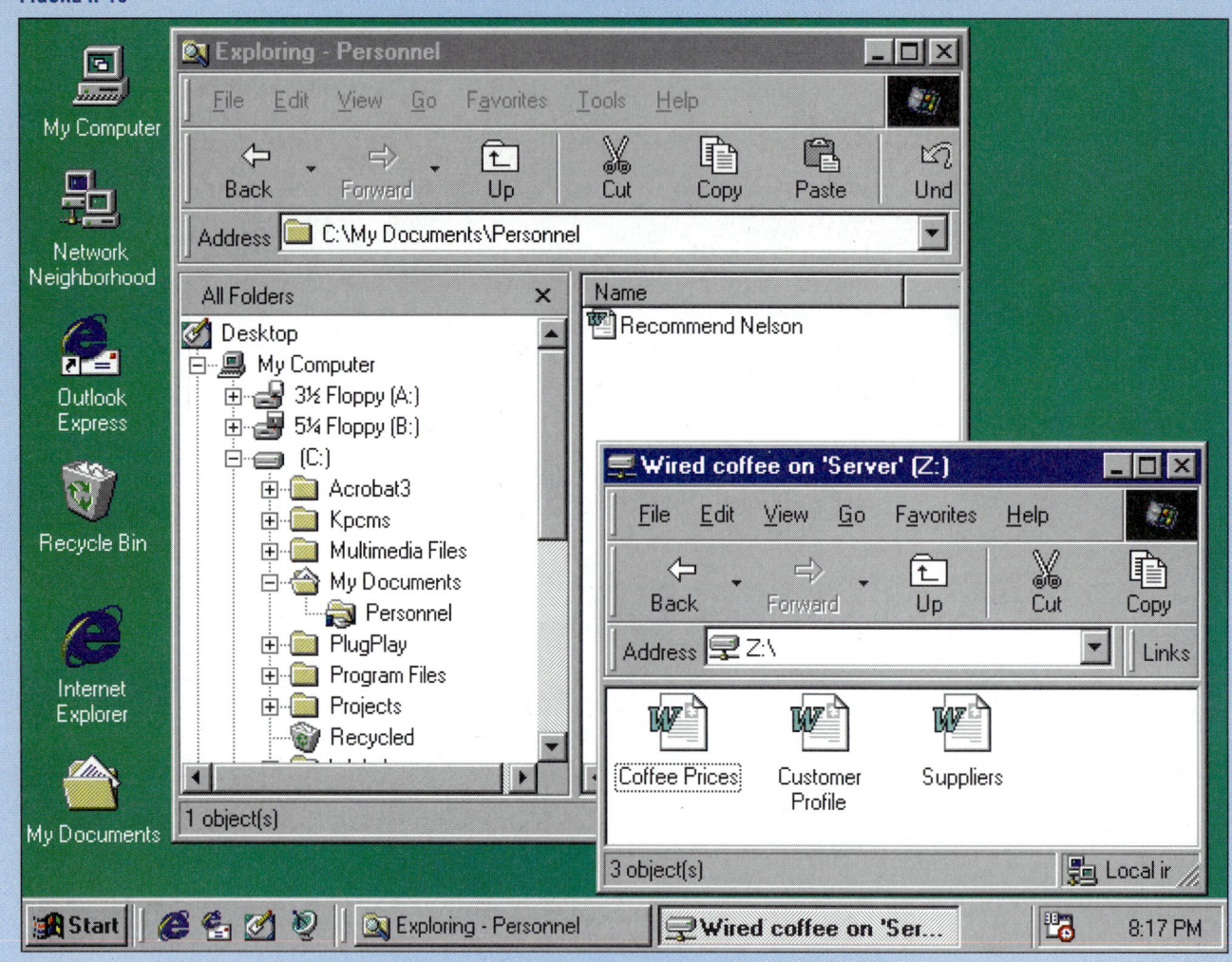

Glossary

Windows 98

Accessories Built-in programs that come with Windows 98.

Active channel A specialized Web page that delivers Internet content from a specific channel, such as Disney, MSNBC, or The Microsoft Network.

Active Desktop The desktop that allows you to access the Internet and view Internet content (Active Desktop items) directly from it.

Active Desktop item An element you can place on the desktop to access or display information from the Internet.

ActiveMovie Control A new media program for Windows 98 that delivers high-quality continuous video playback.

Active program The program that is currently running.

Active window A window that you are currently using; if a window is active, its title bar changes color to differentiate it from other windows, and its program button on the taskbar is highlighted.

Address Book An electronic book where you can store detailed information about a person or company.

Article A newsgroup message.

Auto Hide A feature that helps you automatically hide the taskbar.

Background The surface of your desktop on which icons and windows appear; you can customize its appearance using the Display Properties dialog box.

Backup The process you perform when you want to make copies on a separate disk of frequently used files.

Bitmapped character A character that consists of small dots organized to form a letter.

Browser A program, such as Microsoft Internet Explorer, designed to access the Internet. *See also* Web browser.

Bullet mark An indicator that shows an option is enabled.

Cascading menu A list of commands from a menu item with an arrow next to it. Pointing to the arrow displays a submenu from which you can choose additional commands.

Center A Display properties option that positions the wallpaper picture or pattern in the center of the desktop screen.

Channel Bar The bar on the right side of the desktop that displays the buttons you can use to access the Internet and view Web pages known as active channels (like those on television).

Check box A square box in a dialog box that you click to turn an option off or on.

Check mark An indicator that shows a feature is enabled.

Click To press and release the left mouse button once.

Client A computer that accesses shared resources on a server.

Client/server network   A network setup that provides all users on a network a central location for accessing shared files.

Clipboard   Temporary storage space on a hard drive that contains information that has been cut or copied.

Close   To quit a program or remove a window from the desktop. The Close button usually appears in the upper-right corner of a window.

Command   Directive that provides access to a program's features.

Command button   In a dialog box, a button that carries out an action. A command button usually has a label that describes its action, such as Cancel or Help. If the label is followed by an ellipsis (…), clicking the button displays another dialog box.

Contact   A person or company with whom you communicate.

Contact group   A group of contacts that you can organize together.

Context-sensitive help   Help that relates to the task you are currently working on.

Control Panel   A Windows utility for changing computer settings.

Copy   To place information from a file onto the Clipboard to be pasted in another location, while leaving it in the original location.

Cursor   The blinking vertical line in a document window, such as WordPad, that indicates where text will appear when you type. Also referred to as the Insertion point.

Cut   To remove information from a file and place it on the Clipboard to be pasted in another location.

Cut and paste   To move information from one place to another using the Clipboard as the temporary storage area.

Defragment   A feature that allows you to rewrite the files on your disk to contiguous blocks rather than in random blocks.

Delete   A file or folder that is placed in the Recycle Bin and then removed from the disk.

Desktop   An on-screen version of a desk that provides a workspace for different computing tasks.

Dialog box   A window that appears to request information; many dialog boxes have options you must choose before Windows or a program can carry out a command.

Disk label   Name that you assign to a disk using the Properties dialog box.

Display pane   The bottom pane of Outlook Express that displays the e-mail message selected in the preview pane. *See also* Preview pane.

Document   A file that a program, such as WordPad, creates.

Document window   The part of a program window that displays the current document.

Double-click   To press and release the left mouse button twice quickly.

Download   The process by which you access and display a Web page from the Internet.

Drag   To move an item or text to a new location using the mouse button.

Drive mapping   The process by which you assign drive letters to network folders, making them appear as extra drives.

Edit To change the contents of a file without having to re-create it.

Electronic mail (e-mail) A system used to send and receive messages electronically.

Explorer Bar The pane on the left side of the screen in Windows Explorer that displays all drives and folders on the computer.

Favorite A shortcut to a Web address.

File An electronic collection of information that has a unique name, distinguishing it from other files.

File hierarchy A logical structure for folders and files that mimics how you would organize files and folders in a filing cabinet.

File management The process of organizing and keeping track of files and folders.

File permission A user setting that designates what a user can and cannot do to a file. Two basic types of file permission are read and full. Read permission allows the user to view the file but not to make changes. Full permission allows the user to edit and save changes to the file.

Filter The process of retrieving newsgroup messages from a particular person, about a specific subject, of a certain length, or older than a number of days.

Floppy disk A disk that you insert into the disk drive of your computer (usually drive A: or B:) where you can save files.

Folder A collection of files and/or other folders that helps you organize your disks.

Font The design of a set of characters. For example, Times New Roman.

Format To change the appearance of information but not the actual content.

Graphical user interface (GUI) An environment made up of meaningful symbols, words, and windows that controls the basic operation of a computer and the programs that run on it.

Hard disk A disk that is built into the computer (usually drive C:) where you store programs and files.

Highlight When an item is shaded differently indicating it is selected. *See also* Select.

Home page The first Web page that appears when you open a Web browser.

Hyperlink Highlighted words, phrases, and graphics that open other Web pages. Also known as links.

Icon Graphical representation of a file or another screen element.

Insertion point The blinking vertical line in a document window, such as WordPad, that indicates where text will appear when you type.

Internet A collection of networks that connects computers all over the world using phone lines, coaxial cables, fiber optic cables, satellites, and other telecommunications media. *See also* Network.

Internet service provider (ISP) A company that provides access to the Internet.

Keyboard shortcut A keyboard alternative for executing a menu command. For example, [Ctrl][X] for Cut.

Keyword A word you submit to a search engine that is compared with words found on various Web sites on the Internet. *See also* Search engine.

List box A box in a dialog box containing a list of items. To choose an item, click the list arrow then click the item you want.

Margin The extra space around the edge of a document.

Maximize To enlarge a window so it fills the entire screen. Usually the Maximize button is located in the upper-right corner of a window.

Media Player A program that plays video, sound, or animation files.

Menu A list of available commands in a program.

Menu bar A bar at the top of the program window that organizes commands into groups of related operations.

Message flag An icon associated with an e-mail message that helps you determine the status or priority of the message.

Microsoft Network, The An online service provided by Windows 98.

Minimize To reduce the size of a window. The Minimize button is usually located in the upper-right corner of a window. Double-clicking the Minimize button shrinks the window to an icon on the taskbar.

Mouse A hand-held input device that you roll on your desk to position the mouse pointer on the Windows desktop. *See also* Mouse pointer.

Mouse buttons The two buttons on the mouse (right and left) that you use to make selections and issue commands.

Mouse pointer The arrow-shaped cursor on the screen that follows the movement of the mouse as you roll the mouse on your desk. You use the mouse pointer to select items, choose commands, start programs, and word process in applications. The shape of the mouse pointer changes depending on the program and the task being executed.

Multitasking The ability to run several programs at once and easily switch among them.

My Computer Use to view the files that are available on your computer and how they are arranged. The icon appears on the desktop.

Navigate To reposition the insertion point in a document.

Network Two or more computers connected together in order to exchange and share data, programs, and hardware.

Network Neighborhood An icon on the Windows 98 desktop that lists the computers on the network.

News server A computer located on the Internet where articles on different topics are stored.

Newsgroup Online discussion groups about a particular topic.

Offline When the connection to the Internet is disconnected.

Online services Offer a variety of information using the Internet in the form of news, discussion groups, files, software, and electronic mail capabilities.

Operating system A program that controls the basic operation of your computer and the programs you run on it.

Option button A small circle in a dialog box that you click to select an option.

Outlook Express Start Page A page that displays tools you can use to read e-mail, compose e-mail messages, download the latest newsgroup messages, read newsgroup messages, enter and edit Address Book information, and find people on the Internet.

Pane Part of a window that divides it into two or more sections.

Pattern A design that will display as your desktop background.

Peer-to-peer network A network setup that enables two or more computers to link together without designating a central server.

Point To move the mouse pointer to position it over an item on the desktop.

Pointer trail A mouse setting that adds a shadow to the mouse pointer.

Preview pane The top pane of Outlook Express that displays a list of all the messages in your Inbox.

Printout A document on paper that you printed.

Print Preview A feature that shows the layout and formatting of a document before you print it.

Program Task-oriented software that you use for a particular kind of work, such as word processing or database management. Microsoft Access, Corel WordPerfect, and Microsoft Word are all programs.

Program button The button that appears on the taskbar that represents a program that is minimized but still running.

Properties The characteristics of a specific element (such as the mouse, keyboard, or desktop display) that you can customize.

Protocol A language that the computer uses to communicate with other computers on the network.

Proxy server An Internet connection option that provides a secure barrier between your network and the Internet.

Quick Launch toolbar A toolbar located next to the Start button on the taskbar that contains buttons to quickly start Internet-related programs and show the desktop.

Random access memory (RAM) The memory that programs use to perform necessary tasks while the computer is on. When you turn the computer off, all information in RAM is lost.

Recycle Bin An icon that appears on the desktop that represents a temporary storage area on your hard drive for deleted files. Files remain in the Recycle Bin until you empty it or you restore the file(s).

Restore To reduce the window to its previous size before it was maximized. The Restore button usually is located in the upper-right corner of a window.

Right-click To press and release the right mouse button once quickly.

Scheme A combination of color, fonts, or character designs for window elements.

Screen saver A moving pattern that fills your screen after your computer has not been used for a specified amount of time.

ScreenTip A description of a toolbar button that appears on your screen when you position the mouse pointer over the button.

Scroll bar A bar that appears at the bottom and/or right edge of a window whose contents are not entirely visible. Each scroll bar contains a scroll box and two scroll arrows. You click the arrows or drag the box in the scroll bar in the direction you want the window to move.

Scroll box A box located in the vertical and horizontal scroll bars that indicates your relative position in a window. *See also* Scroll bar.

Search engine A program on the Web that allows you to search through a collection of information found on the Internet.

Select To click and highlight an item in order to perform some action on it. *See also* Highlight.

Server A computer that stores and shares resources, such as programs, files, and folders, with other users on a network.

Service The network component that allows you to share resources on your computer, such as files and printers, with other networked computers.

Shortcut A link that you can place in any location that gives you instant access to a particular file, folder, or program on your hard disk or on a network.

Shortcut menu A menu that appears when you right-click an item on the desktop.

Shut down The action you perform when you are finished working with Windows. After you perform this action, it is safe to turn off your computer.

Start button A button on the taskbar that you use to start programs, find and open files, access Windows Help, and more.

Stretch A Display properties option that displays the wallpaper picture or pattern enlarged across the desktop screen.

Tab A section at the top of the dialog box that separates options into related categories.

Taskbar A bar at the bottom of the screen that contains the Start button and shows which programs are running.

Task Scheduler A tool that enables you to schedule tasks to run at specific times.

Text box A box in a dialog box in which you type text.

Thread A collection of newsgroup messages that consists of the original message on a particular topic along with any responses.

Tile A Display properties option that displays the wallpaper picture or pattern consecutively across the desktop screen.

Title bar The area along the top of the window that contains the filename and program used to create it.

Toggle A button that acts as an on/off switch.

Toolbar A bar that contains buttons that allow you to activate a command quickly.

TrueType character A character that is based on a mathematical equation so the curves are smooth and the corners are sharp.

Uniform Resource Locator (URL) Another name for a Web address.

Wallpaper An image that you display as your desktop background.

Web address A unique address on the Internet where you can locate a Web page. *See also* URL.

Web browser A program that retrieves and displays Web pages. *See also* Browser.

Web page A document that contains highlighted words, phrases, and graphics that link the document to other documents on the Internet.

Web site A computer on the Internet that contains Web pages.

Window A rectangular frame on a screen that might contain icons, the contents of a file, or other usable data.

Windows Explorer A Windows 98 program that lets you manage files, folders, and shortcuts; more powerful than My Computer and allows you to work with more than one computer, folder, or file at a time.

Windows Help A book stored on your computer, complete with an index and a table of contents, that provides information on the features and tasks associated with a Windows program.

Wizard A series of dialog boxes that guide you through steps to complete a task and prompt you for information.

Wordwrap Text that won't fit on one line is automatically placed onto the next line.

Workgroup A group of computers within a network that share resources, such as files and printers.

World Wide Web (Web, or WWW) Part of the Internet that consists of Web sites located on different computers around the world.

Index

Index

Index

Index

Index